Dictionary of
Phrase & Fable

DICTIONARY OF
PHRASE & FABLE

Claremont Books
London

This edition published 1995 by Claremont Books,
an imprint of Godfrey Cave Associates,
42 Bloomsbury Street, London, WC1B 3QJ.

ISBN 1 85471 698 0

Printed in UK

English Idioms.

A

A.—*A 1* – first-class; very good "A 1" at Lloyd's is the term applied to a vessel of the best construction and in the best condition for sailing. Lloyd's Coffee-house in London was the resort of sea-captains, and the name "Lloyd's" is still retained for the headquarters of the shipping interest in London. Here people get the latest shipping intelligence and transact marine insurances.
"One of them takes his five pints of ale a day, and never leaves off smoking, even at his meals."
"He must be a first-rater," said Sam.
"A 1," replied Mr. Roker.—Dickens.

aback—*to take back* to surprise or astonish. Originally a sea phrase; used when the sails were suddenly shifted in order to stop the vessel or give it a backward motion.
Madame Mantilini still said no, and said it, too, with such determined and resolute ill-temper that Mr. Mantilini was clearly taken aback.—Dickens.

A B C—*the A B C of any subject* its rudiments; its elementary principles.
Many farmers seem not at all inclined to observe the very A B C of morality as regards the payment of just debts.— Spectator, 1887.

abide—*to abide by* to fulfil; to refuse to depart from; to carry out.
The rules were fixed, and I must abide by them.—Tyndall.

above—*above-board* openly; without trickery. The man who cheats at cards keeps his hands under the table or board.

"I've no patience with you," he said angrily. "Why can't you be fair and above-board?"—Wm. Black.

Abraham—*to sham Abraham* (a) to feign sickness or distress. An Abraham-man in England was a licensed beggar, who, on account of mental weakness, had been placed in the Abraham Ward of Bethlehem Hospital, and was allowed on certain days to go a-begging. Numerous impostors took advantage of this privilege.
I have heard people say
  That sham Abraham you may,
  But you mustn't sham Abraham Newland.—From an Old Song.
Exp.—*I have heard people say that you may impose on people by a tale of distress, but you must not impose on Abraham Newland (who was cashier to the Bank of England and signed its notes. This, of course, would be a penal offence.)*
—(b) to dissimulate; to pretend ignorance.
"Ay drat it; that you know as well as I do, Gammon," replied Mr. Quirk, with not a little eagerness and trepidation. "Come, come, it's rather late in the day to sham Abraham."—S. Warren.

abroad—*all abroad* (a) in a state of mental perplexity.
He is such a poor, cracked, crazy creature, with his mind all abroad.— A. Trollope.
—(b) having the senses confused; without complete control of one's organism.
At the twelfth round the latter champion

was all abroad, as they saying is, and had lost all presence of mind and power of attack or defence.—Thackeray.

—**The schoolmaster is abroad** good education is spreading everywhere.

Let the solder be abroad if he will, he can do nothing in this age. There is another personage – a personage less imposing; in the eyes of some, perhaps, insignificant. The schoolmaster is abroad, and I trust to him, armed with his primer, against the soldier in full military array.—Lord Brougham.

account—**on account** in part payment. A business phrase, used when two persons have dealings with each other, and the account between them is only partly settled by any payment.

"Give the driver this half sovereign," whispered Captain Ablewhite. "Tell him it is on an account, and that he has a good fare."—B. L. Farjeon.

—**To give a good account of** to be successful with.

The terrier gave a good account of the rats (was successful in killing many of them).

—**To lay one's account with** to expect; to look forward to.

The jurors must have laid their account with appearing (expected to appear) before the Star Chamber.—Hallam.

—**To take into account** to make allowance for.

As to its adventurous beginning, and all those little circumstances which gave it a distinctive character and relish, he took them into account.—Dickens.

acknowledge—**to acknowledge the corn** to admit the truth of a statement.

"What did the man say when you arrested him?" – "He said he was drunk." – "I want his precise words, just as he uttered them. He did not use

the pronoun he, did he?" – "Oh yes, he did; he said he was drunk – he acknowledged the corn." The Court (getting impatient at witness's stupidity), "You don't understand me; I want the words as he uttered them. Did he say, 'I was drunk'?" Witness (zealously), "Oh no, your honour; he didn't say you was drunk. I would not allow any man to charge that upon you in my presence!"—Law Magazine, 1887.

act—**to act a part** to behave hypocritically; to conceal one's real feelings.

Was the young man acting a part, or was he really ignorant of the rumour?—Wm. Black.

—**Act of God**—an event which cannot be prevented by any human foresight, but is the result of uncontrollable natural forces: for example, when a ship is struck by lightning and destroyed.

The act of God, fire, and all the dangers and accidents of the sea, are not accepted as ordinary risks.

—**To have act or part**—another form of **to have art or part.** See **Art**

But I declare I had neither act nor part in applying the thumbscrew to the Spanish captain.—G. A. Sala.

—**Act up to a promise or profession** to behave in a suitable way, considering what promises or profession one has made; to fulfil what one promises or professes to regard as a duty.

It isn't among sailors and fishermen that one finds genuine black-guardism. They have their code, such as it is, and upon the whole I think they act up to it.—W. E. Norris, in Good Words, 1887.

ad—**ad nauseam** until people are tired and sick of the subject.

And so on, and so on ad nauseam, proceeds that anonymous retailer of *petty scandal.—Edinburgh Review, 1887.*

Adam—*the old Adam* the evil nature within a man. Originally a religious phrase.

But Dan was not to be restrained, and breaking into the homespun (colloquial) – a sure indication that the old Adam was having the upper hand – he forthwith plunged into some chaff, etc.—Hall Caine.

—*Adam's ale* or *Adam's wine* pure water.

We'll drink Adam's ale.—Hood.

Some take a glass of porter to their dinner, but I slake my thirst with Adam's wine.

—*Son of Adam* a man.

But as all sons of Adam must have something or other to say to the rest, and especially to his daughters, this little village, though very retired, carried on some dealings with the outer world.—Blackmore.

Exp.—But as all men need to have friendly intercourse with other men, and especially with women, this little village, though very retired, carried on some dealings with the other world.

—*Adam's apple* the projection in the neck under the chin.

Having the noose adjusted and secured by tightening above his Adam's apple.—Daily Telegraph, 1865.

—*Not to know a man from Adam* to be quite unacquainted with him; to be unable to recognize him.

"To my knowledge," again interposed Mr. Lethbridge. "I have never seen his face. I shouldn't know him from Adam if he stood before me now."—B. L. Farjeon.

addresses—*to pay one's addresses to* to court; to approach a lady as a suitor for her hand in marriage.

He was said to be paying his addresses to Lady Jane

Sheepshanks, Lord Southdown's third daughter.—Thackeray.

advantage—*to advantage* favourably; in a good light.

To see the lower portion of this glacier to advantage.—Tyndall.

—*To take advantage of* to use for the furtherance of one's own purposes.

Here was material enough for the craft of William to take advantage of.— Freeman.

affaire—*affaire de cœur* affair of the heart, a love affair. A French phrase.

He had travelled abroad in the interval, and passed through a very serious affaire de cœur.—Quarterly Review, 1887.

after—*after all* nevertheless; when all things are considered. Generally used to introduce some circumstance of a more favourable or pleasing nature.

Yet after all he was a mere mortal.— Washington Irving.

—*After a man's own soul* or *heart* exactly what he likes or admires.

"Give me a kiss, my dear boy," said Fagan, with tears in his eyes. "You're after my own soul."—Thackeray.

afternoon—*an afternoon farmer* one who loses the best time for work; a lazy, dilatory man.

John was too much of an afternoon farmer to carry on the business successfully.

Exp.—John's habits were too dilatory for him to succeed in the business.

age—*to come of age* to reach the age of twenty-one, when the law permits a man to manage his own affairs.

She was now nearly twenty-three. Having, when she came of age, succeeded to her late mother's third of old Talbert's possessions, she was independent both by age and by income.—Hugh Conway.

agog—*all agog* in a state of activity or restless expectation.

*So three doors off the chaise was
stayed,
Where they did all get in;
Six precious souls, and all agog,
To dash through thick and thin.*

                        Cowper.

Exp.—*Six precious souls, and very
eager to dash through every obstacle.*

agreeable—*to make the agreeable to*
to strive to entertain; to be a pleasant
companion to.
*With which laudable and manly
resolution our dashing major
proceeded to make the agreeable to
his guests.*—G. J. Whyte-Melville.

airs—*to give oneself airs* to be conceited or arrogant in behaviour.
*"And these girls used to hold their
heads above mine, and their mother
used to give herself such airs," said
Mrs. Baynes.*—Thackeray.

—*In the air* (a) prevalent; found
everywhere.
*He is alive to the fact that "socialistic
risings" are in the air all over
Europe.*—Spectator, February 18,
1888.

—(b) (in military usage) without support or proper protection.
*The extreme left of the Allied front was,
in military dialect, "in the air" – that is,
protruded into the open country,
without natural or artificial protection
to its outer flank.*—Gardner.

—(c) unsubstantial; visionary; having
no real existence. Generally after the
word **castles**.
*And if our dwellings are castles in the
air, we find them excessively splendid
and commodious.*—Thackeray.

alert—*on the alert* watchful; ready to
observe whatever is passing.
*But those were were stationed at the
look-out were equally on the alert.*—
Thackeray.

all—*all along* See **along**.

—*To be all things to another* to accom-

modate oneself in every way to his
wants, moods, or caprices.
*She had sworn that more than ever she
would be all things to her husband.*—
Marion Crawford.

—*On all fours* See **four**

—*All in all* (a) supreme: all-powerful;
of the first importance.
*The then Prime Minister was all in all
at Oxford.*—A. Trollope.

—(b) the dearest object of affection.
*Desdemona, a happy young wife, till a
wicked enchanter's breath suddenly
wraps her in a dark cloud, is all in all
to (intensely love and admired by) her
husband.*—Blackwood's Magazine,
1887.

I was all in all to him then.—Thackeray.

—(c) (adverbially) completely; en-
tirely.
*Take him for all in all,
I shall not look upon his like again.*

                     Shakespeare.

Trust me not at all or all in all.

                     Tennyson.

—*To be all one* to make no difference.
*Mr. Carker presently tried a canter –
Rob was still in attendance – then a
short gallop. It was all one to the boy.*—
Dickens.

—*All of a heap.* See **heap**.

—*All (in) my eye and Betty Martin*
nonsense; not to be believed. Found
also in the contracted form, all (in)
my eye. This phrase is at least three
hundred years old.
*Says he, "It fairly draws tears from me,"
and his weak eye took to lettin' off its
water. So as soon as the chap went,
he winks to me with t'other one, quite
knowin', as much as to say, You see
it's all in my eye, Slick; but don't let on
to any one about it that I said so.*—
Haliburton.

Exp.—*He said, "It really draws tears
from me," and his weak eye began to
let off its water. So as soon as the man*

went, he winked to me with the other one, quite slyly, as if to say, you see it's all humbug, Slick: but do not tell any one that I said so.

—**All the same** nevertheless; notwithstanding.

The captain made us trim the boat, and we got her to lie a little more evenly. All the same, we were afraid to breathe.—R. L. Stevenson.

—**All serene** very good; all right. At one time a popular street cry in London.

"You will meet me to-night at the railway station, and bring me the money." – "All serene" (Yes, I shall meet you and bring the money).

Tom peeped under the bonnet, and found it, as he expressed himself, all serene.—G. J. Whyte-Melville.

—**All there** clever; able; possessing quick faculties.

Our friend the judge is all there, I can tell you, and knows what he is about.

Exp. —Our friend the judge is a clever man, I assure you, and fully understands how best to act.

—**All and sundry** every one without distinction.

Finally, he invited all and sundry to partake freely of the oaten cake and ale that he had himself brought from Ballymena.—Hall Caine.

Alma—*alma mater* nourishing mother. A name often applied to a university by its graduates. Latin.

The good men – they who have any character, they who have that within them which can reflect credit on their alma mater – they come through (their course of study at the university) scathless.—A. Trollope.

along—*along of* owing to; because of.

"I never had such luck, really," exclaimed coquettish Miss Price, after another hand or two. "It's all along of you, Mr. Nickleby, I think."—Dickens.

—**All along** during its whole existence; the whole time.

This impost was all along felt to be a great burden.—Freeman.

alpha—*alpha and omega* the beginning and the end. These are the first and last letters of the Greek alphabet.

I am Alpha and Omega, the beginning and the ending, saith the Lord.—Rev. i. 8.

The alpha and omega of science.—Herschel.

alt—*to be in alt* to be in an exalted frame of mind. An expression taken from the vocabulary of music.

"Come, prithee be a little less in alt," cried Lionel, "and answer a man when he speaks to you."—Madame D'Arblay.

altar—*to lead to the altar* to marry.

He to lips that fondly falter
Presses hers without reproof;
Leads her to the village altar,
And they leave her father's roof.

Tennyson.

On the 15th of May, in the year 1773, I had the honour and happiness to lead to the altar, Honoria, Countess of Lyndon, widow of the late Right Hon. Sir Charles Lyndon, K.B.—Thackeray

alter—*alter ego* other self; one who is very near and dear to a person; an inseparable friend. Latin.

I am his alter ego – nay, he only sees what I choose to show him, and through the spectacles, as it were, that I place on the bridge of his nose.—J. Payn.

amende—*amende honorable* a sufficient apology and compensation for wrong done. French.

The result of this determined conduct was an amende honorable and peace.—Fortnightly Review, 1887.

amiss—*to take (a thing) amiss* to be offended by it; to resent it.

You will not take it amiss if I take a cousin's privilege.—A. Trollope.

amour—*amour propre* self-esteem. A French phrase.

But, at all events, you should save her amour propre from the shock of any rebuff.—The Mistletoe Bough, 1887.

angel—*to entertain an angel unawares* to be hospitable to a guest whose good qualities are unknown. See the Bible (Gen. xviii.) for the origin of the phrase.

He had always esteemed his sister; but as he now confessed to himself, for these many years he had been entertaining an angel unawares (had not known how very good a woman she was).—J. Payn.

—*Angels' visits* pleasant visits, occurring very rarely.

How fading are the joys we dote upon,
Like apparitions seen and gone;
But those which soonest take their
    flight
Are the most exquisite and strong;
Like angels' visits, short and bright,
Mortality's too weak to bear them long.
              John Morris.

. . . In visits Like those of angels, short and far between.—Blair.

—*The angel of the schools or the angelic doctor* a name given to Thomas Aquinas, the great scholastic philosopher.

—*To write like an angel* to write beautifully (originally of calligraphy, and not of composition).

Here lies poet Goldsmith, for shortness
    called Noll,
Who wrote like an angel, but talked like
    poor Poll.
              Garrick.

animal—*animal spirits* the liveliness that comes from health and physical exhilaration.

She had high animal spirits.—Jane Austen.

ape—*to lead apes* to be an old maid This phrase comes from an old super-stition that unmarried women suffered this punishment after death.

Poor girl, she must certainly lead apes.—Mrs. Centlivre.

appeal—*to appeal to the country* to advise the sovereign to dissolve Parliament and ask the electors to send up new representatives.

As soon as the necessary business could be got through, Parliament would be dissolved, and an appeal made to the country (a new election of representatives made).—Justin M'Carthy.

appearance—*to keep up appearances* to behave in a seemly way before others.

He was terribly afraid, likewise, of being left alone with either uncle or nephew; appearing to consider that the only chance of safety as to keeping up appearances was in their being always all three together.—Dickens.

apple—*apple of Sodom* a specious thing which disappoints. The so-called "apples of Sodom," as described by Josephus, had a fair appearance externally, but when bitten dissolved in smoke and dust.

It will prove, when attained, a very apple of Sodom, dying between the hand and the mouth.

Like to the apples on the Dead Sea shore.

All ashes to the taste.—Byron.

—*Apple of one's eye* a much-prized treasure. The "apple of the eye" is the eye-ball, so called from its round shape: something very delicate and tender.

He kept him as the apple of his eye.—Deut. xxxii. 10.

He would have protected Grace's good repute as the apple of his eye.—Thomas Hardy.

—*To make apple-pie beds* to fold one of the sheets of a bed (removing the other) so as to make it impossible for the intending occupant to stretch his legs; a common practical joke.

No boy in any school could have more liberty, even where all the noblemen's sons are allowed to make apple-pie beds for their masters (disarrange the beds of their teachers).—Blackmore.

—**Apple of discord** something which causes strife. Eris, the goddess of hate, threw a golden apple among the goddesses, with this inscription attached. "To the most beautiful." Three goddesses claimed the prize, and quarrelled over its possession – Hera, Pallas, and Aphrodite (Venus). Paris, son of Priam, was appointed arbiter, and decided in favour of the last.

Not Cytherea (Venus) from a fairer swain
Received her apple on the Trojan plain.
Falconer.

It (the letter) was her long contemplated apple of discord, and much her hand trembled as she handed the document up to him.—Thomas Hardy.

This great and wealthy church constantly formed an apple of discord (a subject of quarrel).—Freeman.

—**Apple-pie order** extreme neatness.

The children's garden is in apple-pie order.—Lockhart.

april—**April fool** one sent on a bootless errand or otherwise deceived on the first of April – a day reserved for such practical joking.

We retired to the parlour, where she repeated to me the strongest assurances of her love. I thought I was a made man. Alas! I was only an April fool!—Thackeray.

apron-string—**tied** or **pinned to a woman's apron-strings** continually in a woman's company, unwilling to quit her side.

If I was a fine, young, strapping chap like you, I should be ashamed of being milksop enough to pin myself to a woman's apron-strings.—Dickens.

apropos—*apropos* to the purpose; appropriately. A French phrase.

—*Apropos de bottes* having no connection with the previous conversation.

The secretary, however, was not the man to own himself vanquished, even in anecdote, but at once began to descant – very much apropos de bottes (without any connection or apparent cause) as it seemed – upon a curious Anglo-French marriage case that had that day appeared in the newspapers.—J. Payn.

—*Apropos de rien* apropos of nothing; irrelevantly.

The story was introduced apropos de rien.

arcadës—*arcades ambo* both of them simpletons. Latin.

He distrusted the people, as much as the aristocracy, and ridiculed the fossilization of Toryism equally with the fluidity of Radicalism.. "Arcades ambo," he used to say, with his serene smile.—Mrs. E. Lynn Linton.

arm—**arm in arm** walking in friendly fashion with the arms linked.

It was an agreeable surprise to her, therefore, to perceive them walking up to the house together arm in arm.—Mrs. Oliphant.

—**In arms** carried about. Generally used with the word **child** or **infant**.

One of these passengers being a child, still young enough to be passed off as a child in arms.—Hugh Conway.

—**At arm's length** at a certain distance; avoiding too great nearness or familiarity.

If she would confide in me, if she would even speak to me of it, I might do something to convince her of her folly . . . But no, she never alludes to

it; she keeps me at arm's length.—
Murray's Magazine, 1887.

—*To lie upon one's arms*. See **lie**.

—*With open arms* warmly; affectionately.

The Stanhopes were all known by name in Barchester, and Barchester was prepared to receive them with open arms.—A. Trollope.

—*In open arms* fighting openly.

Here I sat for some time pondering upon the strange infatuation of wretches who, finding all mankind in open arms against them, were labouring to make themselves a future and tremendous enemy.—Goldsmith.

—*A right arm* See **right**

—*Under arms* bearing arms; in martial array.

In a moment the troops were under arms (in battle array).—Robertson.

—*Up in arms* roused to anger; ready to fight.

If a tramping beggar were set to work in England, and compelled to do it by military discipline, all the philanthropists in the country would be up in arms.—Spectator, 1887.

arrière—*arrière pensée* (a) hidden motives; underlying design. A French phrase.

Our reasons for so doing (placing Mr. Lear above Lewis Carroll as a writer of nonsense) is that no nonsense is so absolutely devoid of arrière pensée as that of Mr. Lear—Spectator, 1887.

—(b) afterthought; something which occurs to one's mind after a thing has been done.

For their sakes and mine, you will not mind very much that you are spared all these arrières pensées.—Sarah Tytler.

arrow—*the broad arrow* the arrow-shaped brand with which the British Government marks its stores.

This jacket moreover, was stamped in various places with the Government broad arrow.—Hugh Conway.

art—*to be* or *have art and part in* to be concerned either in the contrivance or execution of.

"My dear," said she, "it's the foolery of being governor. If you choose to sacrifice all your comfort to being the first rung in the ladder, don't blame me for it. I didn't nominate you; I had no art or part in it" (was wholly unconcerned in contriving or carrying out your nomination).—Haliburton.

ass—*to make an ass of oneself* to behave foolishly. The ass is taken as the type of folly.

Do not make such an ass of yourself as to suppose that.—A. Trollope

—*The asses' bridge* a name given to the fifth proposition of the First Book of Euclid because of the difficulties it presented to beginners. See **Pons Asinorum.**

He could disport himself with trigonometry, feeling confident that Dr. Tempest had forgotten his way over the asses' bridge.—A. Trollope.

assurance—*to make assurance doubly sure* to take every possible precaution.

I'll take a bond of fate and make Assurance double sure.—
Shakespeare.

Now that I had a moment to myself, I lost no time in changing the priming of my pistol; and then, having one ready for service, and to make assurance doubly sure, I proceeded to draw the load of the other and recharge it afresh from the beginning.—R. L. Stevenson.

at—*at all*. See **all**

—*At that* moreover; in addition. A favourite American phrase.

It comes nearest (the Irish car) to riding on horseback, and on a side-saddle at that, of any vehicle travelling I ever saw.—J. Burroughs.

attic—*attic salt* wit or refined pleasantry.

Triumph swam in my father's eyes at the repartee – the Attic salt brought water into them.—Sterne.

Exp.—My father showed triumph in his eyes at the repartee; it was so charmingly witty that it brought tears of pleasure to them.

—*Attic bee* a name given to Sophocles, the Greek dramatist; a sweet poet.

A true Attic bee, he (Milton) made boot on every lip where there was a trace of truly classic honey.—J. R. Lowell.

au—*au contraire* on the contrary. French.

So we have not won the Goodwood cup; au contraire, we were a "bad fifth." if not worse than that.—O. W. Holmes.

—*Au fait* familiar with; accustomed to. French.

She appears to be as au fait to (with) the ways of the world as you or I.—Florence Marryat.

—*Au grand sérieux* in sober earnest. French.

I mean young women of no experience, who take everything au grand sérieux.—Wm Black.

—*Au pied de la lettre* exactly; without deviating from the exact words. French.

—*Au revoir* good-bye for the present; literally, "until we meet again." French.

Arthur took off his hat. "Then we will consider that settled. Good-morning – or perhaps I should say au revoir," and bowing again, he left the office.—H. R. Haggard.

Augean—*to cleanse the Augean stables* to perform a great work of purification. Augeas was a fabulous king of Elis, who imposed on Hercules the task of cleansing his stables, where three thousand oxen had lived for thirty years without any purification.

Hercules performing his task in one day by letting two rivers flow through them.

In short, Malta was an Augean stable, and Ball had all the inclination to be a Hercules.—S. T. Coleridge.

Augustan—*the Augustan age* the period of highest purity and refinement in any national literature. So called from the Emperor Augustus, under whose rule Virgil and Horace wrote their immortal works.

The reign of Queen Anne is often called the Augustan age of England.

auld—*Auld Reekie* a name given to Edinburgh because of the smoke from its chimneys; literally, "Old Smoky."

His (Shelley's) eye was not fascinated by the fantastic outlines of aerial piles seen amid the wreathing smoke of Auld Reekie.—Matthew Arnold.

aut—*aut cæsar aut nullus* either Cæsar or nobody. Latin.

I mean to be aut Cæsar aut nullus (either first or nothing at all) in the concern.

axe—*an axe to grind* a personal pecuniary interest in a matter. The story is told by Franklin that when he was a boy in his father's yard, a pleasant-spoken man came up to him and made himself very agreeable. Among other things, the visitor praised the grindstone, and asked young Franklin to let him see how it worked. He then got the boy to turn the stone, while he sharpened an axe he had with him. The boy was flattered with his compliments and honeyed words, and worked till his hands were blistered. When the man was satisfied he sent the boy off with an oath. That man had an axe to grind – he had a concealed reason for his conduct. All his politeness was prompted by selfish motives.

In the first place, let me assure you, gentlemen, that I have not an axe to grind . . . I can in no way be pecuniarily benefited by your adopting the system of bridges herein proposed.

If the American politician is always ready to grind an axe for his fellow, the Neopolitan is no less convinced of the value of mutual accommodation.—E.S. Morgan, in Fortnightly Review, 1887.

azrael—*the wings of azrael* the approach of death. Azrael, in the Mohammedan Koran, is the messenger of death.

Always, in an hospital, there is life returning and life departing – always may be heard the long and peaceful breathing of those who sleep while health returns, and the sighs of those who listen, in the hushed watches of the night, for the wings of Azrael.—Besant.

B

b—*a b. and s.* a brandy and soda; a wine-glass of brandy in a tumbler of soda-water. See peg.

"They give you weak tea and thin bread and butter, whereas—

"You would rather have a B. and S. and some devilled kidneys," finished Brian.—Fergus W. Hume.

babe—*the babes in the wood* simple, trustful children. An old ballad describes the sad fate of two orphaned children, cruelly treated by a bad uncle.

Yet those babes in the wood, Uncle Sam and Aunt Fanny, trusted six months of our existence to his judgment—Harper's Monthly, September 1887.

back—*to get one's back up* to become roused, angry and obstinate. A cat when irritated and ready to spit and scratch arches its back, the hair becoming erect.

—*to set another's back up* to irritate or rouse him.

I've been to see my mother, and you've set her back up.—Besant.

—*to beak the back* or *neck of* to finish the hardest part of a task. See **Neck**.

I always try to break the back of (finish the hardest part of) my day's work before breakfast.

—*to give* or *make a back* to stoop down, as in the game of leap-frog, that another may jump over you. It is said that Napoleon, who was in the habit of stooping as he walked, was on one occasion used as a back by a volatile student, who mistook the general for one of his companions.

The major was giving a back to Georgy.—Thackeray.

Exp.—The major was stopping so that Georgy might leap over his back.

—*to go back on a person* to betray one. American. See **go**.

I'll not go back on you, in any case.

—*to back the field* (in the language of betting) to bet in favour of the other horses in the field against a single one in particular..

—*to back up* to support.
He prolonged Cæsar's command, and backed him up (supported him) in everything.—Froude

—*to back out* to retreat cautiously from a difficult position; to refuse after consenting.
(He was) determined that Morris should not back out of the scrape so easily.—Scott.

—*on one's back* prostrate; helpless.
The doctor staked his wig that, camped where they were in the marsh, and unprovided with remedies, the half of them would be on their backs before a week.—R. L. Stevenson.

—*to give the back* to leave or quit.
Had even Obstinate himself but felt what I have felt of the powers and terrors of what is yet unseen, he would not thus lightly have given us the back.—Bunyan.

—*to turn ones back upon* to desert; forsake.
"Uncle," said Mrs. Kenwigs, "to think that you should have turned your back upon me and my dear children.—Dickens.

backbone—*to the back-bone* thoroughly; staunchly; essentially.
They told him solemnly they hoped and believed they were English to the backbone.—Hugh Conway.

backstairs—*backstairs influence* private influence of an unworthy nature; underhand intrigue at court. A backstairs minister is one who is not trusted by the country, but is supported by domestic influence in the king's household. For instance, the Earl of Bute was despised as a backstairs minister, because he owed his position to the favour of George the Third's mother.
Which accusation it was easier to get "quashed" by backstairs influence than answered.—Carlyle.

bacon—*to sell one's bacon* to sell one's body.
To the Kaiser, therefore, I sold my bacon.

And by him good charge of the whole is taken.
Schiller.
(translated by Carlyle).
Exp.—*I therefore sold my body to the Emperor, who takes good care of it and me.*

—*to save one's bacon* to escape from personal injury, generally in an undignified way.
*But as he ran to save his bacon,
By hat and wig he was forsaken.*
Coombe.
Exp.—*But, as he ran to escape bodily hurt, he lost his hat and wig.*

bad—*to go to the bad* to become debauched; to sink into poverty and disgrace.
(He) went, as the common saying expressively phrases it, to the bad.—Pall Mall Gazette.

—*to the bad* in debt; having a deficit or loss.
He was between £70 and £80 to the bad.—Pall Mall Gazette, 1884.

—*bad blood* angry and vindictive feelings.
At the battle of Poonah he regained his authority, and whatever bad blood had flowed between them was checked by the prospect of approaching danger.—De Mauley, in Nineteenth Century, 1886.

—*bad debts* debts of which there is no hope that they will ever be paid.
Among his assets he had included a number of bad debts (debts that were hopeless).

—*to go bad* (of meat or food) to spoil.
It goes bad more readily than cooked butcher's meat.—Daily News, 1884.

bag—*bag and baggage* completely; leaving no property behind. The phrase was originally used of the complete evacuation by an army of an enemy's territory, and is now employed generally to signify the wished-for departure of an unwelcome guest.

The Turks . . . their zaptiehs and mudirs . . . their kaimakams and their pashas, one and all, bag and baggage shall, I hope, clear out from the province they have desolated and profaned.—Gladstone.

Exp.—*The Turks and every Turkish official, with all their property and belongings shall, I hope, quit the province (Bulgaria) they have desolated and profaned.*

This expression of Mr. Gladstone's has given rise to what is known as the "bag and baggage policy" in relation to the Turks—to drive them completely out of Europe.

baked—*half-baked* silly; weak in mind.

Hampered withal by a daughter of seventeen not quite right in her head—half-baked, to use the popular and feeling expression.—Besant.

baker—*a baker's dozen* thirteen. See **dozen.**

Formerly called a devil's dozen, and associated with ill-luck.

It is all very well for you, who have got some baker's dozen of little ones, and lost only one by the measles.—Blackmore.

ball—*to open the ball* to begin.

Waltz and the battle of Austerlitz are said to have opened the ball together (commenced the operations of the year together).—Byron.

—*to lead up the ball* to open a dance. Said of the most distinguished couple who occupy the leading place.

Mr. Thornhill and my eldest daughter led up the ball.—Goldsmith.

—*balls* or *the three golden balls* a name given to a pawnbroker's place of business, of which three balls are the sign.

It is not generally known that the three balls at the pawnbroker's shops are the ancient arms of Lombardy. The Lombards were the first money-brokers in Europe.—C. Lamb.

—*to have the ball at one's foot* or *before one* to be in a position to command success; to have things in one's power.

A pretty picture is so much prettier in a gilt frame, and she will probably begin life with the ball at her foot.—G. J. Whyte-Melville.

—*to keep the ball up* or *rolling* to keep a conversation going; to prevent an undertaking from flagging.

If the Spaniards had not lost two armies lately, we should keep up the ball for another year (continue the enterprise for another year).—Wellington.

—*to take up the ball* to take one's turn in speaking or in any social matter.

Rosencrantz took up the ball.—George Eliot.

Exp.—*Rosencrantz took his turn in the conversation.*

Banbury—*to take a child to Banbury Cross* to swing it up and down on one's foot. Grown-up people often amuse children in this way, sitting on a chair or a sofa, and repeating the nursery rhyme:—

Ride a cock-horse
To Banbury Cross,
To see an old woman
Ride on a white horse.
with rings on her fingers
and bells on her toes,
She shall have music
Wherever she goes.

bang—*to bang the bush* to surpass anything that has gone before.

"My," said he, "if that don't bang the bush; you are another-guess chap

from what I took you to be, anyhow."—
Haliburton.

Exp.—*"Really," said he, "if that does
not exceed anything I have yet heard;
you are quite a different fellow from
what I supposed you to be, at any
rate."*

banyan—*banyan-day* a day on which
no meat is served out for rations. A
sea term.

bar—*the bar sinister* the sign of illegitimate birth. In the days of chivalry,
knights of illegitimate birth carried
the arms of their family marked with
a black diagonal bar across from the
right upper corner.

*Why, Philip, my ancestors were princes
of royal blood when yours still herded
the swine in these woods. I can show
more than thirty quarterings upon my
shield, each the mark of a noble house,
and I will not be the first to put a bar
sinister across them.*—H. R. Haggard.

—*to bar out* to refuse to admit the masters of a school. Scholars in England
frequently revolted in this way.

*Revolts, republics, revolutions, most no
graver than a schoolboys' barring
out.*—Tennyson.

—*to eat for the bar.* See **eat**.

bargain—*a wet bargain* an agreement
concluded by the parties drinking
liquor together.

*The recruit took the condition of a
soldier, with a guinea to make it a wet
bargain.*—Windham.

Exp.—*The recruit enlisted, and
received a guinea that he might drink,
on the conclusion of the agreement.*

—*into the bargain* beyond what has
been stipulated; extra; besides.

*If he studies the writings, say, of Mr.
Herbert Spencer into the bargain, he
will be perfect.*—M. Arnold.

—*to make the best of a bad bargain* to
bear adverse circumstances in the
best possible way.

*Men had made up their minds to submit
to what they could not help, and to
make the best of a bad bargain.*—
Freeman.

Exp.—*Men had resolved to submit to
the inevitable, and to bear their bad
luck with the best possible grace.*

bark—*his bark is worse than his bite*
he uses strong language, but acts with
mildness.

*However, I dare say you have learned
by this time that my father's bark is
worse than his bite.*—Sarah Tytler.

barmecide—*a barmecide feast* a banquet where there is nothing to eat.
The name comes from the *Arabian
Nights*, where the story is told of a rich
man, Barmecide, who invited a friend
to dine with him. Dishes were
brought to the table in due order, but
there were no victuals in them. The
host, however, pretended to eat, and
his guest had the politeness to imitate
him. Afterwards a real feast was
served to reward the man for his good
humour.

*A barmecide room, that had always a
great dining-table in it, and never had
a dinner.*—Dickens.

basket—*to be left in the basket* to be
neglected or thrown over.

*Whatever he wants, he has only to ask
it,*
*And all other suitors are left in the
basket.*—Barham.

bat—*on his own bat* on his own
account. Taken from the game of
cricket.

*Titmouse has left Spanker and Co.,
and is now on his own bat (in business
for himself).*

beans—*to know beans; to know how
many beans make five* to be
sagacious; to be worldly-wise.

*I was a fool, I was, and didn't know
how many beans made five. I was
born yesterday, I was.*—B. L. Farjeon.

bear—*to bear one hard* to be unfriendly to.

Cæsar doth bear me hard—Shakespeare.

—*to bear out a man* to lend him support; to back him.

Every one will bear me out in saying that the mark by which you know them is their genial and hearty freshness and youthfulness of character.—Hughes.

—*to bear a bob or a hand* to assist; to join others in work.

We were so short of men that every one on board had to bear a hand.—R. L. Stevenson.

—*to bear down upon* to approach deliberately.

As soon as they got on the quarterdeck Arthur perceived a tall, well-preserved man with an eye-glass, whom he seemed to know, bearing down upon them.—H. R. Haggard.

—*to bear in mind* to remember; recollect.

It will be borne in mind that Mr. Aubrey had given bail to a very large amount.—S. Warren.

—*a bear leader* one who acts as companion to a person of distinction.

Once more on foot, but freed from the irksome duties of a bear leader, and with some of his pay as tutor in pocket, Goldsmith continued his half-vagrant peregrinations through part of France and Piedmont and some of the Italian states.—Washington Irving.

—*to play the bear with* to injure; to damage.

The last storm has played the bear with my crops.

—*a bear garden* a disorderly gathering.

Mr. Trollope visited the chamber whilst at Paris, and heard Soult and Dupin. He thought it a bear garden.—Temple Bar, 1887.

beard—*to beard the lion in his den* to attack a dangerous or much-feared person boldly in his own quarters.

Miss Masterman returned to the inn for lunch, and then prepared for her momentous visit to the rectory; for she had resolved to beard the lion in his den (attack her enemy in his own house), and to denounce him in the presence of his family as a hypocrite.—Chamber's Journal, 1886.

beat—*to beat about the bush* See **bush.**

—*to beat the bush* to search as sportsmen do when in pursuit of game.

Mr. Maurice, again, that pure and devout spirit – of whom, however, the truth must at last be told, that in theology he passed his life beating the bush with deep emotion and never starting the hare.—Matthew Arnold.

—*to beat down* to cause a seller to reduce the price.

Perhaps his patient would try to beat him down (lower his professional charge or fee) and Dr. Benjamin made up his mind to have the whole or nothing.—O. W. Holmes.

—*to beat a retreat* to retire. Originally a military phrase, having reference to the beating of the drums as a sign for making a retreat.

She introduced Percy to him. The colonel was curt but grumpy, and Percy soon beat a retreat.—Reade.

—*to beat the air* to struggle in vain.

So fight I, not as one that beateth the air.—St. Paul (1 Cor. ix. 26).

—*to beat up the quarters of* to visit without ceremony; to "look up."

Sunday coming round, he set off therefore after breakfast, once more to beat up Captain Cuttle's quarters.—Dickens.

—*to beat goose* to thump in arms against the chest in order to get warm.

The common labourers at outdoor work were beating goose to drive the blood into their fingers.—Times, 1883.

—*that beats the dutch* that is astonishing.

It beats the Dutch (it is wonderful) how the thief can have got through so small a hole.

—*to beat a hollow* to vanquish completely.

The Galatea was beaten hollow (completely defeated) by the Mayflower in the last international yacht race.

—*to beat the devil's tattoo* See **tattoo.**

beau—*beau ideal* highest conceivable type; finest specimen. French.

My ambition is to give them a beau ideal of a welcome.—Charlotte Bronte.

beauty—*the beauty sleep* the sleep taken before midnight.

A medical man, who may be called up at any moment, must make sure of his beauty sleep.—H. Kingsley.

—*beauty and the beast* a lovely woman with an ugly male companion. The expression is borrowed from an old nursery tale.

Beauty and the beast was what they called us when we went out walking together, as we used to do every day.—H. R. Haggard.

—*beauty is but skin-deep* beauty is a thing which can be easily destroyed, and should not, therefore, be valued too highly.

Marry a woman for her good qualities; beauty is but skin-deep.

bed—*as you make your bed, you must lie on it* you must bear the consequences of your deliberate actions.

"He has made his bed, and he must lie on it," said the archdeacon.—A. Trollope.

—*a bed of roses* an altogether agreeable position or situation.

A parochial life is not a bed of roses, Mrs. Mann.—Dickens.

Bedfordshire—*to be for Bedfordshire* to be anxious to retire to bed.

'Faith, I'm for Bedfordshire.—Swift.

bee—*in a bee line* following a straight course, as a bee is supposed to do.

I'm going to get home as soon as I can—strike a bee line.—W. D. Howells.

—*to have a bee in one's bonnet* to be crazy in a certain direction.

What new bee will you put under your bonnet next, sir?—A. Trollope.

been—*you've been (and gone) and done it* you have committed an action that may have very serious consequences. A remark generally made half in wonder, half as a warning.

I say, young fellow, you've been and done it, you have.—Dickens.

beer—*to think no small beer of anything* to esteem it very highly.

Miss Arrowpoint coloured, and Mr. Bult observed, with his usual phlegmatic solidity. "Your pianist does not think small beer of himself."—George Eliot.

beg—*to go begging* or *a-begging* (of things) to find no one to claim; to be so plentiful as to be thought not worth accepting. Generally said of things that have been highly prized at other times.

Places like Annerley Hall don't go begging.—Goldsmith.

—*to beg the question* to assume that which requires to be proved; to take for granted the very point of issue.

"Facsimiles!" exclaimed the old man angrily: "why not frankly say that they are by the same hand at once?"

"But that is begging the whole question" (assuming all that requires to be proved), argued honest Dennis, his good and implastic nature leading him into the self-same error into which he had fallen at Charlecote Park.—James Payn.

beggars—*beggars should not be*

choosers those who ask for favours should submit to the terms imposed upon them.

bell—*eight bells* sounded on board ship at noon, four, and eight o'clock.
The unwelcome cry of "All star-bowlines ahoy! eight bells, there below! do you hear the news?" (the usual formula of calling the watch) roused us.—R. H. Dana, Jun.

—*to bear the bell* or *carry away the bell* to be victor in a race or other contest.
There are certain cases, it is true, where the vulgar Saxon word is refined, and the refined Latin vulgar, in poetry – as in sweat and perspiration; but there are vastly more in which the Latin bears the bell.—J. R. Lowell.

—*to bell the cat* at great personal risk, to render a common foe harmless for evil. A phrase borrowed from a well-known fable told upon one historical occasion with great success.
When James III, was king of Scotland, he irritated the old nobility by the favour he showed to painters and architects. One of the latter, named Cochran, who had succeeded to the estates of the Earl of Mar, was especially hated by the nobles. At a meeting in the church of Lander they discussed how best to get rid of him. Lord Gray, afraid that the discussion would lead to no practical result, told the story of the mice and the cat. "A colony of mice, had suffered greatly from the attacks of a cat, who pounced upon them before they had time to escape. They were much concerned over the matter, and resolved to do something to defend themselves. A young mouse rose up and proposed that they should fix a bell round pussy's neck, which would warn them of her approach. This proposal was warmly received, until an old mouse put the pertinent question, 'But which of us will bell the cat?' The orator had not thought of this, and was speechless." When Lord Gray had finished, Archibald, Earl of Angus, a man noted for his bodily prowess and daring, rose up and swore that he would bell the cat. He kept his word, captured Cochran, and had him hanged over the bridge of Lauder. Afterwards he was always known as Bell-the-Cat. And from a loophole while I peep Old Bell-the-Cat came from the keep.—Scott.

belt—*to hit below the belt* to strike another unfairly. A pugilist is not allowed by the rules of boxing to hit his opponent under the waist-belt. This belt is a significant part of a boxer's attire. The champion pugilist of England wears a prize-belt, which he must deliver to any one who vanquishes him.
To refer to his private distresses in a public discussion was hitting below the belt.
Exp.—*It was unfair, in a public discussion, to refer to his private distresses.*

ben—*ben trovato* well found; an ingenious invention. Italian.
If the tale is not true, at least it is ben trovato (ingeniously constructed).

benefit—*without benefit of clergy* During the Middle Ages criminals who could prove that they belonged to the Church, even to the extent of being able to recite a verse of Scripture, were allowed to escape punishment. This privilege was known as *benefit of clergy*. Notorious offenders often escaped on this plea, like Will of Harribee, who knew his *neck-verse* (see *The Lay of the Last Minstrel*). The phrase is now used loosely, as in the following:—
She would order Goody Hicks to take

a James's powder, without appeal, resistance, or benefit of clergy.—Thackeray.

Benjamin—*Benjamin's mess* a specially large portion. For the origin see Gen. xliii. 34: "But Benjamin's mess was five times so much as any of theirs."

berth—*to give a wide berth* to give a ship room to swing at anchor; to avoid a person.

I have had letters warning me that I had better give Ballinascroon a wide berth if I happen to be in that part of Ireland.—Wm. Black.

Bess—*Bess o' Bedlam* a female lunatic vagrant. Bess is a contraction of Elizabeth.

Will you have the goodness to tell me, miss, why you are dressed up after that mad Bess of Bedlam fashion?—A. Trollope.

best—*best man* groomsman; the attendant on a bridegroom.

It was like asking a young gentleman to be best man when he wants to be the bridegroom himself.—James Payn.

—*at the best* taking the most favourable view possible.

I advise you not to accept the situation. At the best (even in the most favourable state of affairs) you will be a mere favourite, removable on the slightest whim of a capricious woman.

—*to have the best of an argument* to gain the advantage in an argument.

"In your argument yesterday, Charles, the strange gentleman had the best of it" (was victor), said his wife.

—*to make the best of one's way* to go as well as can be done in the circumstances.

With these awful remarks, Mr. Kenwigs sat down in a chair, and defied the nurse, who made the best of her way into the adjoining room.—Dickens.

—*to make the best of both worlds* to manage so as to get the good things of earth and be sure of a good place in heaven.

There have been great captains, great statesmen, ay, and great so-called Christians, seeking to make the best of both worlds (being at once worldly and heavenly in their aspirations).—Sarah Tytler.

bet—*you bet* I assure you. American.

My father's rich, you bet.—Henry James, Jun.

bête—*bête noire* pet aversion; object of particular dislike. French.

The ladies of the party simply detest him—if we except Miss Thorneydyke, who cannot afford to detest anything in trousers. Lady Pat, who is a bit of a wit, calls him her bête noire.—Florence Maryat.

better—*for better or for worse* indissolubly, in marriage.

Each believed and indeed pretty plainly asserted, that they could live more handsomely asunder; but, alas! they were united for better or for worse.—Maria Edgeworth.

—*to get the better of* to overcome; to vanquish; to be stronger than.

I got the better of (overcame) my disease, however, but I was so weak that I spat blood whenever I attempted to write.—H. Mackenzie.

—*better half* a man's wife; a complimentary term for a married woman.

"Polly heard it," said Toodle, jerking his hat over his shoulder in the direction of the door, with an air of perfect confidence in his better half.—Dickens.

between—*between you and me and the post* or *the door-post* a phrase used when anything is spoken confidentially.

"Well, between you and me and the door-post, squire," answered his learned visitor. "I am not so sure that

Sir Anthony is quite the rose and crown of his profession."—Blackmore.

The phrase is also found in the more familiar form.—

—*between you and me and the bedpost* don't reveal a word of what I say.

—*between ourselves* speaking confidentially.

Steyne has a touch of the gout, and so, between ourselves, has your brother.—Thackeray.

—*between Scylla and Charybdis* between two menacing dangers. Avoiding one, you fall into the other. Scylla was a rock and Charybdis a whirlpool on the coast of Sicily, and the narrow passage between was very much feared by mariners because of its double danger. Now they are looked on as harmless.

You have your Scylla and your Charybdis, as pastor of the congregation. If you preach the old theology, you will lose the young men; and if you preach the new, you will alienate the old men.

—*between two fires* subject to a double attack; a position of peculiar danger in warfare.

Poor Dawson is between two fires: if he whips the child, its mother scolds him: and if he lets it off, its grandmother comes down on him.

—*to fall between two stools* See **stool.**

—*between wind and water* See **wind.**

bid—*to bid fair* to seem likely; to promise well.

In the eastern counties the old race of small farmers and yeomen have well-nigh disappeared, or rather they bid fair to disappear.—Chambers's Journal, 1887.

big—*a big-wig* a person in authority; a high or powerful person.

Sooner or later one of the big-wigs will take it up, and the point will be settled

done way or other.—Murray's Magazine, 1887.

bird—*a bird in the hand is worth two in the bush* a sure advantage is better than a problematical advantage, even though the latter promises to be twice as good.

—*a bird's-eye or bird-eye view* a general view, such as would be enjoyed by a bird flying over a country.

Viewing from the Pisgah of his pulpit the free, moral, happy, flourishing, and glorious state of France, as in a bird-eye landscape of a promised land.—Burke.

Note.—*Pisgah was the mountain east of the Jordan from the summit of which Moses was permitted to see the promised land of Canaan.*

—*to kill two birds with one stone* to effect two results with one expenditure of trouble.

Sir Barnet killed two birds with one stone.—Dickens.

—*birds of a feather* persons of like tastes.

Birds of a feather flock together.

Exp.—*Persons of like tastes seek one another's society.*

—*jail-bird* a rogue who is oftener in prison than out of it; a hardened offender.

The jail-birds who piped this tune were, without a single exception, the desperate cases of this moral hospital.—Reade.

—*bird of passage* one who shifts from place to place.

No one (here in Shanghai) seems to be living his own life, but something else—something temporary: as if we were all expecting to go home again in the course of the afternoon or the next day, and therefore it does not much matter what we do just for the few hours that remain; or as if we were convicts doing our time; or as if we were political exiles, who might be recalled at any moment; or as if we were in some way birds of passage.—Besant.

—*a little bird whispered it to me* A phrase playfully used of something which has been reported and is repeated. The reference is from the Bible, Eccles. x. 20:—"Curse not the king, no not in thy thought; and curse not the rich in thy bedchamber: for a bird of the air shall carry the voice, and that which hath wings shall tell the matter."

"What a wicked man you are!" smiled Mrs. Jennynge, admiringly. "A little bird told me you could be very severe when you please, though I refused to believe it.".—James Payn.

bishop—*the bishop has set his foot in it* the contents of the dish are burned. A jocular reference to the zeal of bishops for burning heretics.

"Why sure, Betty, thou are bewitched: this cream is burnt too."

"Why, madam, the bishop has set his foot in it."—Swift.

bit—*a bit of one's mind* a good scolding; a serious reproof.

"I shall have to tell her a bit of my mind" (remonstrate sharply with her), he said, as he stepped across the close.—A. Trollope.

—*not a bit of it* by no means; not at all.

"That's rather a sudden pull-up, ain't it, Sammy?" inquired Mr. Weller.

"Not a bit of it," said Sam.—Dickens.

bite—*to bite the thumb at* This was formerly a sign of contempt, often made use of by those who wished to pick a quarrel.

I will bite my thumb at them; which is a disgrace to them, if they bear it—Shakespeare.

—*to bite one's lips* to show signs of disgust and mortification.

The advocates on both sides are

alternately biting their lips (showing chagrin) to hear their conflicting misstatements and sophisms exposed.*—Macaulay.

—*to bite the dust* to fall in battle.

That day three thousand Saracens bit the dust (were slain in battle).

black—*a black sheep* an ill-conducted person; a member of society who is not considered respectable.

I'm forbidden the house. I'm looked upon as a black sheep—a pest, a contamination.—Edmund Yates.

—*Black Monday* the Monday on which school reopens.

She now hated my sight, and made home so disagreeable to me that what is called by schoolboys Black Monday was to me the whitest in the whole year.—Fielding.

—*blackmail* money extorted by threats.

Blackmail, I suppose, is an honest man paying through his nose for the sins of his youth.

—*black draught* a dose formerly given by physicians to relieve stomach ailments.

Go, enjoy your black draughts of metaphysics.—Thackeray.

—*to beat* or *pinch another black and blue* to beat or pinch him until his flesh is discoloured.

"We'll go down arm in arm."

"But you pinch me black and blue," urged Gride.—Dickens.

—*black and white* written definitely on paper in ink.

"I have found it all out! Here is his name in black and white;" and she touched the volume she had just placed on the table with impressive reverence.—James Payn.

blanket—*a wet blanket* one who discourages, who causes others to become disheartened; also, discouragement.

I don't want (said Sir Brian) to be a wet blanket.—W. E. Norris.

blarney—*to have kissed the blarney stone* to be full of flattery and persuasive language. There is a stone in the village of Blarney, near Cork, in Ireland, which was supposed to confer this gift of persuasive speech on those who touched it.

You are so full of compliments to-day that you must have kissed the blarney stone.

bless—*to bless oneself* to be astonished.

Could Sir Thomas look in upon us just now, he would bless himself, for we are rehearsing all over the house.—Jane Austen.

—*to bless oneself with* in one's possession. Generally used of coin, especially of silver coin, which people crossed their palms with for good luck.

The lady hasn't got a sixpence wherewithal to bless herself.—Dickens.

—*bless you* an exclamation of varying significance. Commonly used after sneezing, to avert evil consequences—a superstition common in Ireland.

"Bless you!" murmurs Miss Seymour under her breath—the benediction being called forth by the sneeze, not the demand for mustard.—Rhoda Broughton.

blind—*to go it blind* to act without due deliberation.

blindman—*blindman's buff* an ancient game, still very popular with children. One of the company is blindfolded, and the fun of the game consists in his efforts to capture some one.

Mr. Burchell, who was of the party, was always fond of seeing some innocent amusement going forward, and set the boys and girls to blindman's buff.—Goldsmith.

blithe—*blithe bread* food distributed among guests on the birth of a child in the family. An old custom.

Throughout three long jovial weeks the visitors came and went, and every day the blithe bread was piled in the peck for the poor of the earth.—Hall Caine.

blood—*blood and iron* military compulsion; the force of armies. A phrase usually associated with Prince Bismarck.—Blut und Eisen.

Mr. Carlyle has been heard to say that Rhadamanthus would certainly give Macaulay four dozen lashes when he went to the shades for his treatment of Marlborough. This is quite in character for the Scotch apostle of blood and iron.—J. Cotter Morison.

—*bad blood* See **bad**.

—*his blood was up* he was excited or in a passion.

That is the way of doing business—a cut and thrust style, without any flourish: Scott's style when his blood was up.—Christopher North.

—*a prince of the blood* a nobleman who is a near relative of the royal family.

He had a calm, exhausted smile which—as though he had been a prince of the blood (noble of the highest rank) who had passed his life in acknowledging the plaudits of the populace—suggested the ravages of affability.—James Payn.

—*blood is thicker than water* kinship will cause a man to befriend his relatives; it is better to trust for kind treatment to one's kinsmen than to strangers.

"I am aware there is a family tie, or I should not have ventured to trouble you."

"Blood is thicker than water,' isn't it?—A. Trollope.

—*in cold blood* without passion; deliberately.

The suggestion of such a contingency—which, of course, meant total failure—in cold blood (without any passion) filled up the cup of the antiquary's indignation.—James Payn.

—*blue blood* aristocratic descent.

The blood of the Bunkers has, in yourself, assumed the most azure hue (become most aristocratic).—Besant.

—*to make your blood creep* to fill you with awe or terror.

Jinny Oates, the cobbler's daughter, being more imaginative, stated not only that she had seen the earrings too, but that they had made her blood creep (inspired her with terror).—George Eliot.

blow—*to blow over* to pass off; to be heard of no more.

"Gracious me! an execution!" said Lady Clonbrony: "but I heard you talk of an execution months ago, my lord, before my son went to Ireland, and it blew over; I heard no more of it."—Maria Edgeworth.

—*to blow up* to scold; to reprimand.

If I hadn't been proud of the house, I shouldn't be blowing you up.—Hughes.

blown—*blown upon* having a bad reputation; unsound; damaged.

My credit was so blown upon that I could not hope to raise a shilling.—Thackeray.

blue—*the blue ribbon* (a) the Order of the Garter.

Though he distributed peerages with a lavish and culpable profusion, he (Pitt) never desired one for himself, and he declined the blue ribbon when it was offered him.—Spectator, 1887.

—(b) the phrase is also used to signify "a distinction of the highest kind." P. In 1840 he was elected to a fellowship at Oriel, then the blue ribbon of the university.—Athenæum, 1887.

—(c) a badge worn in England and America by those who do not drink intoxicating liquors.

Of course, Mr. Smith didn't smoke, and sported a blue ribbon as proudly as if it had been the Order of the Garter.—Besant.

—*a blue funk* a state of terrified expectation; a condition of frightened suspense.

Altogether, I was in the pitiable state known by school-boys as a blue funk.—H. R. Haggard.

—*a blue moon* a phenomenon which happens very rarely. Once in a blue moon = very seldom indeed. The real origin of this phrase is unknown.

—*blue moonshine* fantastic nonsense. The subject of a short poem of three stanzas in Haweis's Comic Poets of the Nineteenth Century.

—*blue books* official publications of the British Government. So called because their covers are blue in colour.

At home he gave himself up to the perusal of Blue Books.—Thackeray.

—*in the blues* melancholy; lowspirited.

If we had been allowed to sit idle, we should all have fallen in the blues (had an attack of melancholy).—R. L. Stevenson.

—*the blue and yellow* the *Edinburgh Review*, so called from the colour of its cover.

Shortly afterwards, and very little before the appearance of the Blue and Yellow, Jeffrey made another innovation.—George Saintsbury, in Macmillan's Magazine, 1887.

—*the man in blue* the policeman.

Those kinds of sin which bring upon us the man in blue are such as we think we shall never commit.—Besant.

—*to look blue* to seem disconcerted.

Squire Brown looks rather blue at having to pay two pounds ten shillings for the posting expenses from Oxford.—Hughes.

—*blue-nose* a name given to the inhabitants of Nova Scotia in North America.

How is it that an American can sell his wares, at whatever price he pleases, where a Blue-nose (Nova Scotian) would fail to make a sale at all?—Haliburton.

—*blue-devils* dreadful apparitions which appear to a patient suffering from *delirium tremens.*

The drunken old landlord had a fit of the blue-devils last night, and was making a dreadful noise.

—*blue-stocking* a woman who prides herself on her learning.

Lucy (Hutchinson) was evidently a very superior young lady, and looked upon as the bluest of blue-stockings.—Gentleman's Magazine, 1886.

—*to fly the blue-peter* to be ready to sail (of a vessel). The blue-peter is a small flag run up on the fore-mast of a ship, to announce its departure within twenty-four hours.

The ensign was at her peak, and at the fore floated the blue-peter.—W. Clark Russell.

—*Blue hen* a nickname for the state of Delaware in the United States. A Blue-hen is a native of the state.

"Your mother was a Blue-hen, no doubt," is a reproof to a person who brags, especially of his ancestry.

blush—*to put to the blush* to cause one to redden with shame.

Ridicule, instead of putting guilt and error to the blush (making guilt and error ashamed), turned her formidable shafts against innocence and truth.—Macaulay.

—*at the first blush* or at first blush when one looks hastily for the first time; at the first sudden appearance.

At the first blush the landlord would appear to suffer most, but on nearer examination the tenants are found in the lowest state of poverty.—National Review, 1887.

bo—*to say "bo" to a goose.* See **boo.**

boards—*on the boards* following the profession of an actor.

Lily was on the boards, but Katie could get nothing to do.—Besant.

a bob—a shilling.

The trip cost me a bob and a bender (a shilling and sixpence.)

bodkin—*to sit bodkin.* See **sit.**

body—*to keep body and soul together* to sustain life.

My earnings are so miserable that they scarcely suffice to keep body and soul together (to keep me from starving).

Bohemia—*a flavour of Bohemia* a tone of unconventionality; of neglect of social rules. Bohemia is the name applied in London to the quarter where artists and literary men live as best suits them, wholly neglecting fashion and the elegant world. In France and some other countries Bohemian is the name applied to the gypsy race, who, wherever they go, live a rough kind of life, apart from other people.

Meantime there is a flavour of Bohemia about the place which pleases newcomers. To be sure, Bohemia never had any clubs.—Besant.

bold—*to make bold*—to venture.

"I make bold, young woman," he said as they went away, "to give you a warning about my nephew."—Besant.

—*to make bold with* to tackle; to deal with.

By the time I was twelve years old I had risen into the upper school, and could make bold with Eutropius and Cæsar.

—*as bold as brass* impudent; without modesty or shame.

> Fred Bullock told old Osborne of his son's appearance and conduct. "He came in as bold as brass," said Frederick.—R. H. Thackeray.

bon—*bon gré, mal gré* whether one likes it or not. French.

> Bon gré, mal gré, we had to wait our turn.—R. H. Dana.

—*a bon mot* a clever saying. French.

> The bon mots of the mother were everywhere repeated.—Maria Edgeworth.

—*a bon vivant* an epicure; one fond of good living. French.

> Sir Charles Lyndon was celebrated as a wit and bon vivant.—Thackeray.

bona—*bonâ fide* in good faith; trustworthy. Latin.

> The offer we make is a bonâ fide one (made in good faith).

> But this was a bonâ fide translation.—W. D. Howells.

bone—*a bone of contention* something which causes a quarrel (as a bone does when thrown among dogs).

> The possession of Milan was a bone of contention (cause of quarrel) between the two monarchs.

—*to have a bone to pick with any one* to have some cause of quarrel or complaint against him.

> I consider that I have got a bone to pick with Providence about that nose.—H. R. Haggard.

—*to make no bones* not to hesitate; to publish openly.

> He makes no bones of (publishes openly) his dislike of natives.

bonne—*a bonne bouche* a sweet morsel; something which pleases. French.

> If I could ever believe that Mandeville meant anything more by his fable of the Bees than a bonne bouche of solemn raillery.—S. E. Coleridge.

boo—*to say boo* or *bo to a goose* a test of courage. A man who cannot say boo to a goose has no spirit, and is to be despised for his timidity.

> Now you are always writing, and can't say "bo" to a goose.—C. Reade.

book—*in the books of; in the good books of* in favour with; a favourite of.

> I was so much in his books (in his favour) that at his decease he left me his lamp.—Addison.

—*in the bad* or *black books of* in disfavour with.

> He neglected to call on his aunt, and got into her bad books.

> For some reason or other I am in his black books.—W. E. Norris.

—*to bring to book* to call to account; to accuse of a fault or crime.

> "By the Lord sir," cried the major, bursting into speech at sight of the waiter, who was come to announce breakfast, "it's an extraordinary thing to me that no one can have the honour and happiness of shooting such beggars without being brought to book for it."—Dickens.

born—*all one's born days* during one's whole experience of life.

> At last Nicholas pledged himself to betray no further curiosity, and they walked on, both ladies giggling very much, and declaring that they had never seen such a wicked creature in all their born days.—Dickens.

—*not born yesterday* worldly-wise; not easily gulled.

> She was considerable of a longheaded woman (quite a prudent woman), was mother; she could see as far ahead as most folks. She warn't born yesterday, I guess (was not easily outwitted, I venture to say).—Haliburton.

—*born with a silver spoon in one's mouth*. See **spoon**.

borne—*borne in upon*. See **bear**.

—borne in upon one impressed upon one's mind. Generally used of some foreboding or warning.

It was borne in upon her (impressed upon her mind), as she afterwards expressed it, to beseech the divine compassion in favour of the houseless wretches constrained, perhaps, as much by want as evil habit, to break through and steal.—James Payn.

bosom—a bosom friend a very intimate friend.

"What a strange history that was of his marriage."

"So I have heard; but he is not quite bosom friend enough with me to have told me all the particulars."—A. Trollope.

Botany—Botany Bay the port in Australia to which convicts were formerly shipped.

Who careth that the respectable family solicitor had a grandfather by the maternal side sent to Botany Bay?—Besant.

bottom—one's bottom dollar one's last coin. An Americanism.

I would have parted with my bottom dollar to relieve her.—Besant.

—to be at the bottom of anything to be the chief instigator in any affair.

I am sure Russell is at the bottom of (the chief instigator in) this movement to get rid of our present musical conductor.

—at bottom really; essentially.

He was a kind-hearted man at bottom (under the surface, however roughly he might speak).—James Payn.

bow—to draw the long bow to exaggerate.

Then he went into a lot of particulars, and I begun (began) to think he was drawing the long bow.—W. D. Howells.

—to have a second string to one's bow to be provided with something in reserve in case of an accident happening.

Moreover, in his impatient ambition and indefatigable energy, he had sought a second string to his bow: the public and the publishers showed their sense of his abilities as a pamphleteer and a novelist.—Edinburgh Review.

Exp.—*Moreover, in his impatient ambition and indefatigable energy, he (Disraeli) had sought to have another career open, on which he might fall back if he failed in politics: he was gaining popularity as a pamphleteer and a novelist.*

—to draw a bow at a venture to make an attack blindly; to say or do something without knowing exactly what the result will be. See 1 Kings xxii.

"And your mother was an Indian," said Lady Jane, drawing her bow at a venture.—Mrs. E. Lynn Linton.

bowels—his bowels yearned he felt full of sympathy or affection.

At the sight of his inoffensive sorrow, the mother's bowels began to yearn over (the mother felt her heart drawn to) her son.—C. Reade.

—bowels of mercy or compassion compassionate feelings; pity.

We men of business, you see, Carew, must have bowels of compassion like any other,—Mrs. E. Lynn Linton.

bowl—to bowl out to stop in a successful career. A cricketing phrase.

"Bowled out, eh?" said Routh.

"Stumped sir," replied Dallas.—E. Yates.

—to bowl over to knock down; to overturn.

It was within a day of Thursday's visit that Bennet's last defence was thus placidly bowled over.—Sarah Tytler.

box—in the same box equally embarrassed.

"How is it that you are not dancing?"

He murmured something inaudible about "partner".

"Well, we are in the same box."—H. R. Haggard.

—**to box the compass** to shift round to all quarters. A nautical phrase.

After a week or so the wind would regularly box the compass, as the sailors call it.—Blackmore.

—**to box harry** to avoid the regular hotel table, and take something substantial at teatime to avoid expense. A phrase used by commercial travellers.

boy—*a boy in buttons* a lad who acts as door-servant and waiter in an establishment.

The very boy in buttons thought more of his promotion than of the kind mistress who had housed, clothed, and fed him when a parish orphan.—G. J. Whyte-Melville.

boycott—*to boycott a person* to refuse to deal with a person, in the way of buying or selling, or of social intercourse: from Captain Boycott, a landowner in Ireland, who was so treated during the agrarian war about 1855.

brass—*a brass farthing* a symbol of what is worthless.

He could perceive his wife did not care one brass farthing about him.—H. R. Haggard.

brazen—*to brazen out an act* to refuse to confess to a guilty action, or to boast of it; to be without shame regarding it.

As to Bullying Bob, he brazened the matter out, declaring he had been affronted by the Franklands, and that he was glad he had taken his revenge of them.—Maria Edgeworth.

bread—*to take bread and salt* to bind oneself by oath. An old-fashioned phrase.

—*to break bread* to eat; to be a guest. Old-fashioned in ordinary prose.

As often as Mr. Staunton was invited, or invited himself, to break bread at the Villa des Chataigniers, so often did Violet express her intention of eating her own luncheon or dinner in company with Hopkins, a faithful old servant.—W. E. Norris.

—*bread and butter* material welfare; what sustains life.

Former pride was too strong for present prudence, and the question of bread and butter was thrown to the winds in revolt at the shape of the platter in which it was offered.—Mrs. E. Lynn Linton.

—*bread-basket* a vulgar name for the stomach.

—*bread and cheese* the bare necessaries of life.

—*a "bread-and-cheese" marriage* a marriage to a man who cannot afford to give his wife luxuries.

You describe in well-chosen language the miseries of a bread-and-cheese marriage to your eldest daughter.—G. J. Whyte-Melville.

break—*to break down* (a) to lose control over one's feelings.

"They had better not try," replies Lady Swansdown, and then she suddenly breaks down and cries.—Florence Marryat.

—(b) to fail in health.

I have worked hard since I came here; but since Abner left me at the pinch it hasn't been man's work, Jacky; it has been a wrestling match from dawn to dark. No man could go on so and not break down.—C. Reade.

—*to break in* to interrupt another with a remark.

"Oh, don't talk to me about Rogers!" his wife broke in.—W. D. Howells.

—*to break ground.* **See ground.**

—*to break off with* to cease to have communications with; to renounce the acquaintance of.

Well, then, I consent to break off with Sir Charles, and only see him once more—as a friend.—Reade.

—*to break up* to be near death; to show signs of approaching dissolution.

"Poor Venables is breaking up," observed Sir Brian as they strolled away.—Good Words, 1887.

—(b) to quarrel with; to cease to be friendly with.

"But what cause have I given him to break with me?" says the countess, trembling,—Florence Marryat.

—*to break the ice* to commence a conversation where there has been an awkward silence; to speak first on a delicate matter.

"I will not," said Lochiel, "break the ice. That is a point of honour with me."—Macaulay.

—*to break the news* to impart startling information in a gentle manner; preparing the recipient gradually for the shock.

It suggested to me that I had better break the news to them (of their father's death by the explosion of a boiler), and mechanically I accepted the suggestion and rode away sadly to the Italian villa.—The Mistletoe Bough, 1885.

breakers—*breakers ahead* a cry of danger. The phrase is taken from sealife, where the cry, "Breakers ahead!" announces immediate peril to a vessel. Breakers are waves which go into foam over rocks, or in shallow water.

It made her forget the carking anxieties, the vision of social breakers ahead, that had begun to take the gilding off her position.—Blackmore.

breast—*to make a clean breast of* to make a full and free confession of something that has been kept a secret.

She resolved to make a clean breast

of it (confess the whole affair) before she died.—Scott.

breath—*the breath of one's nostrils* something as valuable as life itself.

The novels were discussed in the society whose flatteries were as the breath of his nostrils.—Edinburgh Review, 1886.

Exp.—The novels were discussed in aristocratic circles, whose flatteries were as dear to Disraeli as his own life.

—*to take away one's breath* to cause surprise or consternation.

He was so polite, he flattered with a skill so surprising, he was so fluent, so completely took away her breath (astonished her), that when he finally begged permission to deliver a valedictory oration to all the young ladies, Miss Billingsworth, without thinking what she was doing, granted that permission.—Besant.

—*under one's breath* very quietly; in fear.

breathe—*to breathe one's last* to die.

It had breathed its last in doing its master service.—Thackeray.

brick—*a regular brick* a good fellow; a pleasant man.

—*like bricks*, or *like a thousand of bricks* with a great impetus or force; violently.

Out flies the fare like bricks.—Dickens.

—*with a brick in one's hat* drunk. American slang.

I think our friend over there has a brick in his hat (is intoxicated).

brief—*to accept a brief on behalf of* to espouse the cause of. A phrase of legal origin.

Not a little to Gilbert's surprise, Mr. Buswell flatly declined to make this concession, alleging that he had not sufficient knowledge of the circumstances to justify him in accepting a brief on behalf of (in defending) the accused.—W. E. Norris.

—*to hold a brief for another* to devote oneself to his defence; to urge all that can be said in his justification.

Professor Dowden holds a brief for Shelley.—Matthew Arnold.

bring—*to bring into play* to cause to act; to set in motion; to give scope to.

The very incongruity of their relative positions brought into play all his genius.—Macmillan's Magazine, 1887.

—*to bring about* to cause to happen; to assist in accomplishing.

There are many who declare that they would be willing to bring about an Anglo-Russian alliance upon the terms of giving Russia her head in the direction of Constantinople.—Fortnightly Review, 1887.

—*to bring round* to restore; to cause to recover.

"How is poor old No. 50 to-day?"

    "Much the same."

    "Do you think you will bring him round, sir?"—C. Reade.

—*to bring up* (of a sailing vessel) to stop; to cease moving.

He was still plunged in meditation when the cutter brought up in the bay.—Good Words, 1887.

—*to bring to bear* to cause to happen; to bring to a successful issue.

There was therefore no other method to bring things to bear but by persuading you that she was dead.—Goldsmith.

—*to bring down the house* to call forth enthusiastic applause.

Every sentence brought down the house as I never saw one brought down before.—J. R. Lowell.

—*to bring to the hammer.* See **hammer.**

—*to bring to the book.* See **book.**

—*to bring to* to resuscitate; to cause to recover.

I once brought a fellow to (made a fellow revive) that was drowned.—Haliburton.

broom—*new brooms sweep clean* those newly appointed to office are apt to make great changes.

If new brooms do not sweep clean, at any rate they sweep away.—Blackwood's Magazine, 1887.

—*to jump the broomstick* to be irregularly married.

This woman in Gerrard Street here had been married very young—over the broomstick, as we say—to a tramping man.—Dickens.

Brown—*Brown, Jones, and Robinson* representatives of Englishmen of the middle class. Their adventures were published in *Punch.*

After the splendid revelry of the mess-table, Captains Brown, Jones and Robinson would turn out in all the glory of red cloth and gold braid.—Mistletoe Bough, 1886.

—*to astonish the Browns* to do something, notwithstanding the shock it will give to the prejudices of one's neighbours.

If we go on to the top of the 'bus, our conduct will astonish the Browns (shock our prejudiced neighbours).

—*to do brown* to hoodwink completely; to gain complete mastery over. See **do.**

His was an imaginative poetical composition, easily scorched enough, but almost incapable of being thoroughly done brown.—G. J. Whyte-Melville.

—*brown bess* a musket.

The British soldier—with his clothing and accoutrements, his pouches, haversack, biscuits, and ammunition, not to mention Brown Bess, his mainstay and dependence—nothing punishes him so much as wet.—G. J. Whyte-Melville.

brutum—*brutum fulmen* a harmless thunderbolt. Latin.

bubble—*bubble and squeak* fried beef and cabbage.
Also used contemptuously of what is little prized.

Rank and title! bubble and squeak! No, not half so good as bubble and squeak—English beef and good cabbage.—Lytton.

buckle—*to buckle to* to set to work at in earnest; to apply oneself diligently to work.

We all buckled to with a will, doing four hours a day.—H. R. Haggard.

bud—*to check* or *nip in the bud* to destroy at an early age; to lose no time in suppressing.

Guessing his intentions, she had received to check them in the bud.—Dickens.

bull—*a bull's eye* the inner disk of a target, surrounded by rings of increasing magnitude. "To make a bull's eye" = to fire a highly successful shot; to score a great success; to gain a striking advantage.

The Republicans had made a bull's eye, and were jubilant.—New York Herald, August 1, 1888.

—*a bull in a china shop* something in a place where it will do an excessive amount of damage.

Poor John! he was perfectly conscious of his own ponderosity—more so perhaps than his sprightly mother-in-law gave him credit for. He felt like a bull in a china shop.—Murray's Magazine, 1887.

—*to take the bull by the horns* to attack something formidable in a bold and direct fashion.

Happening therefore, to meet Monckton one windy morning when he was walking into Kingscliff to keep an appointment, he resolved to take the bull by the horns.—W. E. Norris, in Good Words, 1887.

bullet—*every bullet has its billet* it is

appointed beforehand by fate what soldiers will fall in battle; it is no use contending against fate.

"Well," he remarked consolingly, "every bullet has its billet."—H. R. Haggard.

bundle—*to bundle in* to enter in an unceremonious fashion.

I say, Frank, I must have a dip; I shall bundle in.—G. J. Whyte-Melville.

Buridan—*Buridan's ass* a man of indecision. Buridan, the Greek sophist, maintained that if an ass could be placed between two haystacks, so that its choice was evenly balanced between them, it would starve to death.

He was a Buridan's ass of a man, and seldom came to a decision till it was too late.

burn—*to burn one's fingers* to suffer loss or hurt by meddling with something out of one's own sphere, as by investing in some plausible financial speculation, or taking part in another's quarrel.

He has been bolstering up these rotten iron-works too long. I told him he would burn his fingers.—Mrs. E. Lynn Linton.

—*to burn the candle at both ends* to expend one's resources in two directions; to consume one's energies in a double way.

Washington Irving talks of Goldsmith burning the candle at both ends in the heading to chapter xxiii, of his Life.

—*to burn one's boats* to leave no means of retreat; to act irrevocably.

Then he took the perforated cardboard and tore that likewise into small pieces. "Now I have burned my boats with a vengeance" (certainly left myself no way of retreat), he added grimly.—James Payn.

—*A burned child dreads the fire* those who have suffered are wary.

bury—*to bury the hatchet* to cease fighting. The phrase comes from a Red Indian custom in warfare.

But the Harcourts and the Ellacombes, the Gaysworthys and Fitz-George Standish, were among the more familiar of the guests invited to this dinner, which was essentially a well-dressed pow-wow (council) to witness the burying of the hatchet and the smoking of the calumet.—Mrs. E. Lynn Linton.

bush—*to beat about the bush* to avoid a direct statement of what must be said; to convey one's meaning in a roundabout fashion.

No: give me a chap that hits out straight from the shoulder. Can't you see this is worth a hundred Joneses beating about the bush and droning us all to sleep?—C. Reade.

—*good wine needs no bush* a good thing requires no advertisement; it commends itself. Formerly the branch of a tree was hung out in front of a tavern to indicate that liquor was for sale.

If it be true that good wine needs no bush (is its own recommendation), 'tis true that a good play needs no epilogue.—Shakespeare.

bushel—*under a bushel* secretly; without others knowing it.

Ah, you can't give a dinner under a bushel.—W. D. Howells.

business—*to go about one's business* to go off. The phrase is generally used in dismissing an intruder.

Bidding the soldiers go about their business and the coach to drive off, Hill let go of his prey sulkily, and waited for other opportunities of revenge.—Thackeray.

—*a man of business*—(a) a man gifted with powers of management; one who can prudently direct the details of an enterprise or undertaking.

He was one of the most skilful debaters and men of business in the kingdom.—Macaulay.

—(b) a legal adviser.

The tenant resolved to consult his man of business.

—*to do the business for a man* to kill a man.

His last imprudent exposure of himself to the night air did the business for him (put an end to his life).

—*to have no business in a place,* or *no business to do anything*—(a) to have no occupation calling one thither, or no right to do the thing.

You had no business to meet Mr. Campion without my knowledge: it was disgraceful of you.—F. Anstey.

—(b) figuratively of things.

A frown upon the atmosphere that hath no business (ought not) to appear where skies are blue and earth is gay.—Byron.

—*to mean business* to have serious intentions; to be bent on executing a project.

He really felt very much hurt and seriously alarmed, because it never had occurred to him that the other two should also mean business (have serious intentions—of marrying Clair).—Besant.

butter—*buttered fingers* fingers through which a ball slips. Used contemptuously of a cricket player who fails to hold a ball.

—*to look as if butter would not melt in one's mouth* to look unconcerned; harmless and innocent.

These good young ladies, who look as if butter wouldn't melt in their mouths, are not a whit better than the rest of us.—Blackmore.

—*to know on which side one's bread is buttered* to be well aware of one's own interests; to be full of worldly wisdom as far as regards oneself.

"Pshaw!" answered his mercurial companion, "he knows on which side his bread is buttered.—Dickens.

—*to butter both sides of one's bread* to gain advantages from two parties at one time.

buy—*to buy in* to purchase goods at an auction on behalf of the person selling.

The articles were mainly those that had belonged to the previous owner of the house, and had been bought in by the late Mr. Charmond at the auction.—Thomas Hardy.

—*to buy the refusal of anything* to give money for the right, at a future time, of purchasing it for a fixed price.

I have bought the refusal of the neighbouring piece of land for fifty dollars. Its price is five hundred.

—*to buy off a person* to cause one to cease from opposition by giving him a sum of money, or other benefit.

It was the potential destroyer of their house whom they had to propitiate—the probable possessor of their lands

whom they had to buy off as best they could.—Mrs. E. Lynn Linton.

—*to buy up* a stronger form of **buy**, signifying the complete purchase of a quantity of goods.

I was so delighted with his last box of curios that I bought them up (purchased the whole lot).

by—*by this* when this took place.

By this, John had his hand on the shutters.—R. L. Stevenson.

—*by-and-by* after a time.

He hoped, could he overtake them, to have company by-and-by.—Bunyan.

—*by-the-bye* this phrase is used to introduce a new subject for which the hearers are not prepared.

By-the-bye, gentlemen, since I saw you here before, we have had to weep over a very melancholy occurrence.—Dickens.

bygones—*to let bygones be bygones* to ignore the past.

Can't we let bygones be bygones and start afresh?—W. E. Norris.

C

Cæsar—*Cæsar's wife should be above suspicion.* When Cæsar, whose own reputation was not above reproach, was remonstrated with for putting away his wife on a mere suspicion, he replied that it did not matter for Cæsar, but Cæsar's wife should be above suspicion in matters of morality. The phrase is now used in a general way to express the need there is that those immediately connected with great men should have a flawless reputation.

"Cæsar's wife," you remember the Roman dictator said—"Cæsar's wife must be above suspicion." Surely, if even a heathen thought that, we, Charlotte, with all our privileges (the speaker was a bishop), ought to be very careful on what sort of man we bestow Iris.—Cornhill Magazine, 1887.

cæteris—*cæteris paribus* other things being equal. Latin.

A very rich man, from low beginnings, may buy his election in a borough, but, cæteris paribus, *a man of family will be preferred.*—Boswell.

Cain—*the curse of Cain.* See **curse.**

cake—*you can't both have* or *keep your cake and eat it* a common proverb, signifying the impossibility of reaping the advantages of two wholly opposite courses of conduct. A person must choose which course he will follow, and which set of advantages he prefers and be prepared to resign any claim to the other set of advantages.

Slave-holders in rebellion had alone among mortals the privileges of having their cake and eating it.—J. R. Lowell.

—*my cake is dough* I am quite disappointed.

Notwithstanding all these traverses, we are confident here that the match will take, otherwise my cake is dough.—Howell's Letters.

—*to take the cake* to be first in a contest; to secure the first place in a competition. An Americanism.

The Wesleyans, however, take the cake, having by far the finest church building in their city—a Gothic structure of graceful design.—Boston Commercial Bulletin, May 26, 1888.

calf—*to eat the calf in the cow's belly* to be too ready to anticipate; to be over-sanguine of obtaining something.

I ever made shift to avoid anticipations; I never would eat the calf in the cow's belly.—S. Richardson.

—*calf love* the juvenile passion of a young man.

I thought that it was a childish besotment you had for the man—a sort of calf love, that it would be real kindness to help you out of.—Rhoda Broughton.

call—*to call at a place* to visit it. Said both of persons and of vessels.

"I shall have the honour of calling at

the Bedford, sir, if you'll permit me," said the major.—Dickens.

—*to call to account* to censure; to demand an explanation from.

She can't call Ensign Bloomington to account; can she, hey?—Maria Edgeworth.

—*called to one's account* removed by death.

—*at call* This phrase is used with regard to money which is deposited and can be drawn at any time without previous notice given.

—*to call down* to invoke; to pray to Heaven for.

—*to call for* (a) to need or demand.

I do not think this letter calls for an answer.

—(b) The phrase is used where a visit is paid with a special purpose. For instance, a parcel is often labelled, "To be left till called for."

—*to call forth* to bring out; to cause to appear; to elicit.

She was conscious that few women can be certain of calling forth this admiration.—Besant.

—*to call names* to speak disrespectfully to or of a person.

When he called his mother names because she wouldn't give up the young lady's property, and she relenting caused him to relent likewise and fall down on one knee and ask her blessing, how the ladies in the audience sobbed.—Dickens.

—*to call on* or *upon* (a) to invoke the aid of.

What signifies calling every moment upon the devil, and courting his friendship?—Goldsmith.

—(b) to pay a visit to.

—*to call out* to challenge to fight a duel.

My master was a man very apt to give a short answer himself, and likely to call a man out for it afterwards.—Maria Edgeworth.

—*to call a person to order* (of the chairman of a meeting) to declare that the person has broken the rules of debate, or is behaving in an unseemly manner.

He had lost his temper in the House that evening; he had been called to order by Mr. Speaker.—Wm. Black.

—*to call over* to recite a list of names.

We were now prevented from further conversation by the arrival of the jailer's servants, who came to call over the prisoners' names.—Goldsmith.

—*to call over the coals* to find fault with.

He affronted me once at the last election by calling a freeholder of mine over the coals.—Maria Edgeworth.

—*to call in question* to throw doubt upon; to challenge the truth of.

If the moral quality of his hero could not in safety be called in question (doubted), any suggestion of weakness in him as a writer was still more unendurable.—James Payn.

—*to call up* to revive the memory of; to bring to remembrance.

camel—*to break the camel's back* to be the last thing which causes a catastrophe. The proverb runs: "It is the *last* straw that breaks the camel's back.'

camp—*to camp out* to live in a tent in the open country.

candle—*to hold* or *show a candle to any one* to be in any way comparable with him.

I say she's the best, the kindest, the gentlest, the sweetest girl in England, and that, bankrupt or no, my sisters are not fit to hold candles to her.—Thackeray.

—*to hold the candle* to act as assistant; to aid and abet.

I'll be a candle-holder, and look on.—Shakespeare.

—*to burn the candle at both ends.* See **burn.**

—*to hold a candle to the devil* to diverge from what is strictly right or moral; to do knowingly what is wrong.

Here I have been holding a candle to the devil, to show him the way to mischief.—Scott.

cannot—*I cannot away with this* I detest it; I abominate it.

Couriers and ladies' maids, imperials and travelling carriages, are an abomination to me; I cannot away with them.—Hughes.

canvas—*to get or receive the canvas* an obsolete phrase signifying the same as the modern **to get the sack.**

I lose my honour, if the Don receives the canvas.—Shirley.

cap—*the cap and bells* these were carried by fools in the middle ages, as tokens of their office. The "fools" were licensed jesters. (See *King Lear.*)

And, look you, one is bound to speak the truth as far as one knows it, whether one mounts a cap and bells or a shovel-hat (is a fool or a bishop).—Thackeray.

—*to cap the globe* to surpass everything.

"Well," I exclaimed, using an expression of the district, "that caps the globe, however."—C. Brontë.

—*if the cap fits, wear it* if the remark applies to you, consider it well.

The truth is, when a searching sermon is preached, each sinner takes it to himself. I am glad Mr. Hawes fitted the cap on.—Reade.

—*cap in hand* in the submissive attitude of one who has a favour to ask.

And Tulliver, with his rough tongue filled by a sense of obligation, would make a better servant than any chance fellow

who was cap in hand for a situation.—
George Eliot.

—*to set one's cap at* (of a woman) to
try to captivate; to try to obtain as a
husband.
The girls set their caps at him, but he
did not marry.—Reade.

—*to cap verses* to compose or recite a
verse beginning with the final letter
of a verse given by the previous
speaker. A favourite pastime.
They had amused themselves during
their daily constitutionals by capping
Greek and Latin verses.—Macmillan's
Magazine, 1886.

capital—*to make capital out of anything* to use anything for one's own
profit.
I suppose Russia was not bound to
wait till they were in a position to make
capital out of her again (use her for
their own advancement again).—M.
Arnold.

caput—*caput mortuum* a worthless
residue. Latin.

card—*on the cards* probable; expected
to happen; spoken about or announced.
What if Mr. Slope should become dean
of Barchester? To be sure, there was
no adequate ground—indeed, no
ground at all—for presuming that such
a desecration could even be
contemplated; but nevertheless it was
on the cards (probable).—A. Trollope.

—*a great card* a popular or prominent
man; a man much talked about and
admired.
Captain D'Orville, the great card of the
regiment, came clanking into the
porter's lodge to get a glass of water
for the dame.—G. J. Whyte-Melville.

—*to speak by the card* to be careful
with one's words. Probably a sea
phrase, *card* here being the mariner's
compass, which gives the ship's direction exactly.

How absolute the knave is! We must
speak by the card, or equivocation will
undo us.—Shakespeare.

—*to throw up one's cards* to cease to
struggle; to despair of success in any
enterprise; to confess oneself vanquished.
He perceived at once that his former
employer was right, and that it only
remained for him to throw up his
cards.—W. E. Norris.

care—*care killed a cat* this proverb
refers to the depressing effects of care
upon the bodily health; it even killed
a cat, which has *nine* lives. See **cat**
"Come, come," said Silver, "stop this
talk . . . Care killed a cat. Fetch ahead
for the doubloons."—R. L. Stevenson.

carpet—*on the carpet* under discussion.
on the tapis is an equivalent phrase.
The talk was all of him; of his
magnificence, his meanness, his
manners, his principles, his daughter
and her future marriage—already on
the carpet of discussion and
surmise.—Mrs E. Lynn Linton.

—*to come or be brought on the carpet*
to be introduced. *carpet* was formerly
used for table-cloth.
He shifted the discourse in his turn and
(with a more placid air) contrived to
bring another subject upon the
carpet.—Graves.

—*a carpet-bagger* a Yankee speculator
who, after the great United States
Civil War, went to the South to make
money out of the impoverished
country.
At election times he was the terror of
Republican stump-orators and carpet-
baggers.—Blackwood's Magazine,
1887.

—*a carpet-knight* a gentleman who
receives the honour of knighthood
from his sovereign, not for services
on the battlefield, but for services at
court or as a peaceful citizen.

By heaven, I change
My thought, and hold thy valour light
As that of some vain carpet-knight,
Who ill deserved my courteous care,
And whose best boast is but to wear
A braid of his fair lady's hair.—Scott.

carriage—*a carriage-and-four* a carriage drawn by four horse.

"A carriage-and-four, papa; pray come and look."

"Four horses!" exclaimed Mrs. Armytage, in the excitement of the moment forgetting her own canons of etiquette, and rising from her chair to obtain a better view of the approaching vehicle.—James Payn.

—*carriage company* people who are wealthy enough to keep private carriage.

There is no phrase more elegant and to my taste than that in which people are described as "seeing a great deal of carriage company."—Thackeray.

carry—*to carry all before one* to be completely successful or popular.

Adelina Patti carries all before her (is popular with every one) wherever she goes.

—*to carry the day* to win a victory; to prove superior.

When such discussions arise, money generally carries the day—and should do so.—A. Trollope.

—*to carry anything too far* to exceed the proper bounds in anything.

Of course you may carry the thing too far, as (in the well-known story) when Mr. A. was twitted by Mr. B. and having sent a man to sleep in his (Mr. B.'s) church.— Cornhill Magazine, 1888.

—*to carry off*—(a) to help to pass; to aid; to supplement or supply what is lacking.

She was one who required none of the circumstances of studied dress to carry off aught (supply anything

deficient) in her own appearance.—A. Trollope.

—(b) to cause the death of.

The change of air carried him off.— Temple.

—*to carry it off* to refuse to succumb; to pretend indifference. The phrase is used when a person is placed in an awkward or humiliating position, and tries to hide his feelings of shame or confusion.

Frightened too—I could see that—but carrying it off, sir, really like Satan.— R. L. Stevenson.

—*to carry on*—(a) to conduct; to manage.

The internal government of England could be carried on only by the advice and agency of English ministers.— Macaulay.

—(b) to behave in a particular fashion, so as to call attention to one's conduct; to misbehave.

It was Mrs. Emptage; and how she carried on, with tears and congratulations.—Besant.

—*to carry out* to bring to completion; to give practical effect to.

To carry out the aims he had in view, he tolerated and made use of persons whose characters he despised.— Westminster Review, 1888.

—*to carry one's point* to succeed in one's aim.

They were bent upon placing their friend Littleton in the Speaker's chair; and they had carried their point triumphantly.—Macaulay.

—*to carry through* to bring to completion.

The whole country is filled with such failures – swaggering beginnings that could not be carried through.— Thackeray.

—*carried away by one's feelings* under the guidance of emotion and not of reason; overcome by emotion.

Having an honest and sincere mind, he was not carried away by a popular prejudice.—Tillotson.

cart—*to put the cart before the horse* to put the wrong thing first.

carte—*carte blanche* full freedom; perfect liberty to act in anything as one pleases. French

There is carte blanche *to the schoolhouse fags to go where they like.*—Hughes.

cast—*to cast about*—(a) to devise or plan.

He cast about all that day, and kept his brain working on the one anxious subject through all the round of schemes and business that came with it.—Dickens.

—(b) to look around one; to search mentally or actually.

Here he cast about for a comfortable seat.—R. L. Stevenson.

—*cast down* dejected; in low spirits.

For my part I was horribly cast down.—R. L. Stevenson.

—*to cast out* to quarrel.

The goddesses cast out (quarrelled) over the possession of the golden apple.

—*to cast up*—(a) to reproach or upbraid. Scotch.

For what between you twa has ever been,

    Nane to the other will cast up, I ween.
               Ross.

Exp.—*For no one, I think, will reproach the other for past transactions.*

—(b) to add arithmetically; to compute.

William gave him a slate and a slate-pencil, and taught him how to make figures and to cast up sums.—Maria Edgeworth.

—(c) to turn up; to appear unexpectedly.

Nor, though last not least, must we omit to mention the élite of Bubbleton, who have one and all cast up from "the

Spout," as that salubrious town is sometimes denominated.—G. J. Whyte-Melville.

—*a casting vote* a vote which decides when the voting is otherwise equal. The chairman of a meeting often exercises this power.

caste—*to lose caste* to cease to enjoy the consideration of one's associates; to be thrown out of the society of one's equals.

You may do anything you please without losing caste.—Dickens.

castles—*castles in the air* visionary schemes.

These were but like castles in the air, and in men's fancies vainly imagined.—Sir W. Raleigh.

—*castles in Spain* possessions that have no real existence; also generally of what is visionary and unsubstantial. From the French *châteaux en Espagne.*

Dick is going to Cork to-day to join his regiment (happy, happy Cork!); but he is going to write to me, and I am to write to him. Is not this brick and mortar enough to build quite a big Spanish castle with?—Rhoda Broughton.

casus—*casus belli* ground of quarrel. Latin.

cat—*a cat has nine lives* a proverb expressing the prevailing belief that it is very difficult to kill a cat. see **care**.

He struggled hard, and had, as they say, as many lives as a cat.—Bunyan.

—*to let the cat out of the bag* to disclose a secret.

Letting the cat of selfishness out of the bag of secrecy.—Thackeray.

—*a cat-and-dog life* a life of petty quarrels and bickerings.

I am sure we (England and Ireland) have lived a cat-and-dog life of it.—S. T. Coleridge.

—*to rain cats and dogs* to rain heavily.

"But it'll perhaps rain cats and dogs (it will perhaps rain very heavily) to-morrow, as it did yesterday, and you can go," said Godfrey.—George Eliot.

—*to make a cat's paw of* to use as a mere tool. The phrase is taken from the fable of the cat and the monkey. The latter wished to reach some chestnuts that were roasting on the fire, and used the paw of his friend the cat to get at them.

She's made a cat's paw of you; that's plain enough.—Florence Marryat.

—*to see how the cat jumps* to see exactly how and why a thing happens.

I see how the cat jumps (the real state of affairs): minister knows so many languages he hain't (has not) been particular enough to keep 'em (them) in separate parcels.—Haliburton.

—*to grin like a Cheshire cat* to be always smiling, displaying the gums and teeth.

He lay back in his chair, tapped his boot with his cane, and with a grin on his face such as a Cheshire cat might wear who feels a mouse under her claw.—James Payn.

—*to fight like Kilkenny cats* to fight with deadly desperation. The Kilkenny cats are said to have fought until only their tails remained.

They fight among each other like the famous Kilkenny cats, with the happy result that the population never outgrows the power of the country to support it.—H. R. Haggard.

—*to shoot the cat* to vomit.

—*to turn a cat-in-pan* to execute a somersault; to veer round suddenly.

When George in pudding time came o'er,
And moderate men looked big, sir,
I turned a cat-in-pan once more,
And so became a Whig, sir.—The Vicar of Bray.

—*a cat-o'-nine-tails* an instrument of punishment, so called from the nine pieces of leather or cord which compose it.

Gangs tramping along, with bayonets behind them, and corporals with canes and cats-o'-nine-tails to flog them to barracks.—Thackeray.

catch—*to catch at anything* to try eagerly to seize; to welcome.

Drowning men will catch at straws.—W. E. Norris.

—*to catch it* to be punished; to suffer unpleasant consequences; to be treated roughly.

"Poor Sir Bate! catching it again," he says, smiling.—Florence Maryat.

—*to catch another's eye* to attract his attention. The intending speaker who first catches the chairman's eye at a meeting receives permission to speak.

A florid-faced gentleman, with a nice head of hair, from the south of Ireland, had succeeded in catching the Speaker's eye by the time that Mr. Warding had got into the gallery.—A. Trollope.

Note.— The Speaker is the chairman of the House of Commons.

—*to catch napping* to gain an advantage through the temporary carelessness of another.

Oldfield looked confused; but Somerset, full of mother-wit, was not to be caught napping (taken at a disadvantage).—C. Reade.

—*to catch up*—(a) to overtake.

It is not that the Mohammedan boy is duller than the Hindu boy; but he does not begin (his studies) so soon, and he has not caught up (overtaken) his rival by the time earlier educational honours are distributed.—Calcutta Englishman, 1886.

—(b) to interrupt a speaker with a critical remark; to disagree with one who is speaking.

As for thoughtfulness, and good

temper, and singing like a bird, and never being cross and catching a person up, or getting into rages, as Melenda did, there was nobody in the world like Polly.—Besant.

—*to catch a crab.* See **crab**.

—*to catch a Tartar.* See **Tartar**.

cause—*cause célèbre* a famous law case. A French phrase.

We greatly fear matters will remain in their present disgraceful condition, and that the Campbell cause célèbre will have no result except to vitiate still more the already vitiated atmosphere of society.—Spectator 1886.

—*to make common cause with* to side with and support.

Thus the most respectable Protestants, with Elizabeth at their head, were forced to make common cause (associate themselves) with the Papists.—Macaulay.

caution—*a caution* something to be avoided or dreaded.

Sometimes it doesn't rain here for eight months at a stretch, and the dust out of town is a caution (is dreadful).

cave—*to cave in* to succumb; to give way.

A puppy joins the chase with heart and soul (very eagerly), but caves in (desists) at about fifty yards.—H. Kingsley.

caveat—*caveat emptor* let the purchaser beware of what he is buying. Latin.

caviare—*caviare to the general* not pleasing to ordinary people. Caviare is a substance prized by epicures, and made from the roes of sturgeons and other fish caught in the rivers of Russia.

For the play, I remember, pleased not the million; 'twas caviare to the general.—Shakespeare.

chaff—*to catch with the chaff* to deceive easily.

With which chaff our noble bird was by no means to be caught.—Thackeray.

chair—*to take the chair* to assume the position of president at a meeting.

The committee of the Commons appointed Mr. Pym to take the chair (to be president of the meeting).—Clarendon.

chalk—*by a long chalk* or *by long chalks* clearly; indisputably; by a great interval.

Here, Polly! Polly! Polly! take this man down to the kitchen, and teach him manners if you can; he is not fit for my drawing-room, by a long chalk.—Reade.

challenge—*to challenge the array* to protest against the whole body of jurymen selected. A legal phrase.

chancery—*to get into chancery* to be completely at the mercy of another in a boxing match. When a combatant's head is tucked under the arm of his opponent, and receives a succession of blows, the poor fellow is said to be in chancery.

The Chicken himself attributed this punishment to his having had the misfortune to get into chancery early in the proceedings.—Dickens.

change—*to ring the changes.* See **ring**.

—*to put the change upon a person* to deceive him.

You cannot put the change on me so easy as you think, for I have lived among the quick-stirring spirits of the age too long to swallow chaff for grain.—Scott.

chapter—*to the end of the chapter* to the very end; uninterruptedly.

—*the chapter of accidents* chance; what happens without the possibility of being foreseen and prepared for.

Away runs Jack, shouting and trusting to the chapter of accidents.—Hughes.

—*to give chapter and verse for any-*

thing to give exact particulars of its source.

To clench the matter by chapter and verse, I should like to recall what I have said of these theories and principles in their most perfect and most important literary version.—John Morley, in Nineteenth Century, 1888.

character—*in character* appropriate; suitable.

Read it; is it not quite in character (appropriate)?—Disraeli.

—*out of character* unsuitable; inappropriate.

charge—*to give in charge* to hand over to the police.

châteaux—*châteaux en espagne* something having no real existence. French. See **castles in Spain**.

cheap—*to be cheap of anything* to have received no more than one's deserts in the way of affronts or punishment.

The thief got ten days' imprisonment, and the rogue was cheap of it (deserved all he got).

—*to feel cheap* to be affronted or ashamed.

cheek—*cheek by jowl* in close proximity.

Here was a doctor who never had a patient, cheek by jowl with an attorney who never had a client.—Thackeray.

cheese—*to get the cheese* to receive a check or a disappointment. The phrase is said to have its origin in the history of Beau Brummel, the friend of George IV. Presuming on his acquaintance with the Prince Regent, Brummel used to take the liberty of arriving late at formal dinners, and always expected that the party would await his arrival. On one occasion he arrived in this fashion at the Marquis of Lansdowne's, but found that the company were already far advanced with dinner. The host, turning to

Brummel, asked him if he would have some cheese (a late course). The crestfallen look of the Beau is said to have given rise to the expression, "He got the cheese."

—*the cheese* what is excellent or first-rate.

Ain't I the cheese, oh! ain't I the cheese, As I walk in the park with my pretty Louise?—London Song.

chef—*chef-d'œuvre* a masterpiece; the best work of the kind. French.

The dishes were uncovered. There were vegetables cooked most deliciously; the meat was a chef-d'œuvre – a sort of rich ragout done to a turn, and so fragrant that the very odour made the mouth water,—C. Reade.

cherry—*to make two bites of a cherry* to divide what is so small as scarcely to be worth dividing.

chew—*to chew the rag* to be sullen and abusive. A phrase common in the army.

—*to chew the cud* to ruminate on some memory.

It is possible she was only pretending to sleep, in order to chew the cud (enjoy the memory) of some sweet thought at greater leisure.—James Payn.

chicken—*no chicken* not youthful.

But John Niel was no chicken, nor very likely to fall in love with the first pretty face he met.—H. R. Haggard.

—*count not your chickens till they are hatched* be sure that a thing is actually in your possession before you speak of it as yours, or act as it were yours.

But aren't we counting our chickens, Tag, before they're hatched? If Titmouse is all of a sudden become such a catch, he'll be snapped up in a minute.—S. W. Warren.

child—*from a child* from infancy.

—*child's play* something very easy; work demanding no effort.

It's child play to find the stuff now.—R. L. Stevenson.

Chiltern—*to apply for the Chiltern Hundreds* to resign a seat in Parliament. The hundreds (or districts) of Bodenham, Desborough, and Stoke, in Buckinghamshire, known as the Chiltern Hundreds, have attached to them a stewardship, with the duty of keeping down the robbers who infested the woods of the Chiltern Hills. This office is now a merely nominal one, but it is put to a strange use. When a Member of Parliament wishes to resign his seat—an impossible thing by law, unless he can disqualify himself—he applies for this stewardship, an office under the Crown, the assumption of which requires resignation of a seat in the House of Commons. This practice dates from the year 1759.

This letter was despatched on the 19th of January; on the 21st he applied for the Chiltern Hundreds.—Trevelyan, in *Life of Lord Macauley.*

chime—*to chime in with* to harmonize with.

As this chimed in with Mr. Dombey's own hope and belief, it gave that gentleman a still higher opinion of Mrs. Pipchin's understanding.—Dickens.

chip—*a chip of the old block* a child possessing the characteristics of its father.

"He will prove a chip of the old block (a model of his father), I'll warrant" he added, with a sidelong look at Margaret.—James Payn.

chisel—*full chisel* in haste. American slang.

They think they know everything, and all they have got to do, to up Hudson like a shot, into the lakes full split (in a hurry), off to Mississippi, and down to New Orleans full chisel (in haste).—Haliburton.

—*to chisel* to cheat or defraud.

Why is a carpenter like a swindler? Because he chisels a deal (cheats much).

Note.—A pun is here made on the word chisel and on the word deal (wood).

choke—*to choke off* to get rid of in a summary way.

Indeed, the business of a war-nurse especially is so repulsive that most volunteers were choked off at once.—Cornhill Magazine, 1888.

chop—*first chop* in the first rank; first-class.

He looks like a first-chop article.—Haliburton.

—*to chop logic* to argue in a pedantic fashion.

He was angry at finding himself chopping logic about this young lady.—H. James.

—*to chop upon* to meet suddenly.

I know not what my condition would have been if I had chopped upon (chanced to meet) them.—Defoe.

—*to chop yarns* to tell stories.

Described as a carpenter, but a poor workman, Clara Martha, and fond of chopping yarns, in which he was equalled by none.—Besant.

chronicle—*to chronicle small beer* to register or notify insignificant events.

All the news of sport, assize, and quarter-sessions was detailed by this worthy chronicler of small beer.—Thackeray.

chuck—*to chuck up*—(a) to abandon; to discontinue; to surrender.

Ain't you keeping company with poor old Mrs. Lammas's daughter? unless perhaps you mean to chuck the girl up now because you have been asked for once to meet women of rank.—Justin M'Carthy.

—(b) to give in or surrender. Some-

times corrupted into **jack up**. Probably the word **sponge** is understood. See **sponge**.
At the third round Joe the Nailor chucked up (declared himself beaten).

chum—*to chum up with* to make friendly advances to.

circumstances—*circumstances alter cases* it is necessary to modify one's conduct by the particular circumstances or conditions of each case.
London between August and April is looked upon as a nightmare. But circumstances alter cases; and I see that it will be the best and most convenient place for you.—Mrs. Henry Wood.

claret—*one's claret jug* a slang term for the nose. To tap one's claret (jug)= to cause a man's nose to bleed.
He told Verdant that his claret had been repeatedly tapped.—Verdant Green, ch. xi.

clay—*the feet of clay* the baser portion; the lower and degrading part. See Dan. ii. 33: "This image's head was of fine gold, his breast and his arms of silver, his belly and his thighs of brass, his legs of iron, his feet part of iron and part of clay."

clean—*to make a clean breast of anything* to make a complete confession.
For several days he had made up his mind (resolved) that when he should be questioned upon the subject, he would earn the credit of candour and grace of womanly gratitude by making a clean breast of it (confessing everything).—Blackmore.

—*to show a clean pair of heels* to run off.
These maroons were runaway slaves who had bid a sudden goodbye to bolts and shackles, whips and rods, and shown their tyrants a clean pair of heels.—G. A. Sala.

—*to clean out* to ruin or render bankrupt; to take away all available money from.
"A hundred and forty pounds?" repeated Mrs. Carruthers, in a terrified tone.
"Yes, precisely that sum; and I have not a pound in the world to exist on in the meantime. I am cleaned out, and that's the fact."—E. Yates.

clear—*to clear out* to go off entirely; to go away.
"It would be a pity, sir, if we had to clear out and run," said Maurice.—Mrs. E. Lynn Linton.

climacteric—*the grand climacteric* the most critical period in a man's life (sixty-three years of age). Multiples of 7 or 9 were considered dangerous years in a man's life, 7, 9, 14, 18, 21, 27, 35, 36, 49, etc.: 7×9 was therefore eminently bad. Recognized by Hippocrates.
Our old friend was even now balancing on the brink of an eventful plunge (a proposal of marriage), which, if not made before "the grand climacteric," it is generally thought advisable to postpone sine die.—G. J. Whyte-Melville.

close—*to close with* to agree to.
This offer was at once closed with by the delighted rustic.—W. E. Norris.

cloth—*the cloth* clergymen; the position of clergyman.
And for the sake of the poor man himself too, and for his wife, and for his children, and for the sake of the cloth.—A. Trollope.

clothes—*in long clothes* still a young infant.

cloud—*to be in the clouds* to dream of what is impracticable; to build castles in the air.

—*under a cloud* in disgrace.
Though Cæsar was not, for various reasons, to be pronounced a tyrant, Cicero advised that he should be

buried privately as if his name was under a cloud.—Froude.

The greatest city of the world exercises a strong power of attraction over all manner of men under a cloud.—Nineteenth Century, 1887.

—*every cloud has a silver lining* the darkest prospect has some redeeming brightness; nothing is wholly dark.

"Oh, even the Lapham cloud has a silver lining," said Corey.—W. D. Howells.

cloven—*the cloven foot* the mark of an evil or devilish nature. See **foot**.

Yet although the cloven foot would constantly peep out, and no one could believe either in his principles or his morals, in his way the baron was as much in favour with the fair sex as the honourable and hospitable Lord Skye.—Edinburgh Review, July 1882.

clover—*to live* or *be in clover* to be happily situated; to be surrounded with every luxury.

Now he has got a handle to his name, and he'll live in clover all his life.—A. Trollope.

—*to go from clover to ryegrass* to exchange a good position for a bad. Said of second marriages.

coach—*to drive a coach-and-four* or *a coach-and-six through* to break the provisions of; to find a safe means of evading.

You may talk vaguely about driving a coach-and-six through a bad young Act of Parliament.—Dickens.

—*a coach-and-six* a coach drawn by six horses, such as only very wealthy people formerly used.

"This," said he, "is a young lady who was born to ride in her coach-and-six" (enjoy great wealth).—H. Mackenzie.

coals—*to call, haul,* or *bring over the coals* to administer rebuke; to find fault with.

"Fine talking! fine airs, truly, Miss Patty! This is by way of calling me over the coals for being idle, I suppose!" said Sally.—Maria Edgeworth.

—*to carry coals to Newcastle* to take a thing where it is already plentifully.

"Sure, sir," answered the barber, "you are too wise a man to carry a broken head thither (to the wars), for that would be carrying coals to Newcastle" (taking a broken head to where there are plenty broken heads).—Fielding.

—*to heap coals of fire on one's head* to return benefits where ill-treatment has been received, and thus to make an enemy ashamed of his conduct.

If thine enemy be hungry, give him bread to eat; and if he be thirsty, give him water to drink: for thou shalt heap coals of fire upon his head (make him ashamed of his enmity), and the Lord shall reward thee.—Prov. xxv, 21, 22.

coast—*the coast is clear* there is no danger of interference.

Wait till the coast is clear, then strike tent and away.—Reade.

coat—*to cut one's coat according to one's cloth* to regulate one's expenses by one's income.

Uncle Sutton was displeased. "Debt is dishonest," said he. "We can all cut our coat according to our cloth" (limit our expenses to the size of our incomes).—Reade.

—*to turn one's coat* to change to the opposite party.

This is not the first time he has turned his coat (changed sides).

—*to dust a man's coat for him* to give him a castigation.

Father Parson's coat well dusted: or, short and pithy animadversions on that famous fardel of abuse and falsities, entitled Leicester's Commonwealth—Advertisement quoted by I. Disraeli.

cock—*all cock-a-hoop for anything* very much excited and eager for it.

"All cock-a-hoop for it," struck in Cattledon, *"as the housemaids are."*—Mrs. Henry Wood.

—*that cock won't fight* that expedient will not do.

I tried to see the arms on the carriage, but that cock wouldn't fight (this was of no avail),—C. Kingsley.

—*the gallic cock* the cock is the national bird of France, as the bull is the national animal of England.

—*cock of the walk* chief in a small circle.

Who shall be cock of the walk?—Heading to ch. xvii. of Trollope's *"Barchester Towers."*

—*a cock-and-bull story* an absurd tale.

I did hear some cock-and-bull story the other day about the horses not having run away at all.—Rhoda Broughton.

—*to live like a fighting cock* to live in luxury.

—*a cock is always bold on its own dunghill* every one fights well when surrounded by friends and admirers.

—*to beat cock-fighting* to surpass anything conceivable.

The squire faltered out, "Well, this fights cock-fighting" (is something extraordinary),—Lytton.

—*to knock into a cock* or *a cocked hat* to bruise out of shape; to defeat completely.

I never knew a Welsh girl yet who couldn't dance an Englishman into a cocked hat (who was not vastly superior to an Englishman in dancing).—Reade.

—*to cock* or *turn up one's toes* to die.

Cocker—*according to Cocker* in accordance with the present system of figures. Cocker's Arithmetic, first published in 1677–8, was for long the standard work on the subject, and passed through sixty editions.

cockle—*to warm the cockles of one's heart* to give a pleasant inward feeling.

The sight, after near two months' absence, rejoiced the very cockles of Jerry's heart.—Graves.

—*hot cockles* a game in which one covers one's eyes and guesses who strikes him. Probably from the French *hautes coquilles* (high shells).

cockpit—*the cockpit of Europe* a name applied to Belgium because of the number of great battles that have been fought on its soil. The cockpit is an enclosed area where game-cocks fight, and in ships of war the room in which wounds are dressed.

coin—*to pay a man back in his own coin* to serve him as he has served you.

—*to coin money* to make money very rapidly.

With the new contracts he has secured, Johnson is coining money (making money very quickly).

cold—*cold without* spirits in cold water without sugar.

I laugh at fame. Fame, sir! not worth a glass of cold without.—Lytton.

collar—*against the collar* difficult; causing fatigue. A phrase taken from a horse's harness: when a horse goes uphill the collar pulls on his neck.

The last mile up to the head of the pass was a good deal against the collar (somewhat fatiguing).

—*in collar* employed.

The workman you spoke of is not in collar (out of employment) at present.

colour—*with the colours* under the flag; serving as a regular soldier.

With this view the period of engagement was raised from seven to nine years, five years being passed with the colours (in regular service) and four in the reserve.—Edinburgh Review, 1886.

—*to change colour*. See **change**.

colt—*to have a colt's tooth* (of an elderly person) to have juvenile tastes.

comb—*to cut a man's comb* to humble him.

He'll be a-bringing (he is sure to bring) other folks to preach from Treddleston, if his comb isn't cut a bit (if he is not taught his proper place).—George Eliot.

—*to comb a man's head* to give him a thrashing.

I'll carry you with me to my country-box, and keep you out of harm's way, till I find you a wife who will comb your head for you.—Lytton.

come—*to come about* to result; to happen.

How comes it about (happens it) that, for about sixty years, affairs have been placed in the hands of new men?—Swift.

—*to come at* to get; to obtain.

By the time Abraham returned, we had both agreed that money was never so hard to come at as now.—Goldsmith.

—*to come by* to obtain.

*How came she by that light?
—Shakespeare: Macbeth.*

—*to come down* to subscribe; to give money to an object.

Selcover would be certain to come down handsomely (give a handsome subscription), of course.—Macmillan's Magazine, 1886.

—*a come-down* a fall; a lowering of a person's dignity.

"Now I'm your worship's washerwoman." The dignitary coloured, and said that this was rather a comedown.—Reade.

—*to come in* to prove; to show itself. Used with adjectives like **handy** or **serviceable**.

A knowledge of Latin quotations comes in handy sometimes.

—*to come off*—(a) to happen; to take place.

A day or two afterwards he informed Allen that the thing he had in his mind was really coming off (going to take place).—Besant.

—(b) to end by being; to close a struggle as.

It is time that fit honour should be paid also to him who shapes his life to a certain classic proportion, and comes off conqueror on those inward fields where something more than mere talent is demanded for victory.—J. R. Lowell.

—*to come over* to obtain great influence with; to fascinate.

Miss Gray has "come over him," as Lamb says, where that vulnerable region is concerned.—Sarah Tytler.

—*to come . . . over one* to act like . . . to one.

Also his ideas of discipline were of the sternest, and, in short, he came the royal naval office over us (acted towards us as if he were an officer of the royal navy set in authority over us) pretty considerably, and paid us out amply for all the chaff we were wont to treat him to on land.—H. R. Haggard.

—*to come out*—(a) (of a young lady) to enter into society.

You have lost your fairy godmother, look! Is it coming out (entrance into society) that has done it, or what?—A. Keary.

—(b) to be discovered; to become public.

Nobody can prove that I knew the girl to be an heiress; thank goodness, that can't come out.—Besant.

—*to come round* (*a person*) to cajole; to deceive.

His second wife came round (cajoled) the old man and got him to change his will.

—*to come round* (intrans.) to recover from an attack of sickness.

She was on her bed; she turned her head and saw blood on the pillow, and turned again and saw the face of Nelly. "You're come round at last, are you?" said the woman.—S. Baring-Gould.

—*to come to oneself* to recover consciousness.

She began to hear the voices and to feel the things that were being done to her before she was capable of opening her eyes, or indeed had come to herself (recovered consciousness).—Mrs. Oliphant.

—*to come to* to recover (almost the same as to come to oneself).

Then you, dear papa, would have to put your daughter on the sofa—for of course she would be in a dead faint—remove the pillow, and burn feathers under her nose till she comes to (recovers).—James Payn.

—*to come to grief* to be unsuccessful; to utterly fail.

The Panama Canal scheme is likely to come to grief (prove a failure) owing to want of funds.

—*to come and go upon* to rely upon.

You have an excellent character to come and go upon (depend upon in making your way in the world).

—*to come to hand* to be received. A phrase much used in letter-writing.

"Your letter came to hand yesterday morning, Dr. Tempest," said Mr. Crawley.—A. Trollope.

—*to come to light* to be disclosed; to become public. Generally used of some secret.

The reader need not fear, however; he shall not be troubled with any long account of Mr. Fraser's misfortune, for it never came to light or obtruded itself upon the world.—H. R. Haggard.

—*to come upon the parish* to become a pauper.

—*to come to pass* to happen.

What thou hast spoken is come to pass (has happened); and, behold, thou sees it.—Jer. xxxii. 24.

—*to come to the point* to speak plainly on the real question, without circumlocution. The opposite of beating about the bush.

After a good many apologies and explanations, he came to the point (stated exactly what he had come for), and asked me for the loan of my horse.

—*to come it strong* to exaggerate; to ask a person to credit something impossible.

What! little Boston ask that girl to marry him! Well, now, that's comin' of it a little too strong.—O. W. Holmes.

comme—*comme il faut* as it should be; proper; well-dressed and good-mannered. French.

To have been told that she was not comme il faut is worse evidently a hundred times than if she had been told she was a thief.—Murray's Magazine, 1887.

commission—*to put a ship in commission* to send a ship on active service.

commit—*to commit for contempt* to send a person to prison because he is disobedient or disrespectful in a court of justice.

And even over the august person of the judge himself there hangs the fear of the only thing that he cannot commit for contempt, public opinion.—H. R. Haggard.

—*to commit to memory* to learn by heart.

When young, he committed to memory (learned by heart) the whole of the Psalms and part of Proverbs.

common—*in common* held equally with others; shared indiscriminately.

Poor people, who have their goods in

common, must necessarily become quarrelsome.—Maria Edgeworth.

—*out of the common* unusual; strange.
She was a simple-hearted woman, on whom whatever chanced to her ears out of the common (that was unusual) made a great impression.—James Payn.

—*on short commons* scantily provided with food.
Our men not being yet on short commons, none of 'em had stomach enough to try the experiment.—G. A. Sala.

company—*to keep company* See **keep**.

compare—*to compare notes* to exchange opinions or views on a subject of interest.
It is the hour between daylight and the dinner-bell, when the men have not yet returned from shooting and the women have not retired to dress—the best hour of all in a good old-fashioned country-house, when the guests have tired themselves with out-door amusements, and are ready to compare notes and exchange confidences in the mysterious gloaming.—Florence Marryat.

compliment—*to return the compliment* to say or do something pleasant in return for a previous favour.
Mr. Frank Churchill was one of the boasts of Highbury, and a lively curiosity to see him prevailed; though the compliment was so little returned (he had so little desire to see Highbury) that he had never been there in his life.—Miss Austen.

con—*con amore* with good will; heartily. Italian.
What is distasteful rarely sticks in the memory. What is done cone amore (willingly) is twice and trebly blest.—Journal of Education, 1886.

conceit—*out of conceit* dissatisfied.
Hartfield will only put her out of conceit (make her dissatisfied) with all the other places she belongs to.—George Eliot.

confusion—*confusion worse confounded* a still worse state of disorder.
With ruin upon ruin, rout on rout, Confusion worse confounded.—Milton.

conscience—*conscience-money* money paid anonymously by ratepayers who have cheated the revenue at some previous time.
A child, still young enough to be passed off as a child in arms by all, save perhaps, those tender-minded persons who send conscience-money to the Chancellor of the Exchequer.—Hugh Conway.

—*in all conscience* assuredly.
Plain and precise enough it is, in all conscience.—M. Arnold.

contact—*to come in contact with* to meet; to have dealing with.
Now it must be remembered that this was a man who had lived in a city that calls itself the metropolis, one who had been a member of the State and National Legislatures, who had come in contact with men of letters and men of business, with politicians and members of all the professions, during a long and distinguished public career.—O. W. Holmes.

cook—*to cook one's goose.* See **goose**.

cool—*to cool one's heels* to be made to wait while paying a visit to some important personage.
We cooled our heels (were kept waiting) during the ordinary and intolerable half-hour.—G. A. Sala.

—*a cool hundred* (or any sum) the large sum of a hundred pounds (or any sum).
The knowing ones were cursedly taken in (very much deceived) there. I lost a cool hundred (the large sum of £100)

myself, faith (I assure you).—
Mackenzie.

—cool as a cucumber not agitated; perfectly cool and composed.
"Never fear, Miss Nugent dear," said Sir Terence: "I'm as cool as a cucumber."—Marie Edgeworth.

copy—*to make copy of* to turn into manuscript for the printer.
He would have made copy of his mother's grave (have written an article about it, for which he would be paid).

corn—*to tread on another's corns* to annoy him where he is most easily annoyed.
Hence the reputation he enjoyed of being something more than blunt-spoken—of being, in fact, a pretty good specimen of the perfervid Scotchman, arrogant, opinionated, supercillious, and a trifle too anxious to tread on people's corns.—Wm. Black.

—corn-stalk a name given to the children of Australian settlers, specially in New South Wales.

—corn in Egypt a plentiful supply of provisions. A familiar phrase borrowed from the Bible.
"Uncle's box has arrived," said the minister; "there is corn in Egypt (plenty of food) to-day."

corner—*to drive into a corner* to embarrass; to place in a position where escape is impossible.
"I don't want to act the constable," said the farrier, driven into a corner (embarrassed) by this merciless reasoning, "and there's no man can say it of me if he'd tell the truth."—George Eliot.

—the chief corner-stone the most important support of anything.
*Jesus Christ himself being the chief corner-stone (principal support)—*Ephes. ii. 20.

corpus—*corpus vile* the subject of an experiment. Latin.
It is a tedious process for the inquirer, still more so for the corpus vile of the investigation (poor fellow who is subjected to these inquiries), whose weak brain soon tires.

cotton—*to cotton to a person* to fawn upon him; to make advances to him.
Lady Mansfield's maid says there's a grand title or something in the family. That's why she cottons to (fawns upon) her so, I suppose.

—a cotton lord a wealthy Manchester manufacturer.

couleur—*couleur de rose* rose colour; highly flattering. French
When we begin to tint our final pages with couleur de rose, as in accordance with fixed rule we must do, we altogether extinguish our own powers of pleasing.—A. Trollope.

counsel—*to keep one's own counsel* to preserve a discreet silence.
Old Sedley had kept his own counsel.—Thackeray.

count—*to count upon* to trust to; to look for with confidence.
"Count upon me," he added, with bewildered fervour.—R. L. Stevenson.

—to count out to declare the House of Commons adjourned because there are not forty members present. When the Speaker has his attention drawn to this fact, he must count the number present, and finding it under forty, must declare the sitting over.
Adelina Pattie made her début, May 14, 1861, when Mr. Punch counts out the House and adjourns to Mr. Gye's theatre.—Fortnightly Review, 1887.

countenance—*to keep one countenance* **or** *in countenance* to lend moral support to.
Flora will be there to keep you countenance.—R. L. Stevenson.

—to keep one's countenance to preserve one's gravity; to refrain from laughing.

The two maxims of any great man at court are, always to keep his countenance, and never to keep his word.—Swift.

—*his countenance fell* he looked disappointed.

—*to put out of countenance. See put.*

"To-morrow—you said to-morrow, I think—we will devote to recitation. William Henry's countenance fell (William Henry showed signs of disappointment). He had heard Mr. Reginald Talbot's recitations before.—James Payn.

counter—*a counter-jumper* a shopkeeper's assistant; a retail dealer's shopman.

Confound that impudent young counter-jumper (shopkeeper's lad); but I suppose there's nothing we can do, uncle? They're married by this time.—Longman's Magazine, 1887.

country—*to appeal to the country* to advise the Sovereign to dissolve Parliament in order to ascertain by a new election whether a certain policy is approved by the constituencies.

As soon as the necessary business could be got through, Parliament would be dissolved, and an appeal made to the country (a new election of representatives made).—Justin M'Carthy.

—*to put oneself on one's country* to stand one's trial before a jury.

An outlaw who yielded himself within the year was entitled to plead not guilty, and to put himself on his country (demand a trial by jury).—Macaulay.

coup—*coup de théâtre* a dramatic effect. French.

Perhaps he was not sorry to be able to show his clever coadjutor that she was not the only person who could achieve a coup de théâtre upon occasion.—W. E. Norris.

—*coup d'état* a sudden stroke of policy. French.

The coup d'état of 1852 laid the foundation of the second French Empire.

—*coup de main* a sudden bold attack, without previous approaches. French.

He expected a little more delay and coquetry; and, though he meant to make his approaches very rapidly, it had not entered his mind to carry the widow's heart by a coup de main (sudden proposal of marriage).—James Payne.

—*coup de grâce* a finishing stroke. French.

Two others were told off to give me the coup de grâce, in the event of my not being killed by the firing-party.—All the Year Round, 1867.

courage—*to have the courage of one's opinions* to be fearless in the expression of one's beliefs.

He (Quincy) had not merely, as the French say, the courage of his opinions.—J. R. Lowell.

course—*of course* (a) connected with ordinary matters; unimportant.

After a few words of course, they sailed into the street.—Dickens.

—(b) naturally.

"A fair challenge," cried the marquis joyously. "And I back the gentleman." "Oh, of course" (naturally), said his daughter.—C. Reade.

—*in course* in regular order.

You will receive the other numbers of the journal in course (when the due time for their publication arrives).

—*in due course* at the proper time.

When the boys got promotion, which came in due course (at the proper time), Allen began to buy books.—Besant.

court—*to bring into court* to adduce as an authority.

But in the case of the Ainos, the beards

alone were brought into court (brought forward as evidence).—B. H. Chamberlain.

courtesy—*courtesy-titles* titles assumed by the family of a noble, and granted to them by social custom, but not of any legal value. Thus, the eldest son of the Duke of Devonshire is Marquis of Hartington in ordinary speech, but merely William Spencer Cavendish, a commoner, according to strict law. As a commoner, he sits in the House of Commons. The eldest son of a marquis is allowed the courtesy-title of earl; the eldest son of an earl, that of viscount. Younger sons of peers are allowed the courtesy-title of lord or honourable, and the daughters that of lady or honourable.

cousin—*Cousin Betsy* a half-witted person.
I do not think there's a man living—or dead for that matter—that can say Foster's wronged him of a penny, or gave short measure to a child or a Cousin Betsy.—Mrs. Gaskell.

—*to call cousins* to claim relationship.
My new house is to have nothing Gothic about it, not pretend to call cousins with the mansion-house.—H. Walpole.

—*Cousin Michel or Michael* the nickname given to a German, as "John Bull" to an Englishman and "Brother Jonathan" to an American.
These were truly the days for Cousin Michael, corresponding in a measure to the "good old colonial times" of New England.—Anon.

coûte—*coûte que coûte* at any cost. French.
Mr. Child has fallen into the same mistakes as the proprietress of the Nouvelle Revue, though with less evident desire to abuse and vilify coûte que coûte (at all hazards).—National Review.

Coventry—*to send to Coventry* to exclude from companionship; to have no dealings with. **Sent to Coventry** signifies "in disgrace or disfavour with one's associates." Mostly used by schoolboys, who inflict the punishment frequently on their fellows. See **boycott.**
In fact that solemn assembly a levy of the school, had been held, at which the captain of the school had got up and given out that any boy, in whatever form, who should thenceforth appeal to a master, without having first gone to some prepositor and laid the case before him, should be thrashed publicly, and sent to Coventry.—Hughes.

cover—*covers were laid for so many* dinner was prepared for so many guests.
Covers were laid for four.—Thackeray.

crab—*to catch a crab* to be struck with the handle of the oar in rowing and to fall backwards. This accident occurs if the oar be left too long in the water before repeating the strokes.
I thought you were afraid of catching the wrong one, which would be catching a crab, wouldn't it?—Besant.

crack—*to crack a crib* to break into a house with the intention of robbing it.
Any man calls himself a burglar when he's once learned to crack a crib.—Besant.

—*to crack a bottle* to drink in a friendly way.
He was always ready to crack a bottle (drink) with a friend.

—*to crack up anything* to praise it highly.
Then don't object to my cracking up the old schoolhouse, Rugby.—Hughes.

—*a crack hand* one who is expert; an adept.

He is a crack hand (very clever) at entertaining children.

—to crack a crust to get along fairly well in the world; to make a small but sufficient income.

—in a crack instantaneously.

Poor Jack Tackle's grimy ghost was vanished in a crack (at once).—Lewis.

creature—creature comforts what makes the body comfortable; good food and clothing, and other necessaries and luxuries.

For the first time her own sacrifice of work and time could do nothing for her friend compared with the soft words, the grapes, and the creature comforts so freely bestowed by the newcomer.—Besant.

credat—credat judæus a phrase implying disbelief. Latin. The quotation is from Horace—*Credat Judæus Apella*, "Apella the Jew may believe it!" (but no one else will.)

creeps—to give one the creeps to cause one to shudder.

They give me the creeps, the whole lot of them, and that's a fact.—Haggard.

Crispin—a son or **knight of St. Crispin** a shoemaker.

crocodile—crocodile tears hypocritical tears shed by an unfeeling person.

He (Lord Lovat) laid all the blame of the Frasers' rising upon his son, saying with crocodile tears, that he was not the first who had an undutiful son.—G. A. Sala.

crooked—a crooked sixpence a lucky thing; a talisman. It used to be considered lucky for one to carry about a crooked sixpence on his person.

You've got the beauty, and I've got the luck; so you must keep me by you for your crooked sixpence (to bring you good luck).—George Eliot.

crop—to crop out to appear above the surface. In geology, inclined strata which appear above the surface are said to crop out.

The prejudice of the editor of the newspaper against America crops out (displays itself) in everything he writes.—Hiogo News, 1887.

—to crop up—(a) to rise in different places unexpectedly.

He did not, he said, want to have mushroom watering-places cropping up under his nose.—Good Words 1887.

—(b) to happen or appear unexpectedly.

But curious complications were to crop up yet.—Mrs. Henry Wood.

cropper—to come a cropper to get a fall; to tumble at full length; to meet with a sudden collapse.

He came a cropper yesterday while out riding.

cross—to cross swords to have a duel.

Captain Richard would soon have crossed swords with the spark had any villainy been afloat.—G. A. Sala.

—to cross the hand with silver fortune tellers, who in England and other countries are most frequently of gypsy race, begin their operations by having their hands crossed with a silver coin. They pretend that this is an indispensable preliminary to divination.

The tawny sibyl no sooner appeared, than my girls came running to me for a shilling a-piece to cross her hand with silver.—Goldsmith.

—on the cross unfair; dishonest. Opposed to *on the square*.

crow—crow's feet the wrinkles which age or trouble causes to form about the eyes.

—to eat crow to do what is excessively unpleasant. American. The crow has long been the emblem of contention; as Hudibras says:—

"If not, resolve before we go

That you and I must pull a crow."
The same idea is suggested in *Comedy of Errors*, act iii.:—

"We'll pluck a crow together."

—*to have a crow to pluck with any one* to have some fault to find with one; to have a matter requiring explanation.

Ah, Master George, I have a crow to pluck with you.—Florence Maryat.

—*as the crow flies* directly; without any deviation from the straight line to one's destination.

He went, as the crow flies (in a straight line), over the stubble and by the hedge-sides, never pausing to draw breath.—Mrs. Oliphant.

—*to crow over* to triumph over; to be exultant towards.

The colonel, instantly divining the matter, and secretly flattering himself, and determining to crow over Polly (prove that he was more knowing than Polly), said, to help him out, "Aha, you rogue, I knew it."—Harper's Magazine, 1886.

cry—*to cry off* to retreat from a bargain; to refuse to carry out an engagement.

Osborne will cry off now, I suppose, since the family is smashed.—Thackeray.

—*to cry cupboard* to be hungry.

"Madam, dinner's upon the table."
"Faith I'm glad of it; my belly began to cry cupboard."—Swift.

—*to cry quits.* See quits.

—*to cry over spilt milk* to spend time in useless regrets.

What's done, Sam, can't be helped; there is no use in crying over spilt milk (indulging in unavailing regrets.)—Halburton.

—*to cry up* to praise highly; to puff.

I was prone to take disgust towards a girl so idolized and so cried up (praised), as she always was.—Jane Austen.

—*to cry "wolf"* to raise a false alarm. A phrase taken from one of Æsop's Fables. A shepherd boy, who watched a flock of sheep near a village, called out, "Wolf! wolf!" When his neighbours came to help him, he laughed at them for their pains. The wolf, however, did truly come at last. Then the shepherd boy called out in earnest for help, but no one paid any attention to his cry. They had got accustomed to it, and despised it. He lost nearly all his flock.

cudgel—*to take up the cudgels on behalf of another* to defend him warmly.

On my showing him the correspondence, Delane immediately took up the cudgels for the widow (espoused in the widow's cause.)—Blackwood's Magazine, 1886.

—*to cudgel one's brains* to make a painful effort to remember.

Cudgel thy brains no more about it.—Shakespeare.

cue—*to give the cue* to give a hint; to furnish an opportunity. The cue, in the parlance of the stage, is the catchword, from which an actor knows where his part comes in.

This admission gave the cue to Todhunter (gave Todhunter an opportunity) to take up his parable and launch out into one of his effusive laudations of Parr and all his works.—Macmillan's Magazine.

cui—*cui bono?* to whom will it do any good? Latin.

For the last generation or two a feeling of cui bono had led to the discontinuance of the custom.—Thomas Hardy.

cum—*cum grano salis* with a grain of salt; making some allowance. Latin.

cup—*his cup runs over* he has more than enough. A phrase borrowed from the Bible (Ps. xxiii.).

—*in one's cups* intoxicated.

He had often signified, in his cups (when drinking hard), the pleasure he proposed in seeing her married to one of the richest men in the county.—Fielding.

cupboard—*cupboard love* affection springing from an interested motive.

A cupboard love is seldom true,
A love sincere is found in few.

           Nares.

curled—*curled darlings* petted and pampered young men.

He would show them of what a man in his own right is capable and he would go far past the "curled darlings" who owed everything to fortune and nothing to themselves.—Mrs. E. Lynn Linton.

curry—*to curry favour* to use mean arts to obtain patronage.

curse—*the curse of Cain* Cain, for the murder of his brother Abel, was condemned to be a wanderer and vagabond on the earth.

Those in the provinces, as if with the curse of Cain upon their heads, came, one by one, to miserable ends.—Froude.

—*the curse of Scotland* a name given to the playing-card called the nine of diamonds—the winning card in a gambling game which ruined many Scottish families; or, according to another explanation, the card on the back of which was written the message authorizing the massacre of Glencoe.

curtain—*curtain lectures* private admonitions given by a wife to her husband. The phrase, though of earlier origin, is immortalized in the celebrated *Mrs. Caudle's Curtain Lectures*, by Douglas Jerrold, published in the columns of *Punch*, 1845.

—*the curtain falls* the performance closes; the scene comes to an end.

Here the conversation ought to have ended; the curtain ought to fall at this point. What followed was weak—very weak.—Besant.

cut—*to cut in* to make a remark before another speaker has finished; to throw in a remark suddenly.

"Worked in the fields summers, and went to school winters: regulation thing?" Bartley cut in.—W. D. Howells.

—*to cut off with a shilling* to leave a small sum as a legacy.

Because I'm such a good-natured brother, you know I might get you turned out of house and home, and cut off with a shilling (disinherited) any day.—George Eliot.

—*to cut one short* to interrupt another while speaking.

Tom pulled himself together, and began an explanation; but the colonel cut him short (interrupted him).—Harper's Magazine, 1886.

—*to cut* or *to cut dead* to refuse to recognize an acquaintance in public.

She would cut her dearest friend (pass her dearest friend without recognition) if misfortune befell her, or the world turned its back (society frowned) upon her.—Thackeray.

—*to cut a figure, a dash* or *a dido* to make oneself prominent; to do something to attract notice. The last is a slang phrase, the two first are conversational.

It seems my entertainer was all this while only the butler, who, in his master's absence, had a mind to cut a figure.—Goldsmith.

—*to cut up rough* to resent any treatment; to show a disposition to quarrel.

He'll cut up so rough, Nickleby, at our talking together without him.—Dickens.

—*to be cut up* to be distressed.

Poor master! he was awfully cut up (sorry) at having to leave you.

Well then, of course, I was awfully cut up (in great affliction). I was wild.—C. Reade.

—*to cut one's eye-teeth* to become knowing; to learn how to cheat another man.

Them 'ere fellers (those fellows there—Scotsmen) cut their eye-teeth (learned crafty ways) afore they ever set foot in this country (America), I expect.—Haliburton.

—*the cut of one's jib* one's rig, or personal appearance; the peculiarities of one's dress and walk. A sailor's phrase.

—*cut and come again* a hospitable phrase, signifying that there is plenty for all guests. Jane Carlyle uses the expression in one of her letters.

Cut and come again (a profuse hospitality) was the order of the evening (marked all the proceedings that evening).

—*to cut the (Gordian) knot* to solve a difficulty in a speedy fashion. There was a knot tied by a Phrygian peasant, about which the report spread that he who loosed it should be king of Asia. It was shown to Alexander the Great, who cut it in two with his sword, saying, "'Tis thus we loose our knots."

—*to cut the ground from under one* to leave one in an illogical position, with no reasonable argument in his favour.

—*to cut out* to supplant; to secure another's place or privileges.

In a few weeks some fellow from the West End will come in with a title and a rotten rent-roll and cut all us city men out, as Lord Fitzrufus did last year with Miss Grogram, who was actually engaged to Podder, of Podder and Brown's.—Thackeray.

—*to cut one's throat* to act so as to ruin oneself.

He saw it all now; it had let the old man die after he had executed the fresh will disinheriting him. He had let him die; he had effectually and beyond redemption cut his own throat (ruined himself by his own action).—H. R. Haggard.

—*cut and thrust* keen; forcible.

That is the way of doing business—a cut-and-thrust style, without any flourish: Scott's style when his blood was up.—Professor Wilson.

—*to cut and run* to go off quickly; to run off immediately.

I must cut and run, whatever happens.—G. J. Whyte-Melville.

—*to draw cuts* to decide a matter by drawing papers of unequal length, presented so as to have the same appearance; equivalent to tossing up.

They drew cuts who should go out of the room.

D

dab—*a regular dab at anything.*

"I'm a regular dab at figures you know," said Jeremiah to his mother.—B. L. Farjeon.

daggers—*to look* or *speak daggers* to glare at; to gaze upon with animosity.

I will speak daggers to her; but will use none.—Shakespeare: Hamlet.

—**at daggers drawn** bitterly hostile.
*Lord Shelburne had always desired to
keep the Bedfords at a distance, and
had been at daggers drawn with
(bitterly hostile to) them ever since
their introduction into the
Government.*—Trevelyan.

damn—*to damn with faint praise* to
condemn anything by praising it very
slightly.
*For the first hour all had been
compliment, success, and smiles;
presently came the buts, and the
hesitated objections, and the damning
with faint praise.*—Maria Edgeworth.

Damocles—*the sword of Damocles* a
sword suspended by a single thread,
and ready to descend and kill the
person sitting below it. See **sword**.

Damon—*Damon and Pythias* sworn
friends. The classical name of Pythias
is Phintias. He offered to die for his
friend Damon.
*"Such unscientific balderdash," added
the doctor, flushing suddenly purple,
"would have estranged Damon and
Pythias."*—R. L. Stevenson.

dance—*to dance attendance on* to pay
assiduous court to. A phrase used in
contempt.
*Welcome, my lord; I dance attendance
(wait obsequiously) here.*
—Shakespeare.

—*to dance and pay the piper* to labour
to amuse, and have the expense of the
entertainment besides.

—*to lead a person a dance* or *a pretty
dance* to cause him unnecessary
trouble.

dander—*to get one's dander up* to grow
angry; to lose one's temper. Dander
= dandriff, scurf on the head.
*"I don't understand such language,"
said Alden, for he was fairly riled
(irritated) and got his dander up (lost
his temper).*—Haliburton.

Darby—*Darby and Joan* a happy old

couple devoted to each other. They
are characters in a popular ballad.
*You may be a Darby, but I'll be no Joan
(devoted wife), I promise.*—Goldsmith.

dark—*a dark horse* a competitor about
whose chance of winning the world
knows nothing. A sporting phrase.
*You see I was dipped pretty deep, and
duns after me, and the Derby my only
chance, so I put the pot on (betted
heavily on the favourite horse); but a
dark horse won.*—C. Reade.

—*to keep another in the dark* to keep
him in ignorance of an event.

—*to keep dark about anything* to preserve secrecy about it.
*If you will (fight me), I'll keep dark about
it (never speak about our fight).*—
Haliburton.

darken—*to darken another's door* to
cross the threshold of his house.
*He is a dishonourable scoundrel; and
if, after this assurance, you receive
him, I shall never darken your door
again.*—C. Reade.

David—*David and Jonathan* inseparable friends. A Biblical parallel to the
classical friendship of Damon and
Pythias.
*I was—everybody knows that—I was
his confidential factotum and his
familiar friend, as David was to
Jonathan.*—Besant.

Davy—*Davy Jones* a sailor's term for
death.
*Keep my bones from Davy
Jones (death).* Popular Song.

—*Davy Jones's locker* the place
where dead men go. A common
expression with sailors. It is also used
for the sea, the common receptacle of
everything thrown overboard.
*I tell thee, Jack, thou'rt free; leastways,
if we get to Jamaica without going to
Davy Jones's locker.*—G. A. Sala.

day—*to have had one's day* to be past
one's prime; to be no longer "in the

swim;" to be old-fashioned; to be discarded for something newer.

"Old Joe, sir," said the major, "was a bit of a favourite in that quarter once; but Joe has had his day."—Dickens.

—*every dog has his day.* See **dog**.

—*this day week* (**or** *year,* **or** *six months*) a week counting from this day; the corresponding day of last or next week.

Almost on that day year (the corresponding day of the last year) it (the House of Commons) had been cheering Pitt while he declaimed against the folly of a Hanoverian war.—Macaulay.

—*his days are numbered* he has only a short time to live.

Marocco alone yet bars the way, and Marocco's days are practically numbered.—Grant Allen, in Contemporary Review 1888.

—*to carry the day* to be victorious; to win a victory.

It was the cry of "free education" that carried the day (won the victory).

—*day of grace* a day allowed by the law before money is called in, or the law is put in execution. Three days of grace are generally allowed for the payment of a bill beyond the date actually mentioned in the paper. Thus a bill in which payment is promised on the 1st November is duly paid on the 4th.

—*a day after the fair* too late to see anything.

daylight—*to throw daylight upon* to reveal; to display to view.

But for that accident, the mystery and the wrong being played out at Caromel's farm might never have had daylight thrown upon it.—Mrs. Henry Wood.

de (French)—*de haut en bas* in a lofty, condescending fashion. French.

She used to treat him a little de haut en bas.—C. Reade.

—*de trop* in the way; not wanted; superfluous. French.

To turn a young lady out of her own drawing-room without assigning any reason for it, except that she is de trop (her presence is not wished for), is a very difficult operation.—James Payn.

—*de rigueur* strictly required. French.

His face was rather soft than stern, charming than grand, pale than flushed; his nose, if a sketch of his features be de rigueur for a person of his pretensions, was artistically beautiful enough to have been worth doing in marble by a sculptor nor over-busy.—Thomas Hardy.

De (Latin)—*de jure* legal; having the sanction of law. Latin.

—*de facto* real; having actual possession. Latin.

It was, we believe, impossible to find, from the Himalayas to Mysore, a single Government which was at once a Government de facto and a Government de jure.—Macaulay.

—*de mortuis nil nisi bonum* say only what is good of the dead. Latin.

The proverb of de mortuis is founded on humbug.—A. Trollope.

—*de novo* from a new point; afresh. Latin.

dead—*dead drunk* stupefied with liquor.

—*the dead-letter office* the department in the post-office where unclaimed letters are kept.

May not these wanderers of whom I speak have been sent into the world without any proper address at all? Where is our dead-letter office for such?—J. R. Howell.

—*to pull the dead horse* do work for wages already paid.

—*dead as a herring* **or** *as a door-nail* stone dead; without any life. The herring is a fish which dies immediately after it leaves the water.

"What! is the old king dead?"

"As nail in door."—Shakespeare: 2 Henry IV.

—**Dead Sea fruit** fruit fair to the eye, but crumbling to dust when the skin is broken. See **apple of Sodom.**

He had come across the fruits of the Dead Sea, so sweet and delicious to the eye, so bitter and nauseous to the taste.—A. Trollope.

—**dead hand** the mysterious influence of a dead person whom one has injured. An old superstition of this kind still lingers.

She must have been led, he thought, to his office by the dead hand of Tom himself.—Besant.

—**in a dead hand** said of land or property held by a corporation (for example, the Church) and not by a personality. Latin, *in manu mortuo.*

—**a dead letter** something no longer in force; a rule never attended to.

The rule about ready money was soon a dead letter (soon fell into disuse).—Trevelyan.

—**a dead-head** a person who obtains entrance into entertainment without paying; a sponger.

Poor, hopelessly abandoned loafers, wearing plainly the stamp of dead-head on their shameless features.—A. Grant.

—**a dead-heat** a contest where it is impossible to decide who is victor.

He was up in a moment; but he was already overlapped, and although he made up the difference, it was a dead-heat, and they were in neck-and-neck.—Besant.

—**dead beat** thoroughly exhausted.

I could not move from the spot. I was what I believe seldom really happens to any man—dead beat, body and soul.—C. Reade.

—**dead man's part** in law, the portion of an intestate person's movables beyond the share which goes by right to his wife and children. A technical phrase.

—**dead men** empty bottles.

Lord Smart. Come, John, bring me a fresh bottle.

Colonel. Ay, my lord; and pray, let him carry off the dead men, as we say in the army (meaning the empty bottles).—Swift.

dear—**dear me! oh dear!** or simply, **dear!** an exclamation of surprise, commiseration, or weariness, according to the tone in which it is uttered.

"Did you ever have your likeness taken, Harriet?" said she.

"Oh dear! no—never." (An exclamation of surprise.)

"You haven't got an egg upon you, Mrs. Bormalack, have you? Dear me! (how surprising!) one in your lap. Actually in a lady's lap!—Besant.

death—**to do to death** to kill.

This morning a boy of fifteen was done to death by Mr. Hawes.—C. Reade.

—**weary to death** excessively fatigued. This phrase really contains no reference to actual dying.

The houses themselves were mostly gable-roofed, with latticed windows, which served excellently to exclude the light, and which gave a blank and lack-lustre look to the edifices, as though they were weary to death of the view over the way.—W. Clark Russell.

—**to the death** fatally.

—**at death's door** very near dying; on the point of expiring.

Greaves had taken her marriage to heart, and had been at death's door (very dangerously ill) in London.—C. Reade.

—**in at the death** present at the final act of any exciting series of events.

The phrase is borrowed from fox-hunting.

—death on anything having a great inclination for anything; skilful or sure in performance.

He wandered about all day, stepping now and then, as he had promised his mother, into the business places to inquire for employment; but no one wanted an honest lad who could read, write and was "death on figgers" (clever at counting).—Life of President Garfield.

—he will be the death of me he will cause me to die. Generally used in a joking way.

Mrs. Squallop stared at him for a second or two in silence, then, stepping back out of the room, suddenly drew to the door, and stood outside, laughing vehemently. . . . "Mr.—Mr. Titmouse, you'll be the death of me (kill me with your laughter), you will—you will!" gasped Mrs. Squallop, almost black in the face.—S. Warren.

debt—*to pay the debt of nature* to die. See **pay**.

delirium—*delirium tremens* a dreadful disease resulting from hard drinking. Also known as D.T. and **blue devils**.

I am an Englishman and proud of it, and attached to all the national habits, except delirium tremens.—C. Reade.

demand—*in demand* much sought after.

—on demand when asked for.

He sent me a bill payable on demand (when presented at the proper time).

depend—*depend upon it* you may be certain; I assure you.

"If so," returned he, "depend upon it you shall feel the affects of this insolence."—Goldsmith.

deuce—*play the deuce with* disorganize; ruin. Deuce was a dæmon among the Brigantes, a tribe of the early Britons.

"Yonder is the inn," he exclaimed, "a handsome house enough, one must allow, and standing in quite a little park of its own; but for all that I have a presentiment that the cooking will play the deuce with (completely spoil) my digestion, and that we shall be poisoned with bad wine."—James Payn.

deus—*deus ex machina* an unexpected deliverer or helper, who comes just at the very time of danger or difficulty. Latin. The phrase is a classical one, and alludes to the supernatural deliverance of heroes on the Roman stage by the descent of a god, by mechanical contrivance, who bears them off in safety.

Where, in this case, were we to look for the deus ex machina who should fulfil the father's vow and sever the daughter's chains by one happy stroke?—W. E. Norris.

devil—*the devil's advocate* the person in an ecclesiastical assembly who had the ungracious office of opposing the canonization of some saint. The Latin form of the word is *advocatus diaboli*. The *advocatus diaboli* tried to throw doubt on the sanctity and miraculous powers of the proposed saint. In the following extract *devil's advocate* signifies "one who tries to prove the existence of unpleasant qualities":—

Mill was one of the sternest and most rigid representatives of that northern race which, notwithstanding the very different qualities which make it illustrious, has so continued to retain its conventional reputation for harshness and coldness that we are almost forced to believe there must be some truth in the imputation. There would be so if the devil's advocate could produce many such men as

James Mill to counter-balance Scott and Mackintosh as specimens of the character of their countrymen.—Mrs. Oliphant.

—**devil take the hindmost** the one who is last must suffer.

—**the devil to pay** a heavy sum to pay back; very serious consequences.

"There will be the devil to pay at the hall," said Paston. "You don't pump out a mine for a trifle, and with all that building on hand."—Mrs. E. Lynn Linton.

—**devils' luck** great good fortune; astonishing luck.

Mark my words, Gride: you won't have to pay his annuity very long. You have the devil's luck in bargains always.—Dickens.

—**the devil** a phrase used to contradict a statement that has just been made, or to express dissent from it.

"I'm Paddy Luck, and it's meself (myself) will sell the baste (beast) for twelve pounds, and divil a ha'penny less" (not one halfpenny under that sum).—C. Reade.

—**a devil of a temper** a very bad temper.

Mrs. Churchill had no more heart than a stone to people in general and a devil of a temper (very bad temper).—Miss Austen.

—**between the devil and the deep sea** between two menacing dangers.

Rupert's position was desperate: his friends had forsaken him; he was caught between the devil and the deep sea.—Gentleman's Magazine, 1886.

—**to whip the devil round the post** to evade rules or provisions.

—**devil-may-care** reckless; heedless.

I once had the honour of being on intimate terms with a mute, who, in private life and off duty, was as comical and jocose a little fellow as ever

chirped out a devil-may-care (reckless) song.—Dickens.

—**give the devil his due** allow even the worst man credit for what he does well.

Arthur Brooke was a straightforward and just young fellow; no respecter of persons, and always anxious to give the devil his due.—W. E. Norris.

—**to beat the devil's tattoo** to drum with the fingers on a window or a table. See **tattoo.**

diamond—*a rough diamond* a person with an unattractive exterior who possesses good qualities of mind and heart.

As for Warrington, that rough diamond had not had the polish of a dancing master and he did not know how to waltz.—Thackeray.

—**diamond cut diamond** a phrase used when one sharp person outwits another.

Notwithstanding their difference of years, our pair are playing a game very common in society, called diamond cut diamond.—G. J. Whyte-Melville.

dickens—*what the dickens* what the devil. A strong form of **what.**

I cannot tell what the dickens his name is.—Shakespeare.

die—*the die is thrown* or *cast* the decision is made; the decisive step is taken.

At all events, what use was there in delaying? The die was thrown, and now or to-morrow the issue must be the same.—Thackeray.

—**to die by inches** to die slowly; to waste away slowly but steadily.

At the time a sudden death always seems something strange and horrible, like a murder; although probably most of us, if we could choose, would rather be killed at a blow than die by inches.—W. E. Norris.

dine—*a diner-out* a man who generally dines with friends.

—*to dine with Democritus* to be cheated out of one's dinner.

—*to dine with Sir Thomas Gresham* to go without a dinner. The London Exchange was founded by Sir Thomas Gresham, a merchant in Queen Elizabeth's time, who gave his name to "Gresham's Law" in political economy. The Exchange was a favourite lounging-place for penniless men.

—*to dine with Duke Humphrey* to get no dinner at all. Some gentlemen were visiting the tomb of Duke Humphrey of Gloucester, and one of the party was by accident shut in the abbey. His whereabouts remained undiscovered until the party had risen from dinner. The poor fellow had been with Duke Humphrey, and had got no dinner at all—hence the phrase.

—*to dine with Mohammed* to die.

—*to dine with the cross-legged knights* to have no dinner to go to. A London phrase.

dip—*to dip in gall* to make very bitter.
The famous Shakespearian critic Malone was the object of his special aversion, which was most cordially reciprocated, and often had they transfixed one another with pens dipped in gall (full of rancour).—James Payn.

dirt—*dirt cheap* at an excessively low price.
Thirty pounds a week. It's too cheap, Johnson; it's dirt cheap.—Dickens.

—*to eat dirt* to submit to insult.
Though they bow before a calf, is it not a golden one? Though they eat dirt, is it not dressed by a French cook?—G. J. Whyte-Melville.

discount—*at a discount* (a) not in demand; not valued highly; unpopular.

There can be no doubt that the old-fashioned ideas of English policy in the East are at a discount.—Fortnightly Review, 1887.

—(b) sold at less than the market value.

dispose—*to dispose of* (a) to get rid of; to free oneself from.
But Wilkes had still to be disposed of.—Percy Fitzgerald.

—(b) to sell.
Madam is ready to dispose of her horse and carriage if a good price is offered.

ditch—*to die in the last ditch* to resist to the uttermost; to make a desperate resistance.

ditto—*to say ditto to* to acquiesce in; to accept the conclusions or arrangements of others.
Dr. Lavergne was a convinced Republican; his wife's convictions resembled those of the wise and unassuming politician who was content to say ditto to Mr. Burke.—W. E. Norris.

divine—*divine right of kings* a theory, first explicitly held by James I, of England, that the king is above the law, and answerable for his actions to no one. See Macaulay's *History of England*, Introduction.

Dixie—*Dixie's land* a land of plenty and happiness, celebrated in negro songs. Dixie was a planter in Manhattan Island, who removed his slaves to one of the Southern States, where they had less to eat and more to do, and therefore sighed for their old home.
In Dixie's land I take my stand,
I'll live and die for Dixie.
Popular Song,

do—*to do up* (a) to make tidy.
"But who is to do up your room every day?" asked Violet.—Besant.

—(b) to ruin; to make bankrupt.
He observed that there was a pleasure in doing up a debtor which none but a

creditor could know.—Maria Edgeworth.

—(c) to weary.

The widow felt quite done up (fatigued) after her long walk.

—_to do away with_ to remove; to get rid of.

Delightful Mrs. Jordan, whose voice did away with (banished) the cares of the whole house before they saw her come in.—James Payn.

—_to do for a man_ to ruin him.

—_to have to do with_ to be interested in; to have business with.

We have, however, to do with (our business is with) only one pair who were sitting together on the banks opposite Trinity.—Besant.

—_to do (well) by_ to behave (well) towards.

One does as one is done by.—W. Black.

—_well-to-do_ in comfortable circumstances.

He's growing up fast now, and I am pretty well-to-do (in fairly good circumstances).—Haliburton.

—_to do a person in the eye_ to cheat him.

doctor—_to put the doctor on a man_ to cheat him.

Perhaps ways and means may be found to put the doctor upon the old prig.—Tom Brown.

—_Doctors' Commons_ the Government office in London where wills are kept and marriages registered. So called because the Doctors of Civil Law were required to dine together (hold their common meal) four days in each term, called "eating their terms."

She had a superstitious kind of notion that she would do better in a future state if she would be recognized by the social law in this, and that the power of Doctors' Commons extended beyond the office of the registrar-general.—Mrs. E. Lynn Linton.

—_doctors differ_ or _disagree_ there exists a grave difference of opinion. A phrase in common use, employed somewhat playfully.

Who shall decide, when doctors disagree?—Pope.

doe—_doe_ See **John Doe**.

dog—_the dog of Montargis_ a dog whose master was slain, and which showed wonderful intelligence and ferocity in its behaviour to the murderer. Its name was Dragon; its master's name was Captain Aubri de Montdidier. The murderer's name was Richard Macaire.

No doubt Diogenes is there, and no doubt Mr. Toots has reason to observe him; for he comes straightaway at Mr. Toots's legs, and tumbles over himself in the desperation with which he makes at him, like a very dog of Montargis.—Dickens.

—_a dog-in-the-manger_ a selfish man, who refuses to allow his neighbour to enjoy even what he himself has no use for. Used as an adjective—"a dog-in-the-manger course of conduct."

A dog lay in a manger, and by his growling and snapping prevented the oxen from eating the hay which had been placed for them. "What a selfish dog!" said one of them to his companions. "He cannot eat the hay himself, and yet refuses to allow those to eat who can."—Æsop's Fables.

—_to dog-ear a book_ to turn down the corners of its pages so that they resemble a dog's ears.

—_a dog-in-a-blanket_ a kind of pudding made of dough and suet, and enclosing jam. Also called _roly-poly._

—_dog cheap_ very cheap. A corruption of _god-chepe_, a good bargain.

—**dog's nose** a drink composed of gin and beer.

—**the dogs of war** famine, sword, and fire.

And Cæsar's spirit, ranging for revenge, With Atë by his side, come hot from hell, Shall in these confines, with a monarch's voice, Cry, "Havoc" and let slip the dogs of war.— Shakespeare.

Note.—*Atë is the goddess of revenge. To cry "Havoc" signifies "to order slaughter without mercy."*

—**to go to the dogs** to go to ruin.

—**to lead the life of a dog or a dog's life** to pass a miserable existence.

I am afraid I led that boy a dog's life (made that boy's existence miserable).—R. L. Stevenson.

—**every dog has his day** the period of enjoyment allowed to any creature is a short one.

"Let Hercules himself do what he may, The cat will mew, and the dog will have his day."

Shakespeare: *Hamlet.*

—**dog latin** a debased medieval form of Latin, used by physicians, lawyers, and others, to whom the language was only partially familiar.

It was much as if the secretary to whom was intrusted the direction of negotiations with foreign powers had a sufficient smattering of dog Latin to make himself understood.—Macaulay.

—**give a dog an ill name and hang him** when a person's reputation is bad, all his actions, even though well-intentioned, are viewed with suspicion. It is better to get rid altogether of a man who has lost his good name, existence being thenceforth a burden to him.

You may say what you like in your kindness and generosity—it is a case of "give a dog an ill name and hang him."

dolce—*dolce far niente* sweet do nothing, or idleness. Italian.

don't—*don't you know?* a phrase frequently inserted in conversation, sometimes to secure the better attention of the listener.

"Oh, you don't know what Brighton is at this time of year," said Mr. Tom. "All the resident people like ourselves keep open house, don't you know? and very glad to."—Wm. Black.

door—*to lay at one's door* to charge one with.

A great many faults may be laid at their door, but they are not fairly to be charged with fickleness.—J. R. Lowell.

—*next door to anything* approaching closely to it.

A seditious word leads to a broil, and a riot undiminished is but next door to (closely resembles) a tumult.— L'Estrange.

Dorcas—*a Dorcas society* a woman's association for providing poor people with clothing. It receives the name from Dorcas, or Tabitha, who made clothes for the poor (Acts ix. 39).

About a year ago the ladies of the Dorcas society at our church made up a large quantity of shirts, trousers, and socks.—Max Adeler.

dot—*dot and carry one* irregularly; spasmodically.

I was not new to violent death. I have served His Royal Highness the Duke of Cumberland, and got a wound at Fontenoy; but I know my pulse went dot and carry one.—R. L. Stevenson.

double—*to take a double-first* to pass for a degree at Oxford with the highest honours in two schools or departments.

For instance, though I firmly believe that you could at the present movement take a double-first at the university, your knowledge of English literature is almost nil.—H. R. Haggard.

—*a double entendre* a remark covering a concealed meaning, which has generally a questionable reference. French.

An agreeable old gentleman, who did not believe in anything particular, and had a certain proclivity toward double entendres.—Rhoda Broughton.

—*the double lines* the name given in Lloyd's publications to the record of losses and accidents.

One morning the subscribers were reading the "double lines," and among the losses was the total wreck of this identical ship.—Old and New London.

—*double or quits.* When two persons have been playing for a stake, the loser or the winner may give a second challenge for the same amount. The result of the second venture either leaves the loser twice as badly off as before, or makes both parties even. In making this second challenge the phrase "double or quits" is used.

—*double-dealing* duplicity; trickery.

This young lady was quite above all double-dealing; she had no mental reservation.—Maria Edgeworth.

down—*to be down upon a person* to reprove or find fault with him.

Poor Buswell! his appearance isn't aristocratic, I admit, and Mrs. Greenwood was rather down upon me for asking him here.—Good Words, 1887.

down on their luck (a) in an evil plight; very unfortunate.

I wouldn't turn you away, Alan, if you were down on your luck.—R. L. Stevenson.

—(b) in low spirits.

The order for their execution arrived, and they were down upon their luck terribly.—C. Reade.

—*down in the mouth* dispirited; sad.

Well, I felt proper (very) sorry for him, for he was a very clever man, and looked cut up dreadfully, and amazin' (exceedingly) down in the mouth (melancholy).—Haliburton.

downy—*to do the downy* to lie in bed; to sleep.

And then, being well up, you see, it was no use doing the downy again, so it was just as well to make one's twilight (toilet) and go to chapel.— Verdant Green, ch. vii.

dozen—*a baker's dozen* thirteen. Formerly bakers gave an extra loaf or bun with every dozen sold to customers. Giving a man a baker's dozen is a slang expression for "giving him an extra sound beating."

dragon—*dragons' teeth* things which bring future destruction. Cadmus, the founder of Thebes, succeeded in killing a redoubtable dragon, by Athene's aid, and sowed its teeth in the plain. From these teeth sprang up armed men, who killed each other, all except five, the ancestors of the Thebans.

French Clinton plunged headlong into the abyss, and orders went forth like so many dragons' teeth sown by a financial Cadmus.—Mrs. E. Lynn Linton.

draw—*to draw on* to approach (of time).

And so the time of departure drew on rapidly.—Dickens.

—*to draw rein* to stop; to check one's course. A phrase used in riding and driving.

Lanfrey drew rein at the door.—Mrs. E. Lynn Linton.

—*to draw up* to stop; to come to a halt. Almost the same as **to draw rein**. There is the notion of gradual slackening of motion, as in a railway train approaching a station.

—*to draw the line somewhere* to refuse to move outside of a certain limit of conduct; to impose an arbitrary restriction on one's behaviour from fear of going too far.

—*to draw a person out* to lead a person to express his real opinions or show his real character.

there are many subjects on which I should like to draw him out (induce him to speak his mind freely).—Haliburton.

—*to draw the wool over* to hoodwink; to deceive.

Sir Henry was the fortunate possessor of what Pat was pleased to call "a nasty, glittering eye," and over that eye Pat doubted his ability to draw the wool as he had done over Celtic orbs.—C. Reade.

—*a drawn game* a game in which neither party wins.

If we make a drawn game of it, every British heart must tremble.—Addison.

dree—*to dree one's weird* to submit to one's fate. Scotch.

Nevertheless, French must dree his weird as a brave man should; and having drawn his lot from the hands of fate, he must obey the mandate written on the card.—Mrs. E. Lynn Linton.

dress—*the dress circle* that part of a place of entertainment which is set apart from the upper classes who come in evening dress.

drive—*to drive at anything* to speak with a certain end in view.

"What are you driving at?" (what is your intention in speaking as you do) he went on. "I show you a bit of my hand (a part of my scheme), and you begin talking round and round" (ambiguously).—Besant.

drop—*to drop in* to pay an informal visit.

If he could drop in (visit us in a friendly way) on Sunday week, he might go home the wiser.—Blackmore.

—*to drop off* (a) to fall asleep.

Every time I dropped off (fell asleep) for a moment, a new noise awoke me.—Mark Twain.

—(b) to leave (in a quiet way); to disappear.

The matrons dropped off one by one, with the exception of six or eight particular friends, who had determined to stop all night.—Dickens.

—*to take a drop too much* to get intoxicated.

He used often to take a drop too much (be the worse for liquor).

drown—*to drown the miller* to mix water and spirits in so unequal proportions as to make the concoction unpalatable (from too much water).

drowning—*drowning men catch at straws.* When a man is in a desperate situation he seeks to save himself by every possible means, even when those which offer are ridiculously inadequate.

Either because drowning men will catch at straws, or because he had really misplaced confidence in my abilities, this assurance seemed to comfort him a great deal.—W. E Norris.

drug—*a drug in the market* an unsaleable commodity.

Watch-guards and toasting-forks were alike at a discount, and sponges were a drug in the market (found no one to buy them).—Dickens.

dry—*a stirring of the dry bones* a revival of life where all seems dead. Biblical. See Ezek. xxxvii. 1–10.

duck—*to make ducks and drakes of a property* to spend it foolishly. Making ducks and drakes is a game played with a flat piece of stone or metal, which when flung with its broad surface almost parallel to smooth water, skips up and down like a bird. It would be foolish to use coins for such a purpose.

A fine thing for her, that was a poor girl

without a farthing to her fortune. It's well if she doesn't make ducks and drakes of it (foolishly spend it) somehow.—George Eliot.

—*a lame duck* a man who cannot pay his debts on the Stock Exchange.

—*a duck's egg* nothing. A phrase used at schools and colleges when a batsman in a cricket-match scores 0.

He got a duck's egg (no marks) at the last examination.

dull—*dull as ditch-water* wholly uninteresting.

What passed through his mind was something like the following: "Heigho! O Lord! Dull as ditch-water! This is my only holiday, yet I don't seem to enjoy it."—S. Warren.

dumps—*in the dumps* sulky; in a bad temper.

dust—*to throw dust in a man's eyes* to try to lead him astray.

He cared to say no more; he had thrown quite dust enough into honest Adam's eyes (deceived honest Adam quite enough).—George Eliot.

—*to raise a dust* to make a commotion.

There was small reason to raise such a dust (cause such a disturbance) out of a few indiscreet words.—Hacket.

Dutch—*a Dutch auction* an auction where goods are started at an extravagantly high price, and then gradually lowered in price until the people show a willingness to buy then. A common method of business among travelling peddlers.

They (the politicians) are always bidding against each other in the Dutch auction by which we are being brought down surely, though by a protracted process, to the abolition of every sort of qualification.—Goldwin Smith, in *Contemporary Review*, 1887.

—*Dutch courage* courage that results from indulgence in strong drink. Probably the phrase arose from the extensive use of Dutch gin, known as Hollands.

You shall have some fizz to give you Dutch courage.—Besant.

—*a Dutch concert* a concert or musical gathering at which each person sings his own song, without reference to that of his neighbour.

—*a Dutch uncle* a clumsy, uncouth man.

Dutchman—*then I'm a Dutchman.* A phrase used after a supposition has been made, in order to show its absurdity.

"Tom," said the other doggedly, "if there is as much gold on the ground of New South Wales as will make me a wedding-ring, I am a Dutchman."—C. Reade.

E

e—*e. and o. e.* errors and omissions excepted. Often added to an account when presented.

ear—*to give ear* to listen.

"Mr. Utterson, sir, asking to see you," he called; and even as he did so, once *more violently signed to the lawyer to give ear.*—R. L Stevenson.

—*about one's ears* in a confused heap; in a falling mass of ruin.

You'll have those universities of yours about your ears soon if you don't

consent to take a lesson from
Germany.—A. Trollope.

—to set by the ears to cause a quarrel.

I little thought when I ran in with Miss
Berry's good news that it would have
the effect of setting us all by the ears
(causing us all to quarrel).—A. Keary.

—by the ears quarrelling.

Take any two men that are by the ears
(quarrelling): they opinionate all they
hear of each other, impute all sorts of
unworthy motives, and misconstrue
every act.—Haliburton.

—little pitchers have long ears. See
pitcher.

ease—*at ease in one's inn* thoroughly
at home and comfortable. An old-
fashioned phrase.

Shall I not take mine ease in mine
inn?—Shakespeare: 1 Henry IV.

—standing at ease a military posture,
which gives rest to the legs.

So the ladies sat in a circle, and the
gentlemen stood at ease, tired out
before the close of the evening.—
Harper's Magazine, March 1888.

—ill at ease in an unquiet state; restless.

But the general is ill at ease; he cannot
get that infernal anonymous letter out
of his head.—G. J. Whyte-Melville.

—to ease away a rope to slacken it
gradually.

easy—*easy come, easy go* what is
gained without difficulty is resigned
or spent without much thought.

eat—*to eat one's words* to take back
what one has said; to retract
assertions too boldly made.

"I will swear by it (my sword) that you
love me; and I will make him eat it that
says I love not you."

"Will you not eat your word?" (repent
of what you have said).—
Shakespeare.

—to eat for the bar to prepare oneself
to be a barrister. Those studying for
entrance to the bar are required to be

present at a certain number of dinners
in the Temple or in Gray's Inn.

If you bind him with leading-strings at
college, he will break loose while
eating for the bar in London.—A.
Trollope.

—to eat out one's heart to suffer
intensely from disappointment and
forced inactivity.

She withdrew, covered with
mortification, to hide her head and eat
out her heart in the privacy of her own
uncomfortable home.—Gentleman's
Magazine, 1888.

edge—*to play with edge-tools* to sport
with what is dangerous.

You jest; ill jesting with edge-tools (on
dangerous subjects).—Tennyson.

—to set the teeth on edge to cause
unpleasant sensations.

I had rather hear a brazen canstick
turned,
Or a dry wheel grate on the axle-tree;
And that would set my teeth nothing on
edge,
Nothing so much as mincing poetry.
                                    Shakespeare.

effect—*in effect* really; actually.

To say of a celebrated piece that there
are faults in it is, in effect (really), to
say that the author of it is a man.—
Addison.

—to take effect to operate; to act as
intended.

The medicine took effect, and the
patient fell into a sound sleep.

egg—*to egg on* to urge; to incite.

She would then be in a better position
to judge how far it was the girl's own
doing, and how far she had been
egged on to it by others.—Murray's
Magazine, 1887.

—as sure as eggs is eggs certainly; assuredly. Perhaps a corruption of "As sure
as x is x"—a dictum in logic.

And the bishop said, "Sure as eggs is

eggs, this here is the bold Turpin."—Dickens.

—*to have all one's eggs in one basket* to risk all one's goods in the same venture; to have everything dependent on the security of one particular thing or one particular undertaking.
I know your happiness depends on her. All your eggs are in that one basket.—C. Reade.

—*a bad egg* a worthless fellow.

El Dorado—*an El Dorado* a golden land; a country full of gold and gems. The expression is a Spanish one, and is generally associated with the discoveries Spanish adventurers made in the fifteenth and sixteenth centuries.
The whole comedy is a sort of El Dorado of wit.—T. Moore.

elbow—*elbow grease* hard scrubbing; hard work.
"Not at all, Mrs. Broughton; success depends on elbow-grease."—A. Trollope.

—*elbow room* room in which to move easily; sufficient space.
"You will have elbow-room out here, eh?" said he. "You will not crowd your neighbours off the pavement."—Wm. Black.

—*out at elbows* shabbily dressed; wearing ragged clothes.
When a man's getting out at elbows (dress becomes shabby) nobody will believe in him.—George Eliot.

elevation—*the elevation of the host* the part of the Mass in which the celebrant raises the consecrated wafer above his head to be adored by the people (Roman Catholic Church).

eleventh—*at the eleventh hour* just in time and no more. See the parable of the Labourers in the Vineyard, Matt. xx.1.

embarras—*embarras de richesse* excess of material; the perplexity which arises from the difficulty of choice among very many things. French.

en—*en rapport* in sympathetic connection. French.
Your primary object is, by organizing your brotherhood and putting it en rapport with the leaders of education in this country, to secure it for it increased respect.—Journal of Education, 1888.

—*en garçon* as a bachelor; in bachelor's style. French.
George came to dinner—a repast en garçon—with Captain Crawley.—Thackeray.

—*en masse* in a body. French.

—*en route* in the course of the journey. French.

end—*on end* in succession; without a break.
Peasants who have begun to save constantly continue the way of living we have described for years on end.—Spectator, 1887.

—*to make both ends meet* to make one's income cover one's expenditure; to keep out of debt.
Even Mr. Whichelo, the head clerk, whose children were often ailing and who had a good deal of trouble to make both ends meet (keep out of debt with his small income), smiled benignly upon Kate.—Mrs. Oliphant.

—*no end of a fellow* a very fine fellow.
Keats was no end of a fellow (a grand man).—Besant.

enough—*enough and enough* more than enough.
The play has wit enough and enough.—Madame D'Arblay.

—*enough is as good as a feast* what is sufficient serves the purpose as well as if there were an excess.
The Koh-i-noor had got enough, which in most cases is more than as good as a feast.—O. W. Holmes.

entre—*entre nous* "between ourselves." Used when a confidential statement is made. French.

equal—*equal to the occasion* not perplexed; able to act.

esprit—*esprit de corps* the desire to defend the institution or company to which one belongs. French.

et—*et hoc genus omne* and everything of the sort; and all similar beings of things. Latin.
And with those forlorn creatures must be taken into account others—older, but in this respect equally forlorn—the whole race of shop-girls, errand-boys, young maidens, et hoc genus omne.—Edinburgh Review, 1887.

event—*at all events* whatever happens; in any case.
At all events (in any case), Constance, you will go on to prove it by your original papers when you publish your researches.—Besant.

ever—*ever and anon* frequently; from time to time.
Ever and anon a pamphlet issued from the pen of Burke.—Henry Morley.

every—every bit quite; altogether.
The copy is every bit (quite) as good as the original.

—*every now and then* frequently; after the lapse of short intervals.
Every now and then a countryman would burst into tears.—Thackeray.

evidence—*in evidence* actually present; before the proper authorities.
The sister whose presence she had relied on was not in evidence.—Blackwood's Magazine.

evil—*the evil eye* malign influence (supposed to exist in the glance of certain persons).
Evelyn himself informs us how Sir Stephen contrived to escape the evil eye (bad influence) which ordinarily pursues a self-made man.—Trevelyan.

ewe—*a ewe lamb* a single possession very much prized by its possessor. See the parable of the Ewe Lamb told by Nathan to King David (2 Sam. xii. 1–14).

ex—*ex cathedra* made with authority; dogmatic. Latin.
So it has happened, not rarely, that criticism has flagrantly blundered and made itself ridiculous in its ex cathedra decisions on the merits of poetry and poets.—Ray Palmer.

—*ex officio* by virtue of one's office. Latin.
All over the Continent the ministers of the crown or of the republic sit ex officio in either house from the day they are appointed.—Spectator, 1887.

—*ex parte* biased; one-sided; partial. Latin.
Or perhaps I ought to have suppressed the note altogether on the ground that it was a mere ex parte statement.—Professor Huxley.

—*ex pede Herculem* we recognize Hercules from the size of his foot; that is, we judge of the whole by a typical part. Latin.
Ex pede Herculem may often prove safe enough, to ex verruca Tullium (to recognize Cicero from the wart on his nose) is liable to mislead a hasty judge of his fellow-men.—O. W. Holmes.

—*ex post facto* after the deed is done. Latin. An *ex post facto* law is a law made to punish deeds already committed.
There were libels, no doubt, and prophecies, and rumours, and suspicions, strange grounds for a law inflicting capital penalties ex post facto (of a retrospective nature), on a large body of men.—Macauley.

exception—*to take exception* to be offended.
Her manner was so perfectly respectful that I could not take exception to (find fault with) this retort.—Farjeon.

execution—*to do execution* to be effective; to secure victims; to win conquests. Generally used of a lady's eyes, which are supposed to capture a man's heart.

Sophia's features were not so striking at first, but often did more certain execution.—Goldsmith.

exeunt— *exeunt omnes* all go out (at the end of a scene). Latin.

expense—*at another's expense* with a view to depreciate the person.

These satirical observations were made simply at Prince Albert's expense (solely with the view of depreciating Prince Albert), and were not intended to reflect upon the Queen or the Royal Family.—Fortnightly Review, 1887.

experimentum—*experimentum crucis* the critical test. Latin.

"Boiled just three hours longer than the other," he said; "six hours in all. This is the experimentum crucis."—O. W. Holmes.

experto—*experto crede* believe one who has gone through the experience. Latin.

eye—*to make eye's at* to gaze upon amorously; to look at in a loving way.

—*the eye of Greece* Athens. A name applied to it by Milton—*Paradise Regained*, bk. iv., 1.240:—

Athens, the eye of Greece, mother of arts.

—*to have a good eye to anything* to look well after it; to be quick in recognizing.

I remember her, however, as a sensible woman, and, having a good eye to the main chance (being careful of money), she had been a capital wife to William.—Hugh Conway.

—*to see with half an eye* to see with great ease.

—*to cast sheep's eyes at* to gaze at in a modest and diffident but longing way, like a bashful lover.

There came a wealthy stockbroker who cast sheep's eyes at Helena.—The Mistletoe Bough, 1885.

—*up to the eyes* completely; fully.

A neighbour's estate, mortgaged up to the eyes, was sold under the hammer (mortgaged to its full value, was sold by auction).—C. Reade.

—*in the wind's eye* directly opposed to the wind.

Proper scared they were to see a vessel, without sails or oars, going right straight ahead, nine knots an hour, in the very wind's eye (right against the wind).—Haliburton.

—*my eye!* an exclamation of astonishment.

—*to see eye to eye* to have the same opinions on any subject. A phrase mostly used in religious circles.

Until we can see eye to eye (have the same views) on this question of Church government, it is better that we should worship apart.

F

face—*a long face* a sad or mournful countenance.

—*to set one's face against* to oppose with determination.

—*to make faces* to contort the countenance.

—*to put a good face* to bear up courageously; to show no signs of flinching.

In a word, Mrs. Bute put a good face against fortune, and kept up appearances in the most virtuous manner.—Thackeray.

—*face to face* in immediate presence of each other.

She sent for Blanche to accuse her face to face (in her presence).—Tennyson.

—*to face a thing out* to refuse to retire through shame or for fear of obloquy.

She thinks with oaths to face the matter out.—Shakespeare.

Exp.—*She thinks that she will be able to maintain her innocence in the matter by taking grave oaths.*

—*to put a bold face upon* to act boldly, as if there was nothing to be ashamed of.

Dundas had little or rather nothing to say in defence of his own consistency; but he put a bold face on the matter, and opposed the motion.—Macaulay.

facings—*to put one through one's facings* to examine; to inspect.

The Greek books were again had out, and Grace, not at all unwillingly, was put through her facings.—Trollope.

fag—*the fag end* the closing piece of any work, where the interest flags.

fair—*fair game* open to attack; deserving of banter or criticism.

Bourrienne is fair game, but the whole of his statements are not worthless.—Spectator, February 18, 1888.

—*fair and square* honest; just.

—*to be on the fair way* or *fair road to anything* to have every chance of attaining anything.

—*to bid fair* to promise well.

The lad bids fair to rival (gives promise of rivalling) his elder brother in scholarship.

—*fair play* courteous and just treatment of competitors or enemies.

I did that to get clear of the crowd, so that I might have fair play at him (struggle with him on equal terms).—Haliburton.

—*fair and softly goes far in a day* courtesy and moderation enable a man to effect a great deal. An Irish proverb.

"Slow and sure," said his friends, "fair and softly goes far in a day. What he has, he'll hold fast; that's more than Marvel ever did."—Maria Edgeworth.

faith—*in good faith* without treachery; honourably.

There was no doubt in any one's mind that Allen's father had acted in good faith (honestly).—Besant.

fall—*to fall away* to degenerate.

The temptations of the lower-fourth soon proved too strong for him, and he rapidly fell away.—Hughes.

—*to fall away from* to abandon; to desert.

"We shall beat him yet," said Hawes, assuming a firmness he did not feel, lest this man should fall away from him, and perhaps bear witness against him.—C. Reade.

—*to fall flat* to cause no amusement or interest.

Her remark fell flat—every one knows the effect of the reproduction of a worn-out jest—and had a sobering effect upon the little company.—James Payn.

—*to fall foul of* to collide with; to dash against; to unwittingly attack; to quarrel with.

In their sallies their men might fall foul of (attack) each other.—Clarendon.

—*to fall in* (a) to take one's place in the ranks. A military phrase.

Ere Charlie had finished his ration, dark

though it was, the men had fallen in.—
G. J. Whyte-Melville.

—(b) to become the property of a person after the lapse of a certain time.

And then the inheritance fell in.—Besant.

—*to fall in with* to meet with; to come across.

"Did you ever fall in with any Yankees?"

"One or two, sir."—C. Reade.

—*to fall off* (a) to diminish; to lose ground; to deteriorate.

One regrets to note that after her engagement to Tom there came a sad falling off in her thirst for knowledge.—Besant.

—*to fall out* (a) to quarrel.

I did upbraid her and fall out with her.—Shakespeare.

—(b) to happen.

And it fell out with me, as it falls out with so vast a majority of my fellows, that I chose the better part.—R. L. Stevenson.

—*to fall through* to be abandoned (of a scheme).

These arrangements would fall through, and it was easy to know what would follow.—Proude.

—*to fall to* to commence with energy (generally said of eating).

—*to fall to the ground* (a) to fall from lack of support; to be abandoned (of some proposition).

You had better let them know that Sir Abraham is of opinion that there is no case at any rate against Mr. Harding, and that as the action is worded at present it must fall to the ground.—A. Trollope.

—(b) to have no practical effect.

These were your words, sir; they did not fall to the ground.—C. Reade.

—*to fall short* to be deficient.

Her place had been supplied by an

excellent woman, who had fallen little short of (nearly equalled) a mother in affection.—Jane Austen.

—*to fall in love with* to become enamoured of.

On our first acquaintance I clearly saw that he was not disposed to pay court to my fortune, and I had also then coolness of judgment sufficient to perceive that it was not probable he should fall in love with my person.—Maria Edgeworth.

—*to fall upon one's feet* to escape injury; to be fortunate. The metaphor is borrowed from the natural fact that a cat, when thrown from a height, alights on its feet, and thus escapes any serious hurt.

family—*a person of family* a well-born person.

And Mr. Irwine's sisters, as any person of family (lady or gentleman) within ten miles of Broxton could have testified, were such stupid, uninteresting women.—George Eliot.

fancy—*fancy free* with the affections not engaged.

In maiden meditation, fancy free.—Shakespeare.

—*the fancy* sporting characters; prize-fighters; dog-fanciers.

The patrons of the fancy (prize-fighting) are proud of their champion's condition.—George Eliot.

far—*far gone* deeply affected by some strong influence, such as disease, drink, or love.

He felt a void in his heart that quite startled him. He had no idea he was so far gone (in love).—G. J. Whyte-Melville.

—*a far cry* a long distance. A phrase borrowed from the well-known saying, "It is a far cry to Lochawe."

It is a far cry from Paris to Kairwan.—Fortnightly Review, 1887.

—*far and away* completely; beyond comparison.

Public opinion is not altogether wrong in crediting the Jews with an amount of wealth larger by a good deal than is their due, and, what is perhaps more to the point, a proportion of rich families far and away beyond anything that is found among Gentiles.—Spectator, 1887.

—*far niente* do nothing; idleness. An Italian phrase. See **dolce far niente**.

The far niente of her Italian life had entered into her very soul.—A. Trollope.

—*far from it* not at all; by no means.

"Mr. Dickson, you say, is not, strictly speaking, handsome?"

"Handsome! Oh no; far from it (anything but that)—certainly plain."—Jane Austen.

farthest—*at farthest; at the farthest* making the largest possible allowance of time.

Parliament will certainly rise the first week in April at farthest (not later than the first week in April).—Chesterfield.

fashion—*after a fashion* to a certain degree; in a certain nominal way (generally said disparagingly).

He knows French after a fashion (has a certain knowledge of French; not a thorough knowledge).

fast—*to play fast and loose* or *at fast and loose* to act in a way inconsistent with one's promises or engagements; to behave with inconstancy; to show no consideration for.

'It's a shame, by heavens!" said George, "to play at fast and loose with a young girl's affections."—Thackeray.

fat—*to live on the fat of the land* to have every luxury.

It is well known that the family of the Slopes never starve: they always fall on their feet like cats; and let them fall where they will, they live on the fat of the land.—A. Trollope.

—*the fat is in the fire* there is a great splutter and confusion.

He's a credit to your nation, that man. He's actually the first pot-hook on the crane: the whole weight is on him: if it weren't for him the fat would be in the fire in no time (things would very quickly be in confusion).—Haliburton.

—*to kill the fatted calf* to prepare the best food in the house for an expected guest. The phrase is used in the parable of the Prodigal Son (Luke XV).

father—*The Father of Waters* the river Nile.

Rasselas was the fourth son of the mighty emperor in whose dominions the Father of Waters begins his course.—Samuel Johnson.

—*to father anything on a person* to ascribe its origin to him.

Of the poor pagan poets, it must be confessed

That time, and transcribing, and critical note,

Have fathered much on them which they never wrote.—Byron.

fault—*to a fault* even more than is required; to excess.

He was kind to a fault.—Thomas Hardy.

—*at fault* puzzled; in a difficulty how to proceed. Said of a dog when it has missed the scent.

And then the two set about foraging for tea, in which operation the master was much at fault (puzzled how to proceed).—Hughes.

—*in fault* to blame; erring.

Is Antony or we in fault (to blame) for this?—Shakespeare.

—*to find fault with* to blame; to be displeased with.

We'd find no fault with (not blame) the tithe-woman, if I were the parson.—Shakespeare.

faux—*a faux pas* a false step; a breach of moral conduct. French.

Then it was he committed a faux pas.—C. Reade.

feast—*feast of reason and flow of soul* intellectual intercourse where the conversation reaches a high point of excellence.

There St. John (pronounce Sinjun) mingles with my friendly bowl,
The feast of reason and the flow of soul.—Pope.

feather—*to feather one's nest* to provide for one's own personal comfort and interests; to lay by money for oneself.

You have forgot this, have you, now you have feathered your nest? (since you have made a sufficient provision for yourself).—Congreve.

—*a feather in one's cap* an honour.

The fellow's very carelessness about these charges (accusations) was, in Margaret's eyes, a feather in his cap (something to be proud of), and proved, for one thing, their absolute want of foundation.—James Payn.

—*in full feather* in elaborate costume.

—*in high feather* in high spirits; exultant.

Martin leads the way in high feather; it is quite a new sensation to him getting companions.—Hughes.

—*to show* or *fly the white feather* to betray signs of fear; to be a coward.

My blood ran a little cold at that but I finished my liquor. It was no use flying a white feather (showing signs of fear); so say I (I said), "Here's to the Corsair's bride."—C. Reade.

Fell—*Dr Fell* a character mentioned in a verse of Tom Brown's (1663-1704), and often referred to in literature. When a person is disliked, but no specific reason can be assigned for this dislike, it is usual to quote the lines—

I do not love thee, Dr. Fell,
The reason why I cannot tell:
But this alone I know full well,
I do not love thee, Dr. Fell.—R. L. Stevenson.

fiddle—*to play first fiddle* to take the lead in anything.

Tom had no idea of playing first fiddle (taking the lead) in any social orchestra (friendly gathering).—Dickens.

—*to play second fiddle* to take a subordinate position.

She had inherited from her mother an extreme objection to playing, in any orchestra whatsoever, the second fiddle (occupying, under any circumstances, a secondary place).—James Payn.

—*scotch fiddle* the itch (so called from the motion of the hand in scratching).

—*fiddle-de-dee* an exclamation of impatience and contempt.

I told him I was discouraged and unhappy; his daughter's heart seemed above my reach.

"Fiddle-de-dee!" (away with such talk), said he. "It all comes of this new system—courting young ladies before marriage spoils them."—Reade.

—*fiddler's news* news that comes very late.

"Have you heard that the Pope is ill?"—*"Oh, that's fiddler's news" (known to every one).*

fiddlestick—*fiddlestick* or *fiddlesticks* an exclamation of impatience; nonsense.

"A question of fiddlestick!" (mere nonsense), cried the doctor angrily, walking about the room.—Mrs Oliphant.

fie—*fie-foh-fum* words such as would be uttered by a bloodthirsty monster; blustering talk.

Fie, foh, and fum,
I smell the blood of an Englishman.
                                    Shakespeare.

field—*to be in the field* to be a competitor for any prize.

From the very first, Mitchell perceived that there could be little hope for him so long as Gilbert Segrave remained in the field (continued to be a competitor).—Good Words, 1887.

—*to keep* or *hold the field* to maintain one's ground against all opponents.

There all day long Sir Pelleas kept the field (proved himself victorious against all competitors).—Tennyson.

—*to take the field* to commence warlike operations.

fig—*a fig for any one* an expression of contempt = "What do I care for him!"

Let it come, i'faith, and I'll pledge you all; and a fig for Peter!—Shakespeare.

fight—*to fight shy of* or to avoid.

If you fight shy of him, miss, you may remember this, that you will fight shy of me at the same time.—A. Trollope.

—*to fight for one's own hand* to struggle for one's personal interests.

Each should fight for his own hand.—Wm. Black.

figure—*to make a figure* to distinguish oneself.

Besides, he would have been greatly hurt not to be thought well of in the world; he always meant to make a figure (distinguish himself), and be thought worthy of the best seats and the best morsels.—George Elliot.

—*to figure out* to ascertain an amount by careful computation.

—*to figure up* to add items into a total.

—*to cut a figure* to make a grand appearance.

He ruined his mother that he might cut a figure (appear splendid) at the university.—Thackeray.

—*to find it in one's heart* to persuade oneself.

I could not find it in my heart (persuade

myself) *to dismiss the old man, who had been about the house so long.*

fine—*in fine* in conclusion; to sum up.

In fine, Rob was despatched for a coach, the visitors keeping shop meanwhile.—Dickens.

finger—*to have a finger in the pie* to be mixed up in any affair.

But then they dearly loved having a finger in the pie parochial.—Hugh Conway.

—*to have at one's fingers' ends* to be able to repeat or use without any trouble (generally of something committed to memory).

He had Greek at his fingers' ends.—A. Trollope.

—*to arrive at one's fingers' ends* to be reduced to poverty; to be in great straits.

fire—*to fire up* to become angry; to show indignation.

Now a high-minded, honest man would have fired up at this.—B. L. Farjeon.

first—*first chop* first-rate; of the highest excellence. An Anglo-Chinese expression.

fish—*neither fish, flesh, nor good red herring* difficult to classify; having no pronounced character.

A phrase used by Tom Brown and Dryden.

Was he a Tory or a Liberal? or was he neither fish, flesh, nor the other thing?

—*neither fish nor fowl* odd; difficult to classify.

—*a fish out of water* Said of a person who is placed in a position which is strange and distasteful to him.

Mr. Dance stood there, as he said, "like a fish out of water."—R. L. Stevenson.

—*a loose fish* a man of dissipated habits.

Mr. Henry Fielding, a writer of plays and novels then much in vogue, but a sad, loose fish.—G. A. Sala.

—*a queer fish* an eccentric person.

"And what sort of fellow did you find Crawley, Uncle Tom?"

"Such a queer fish—so unlike anybody else in the world!"—A Trollope.

—**all's fish that comes to his net** he is not very particular or scrupulous. Everything is fish that comes to Mr. Frey's net.—Spectator, February 18, 1888.

—**to make fish of one and flesh of another** to treat two persons in different fashions; to show partiality.

—**to fish for compliments** to converse in a way that induces people to pay compliments to you; to lead people to praise you, because they see you wish to be praised.

"But you did, perhaps," she added innocently, fishing for a compliment.—Thomas Hardy.

—**other fish to fry** other business to attend to.

"I never asked you about your spill the other night," says she in her loud voice; "I had other fish to fry."—Rhoda Broughton.

fit—**to fit in with** to agree exactly with. Under such temptations careless or ill-educated people, even if they would not invent circumstances or dates, are extremely apt to twist them so as to fit in with what they have undertaken to prove.—Spectator, April 14, 1888.

fits—**by fits and starts** spasmodically; without steady application.

flag—**the flag at half-mast** this is a sign of mourning, observed especially by vessels in harbour, when any personage dies.

—**to hang out the white flag** to show willingness to come to terms, generally in token of surrender.

—**to hang out the red flag** (a) to intimate danger.
The red flat warns of danger.
White is all right,

Red is all wrong,
Green goes gently bowling along.
Mneonic Rhyme for Railway
Signalmen.

—(b) to give signal for battle.

flame—**a flame** a sweetheart.

—**an old flame** a former sweetheart.
I suppose she was an old flame of the colonel's.—Thackeray.

flare—**to flare up** to go into a passion.

flash—**a flash in the pan** an abortive attempt; a failure of some ambitious undertaking. The phrase is taken from a flint-lock gun which, though loaded, fails sometimes to go off when the flint is struck.

—**the flash gentry** thieves; professional rogues.

"Nice boys, both," said their father. "They won't turn up their noses as if they were gentlemen. A pretty kind of flash gentlemen you are!"—Besant.

—**to flash fire** to throw angry or passionate glances; to make the eyes glisten with strong emotion.
The eyes of the Indian monarch flashed fire, and his dark brow grew darker, as he replied, "I will be no man's tributary."—Prescott.

flat—**to fall flat** to fail to cause interest or amusement.
She had a dry, queer humour, and loved a joke; but Phil's fell very flat (his jokes were very far from interesting her) this night.—Blackmore.

flea—**a flea-bite** something trifling; a thing of no importance.
Doubtless to a man of Mr. Aird's fortune such things are but flea-bites.—James Payn.

—**a flea in one's ear** an annoying suggestion; an unwelcome repulse.
"I wouldn't do it, if it was ever so!" exclaimed Mrs. Jennynge, who in this extremity had utterly discarded her French for the vernacular. "You try it yourself, and see if he don't put you

down pretty quick, or send you flying
with a flea in your ear" (with a sharp
rebuke).—James Payn.

flesh—*flesh-pots,* **or** *the flesh-pots of
Egypt* material welfare; sordid considerations. The reference is to the
conduct of the children of Israel in
the desert, many of whom grew weary
of the plain food. See Ex. xvi. 3.

—*flesh and blood* human nature.
Not as I wish to speak disrespectful o'
them as have got the power i' their
hands, but it's more than flesh and
blood (human nature) 'ul bear
sometimes.—George Eliot.

—*to make the flesh creep* to cause a
sensation of dread and horror.
"My dear Mr. Aird, you make our flesh
creep!" (you horrify us), remonstrated
Mrs. Wallace; whereupon he
desisted.—James Payn.

—*to fling over* to desert; to cease to
assist or patronize.
"Of course, the old girl will fling him
over," said the physician.—Thackeray.

—*to have a fling at; to indulge in a
fling at* to attack sarcastically.
I even went so far as to indulge in a
fling at (attack sarcastically) the State
House, which, as we all know, is in
truth a very imposing structure.—
Holmes.

—*to have one's fling* to indulge in fun
or in dissipation.
As for me, all I look forward to is to
have my little fling (indulge in a little
dissipation), and then to give up the
gaieties of London and take a quiet
villa and have a garden.—Besant.

flint—*to fix another's flint for him* to
punish him.
"That is worse still," said I, "because
you can't resent it yourself. Leave him
to me, and I'll fix his flint for him"
(castigate him).—Haliburton.

—*to skin a flint* to be excessively mean
in one's dealings.

floor—*to take the floor* **to rise to
address a public meeting.

—*to have the floor* **to have the right of
addressing a meeting by rising before
other intending speakers.

flotsam—*flotsam and jetsam* goods lost
at sea, and either floating in the water
or cast on shore.

fly—*fly-away* absurd; fantastic.

—*to fly out against* **or** *at* to speak in a
rash, impulsive manner against.
It 'ud ill become a man in a public office
to fly out (speak rashly) again' King
George.—George Eliot.

—*to fly in the face of* to oppose directly
and in a reckless fashion.
Every evening before we left Paris I
saw her, and implored her to trust
herself to me and leave Paris as my
wife . . . But, with all this, she was firm,
and would not fly in her parents' face.—
C. Reade.

—*to fly in the face of providence* to
do a deliberately imprudent thing; to
court danger or death.
Dr. Cooper had told her that to sleep
with the child would be to fly in the
face of Providence; for if any mischief
was really brewing, she would in that
case be certain to suffer from it.—
James Payn.

—*with flying colours* honourably; triumphantly.

—*The Flying Dutchman* the name
applied to the express train running
from London to Exeter on the broad-
gauge railway; so called on account of
its speed. The term originally
belonged to a phantom ship, which
was supposed to fly over the waves
till the day of judgment.

—*to fly off at the handle* to become
excited; to act impulsively.
He was full of crotchets that way, and
the sight of the sea, or even a mere
flower, would make him fly right off at
the handle.—Haliburton.

follow—*to follow suit* to behave in the same manner; to do as the person before you has done. A phrase borrowed from card-playing.
But when the fortunes of Kingscliff began to rise, the fortunes of the gallant admiral followed suit.—Good Words, 1887.

food—*to become food for fishes* to be drowned.
But he was dead enough, for all that, being both shot and drowned, and was food for fish in the very place where he had designed my slaughter.—R. L. Stevenson.

—*to be food for worms* to be in one's grave; to be dead and buried.
The certificates are all genuine: Snawley had another son, he has been married twice, his first wife is dead: none but her ghost could tell she didn't write that letter; none but Snawley himself can tell that this is not his son, and that his son is food for worms.—Dickens.

fool—*to be a fool for one's pains* to take unnecessary and thankless trouble.

—*a fool's paradise* a state of happiness where everything is unreal and certain to be shattered.
Into a limbo large and broad, since called The Paradise of Fools.—Milton, Paradise Lost, bk. iii, 1. 495.

foot—*to put the best foot foremost* or *forward* (a) to walk as rapidly as possible; to exert oneself to the utmost.
The girl made up her mind to put the best foot foremost (put forth all her powers of walking), and run through her terrors at such a pace that none of them could lay hold of her.—R. Blackmore.

—(b) to make the best display possible. Linlithgow put her best foot forward (made her best appearance) last Saturday, when the freedom of that ancient and royal city was presented to the Earl of Rosebery.—St. Andrews Citizen, 1886.

—*to put one's foot in it* to make an awkward mistake; to say something embarrassing.
Women have such confounded queer ways. You're sure to put your foot in it if you intermeddle.—Wm. Black.

—*with one foot in the grave* very feeble; having but a short time to live.
It is sometimes the fate of a poet to succeed, only when he has one foot in the grave (has but a short time to live).—Besant.

—*to put down one's foot*—to refuse to go further; to be firm in refusing.

—*at one's feet* submissive; in a suppliant attitude.
It was all very well to have Mr. Slope at her feet, to show her power by making an utter fool of a clergyman.—A. Trollope.

—*the cloven foot* one of the marks of the devil. To display the cloven foot is to betray an evil purpose.
But they had not long been man and wife ere Tom began to show the cloven foot.—G. J. Whyte-Melville.

—*to foot it* to dance.
Of course they found the master's house locked up and all the servants away in the close, about this time no doubt footing it away on the grass.—Hughes.

—*to put one's foot on another's neck* to crush or trample upon him.
She should tramp the roads as a mendicant. He would put his foot on her neck.—Hall Caine.

—*to fall on one's feet* to meet with unexpected good luck.

—*to foot a bill* to pay the expenses incurred.
Goa, in the case of final French occupation, might continue its work of propagandism, but the Church would

have to look after the work and foot the bill.—*Harper's Monthly, September 1887.*

—*the first-foot* the person who is the first to cross the threshold of a house on New-Year's morning.

It matters not upon which side of the Border it may be—and northward the feeling extends far beyond the Border—there is a mysterious, an ominous importance attached to the individual who first crosses the threshold after the clock has struck twelve at midnight on the 31st of December, or who is the first-foot in a house after the new year has begun.—*Wilson's Tales of the Border.*

—*to pay one's footing* to pay the necessary fees or perquisites on being admitted to any club or society.

force—*to force a man's hand* to compel him to act prematurely, or to adopt a policy he dislikes.

The best guarantee against such a course is the repugnance of the German emperor to engage in a new struggle; but if it were determined on by all but himself, the emperor's hand might be forced (the emperor might be compelled unwillingly to declare war).—*Spectator, 1886.*

—*to come into force* (of a law or regulation) to begin to be enforced.

fore—*to the fore* present; on the scene.

It never did really occur to him that any one would have the wild audacity to run away with one of his sisters, while he, Mr. Tom Beresford, was to the fore.—*Wm. Black.*

forelock—*to take time* or *occasion by the forelock* to avoid delay; to be on the alert for every available opportunity. Time is represented as an old man with a single lock of hair on the forehead, and an hour-glass and a scythe in his hands.

Time flies here with such a frightful

rapidity that I am compelled to seize occasion by the forelock.—*Thackeray.*

forget—*to forget oneself* to be guilty of an unworthy act or word; to lose command of one's tongue or temper.

The little gentleman shocked the propriety of the breakfast-table by a loud utterance of three words, of which the two last were "Webster's Unabridged," and the first was an emphatic monosyllable ("damn"). "Beg pardon," he added—"forgot myself" (I have said hastily what I should not).—*Holmes.*

fork—*to fork out* to hand out money; to take from one's pocket.

forlorn—*a forlorn hope* a desperate venture.

He had not merely, as the French say, the courage of his opinions; but his opinions became principles, and gave him that gallantry of fanaticism which made him always ready to head a forlorn hope.—*J. R. Lowell, on Josiah Quincy.*

form—*in form* in good condition; able to do oneself credit.

"Were you in form, Babs?" asked Mrs. Gaysworthy.—*Mrs. E. Lynn Linton.*

forty—*forty winks* a short sleep during the day.

Then came forty winks; and afterwards he would play whist for high stakes.—*Saturday Review, 1888.*

fours—*to go on all fours* (a) to crawl on the hands and feet or on the hands and knees.

He looked up, and beheld what he judged, by the voice, to be Mrs. Armitage: her face was averted from him, and kept close to the cliff, down which she had been proceeding backward, and on all fours (using hands as well as feet), until fear and giddiness had checked her progress.—*James Payn.*

—(b) to be exactly apposite.

*What was it Brabantio said to Othello
after the council scene? "She has
deceived her father, and may thee."
The quotation isn't quite on all fours,
but it's near enough.*—F. Anstey.

fourth—*the fourth estate* the press;
newspapers.

*All these I have had to pass by and to
confine myself to a broad and general
description of the origin of those higher
representatives of journalism which
we all have in our minds when we
speak of the activity and power of the
fourth estate.*—Charles Peabody, *in
English Journalism*.

—*the Fourth of July* the United States'
national holiday.

*We may prove that we are this, and
that, and the other—our Fourth of July
orators have proved it time and again—
the census has proved it.*—J. R.
Lowell.

free—*a free fight* a fight joined in by a
whole crowd; a promiscuous combat.

*So many free fights, brave robberies,
gallant murders, dauntless kickings.*—
Besant.

—*to make free* to venture; to be bold
enough.

*My landlord made free to send up a jug
of claret without my asking.*—
Thackeray.

freedom—*the freedom of a city*
immunity from county jurisdiction,
and the privilege of corporate taxation and self-government held under
a charter from the crown. The right to
share in these privileges is conferred,
with the parliamentary franchise or
right of voting, on distinguished persons whom the city desires to honour.

*Linlithgow put her best foot forward last
Saturday, when the freedom of that
ancient and royal city was presented to
the Earl of Rosebery.*—St Andrew
Citizen, 1886.

French—*to take French leave*—(a) to
go off secretly, without notice or
warning; to elope.

*You must take French leave and run
away from Newly and your charming
wife for six months.*—Austen Pember.

—(b) to enter without invitation; to do
anything without obtaining permission.

*The solicitor, taking French leave, led
us across the spacious vestibule to
the library, much to the amazement of
the servants.*—B. L. Farjeon.

Friday—*a man Friday* a constant and
submissive attendant. See Defoe's
Robinson Crusoe.

friend—*a friend at court* a person with
influence in a powerful quarter.

*"Not in that place, p'raps," returned the
grinder, with a wink. "I shouldn't
wonder—friends at court, you know—
but never you mind, mother, just now;
I'm all right, that's all.*—Dickens.

fry—*small fry* insignificant people.

*The coming of Sheridan was quite
another matter. Compared with him all
other managers were small fry
(insignificant).*—James Payn.

—*out of the frying-pan into the fire*
from a bad position into a worse.

*If it were not for Claire I would jump
out of this frying-pan, which scorches
and broils—yes still, after twenty
years and more—into the fire which
burns.*—Besant.

full—*full dress* the dress worn on
occasions of ceremony. For men, a
black suit with swallow-tail coat, and
open vest, and a white necktie constitute full dress. Ladies' full dress
leaves the shoulders bare.

*One round white arm rested on the
window-ledge, and her long black hair
fell in loose masses over the snowy
garments which, constituting a lady's
déshabille, reveal her beauties far less
literally than the costume she more*

inaptly terms "full dress."—G. J. Whyte-Melville.

—*to the full* quite as much, certainly not less.

This place was a prison for debtors as well as criminals, and was to the full as foul as the Tophet-pit at Aylesbury yonder.—G. A. Sala.

—*in full cry* hurrying fast; in hot pursuit. Cry here means a pack of hounds.

Seven mutineers—Job Anderson, the boatswain, at their head—appeared in full cry at the south-west corner.—R. L. Stevenson.

—*full fig* elegantly; making a great display.

So all of us cabin party went and dressed ourselves up full fig, and were introduced in due form to the young queen.—Haliburton.

—*in full swing* at its busiest; busy and thronged.

The street market was in full swing.—Besant.

funk—*to put in a funk* to frighten; to cause a tremble.

Matcham said "he'd only been drunk"—that his spirits had sunk At the thunder—the storm put him into a funk.—Barham.

—*in a funk* frightened; put about.

If I were Foxy, I should be in a funk myself.—Besant.

funny—*the funny bone* that part of the elbow which is exposed to nervous shocks.

They smack and they thwack, Till your funny bones crack, As if you were stretched on the rack.

Barham.

G

gab—*the gift of the gab* readiness of speech; fluency.

I always knew you had the gift of the gab (were ready in speech), of course.—Dickens.

gad—*upon the gad* restless; always moving hither and thither.

I have no good opinion of Mrs. Charles's nursery-maid. I hear strange stories of her; she is always upon the gad.—Miss Austen.

—*to gad about* to spend one's time in frivolous visiting of friends or places.

By this time our friends had grown rather weary of gadding about—Hugh Conway.

gaff—*to blow the gaff on* to inform against.

If I do not induce you and your brother scoundrel to surrender your present devices, I will take it upon myself to blow the gaff on the whole rascally three of you.—D. Christie Murray.

gain—*to gain ground* to advance; to make progress.

The Jews are not only extraordinarily powerful and numerous there (in Galicia), but are gaining ground day by day.—Fortnightly Review, 1887.,

gall—*gall and wormwood* said of what is excessively bitter and distasteful.

The talk eddied even to the aristocratic back-waters of Clinton Hall, where it was so much gall and wormwood to the family.—Mrs. E. Lynn Linton.

gallows—*gallows-bird* a person who

looks like a condemned criminal; a person of abandoned appearance.

"It is ill to check sleep or sweat in a sick man," said he: "I know that far, though, I ne'er minced ape nor gallows-bird."—C. Reade.

game—*game for anything* ready to venture upon anything; full of life.

If you don't stop your jaw about him, you'll have to fight me; an that's a little more than you're game for, I'm thinking."—H. Kingsley.

—*the game is worth the candle* the results are worth striving for; one will be repaid for one's trouble.

George can never take what I mean to offer; if he should, the Egyptian will be spoiled indeed, and the game will be worth the candle.—H. R. Haggard.

—*to die game* to die in a courageous manner.

I say that coachman did not run away, but that he died game.—Dickens.

—*a game at which two can play* a course of action equally open to another person.

"I'll have you both licked when I get out, that I will," rejoined the boy, beginning to snivel.

"Two can play at that game, mind you," said Tom.—Hughes.

—*to make game of* to ridicule; to turn into sport.

Now in the Fleet Prison, where I write this, there is a small man who is always jeering and making game of me.—Thackeray.

gang—*to gang a-gley* to go wrong. Scottish dialect.

The best laid schemes o' mice and men

Gang aft a-gley.—Burns.

As many things gang a-gley with us in our plans and desires while alive, it is not surprising that matters turn out contrary to our expectations after death.—James Payn.

gapes—*the gapes* a fit of yawning.

Another hour of music was to give delight or the gapes, as real or affected taste for it prevailed.—Jane Austen.

gate—*to break gates* to remain outside the college gates after the hour for closing. An Oxford and Cambridge University phrase.

If you break gates again we shall have you rusticated (temporarily expelled).

—*the gate of horn* a mythological term, signifying the gate by which true dreams came forth. From the gate of ivory deceptive dreams proceeded.

—Then he (Laud) dreamed that he had turned Papist, of all his dreams the only one, we suspect, which came through the gate of horn (was likely to prove true).—Macaulay.

gather—*gathered to one's fathers* dead and buried.

When his glitter is gone, and he is gathered to his fathers, no eye will be dim with a tear, no heart will mourn for its lost friend.—A. Trollope.

gaudy—*a gaudy-day* a holiday or festival. Old-fashioned, but still in use at some of the universities.

Just at one time, about 1641, we hear from our best authority, Phillips, of his keeping a gaudy-day.—Mark Pattison.

gauntlet—*to throw down the gauntlet or glove* to challenge.

The company threw down the gauntlet to (defile) all the maritime powers of the world.—Macaulay.

—*to take up the gauntlet or glove* to accept a challenge.

—*to run the gauntlet* to pass through a severe course of treatment in the way of criticism or obloquy. The phrase used in this figurative sense comes from the custom of inflicting a punishment bearing this name. A prisoner, stripped to his waist, had to run between two lines of soldiers armed with gloves, and with sticks and other weapons, with which they struck him as he passed.

We went to the jetty to see the 'usband's boat come in, and formed part of the long row of spectators, three deep, who had assembled to watch the unfortunate passengers land and run the gauntlet of unscrupulous comment and personal remarks all down the line.—The Mistletoe Bough, 1865.

gear—*to throw out of gear* to disturb the working of.

Such delusions have happened to many of us, and most commonly when the mind has been disturbed and thrown out of gear (put out of good working order) by unwonted circumstances.—James Payn.

gentle—*gentle and simple* high-born and low-born; noble and peasant.

So, too, I am afraid it is a true bill that torture was, in the bad old days, indiscriminately used towards both gentle and simple in some gloomy underground places in this said Tower.—G. A. Sala.

get—*go along! or get along with you!* an exclamation of impatience, often used in a bantering way.

"Oh, get along with you, Mr. Segrave," returned Buswell, much delighted by this delicate piece of flattery.—W. E. Norris, in Good Words, 1887.

—*to get along* to fare; to be in a good condition.

'Well, doctor, how has the poor patient been getting along (progressing) lately?"

"Only fairly; she is still very weak."

—*to get at* to obtain; to find.

When a doctor could be got at, he said that, but for Mrs. Lapham's timely care, the lady would hardly have lived.—W. D. Howells.

—*to get on*—(a) to succeed; to rise in life.

Throughout the Continent, in England, and in America, the enormous majority of the population are striving for success in their several professions and callings; every man, with the doubtful exception of a few Trappist monks, is trying to get on. —Spectator, 1887.

—*to get on*—(b) to make progress; to improve.

He soon got on so well that he discarded the other (crutch).— Murray's Magazine, 1887.

—*to get on with any one* to find oneself in congenial company.

She could not get on with Mr. Adair (Mr. Adair and she were not congenial to each other).—James Payn.

—*to get under* to obtain the mastery over; to suppress.

Towards three o'clock the fire was got under, and darkness and silence succeeded.—Maria Edgeworth.

—*to get up*—(a) to prepare with a special practical object in view—as, to get up Shakespeare's *Hamlet* for a college examination.

His readers are candidly informed in the preface what books he has consulted; and it appears that he has got up the reign of Henry VIII, from Brewer, Hook, Canon Dixon, Ranke, Froude, and Friedmann.—Athenæum, 1887.

—(b) to organize; to arrange.

A few days afterwards a committee, consisting of Lady Mona, "Beauty" Strutt, and Mrs. Walter Pullen, is assembled in Lady Swansdown's boudoir to discuss the best means of getting up the proposed theatricals.— Florence Marryat.

—*to get oneself up* to appear in a striking or elaborate costume.

Like most men who are not in the habit

of "getting themselves up" every day, he was always irritable when thus clothed in his "best".—G. J. Whyte-Melville.

—*get-up* style of dress; fashionable way of dressing.

There is none of the colour and tastiness of get-up which lends such a life to the present game at Rugby.—Hughes.

—*to get over* to recover from.

She had been out of health for some time. Her mother called it "general debility;" but I firmly believed that it was that love affair with Frank Hayles which she had never got over (recovered from).—The Mistletoe Bough, 1885.

—*to get over a person* to ingratiate oneself with him.

How you've managed to get over your mother-in-law is a mystery to me.—Dickens.

—*to get off* to escape.

He will get off. I'm the only witness. A jury won't believe a black man in this country.—H. R. Haggard.

—*to get one's back up* to be irritated; to be angry.

"Are you?" I said, beginning to get my back up.—H. R. Haggard.

—*to get by heart* to commit to memory.

"It is a very long play."

"The longer the better," murmured the antiquary.

"But not when one has to get it by heart" (commit it to memory), observed William Henry dryly.—James Payn.

—*to get religion* to become pious; to be religious. A colloquial American phrase.

Irene Pascoe once met a knight on a missionary platform, and found he'd got religion (he was a pious man).—Besant.

ghost—*to give up* or *yield up the ghost* to die.

So, underneath the belly of their steeds,
That stained their fetlocks in his smoking blood,
The noble gentleman gave up the ghost (died).—Shakespeare.

—*to have not a ghost of a chance* to have no reasonable prospect.

You do not tell me that Carswell is applying for the Hebrew chair. He has not a ghost of a chance (his candidature is hopeless).

gift—*better not look a gift-horse in the mouth* do not examine too critically what is given to you as a gift.

The poet gives as well as makes; the rest of us only receive: we criticise these gifts; we venture to look into the mouth of the fairest gift-horse (criticise the finest poems that are given us).—Besant.

gild—*to gild the pill* to make an unpleasant thing appear attractive.

I just lay myself out to get to the blind side of them, and I sugar and gild the pill so as to make it pretty to look at and easy to swallow (say things in so flattering a way that I can coax them into doing anything).—Haliburton.

gills—*rosy* or *red about the gills* flushed with drink. By the "gills" understand the flesh about the jaws.

—*white in the gills* showing signs of terror or sickness.

"What's the matter, young 'un?" asked Joe, surprised. "What makes you so white in the gills?"—Besant.

gird—*to gird up the loins* to prepare oneself for hard work. A Biblical expression.

The house awakes, and shakes itself, girds up the loins for the day's work.—Rhoda Broughton.

give—*to give away* to act the part of father to the bride at a marriage.

Waxy came down to ratify the deeds; Lord Southdown gave away his sister. She was married by a bishop, and not by the Rev. Bartholomew Irons, to the disappointment of the irregular prelate.—Thackeray.

—*to give oneself away* to make oneself absurd by a heedless remark; to say unwittingly what damages one's own cause. In the following extract the absurdity lies in the "swell" unwittingly confessing that he had dealings with a pawnbroker:—

Swell. I am going to resign from my club.

Friend. I thought you liked it so much.

Swell. Used to be all right, but society is getting too mixed. Why, I met my pawnbroker there the other night.—*Harper's Monthly, May 1888.*

—*to give it to a person* to scold or punish him; to attack him with angry words or with blows.

M'Gregor pitched into him so when he said it—gave it him right and left (reproved him in the severest manner).—Rhoda Broughton.

—*to give up to* or *upon* to lead into; to open upon.

Then we passed on up this till at last we reached the top, where we found a large standing space to which there were three entrances, all of small size. Two of these gave on to (led into) rather narrow galleries or roadways cut in the face of the precipice.—H. R. Haggard.

—*to give oneself out as* or *for* to proclaim oneself to be.

He gives himself out, sir, for what nowadays they call a patriot—a man from East Prussia.—R. L. Stevenson. *Last winter he called himself Lord Charles Templeton, and took in the whole society of Florence. This year, as you are aware, he has selected Cannes as his field for operations, and has given himself out as a cousin of*

Lord Bellingham's, with whom, I need hardly tell you, he is in no way connected.—W. E. Norris.

—*to give up*—(a) (transitive) to discontinue the use of; to abandon.

—(b) (intr.) to surrender; to confess oneself beaten.

Then, for fear of her place, and because he threatened that my lady should give her no discharge without the sausages, she gave up (yielded) and from that day forward always sausages, or bacon, or pig-meat in some shape or other, went up to the table.—Maria Edgeworth.

—*a give-and-take policy* a policy of mutual accommodation and forbearance.

Nothing can be more annoying to an ordinary man than to find the wife of his bosom, who has jogged along with him very comfortably in a give-and-take (mutual forbearance) style for many years, suddenly turn round and lecture him upon his amiable little weaknesses (faults).—Hugh Conway.

—*to give forth* or *give out* to announce or publish.

Soon after it was given forth (announced), and believed by many that the king was dead.—Hayward. *She gives it out (states publicly) that you shall marry her.*—Shakespeare.

—*to give out* to come to an end.

But before they had covered half a mile poor Mrs. Mordaunt's strength gave out (failed).—English Illustrated Magazine, 1887.

—*to give in* to cease exertions; to confess oneself vanquished.

They did not yet give in (confess themselves beaten); they had hitherto gone only about the streets; they would go to places where people meet together.—Besant.

—*to give over*—(a) (of a sick person) to cease hoping for his recovery.

Valence told me that he had been given over—that he could not live more than six months or so.—Florence Marryat.

—(b) to yield; to commit.

They (the Protestant clergy) might have attained to the influence which is now given over entirely to the priest.—Thackeray.

—*to give oneself up*—(a) to surrender to the police.

News came that the Brighton murderer had given himself up (surrendered himself to the police).

—(b) to lose hope of saving one's life.

When I saw that the floods had carried away the bridge, I gave myself up for lost (abandoned) hope.

—*to give a person up*—(a) to despair of seeing him.

It was at that unheard-of hour (11 p.m.) that Miss Huntly, whose experience of provincial habits was limited, thought fit to put in an appearance, and her hostess's ejaculation of "At last! Why, we gave you up more than an hour ago!" drew forth no apology from her.—Good Words, 1887.

—(b) to renounce; to repudiate; to refuse to acknowledge.

He had been living what was a wild, college life even in these wild days; and his family had almost given him up.—E. Yates.

—*to give way* to yield; to break down.

I wished I had not given way (yielded) to her in the matter of a private sitting-room (which she would not consent to have).—The Mistletoe Bough, 1885.

On one occasion, as she was being brought down from her look-out chamber in a new carrying-chair, it gave way.—S. Baring-Gould.

gizzard—*to fret one's gizzard* to be anxious; to worry oneself. Gizzard (primarily a fowl's stomach) is used of the temper or disposition.

He'll fret his gizzard green if he don't

soon hear from that maid of his.—Thomas Hardy.

Glasgow—*a Glasgow magistrate* a salt herring. It is said that when George IV. visited Glasgow, some salt herrings were placed, in joke, on the iron guard of the carriage belonging to a well-known Glasgow magistrate, who formed one of a deputation to receive the king.

glass—*he has taken a glass too much* he is intoxicated.

—*those who live in glass houses should not throw stones* people who are themselves open to criticism ought not to criticize. Compare the opening verses of Matthew vii.

And there is an old proverb about the inexpediency of those who live in glass houses throwing stones.—Florence Marryat.

glove—*to throw the glove or gauntlet to* to challenge; to show readiness to fight with.

I will throw my glove to Death itself (challenge Death itself to prove), that there's no maculation in thy heart.—Shakespeare.

She was now, at the age of twenty-two, very different from the girl who so hastily threw down the glove to her stepmother.—Hugh Conway.

—*to take up the glove or gauntlet* to accept a challenge to fight.

On the other hand, Austria had only to conclude an offensive and defensive alliance with King Milan, and the Czar must take up the glove thus, as it were, thrown in his way.—Spectator, December 12, 1888.

—*to be hand and glove with.* See **hand**.

—*to put on or wear glove* to attack an adversary in a mild or generous way.

He (Macaulay) put on no gloves, took in hand no buttoned foil, when on well-chosen occasions, he came down to the House to make a speech.—J. Cotter Morison.

glut—*to glut the market* to furnish an excess of goods for the market, so that a sale cannot be found for them.

go—*a go* a curious or embarrassing state of affairs.

Well, I am blessed (to be sure), here's a go (the position is embarrassing).— C. Reade.

—*no go* a failure. Said of what is unworkable or impossible.

"What's a caveat?" inquired Sam.—"A legal instrument, which is as much as to say it's no go," replied the cobbler,— Dickens.

Exp.—A legal instrument, or, in other words, something which does nothing and with which nothing can be done.

Of course, under the circumstances, no go for (I cannot give you) the fifteen thousand,—*Truly yours, Arthur.—The Mistletoe Bough,* 1885.

—*go along* an exclamation of (feigned) anger or impatience. See **get along**.

*"May its poppet come in and talk?"—"Certainly not," replied madam; "you know I never allow you here. Go along."—*Dickens.

—*to go bail for another* to become legal security for an accused person's appearance at his trial.

*The world has not gone bail for us, and our falling short involves not the ruin of others.—*C. Lever.

—*to go hard with one* to prove a troublesome matter to one.

*He jumped up with a great exclamation, which the particular recording angel who heard it pretended not to understand, or it might have gone hard with (proved a serious matter for) the Latin tutor some time or other.—*Holmes.

—*to go home to* to appeal directly to.

Mrs. Wallace spoke very slowly, because it was not an easy matter

with her to express her ideas, and with a certain gentle earnestness that went home (appealed directly) to the young girl's heart, at least as much as the logic of her argument.—James Payn.

—*go-to-meeting air* or *clothes* such as people have on when they go to church; respectable.

*Tom (was) equipped in his go-to-meeting roof (respectable hat), as his friend called it.—*Hughes.

—*to go with the stream* to do as people around one do.

And then it is so much easier in everything to go with the stream, and to do what you are expected to do.— Mrs. Oliphant.

—*to go without saying* to be an understood thing; to be an evident fact, or natural conclusion. Translated from the French, *Cela va sans dire.*

Imagine all this, and you will have some idea of the shackles with which the literary class in Japan have shackled their countrymen. It goes without saying (the conclusion is inevitable) that, under such circumstances, a lively, natural style is impossible.—Japan Mail, 1887.

—*to go by the board* to be lost. A nautical phrase, now in ordinary use.

During that long sickness my wardrobe, and jewellery, and everything went by the board (I had to give up my wardrobe, and jewellery, and everything).

Her rattling shrouds, all sheathed in ice,

With the masts, went by the board.— Longfellow.

—*to go out of one's way* to trouble oneself; to discompose oneself.

"My dear, I am sorry you did not smell it; but we can't help that now," returned my master without putting himself in a passion or going out of his way (showing signs of

discomposure), but just fair and easy helped himself to another glass.—Maria Edgeworth.

—*to go all lengths* to hesitate at no act.
He is ready to go all lengths (risk everything) in his advocacy of the temperance question.

—*to go to the bad* to become a wreck.
Think of my case, Miss Rawdon—linked for life to a woman whom I married to give myself a home, because all ties that bound me to domestic life seemed broken when I lost my darling, and because otherwise I should eventually have gone to the bad.—The Mistletoe Bough, 1885.

—*to go to the wall* to be discomfited; to have to retire.
Everybody must go to the wall who cannot serve that interest.—North American Review, 1887.

—*to go further and fare worse* to take extra trouble and find oneself in a worse position than before.
Well upon my word, I don't blame you; you might have gone further and fared worse.—H. R. Haggard.

—*all the go* popular; fashionable.
Folks ain't thought nothin' of (are held of no account), unless they live at Treemont: it's all the go (that place is very fashionable).—Haliburton.

—*on the go* active; running about continually; indulging in liquor.
"Ma'ame Richard was on the go," as one of them said when he helped to pick her out of the gutter and carry her dead drunk into the back kitchen, where she and others made their filthy lair.—Mrs. E. Lynn Linton.

—*to go back on* to be unfaithful to; to fail to keep, especially of promises. See **back**.
Why don't you know, boss (master)? They said they'd take me instead of you, and they won't go back on their

word (break their promise).—Temple Bar, 1886.

—*to go down* to be accepted; to be received with favour.
Fletcher, Ben Jonson, and all the plays of Shakespeare, are the only things that go down.—Goldsmith.

—*to go for a man* to attack him.
When he began to rail against American institutions, I went for (attacked) him.

—*to go in for* to give one's attention to; to apply oneself to.
Skating was an accomplishment he had never gone in for (attempted to acquire).—Blackwood's Magazine, 1887.

—*to go it* to be extravagant or headstrong in behaviour.
I heard Master George was going it, from the Saunders.—Maryatt.

—*to go off* to happen; to take place.
The wedding went off (happened) much as such affairs do.—Mrs. Gaskell.

—*to go out*—(a) to be discontinued; to cease.
I think I must tell you, as shortly as I can, how the noble old game of backsword is played; for it is sadly gone out of late.—Hughes.

—(b) to go out to service; to become a domestic servant.
"I think you have mistaken my aunt," put in that young person. "She would be the last to hinder me or any of us going out, if it were for our good."—Mrs. J. H. Riddle.

—*to give one the go-by* to neglect him; to refuse to acknowledge him.
But being made an honest woman of, so to speak, Becky would not consort any longer with these dubious ones, and cut Lady Crackenbury when the latter nodded to her from her opera-box, and gave Mrs. Washington White the go-by in the ring.—Thackeray.

God—*God's acre* the churchyard.

As her eye roamed from sea to land it fell upon the little church immediately beneath her, into whose God's acre the footpath descended.—James Payn.

golden—*the golden State* California.

—*the golden rule* "Do unto others as you would have others do unto you."

My dear boy, have you not learned the golden rule? In all human actions look for the basest motive, and attribute that. (This is said in satire; the real golden rule is as above).—Besant.

—*the golden bowl is broken* a euphemistic expression for death. Taken from the Book of Ecclesiastes (xii. 6): "Or ever the silver cord be loosed, or the golden bowl be broken, or the pitcher be broken at the fountain, or the wheel broken at the cistern. Then shall the dust return to the earth as it was; and the spirit shall return unto God who gave it."

And thus they go on from year to year, until the golden bowl is broken (they die).—H. R. Haggard.

—*to worship the golden calf* to bow down before something unworthy. The reference is to the action of the children of Israel at Mount Sinai. See Exodus xxxii.

The bourgeois mind is instantly prostrated before the golden calf of commercial prosperity.—Wm. Black.

gone—*a gone 'coon* on who is lost or ruined. 'Coon is short for racoon.

Mr. Winchester did not stop there—he forced a hundred pounds upon George. "If you start in any business with an empty pocket, you are gone 'coon."—C. Reade.

—*a gone case* something hopeless; a person who is despaired of.

When officers are once determined to ride a man down, it is a gone case with him (there is no hope for him).—R. H. Dana.

—*too far gone* in a hopeless or desperate condition.

To use a phrase not often applied to a young lady, she was too far gone (hopelessly in love).—James Payn.

good—*as good as a play* very interesting; exceedingly amusing.

He swore it was as good as a play to see her in the character of a fine dame.—Thackeray.

—*as good as gold* thoroughly good and trustworthy. Generally used of persons.

Having said this, Grace walked slowly out of the room, and neither Mrs. Dale nor Lily attempted to follow her.

"She's as good as gold," said Lily, when the door was closed.—A. Trollope.

—*a good thing* a clever saying.

When we say a good thing, in the course of the night, we are wondrous lucky and pleased. Flicflac will trill you off fifty in ten minutes.—Thackeray.

—*good lady* wife; madam.

His good lady, indeed, was the only person present who retained presence of mind enough to observe that if he were allowed to lie down on Mr. Squeers's bed for an hour or so, and left entirely to himself, he would be sure to recover again almost as quickly as he had been taken ill.—Dickens.

—*as good as* virtually; essentially; in every essential respect.

She said that he was as good as engaged to a girl out there, and that he had never dreamt of her.—W. D. Howells.

—*for good* altogether; completely.

"You are going away for good (never to return), Mrs. Fortress?" I said.

"Yes, sir," she answered, "for good."—English Illustrated Magazine, 1886.

—*for good and all* finally; never to be reversed.

When they were made sensible (understood) that Sir Condy was going to leave Castle Rackrent for good and all (never to return), they set up a whillalu (shout) that could be heard to the farthest end of the street.—Maria Edgeworth.

—*good for any sum* able or willing to pay the sum.

One day a gentleman and lady came in to lunch. A nice, quiet, tidy little lunch they had, just the same as in a good house of their own. By-and-by I bring in the bill, and wonder what they are good for (how much money they will give me).—All the Year Round.

—*to the good* on the profit side.

"Well," says I, "are you done up stock and fluke—a total wreck?"—

"No," says he; "I have two hundred pounds left to the good."—Haliburton.

—*good gracious!* an exclamation of astonishment.

"Twenty years! Good gracious, papa, I shall be six-and-thirty, so frightfully old to talk about anything!"

Papa looked a little grave. "Oblige me, my dear, by not saying good gracious; it is very unladylike."—The Argosy, 1886.

—*a good Samaritan*. See **Samaritan**.

—*good-morning to anything* farewell to it.

When anything's upon my heart, good-morning to my head: it's not worth a lemon.—Maria Edgeworth.

Exp.—The speaker means to say that his head or judgment takes its departure when his heart or feelings are interested.

—*as good as one's word* performing one's promises.

It was evident to her that Frank Muller would be as good as his word.—H. R. Haggard.

goody—*goody-goody* weakly virtuous; good, but feeble.

goose—*his geese are swans* he places too high a value on his own possessions; he overestimates what is his own.

He (Dr. Whately) was particularly loyal to his friends, and, to use the common phrase, all his geese were swans.—Cardinal Newman.

—*the goose that lays the golden eggs* the source of one's wealth or most cherished possessions.

This affectionate anxiety was partly due to a certain apprehension the old gentleman experienced when the goose that laid the golden eggs for him was out of sight.—James Payn.

—*to kill the goose that laid the golden egg* to destroy the source of one's income or profit. A phrase taken from one of Æsop's Fables.

If Brian had only known how immensely he had risen in her respect by the not very extraordinary display of talent and ability which he had just made, he would doubtless have hastened to kill the goose that laid the golden eggs by playing classical compositions until he wearied her.—Good Words, 1887.

—*to cook a person's goose for him* to cause his death.

"You see," said Tom, "that if you should happen to be wrong, our goose is cooked without the least doubt."—Besant.

—*it's a gone goose with any one* there is no more hope for him.

Well, he took the contract for beef with the troops; and he fell astern (failed to make it profitable), so I guess it's a gone goose with him.—Haliburton.

gooseberry—*to play up old gooseberry with people* to defeat them or silence them sharply.

He began to put on airs, but I soon

played up old gooseberry with him (snubbed him).

She can squander the income as she pleases, and play old gooseberry up to a certain point.—Miss Braddon.

—*to play gooseberry* to act as a third person for the sake of propriety; to appear with two lovers in public.

There was Helena out of her chair standing by a gentleman . . . while I was reduced to that position which is vulgarly but expressively known as playing gooseberry.—The Mistletoe Bough, 1885.

—*a gooseberry-picker* one who plays gooseberry.

What do I care for old Thresher? I brought Thresher to-day as a gooseberry-picker.—S. Baring-Gould.

—*like old gooseberry* with great energy.

Take them by the tail . . . and lay on like old gooseberry.—H. Kingsley.

—*as green as a gooseberry* very ignorant of life; raw and uneducated.

His name was Green, and he was as green as a gooseberry.—Captain Marryat.

Gordian—*to cut the Gordian knot* to solve a difficulty in a bold or unusual fashion.

Frank Muller must die, and die before the morning light. By no other possible means could the Gordian knot be cut.—H. R. Haggard.

grace—*to say grace* to ask the Divine blessing before commencing a meal.

Mr. Pickwick, having said grace, pauses for an instant and looks round him.—Dickens.

—*to get into a person's good graces* to gain his favour or friendship.

Major D'Orville is rapidly gaining ground in the good graces of all the Newton Hollows party.—G. J. Whyte-Melville.

—*with a good grace* gracefully; graciously.

—*with a bad grace* ungraciously, so as to leave an unpleasant impression.

What might have been done with a good grace would at last be done with a bad grace.—Macaulay.

—*the throne of grace* a figurative expression, meaning God's seat, heaven. To come to the throne of grace is to pray.

—*the means of grace* opportunities of hearing the gospel. A religious expression.

The shop is next door but one to a chapel, too. Oh, how handy for the means of grace!—Besant.

grain—*against the grain* unpleasant; contrary to one's bias or inclination.

I am deficient in the auri sacra fames—the passion for dying a millionaire that possesses so many excellent people. I had rather have a little, and do what I like, than acquire a great deal by working against the grain (doing work which is unpleasant).—James Payn.

—*with a grain of salt* with some reservation. Translation of the Latin phrase *Cum grano salis.*

Some of the adventures narrated may require to be taken with a grain of salt.—Spectator, September 3, 1887.

grape—*sour grapes* something which is despised because it is unattainable. See **sour**.

"So it has got its big wax doll after all, has it?" asks she with a sneer; "curly wig and long legs, and all!"

I am roused to retort. I turn and rend her.

"Sour grapes!" cry I, with red cheeks, and in an elevated key.—Rhoda Broughton.

grass—*to let the grass grow under one's feet* to be inactive; to be idle and lazy.

Captain Cuttle held on at a great pace, and allowed no grass to grow under his feet.—Dickens.

—*grass widow* a lady whose husband is

temporarily absent. An Eastern term, especially used in India.

A grass widow finds herself in need of consolation for the cruel absence of her liege lord.—The Mistletoe Bough, 1885.

grease—*to grease the palm of* to bribe; to use money for the purpose of corrupting.

Greek—*the Greek Kalends* future time which will never arrive. The Kalends occurred at the beginning of the month with the Latin system of reckoning time; hence the term *Calendar*—a table announcing when the first day of each month fell. The Greeks had no Kalends.

The London School Board have since executed a strategical movement to the rear, suspending the obnoxious notice for a month, which is the English equivalent for the Greek Kalends.—Journal of Education, 1887.

—*when Greek meets Greek, then comes the tug of war* when one strong champion meets another of equal prowess the fight is a keen one.

When Greeks joined Greeks, then was the tug to war.—Nathaniel Lee.

—*Greek to any one* unintelligible to him. See Shakespeare's *Julius Cæsar*, act i. scene 2.

Cassius. Did Cicero say anything?
Casca. Ay, he spoke Greek.
Cassius. To what effect?
Casca. Nay, an I tell you that I'll ne'er look you in the face again; but those that understood him smiled at one another and shook their heads; but, for mine own part, it was Greek to me.

green—*the green-eyed monster* jealousy.

Cherry was green with jealousy, but tried to hide it under protestations of admiration.—The Mistletoe Bough, 1885.

—*to see green in another's eye* to consider him a simple, gullible fellow.

"Now, soldier-boy," said I.
"Do you see green in my eye?
Oh, pray excuse the slang!"
                                    T. Davidson.

—*the wearing of the green* green is the Irish national colour. To wear it shows patriotic or rebel sympathies.

They are hanging men and women for the wearing of the green.—Popular Song.

—*a green hand* a raw fellow unaccustomed to the work he undertakes.

"I thought everybody knew Job Terry," said a green hand who came in the boat with me, when I asked him about his captain.—R. H. Dana.

—*the green room* the private chamber where actors dress and undress. This room is a notorious place for gossip.

There was only one topic on which Sir Henry could converse, and he was uncertain how it would be received if he was to start it—namely, actors' gossip and green-room whispers.—Besant.

grief—*to come to grief*—to be ruined; to fail completely.

France and Bonaparte, driven by the French fat (fool), as you are driven by the British Philistine,—and the French fat has proved a yet more fatal driver than yours, being debauched and immoral, as well as ignorant,—came to grief (were ruined).—M. Arnold.

grin—*to grin and bear it* to suffer anything painful in a manly way, without complaint.

"You scoundrel," he said between his teeth, "you have made a fool of me for twenty years, and I have been obliged to grin and bear it." H. R. Haggard.

grind—*to grind the face of* to oppress; to tyrannize over.

The agent was one of your middle-men

who grind the face of the poor.—Maria Edgeworth

—**hard grinder** a hard-working student or professional man.

Besides, there is a pension looming ever so far ahead which I must go back and grind for.—Murray's Magazine, 1887.

—**to grind one's teeth** to have feelings of disgust, disappointment, or rage.

Everything annoyed and angered me that day. . . . I ground my teeth (was intensely irritated) at the luncheon-table, which would have feasted half-a-dozen families. The Mistletoe Bough, 1885.

grips—*at grips with* struggling hard against.

Tom was daily growing in manfulness and thoughtfulness, as every high-couraged and well-principled boy must, when he finds himself for the first time consciously at grips with self and the devil.—Hughes.

grist—*to bring grist to the mill* to procure needful supplies; to be a source of profit.

A sly old Pope created twenty new saints to bring grist to the mill of (constitute a source of income for) the London clergy.—Bishop Horsley.

grog—*grog-blossoms* the red pimples on a drunkard's nose.

A few grog-blossoms marked the neighbourhood of his nose.—Thomas Hardy.

ground—*to break ground* to commence operations; to take the first step in any undertaking.

—*to gain* or *get ground* to advance; to make progress.

It was very tiring and slow work, yet I did visibly gain ground.—R. L. Stevenson.

—*to lose ground* to retreat; to give way; to become less powerful.

But, on the whole, I am unable to deny

that the state and the nation have lost ground with respect to the great business of controlling the public charge.—Gladstone.

—*to have the ground cut from under one's feet* to see what one relies on for support suddenly withdrawn.

His was not a practical mind, and it was sure to take him some time to realize what it means to have the ground cut from under your feet.—Good Words, 1887.

—*to hold one's ground* to maintain one's authority or influence.

Having shipped for an officer when he was not half a seaman, he found little pity with the crew, and was not man enough to hold his ground among them.—R. H. Dana, Jun.

—*to stand one's ground* to be firm; to be unyielding.

But she made a supreme effort over herself, and did her best to stand her ground.—Mrs. E. Lynn Linton.

—*down to the ground* completely.

"America is the place," he said to himself. "Some sea-coast city in South America would suit me down to the ground."—Miss Braddon.

grow—*to grow upon* to obtain great influence over; to become prized.

It was a face rather lovable than beautiful, rather sensitive than intellectual – a face which grew upon you as you looked at it, and which was always pleasant to look upon.—W. E. Norris.

grub—*Grub Street* the name of a low quarter in London inhabited formerly by poor authors. As a noun, Grub Street signifies poor, mean authors; as an adjective, mean, poor, low. The street is now called Milton Street.

Johnson came among them the solitary specimen of a past age, the last survivor of the genuine race of Grub Street hacks.—Macaulay.

—*grub and bud* victuals and drink.

gruel—*to give a person his gruel* to punish a person severely; to kill him.

> He refused, and harsh language ensued,
> Which ended at length in a duel,
> When he that was mildest in mood
> Gave the turbulent rascal his gruel.
>   Barham.

Grundy—*Mrs. Grundy* jealous neighbours; the scandal-loving portion of the community. The name comes from Morton's novel *Speed the Plough* (1798), where one of the characters, Mrs. Ashfield, is always exclaiming, "What will Mrs. Grundy say?" Mrs. Grundy was her neighbour.

> These awful rules of propriety, and that dreadful Mrs. Grundy (the thought of what one's neighbours will say), appear on the scene, and of course spoil everything.—Blackwood's Magazine, 1887.

guard—*to be on one's guard* to be watchful and prepared for an attack.

> Their pa and ma being seized
> With a tiresome complaint, which, in some seasons,
> People are apt to be seized
> With, who're not on their guard against plum-seasons,
> Their medical man shook his head,
> As he could not get well to the root of it.
>   Barham.

—*to put a man on his guard* to warn him; to make him careful.

> It was in such an outburst of rage that he had assaulted John in the inn-yard of Wakkerstrom, and thereby put him on his guard against him.—H. R. Haggard.

—*off one's guard* heedless; forgetful; in a careless state.

> Isaac caught both faces off their guard, and read the men as by a lightning flash to the bottom line of their hearts.—C. Reade.

gulf—*a great gulf fixed* a complete and permanent cause of separation; a radical difference and divergence. The phrase comes from the parable of Dives and Lazarus. See Luke xvi.26.

> For forty years and more I lived among savages and studied them and their ways; and now for several years I have lived here in England, and have in my own stupid manner done my best to learn the ways of the children of light, and what have I found? A great gulf fixed? No, only a very little one.—H. R. Haggard.

gun—*a great gun* a noted personage.

> Time flew on, and the great guns one by one returned – Peel, Graham, Goulbourn, Hardinge, Herries.—Beaconsfield.

—*to blow great guns* to be very stormy; to blow a heavy gale.

> At last it blew great guns; and one night, as the sun went down crimson in the Gulf of Florida, the sea running mountains high, I saw Captain Sebor himself was fidgety.—C. Reade.

guts—*to have guts in the brain* to have sense; to be full of intelligence. Old-fashioned.

> The fellow's well enough, if he had any guts in his brain.—Swift.

gutter—*out of the gutter* of low origin.

> "We could never have supposed one of our blood would commit the crime of marrying a plebeian – and for love!"
>
> "Then why do you marry your sons to girls out of the gutter?" (low-born girls), was sometimes the rejoinder.—National Review, 1887.

H

hack—*at hack* (or *heck*) *and manger* profusely; extravagantly. Heck, or hack, is Scotch for a manger. The word is of Scandinavian origin.
The servants at Lochmarlie must be living at hack and manger.—Miss Ferrier.

hail—*hail-fellow well-met* familiar; on terms of easy intimacy. Also used as a noun.
It was not, I will frankly admit, a very righteous beginning to a young life to be hail-fellow well-met with a gang of deer-stealers.—G. A. Sala.

hair—*to a hair* to an extreme nicety.
Oh! that's her nose to a hair, – that's her eye exactly.—Haliburton.

—*to split hairs* to dispute over petty points. A *hair-splitter* is a caviller.
Pray, don't let us be splitting hairs.—A. Trollope.

—*both of a hair* both alike.
For the peddler and tinker, they are two notable knaves, both of a hair, and both cousin-germans to the devil.—Greene.

—*hair standing on end* this is a sign of terror. See **stand**.

—*to take a hair of the dog that bit you* This was at one time supposed to be a cure for hydrophobia. The expression is commonly used now when a man, after heavy drinking, is advised to take a little more brandy or other liquor.
Decidedly, too, the homœopathic system must be founded on great natural facts, and there is philosophy, born of the observation of human nature, in the somewhat vulgar proverb that recommends a hair of the dog that bit you.—H. R. Haggard.

—*to turn a hair* to show signs of fatigue. A phrase taken from horsemanship, and properly only applicable to a horse, but now used generally.
Then the fiddlers began – the celebrated fiddlers, who, given free stripping, could play from sunset to dawn without turning a hair.—R. D. Blackmore, in *Murray's Magazine*, 1888.

half—*half-seas over* in a semi-drunken state; confused with drink.
But Jason put it back as he was going to fill again, saying, "No, Sir Condy, it shan't be said of me I got your signature to this deed when you were half-seas over."—Maria Edgeworth.

—*a bad halfpenny* something which is supposed to return to the owner, however often he tried to get quit of it.
It was not the first time, nor the second, that I had gone away – as it seemed, permanently – but yet returned, like the bad halfpenny.—N. Hawthorne.

—*half the battle* no small part of the difficulty overcome.
To provide the patient with a good bed, fresh air, and suitable warmth is half the battle (will do as much as all things else for his recovery).

—*better half* a wife. See **better**.

halloo—*don't halloo till you're out of the wood* be careful about showing premature signs of exultation. A favourite saying of the Duke of Wellington.

When Wellington had driven the
French out of Portugal, the
Portuguese issued a print of the Duke,
bearing the legend underneath –
"invincible Wellington, from grateful
Portugal." A friend having sent the
Duke a copy of the print, he struck out
the word "Invincible" with a dash of
his pen, and wrote below, "Don't halloo
till you're out of the wood."

halting—*the halting foot of justice* an
expression borrowed from Latin
literature, signifying the slow but sure
punishment which follows wrong-
doers.

Justice, though with halting foot, had
been on his track, and his old crime
of Egyptian days found him out at
last.—The Times, 1887.

hammer—*to go it hammer and tongs*
to act violently and recklessly; to
throw all one's energies into anything.
The ancient rules of a fair fight were
utterly disregarded; both parties went
at it hammer and tongs, and hit one
another anywhere with anything.—
James Payn.

—*to bring to the hammer* to sell by
auction.
All Digg's penates (household effects),
for the time being, were brought to the
hammer.—Hughes.

—*to sell under the hammer* to sell by
auction.
He threatened to foreclose, and sell the
house under the hammer.—C. Reade.

hand—*in hand* (a) under control.
The other was laughed at behind his
back, and outwitted by the young man
he thought he had so well in hand
(completely under control).—Jane
Austen.

—(b) in present possession; ready for
use.
"You are in the fortunate position of
having a competence of your own, I
conclude."

"Well, yes; that is, I come into it on
my majority – something in land and
also in hand."—Besant.

—(c) under discussion.
Mrs. Nickleby glided, by an easy
change of the conversation,
occasionally into various other
anecdotes, no less remarkable for
their strict application to the subject in
hand.—Dickens.

—*to keep in hand* to direct or manage.
As keeping in hand the home-farm at
Domwell, he had to tell what every
field was to bear next year.—Jane
Austen.

—*to take in hand* to take charge of; to
pay attention to.
I have asked Herr Hoffman to take me
in hand.—Leisure Hour, 1887.

—*at hand* near; close to one. Used both
of time and of place.
Mr. Woodhouse was to be talked into
an acquiescence of his daughter's
going out to dinner on a day now near
at hand (soon to arrive).—Jane
Austen.

—*to come to hand* to be received.
"Your letter came to hand yesterday
morning, Dr. Tempest," said Mr.
Crawley.—A. Trollope.

—*at first-hand* directly; without any
intermediate process.
Oh, indeed, I should much rather come
here at first-hand if you will have
me.—Jane Austen.

—*at second-hand* not directly; through
an intermediary.
He kept up just so much
communication with them as to inform
them, at second-hand or at third-hand,
which measures to impede and if
possible to defeat.—Trevelyan.

—*out of hand* (a) directly; at once.
Gather we our forces out of hand,
and set upon our boasting enemy.
Shakespeare.

—(b) ended; finished.

Were these inward wars once out of hand (over),
We would, dear lords, unto the Holy Land.

Shakespeare.

—**hand over hand** at a rapid rate.
He made money hand over hand.—Haliburton.

—**hand over head** leisurely; easily.
He set his magnificent main-sail and fore-sail and main-jib, and came up with the ship hand over head, the moderate breeze giving him an advantage.—C. Reade.

—**an old hand** an experienced person.
I am an old Parliamentary hand.—W. E. Gladstone.

—**a great hand at anything** very well skilled in it; very prone to it.
He is a great hand at a flam (an inveterate liar).—Haliburton.

—**with a high hand** arrogantly; imperiously.
We have no time now for such trumpery; we must carry things now with a much higher hand (more imperiously).—Blackmore.

—**to get** or **gain the upper hand** to obtain the mastery.
It seems to me that the old Tory influence has gained the upper hand.—J. Chamberlain, M.P.

—**from hand to mouth** without making any provision for the morrow; consuming every day what is earned.
No winter passes without reports of bitter distress in Korea. The general mass of the inhabitants live from hand to mouth, and can barely support themselves at the best of times.—Japan Mail, 1886.

to fight for one's own hand to look after one's own interests.
He had won the respect of his official superiors by showing that, in case of need, he could fight for his own hand

(struggle on behalf of his own interests).—Trevelyan.

—**hand and glove** or **hand in glove** on very intimate terms.
We thought him just the same man as ever – hand and glove (intimate) with every one.—Maria Edgeworth.

—**to lend a hand** to help.
Here comes a huntsman out of the woods dragging a boar which he has shot, and shouting to the neighbours to lend him a hand.—N. Hawthorne.

—**to bear a hand** to be quick.
"Stop, stop, daddy," said a little half-naked imp of a boy, "stop till I get my cock-shy." "Well, bear a hand then," said he, "or he'll be off; I won't wait a minute."—Haliburton.

—**hand in hand** (a) with the hands joined; close together; linked in friendly fashion.
Now we are tottering down, John;
But hand in hand we'll go,
And sleep together at the foot,
John Anderson, my jo.

Burns.

—(b) in conjunction; in unison.
They were unable to see how parochial affairs could go on unless they worked hand in hand with the curate.—H. Conway.

—**to make a poor hand at** to make little impression upon; to make little progress with.
Notwithstanding the captain's excessive joviality, he made but a poor hand at the smoky tongue.—Dickens.

—**to make no hand of** to be unable to explain.
No, sir, I can make no hand of it; I can't describe him.—R. L. Stevenson.

—**to give one's hand upon anything** to pledge one's honour to fulfil a promise.
The moment I choose, I can be rid of Mr. Hyde; I give you my hand upon

that (*promise you that solemnly*).—R.
L. Stevenson.

—*on hand* in one's possession.
Last year, I believe it was something
awful; you could see at the end of the
season how the mothers were
beginning to pull long faces when they
thought of having to start off for Baden-
Baden with a whole lot of unsaleable
articles on hand.—Wm. Black.

hands—*to hold one's hands* to do
nothing; to refrain from interfering.
So, with something of an ill grace, Lord
Salisbury bade those of his inclining
to hold their hands, and this Land Bill
of 1881 became law.—Justin
M'Carthy.

—*to lay hands on* to seize; to lay hold
of.
Lay hands on the villain.
Shakespeare.

—*to shake hands with* to salute by
grasping the hand.
The monarch is forced to shake hands
with the very politicians who have just
brought before the House the abolition
of the royal prerogative.—Ouida.

—*to have upon one's hands* to be responsible for; to have charge of.
Patty had all the business of the house
upon her hands.—Maria Edgeworth.

—*to take off one's hands* to free from
a burden.
No one will take Ugly Mug off my
hands, even as a gift.—Florence
Marryat.

—*on all hands* everywhere.
I believe it's admitted on all hands that
they (the young men at Oxford) know
what's good, and don't coddle
themselves.—Dickens.

—*my hands are full* I am very busy; I
have plenty of work to do.
Robinson's hands were now full; he
made brushes, and every day put
some of them to the test upon the floor
and walls of the building.—C. Reade.

—*to change hands* to go into the pos-
session of another.
And so they haggled on for a little
longer, but at the end of the interview
Dandy had changed hands, and was
permanently engaged as a member of
Mr. Punch's travelling company.—F.
Anstey.

handle—*to give a handle to* to supply
with an occasion.
The defence of Vatinius gave a
plausible handle (furnished a fair
opportunity) for some censure upon
Cicero.—Malmoth.

—*to handle without mittens* or *gloves*
to treat without any superfluous politeness or gentleness; to attack vigorously.
He declares that it is time for the good
and true men to handle the imposters
without gloves.—North American
Review, 1887.

—*a handle to one's name* a title.
Now he has got a handle to his name,
and he'll live in clover all his life.—A.
Trollope.

—*to go off the handle* to die.
My old gentleman means to be mayor,
or governor, or president, or
something or other before he goes off
the handle.—O. W. Holmes.

handsome—*to do the handsome thing
by another person* to behave liberally
towards him.
She hoped it would be a match, and
that his lordship would do the
handsome thing by his nephew.—
Fielding.

handwriting—*the handwriting on the
wall* the announcement of an
approaching catastrophe. See the
Bible, Dan. v. 5–31. At the feast of
Belshazzar, the king of Babylon,
there "came forth fingers of a man's
hand, and wrote over against the
candlestick upon the plaster of the
wall of the king's palace: and the king

saw the part of the hand that wrote . . . And this is the writing that was written, *Mene, Mene, Tekel, Upharsin.* This is the interpretation of the thing: *Mene*; God hath numbered thy kingdom, and finished it. *Tekel*; Thou art weighed in the balances, and found wanting. *Peres*; Thy kingdom is divided, and given to the Medes and Persians. . . . In that night was Belshazzar the king of the Chaldeans slain. And Darius the Median took the kingdom."

hang—*to hang fire* to delay the accomplishment; to come to no decisive result.

The plot, too, which had been supported for four months by the sole evidence of Oates, began to hang fire.—Green.

—*to hang out* to lodge; to live.

I say, old boy, where do you hang out?—Dickens.

—*to hang in chains* to suspend a criminal's body in an iron frame, as a public spectacle.

They hanged him in chains for a show.—Tennyson.

—*to get the hang of a thing* to understand the general meaning, drift, or principle of anything.

—*to hang by a thread* to be in a very precarious position or condition.

A sailor knows too well that his life hangs by a thread to wish to be often reminded of it.—R. H. Dana, Jun.

—*a hang-dog look* a guilty, depressed appearance.

"He, he!" tittered his friend, "you are so – so very funny!"

"I need be," remarked Ralph dryly, "for this is rather dull and chilling. Look a little brisker, man, and not so hangdog like."—Dickens.

hank—*hank for hank* on equal terms.

happy—*happy-go-lucky* improvident; heedless.

In the happy-go-lucky way of his class.—C. Reade.

—*the happy despatch* suicide; a name commonly given to the Japanese method.

It was to provide Lord Harry Brentwood with a seat (in Parliament) that I was to commit this act of happy despatch (political suicide).—Mistletoe Bough, 1885.

hard—*hard as the nether millstone* very hard; unfeeling and obdurate. Generally applied to human character.

We in the wilderness are exposed to temptations which go some way to make us silly and soft-hearted. Somehow, few of us are certain to keep our hearts as hard as the nether millstone.—Nineteenth Century, 1887.

—*a hard case* an irreclaimably bad person.

He was a fellow-clerk of mine, and a hard case.—R. L. Stevenson.

—*hard and fast* securely.

"You can't mean Smike?" cried Miss Squeers, clapping her hands.

"Yes, I can, though," rejoined her father. "I've got him hard and fast."—Dickens.

—*to go hard with one* Said where any one fares ill or has bad luck.

It will go hard with poor Antonius.—Shakespeare

—*hard by* in the immediate vicinity; close to.

The news next obtained of the elephant was that he had killed several persons hard by.—Chamber's Journal, 1887.

—*hard lines* harsh treatment; unfortunate conditions.

That was hard lines for me, after I had given up everything for the sake of getting you an education which was to be a fortune to you.—George Eliot.

—*hard up* having little money to pay one's debts; in monetary difficulties.

Every man in England who was hard up, or had a hard-up friend, wrote to him for money in loan, with or without security.—Besant.

hare—*as mad as a march hare* crazy; insane.

"Oh," said the admiral, "then he is mad?"

"As a March hare, sir. And I'm afraid putting him in irons will make him worse. It is a case for a lunatic asylum.—C. Reade.

—*the hare's foot* the brush used by ladies for applying rouge.

The heart of poor dear Babs gave a bound which brought a colour into her face brighter than that which the hare's foot had left.—Mrs. E. Lynn Linton.

hark—*to hark back* to return to a subject which has been dropped; to begin again where one has left off.

Had they gone and told Silver, all might have turned out differently; but they had their orders, I suppose, and decided to sit quietly where they were and hark back again to "Lilliburlero" (commence singing "Lilliburlero" again).—R. L. Stevenson.

harness—*to die in harness* to continue at one's occupation until one's death; to refuse to retire from active life.

Nevertheless it was his (Lord Shaftesbury's) constant prayer that he might die in harness, and his last years were full of unceasing activity.—Leisure Hour, 1887.

harp—*to harp on the same string* to continue speaking on the same subject.

His mind, she thought, was certainly wandering, and, as often happens, it continued to harp on the same string.—James Payn.

harum—*harum-scarum* wild; reckless.

They had a quarrel with Sir Thomas Newcome's own son, a harum-scarum

lad, who ran away, and then was sent to India.—Thackeray.

hash—*to settle a man's hash for him* to overthrow his schemes; to ruin him.

At Liverpool she (the elephant) laid hold of Bernard, and would have settled his hash for (killed) him, but Elliot came between them.—C. Reade.

haste—*the more haste the less speed* excessive haste is often the cause of delay.

Women are "fickle cattle," I remember – I am sure my dear wife will excuse my saying so in her presence – and "most haste" is often "worst speed" with them.—Florence Marryat.

hat—*to hang up one's hat in a house* to make oneself at home; to enter into occupation. Visitors usually carry their hats in their hands when making a short visit; to hang up the hat implies special intimacy or a regular invitation.

"Eight hundred a year, and as nice a house as any gentleman could wish to hang up his hat in," said Mr. Cumming.—A. Trollope.

—*to pass round the hat* to solicit subscriptions.

—*a bad hat* a good-for-nothing fellow.

There was a fellow in my Katie's family who was formerly in the army, and turned out a very bad hat indeed.—Besant.

hatches—*to be under hatches* to be in a state of depression or poverty; to be dead.

Well, he's dead now and under hatches.—R. L. Stevenson.

hatchet—*to bury the hatchet* to cease fighting; to become friendly. A phrase borrowed from a Red Indian custom.

Dr. Andrew Marshall made it up with his adversary, and they lived on friendly terms ever afterwards. Why don't some of our living medici bury the hatchet with a like effective ceremony?—Jeaffreson.

—*to dig up the hatchet* to renew hostilities.

—*to take up the hatchet* to make war.

—*to throw the hatchet* to tell fabulous stories.

haul—*to haul over the coals.* See **coal.**

—*to haul in with* to sail close to the wind, in order to approach more closely an object. A nautical phrase.

—*to haul off* to sail close to the wind, in order to avoid an object. A nautical phrase.

—*to haul round* (of the wind) to shift to any point on the compass. A nautical phrase.

—*to haul the wind* to turn the head of the ship nearer to that point from which the wind blows. A nautical phrase.

have—*to have at a person* to try to strike or hit him. A *have-at-him* is a stroke or thrust.

And therefore, Peter, have at thee (I'll hit thee) with a downright blow.—Shakespeare.

—*to have it out (with a person).* (a) to settle a disputed point; to challenge another because of some offence of which he has been guilty.

I marched back to our rooms feeling savagely inclined to have it out with Forbes for (demand from Forbes an explanation of) his selfishness and lack of consideration.—Macmillan's Magazine, 1887.

—(b) to finish it; to enjoy the rest of it.

During the remainder of the day Mr. Browdie was in a very odd and excitable state; bursting occasionally into an explosion of laughter, and then taking up his hat and running into the coachyard to have it out by himself.—Dickens.

—*to have a care* to be cautious.

Have a care, Joe; that girl is setting her cap at you.—Thackeray.

—*to have nothing for it* to have no alternative.

He had nothing for it but to disperse his army.—Burton.

—*he had like to have* he came near having.

Wherever the Giant came, all fell before him; but the Dwarf had like to have been (was nearly) killed more than once.—Goldsmith.

hawk—*to know a hawk from a hernshaw* to be clever; to be wide awake.

A hernshaw is a kind of heron. When the wind is southerly I know a hawk from a hernshaw (or handsaw).—Shakespeare.

hawse—*to come in at the hawse-holes* to enter the navy at the lowest grade.

hay—*to make hay while the sun shines* to take every advantage of a favourable opportunity.

If Patty had not been wise in her generation – if she had not made her hay while the sun shone, and lined her nest while feathers were flying abroad – on the death of her master she would have come to cruel ends.—Mrs. E. Lynn Linton.

—*between hay and grass* in an unformed state; hobble-de-hoy. An Americanism, said of youths between boyhood and manhood.

—*to make hay of* to throw into confusion; to disturb.

Oh, father, you are making hay of my things.—Maria Edgeworth.

head—*to have a head on one's shoulders* to be possessed of judgment and discretion.

To be sure, her father had a head on his shoulders, and had sent her to school, contrary to the custom of the country.—C. Reade.

—*to eat his head off* (of a horse) to do

little or no work; costing more in food than he is worth.

It was my duty to ride, sir, a very considerable distance on a mare who had been eating her head off (resting lazily in her stable).—Blackmore.

—*to take it into one's head* to conceive a sudden notion. See **take.**

Francis had taken it into his head to stroll over to Whitestone's that evening.

—*to turn one's head* to make vain or unreasonable.

Well, he fairly turned Sall's head; the more we wanted her to give him up, the more she wouldn't.—Haliburton.

—*to put out of one's head* to forget; to drive away the thought of.

Emma at last, in order to put the Martins out of her head, was obliged to hurry on the news, which she had meant to give with so much caution.— Jane Austen.

—*heads or tails?* a cry used in tossing up a British coin. The face side and the reverse side of the coin are known respectively as heads (with reference to the King's head stamped on that side), and as tails, a term which has no particular significance.

If you come out heads (says Cripps, addressing an old sixpence which he is about to toss), little Ethy shall go; if you come out tails, I shall take it for a sign that we ought to turn tail in (retreat from) this here job.—Blackmore.

—*to make neither head nor tail of anything* to be unable to understand or find meaning in any statement or event.

You did say some queer things, ma'am, and I couldn't make head nor tail of what you said.—Mrs. Oliphant.

—*over heads and ears* completely.

Kit is over head and ears (in love), and she will be the same with him after that fine rescue.—Blackmore.

—*head-over-heels* hurriedly; before one has time to consider the matter.

This trust which he had taken on him without thinking about it, head-over-heels in fact, was the centre and turning-point of his school life.— Hughes.

—*to give the head to a horse* to allow it freedom.

He gave his able horse the head.

Shakespeare.

—*to let a man have his head* to allow him freedom. A phrase borrowed from the last, and originally only applicable to a horse.

She let him have his head for a bit, and then, when he'd got quite accustomed to the best of everything and couldn't live without it, she turned him into the street, where there is no claret and no champagne.—Besant.

—*head and shoulders* by the height of the head and shoulders.

My son is head and shoulders taller than his mother.

—*to come to a head* to ripen to approach completion.

The plot was discovered before it came to a head.

—*head and front* the outstanding and important part.

"Your good conversation in Christ" — "As he who called you is holy, be ye holy in all your conversation." This is the head and front of the matter with the writer.—M. Arnold.

—*off one's head* crazy; excited, and not under the guidance of one's reason; delirious.

His three companions exchanged a second look of meaning, and one of the men whispered to his mate, "He's clean off his head" (he is no longer sane).—All the Year Round, 1887.

—*to buy* or *sell a property over one's head* to buy or sell without consulting the occupants.

"What will become of Red Windows?"
"It will be sold over my head."—
Chamber's Journal, 1888.

—to keep one's head above water to
avoid bankruptcy.
He is not, like our friend Sir Hyacinth
O'Brien, forced to sell tongue and
brains and conscience to keep his
head above water.—Maria
Edgeworth.

heap—struck all of a heap completely
astonished.
I thought he'd fainted too; he was so
struck all of a heap.—Haliburton.

hear—to hear tell of to hear by report;
to be informed of.
I never heard tell of a man becoming a
dressmaker.—Haliburton.

heart—to take heart to become hope-
ful; to feel encouraged.
It is difficult for the farmer, particularly
in some districts of Fife, to take heart
after the experience of the last few
days with their ceaseless torrents.—
St. Andrews Citizen, 1880.

—to take anything to heart to feel
deeply pained about anything.
I would not shame you by seeming to
take them to heart or treat them
earnestly for an instant.—Dickens.

—to break one's heart to die of disappointment; to be mortally disappointed; to cause bitter grief or
sorrow to one.
But his friend talked, and told the other
officers how Greaves had been jilted,
and was breaking his heart (dying of
grief).—C. Reade.

—in one's heart of hearts in the inmost
recesses of the heart; privately;
secretly.
In his heart of hearts he feared lest
there might be some flaw in the young
man's story.—James Payn.

—to carry or **wear one's heart upon
one's sleeve** to expose one's inmost
thoughts to one's neighbours.

But I will wear my heart upon my sleeve
For daws to peck at.
Shakespeare.

Note – By "daws" are meant captious,
ill-natured people.

—heart and soul enthusiastically.
He went into the scheme heart and
soul (with enthusiasm).

—his heart is in the right place he is of
a kindly and sympathetic disposition.
See **right**.

—to have at heart to be deeply
interested in.
What a touching attachment that is
which these poor fellows show to any
one who has their cause at heart –
even to any one who says he has.—
Thackeray.

—to get or **learn by heart** to commit to
memory.
She fell to laughing like one out of her
right mind, and made me say the
name of the bog over, for her to get it
by heart, a dozen times.—Maria
Edgeworth.

—to have one's heart in one's mouth to
be frightened or startled.
"Old Thady," said my master just as he
used to do, "how do you do?"
"Very well, I thank your honour's
honour," said I; but I saw he was not
well pleased, and my heart was in my
mouth as I walked along with him.—
Maria Edgeworth.

—heart whole not in love.
No young woman could reject such an
offer without consideration, if she were
heart whole.—Florence Marryat.

—to take heart of grace to feel one's
courage revive.
I told him I was come to the
Queensferry on business, and, taking
heart of grace, asked him to direct me
to the house of Mr. Rankeillor.—R. L.
Stevenson.

—his heart sank into his boots he lost

hope or courage; he became deeply disheartened.

Perhaps it was this – perhaps it was the look of the island, with its gray melancholy woods, and wild stone spires, and the surf that we could both see and hear foaming and thundering on the steep beach – at least, although the sun shone bright and hot, and the shore birds were fishing and crying all around us, and you would have thought any one would have been glad to land after being so long at sea, my heart sank, as the saying is, into my boots; and from that first look onward, I hated the very thought of Treasure Island.—R. L. Stevenson.

—*after one's own heart* just such as one likes; dear to one.

It was, indeed, a representative gathering after the Talberts' own heart.—Hugh Conway.

—*out of heart* heavy; sodden.

The tillage-ground had been so ill managed by his predecessor that the land was what is called quite out of heart.—Maria Edgeworth.

heaven—*in the seventh heaven* in a state of intense delight or exaltation.

William Henry, for his part, was in the seventh heaven ... Those days at Stratford were the happiest days of his life.—James Payn.

—*Good heavens!* an exclamation of surprise.

Sir Henry Steele broke in loudly, "Good heavens! well, he is an extraordinary man.".—C. Reade.

heavy—*heavy in hand* deficient in verve; requiring to be urged on. A phrase originally used in driving.

He was a kind, honest fellow, though rather old-fashioned, and just a trifle heavy in hand.—James Payn.

heels—*laid by the heels* (a) prostrated.

When a very active man is suddenly laid by the heels, sad as the

dispensation is, there are sure to be some who rejoice in it.—Blackmore.

—(b) put under arrest.

—*to take to one's heels* to run off.

Timothy's Bess's Ben first kicked out vigorously, then took to his heels (scampered away), and sought refuge behind his father's legs.—George Eliot.

—*down at heels* or *out at heels* having bad or untidy shoes; in poor circumstances.

I am almost out at heels (in very low circumstances).—Shakespeare.

—*to cool* or *kick one's heels* to be made to wait when calling upon some great personage.

I have been waiting, kicking my heels since the train came in.—Sarah Tytler.

—*to tread upon the heels* to follow closely.

One woe doth tread upon another's heels (follows another closely).—Shakespeare.

—*Achilles' heel* the only vulnerable part. When Thetis dipped her son in the river Styx to make him invulnerable, she held him by the heel, and the part covered by her hand was the only part not washed by the water.

Hanover is the Achilles' heel (only assailable point) to invulnerable England.—Carlyle.

—*to kick up the heels* to die.

His heels he'll kick up,
Slain by an onslaught fierce of hick-up.
                    Robert Browning.

—*to come* or *follow upon the heels of* to follow closely; immediately succeeding.

Bread, I believe, has always been considered first, but the circus comes close upon its heels.—Contemporary Review, 1887.

Exp. – The multitude cries first for food, but soon it demands amusements.

—to get the heels of another to outstrip him.

O rare Strap, thou hast got the heels of me at last.—Smollett.

—to show the heels of to outstrip.

My impatience has shown its heels to my politeness.—R. L Stevenson.

—to show a light pair of heels to abscond.

The day after the discovery of the fraud, Stanton thought it prudent to show a light pair of heels.

helter—*helter-skelter* in haste and confusion.

Colley held up a white handkerchief in his hand, and Breytenback fired, and down went the general all of a heap, and then they all ran helter-skelter down the hill.—H. R. Haggard.

hen—*like a hen on a hot girdle* very restless.

—to sell one's hens on a rainy day to sell at a disadvantage, or foolishly.

"Never mind our son," cried my wife. "Depend upon it, he knows what he is about, I'll warrant, we'll never see him sell his hens on a rainy day. I have seen him buy such bargains as would amaze one."—Goldsmith.

Hercules—*Hercules' labours* Hercules, the mythical strong man of Greece, performed twelve labours or tasks, requiring enormous strength, for his brother Eurystheus. See **Augean**.

That, too, is on the list of Hercules' labours, Peter mine.—Charles Kingsley.

here—*neither here nor there* of no importance.

"Touching what neighbour Batts has said," he began in his usual slow and steadfast voice, "it may be neither here nor there.".—Blackmore.

—here and there scattered about thinly; occurring at rare intervals.

I wind about, and in and out, With here a blossom sailing,

And here and there a lusty trout And here and there a grayling.

Tennyson.

—here's to you I drink to your good health. A somewhat old-fashioned phrase, used before drinking a glass of wine or cordial with a friend.

Here's to budgets, bags, and wallets! Here's to all the wandering train!

Burns.

Exp. – The poet calls upon his hearers to fill their glasses and drink to the health of all jolly beggars.

Herod—*to out-Herod Herod* to be more outrageous than the most outrageous; to pass all bounds; to rant. Herod was the blustering tyrant of the Old English mystery plays. See Shakespeare's Hamlet, act iii, sc. 2.

But Lord Randolph out-Herods Herod in the opposite direction.—Fortnightly Review, 1887.

hic—*hic jacet* two Latin words, signifying *Here lies* which frequently begin the inscription on a tombstone. Inscriptions were formerly very commonly couched in Latin.

On each brutal brow was plainly written the hic jacet of a soul dead within.—E. Bellamy.

hide-and-seek—*to play hide-and-seek with any one* to seem to elude his pursuit. Hide-and-seek is a children's game, in which one hides and the others try to find him, or *vice versa*.

Indeed, the time passed so lightly in this good company that I began to be almost reconciled to my residence at Shaws; and nothing but the sight of my uncle and his eyes playing hide-and-seek with mine revived the force of my distrust.—R. L Stevenson.

high—*on high* aloft; in or to heaven.

Thy seat is up on high (aloft).

Shakespeare.

—high jinks uproarious fun; great sport.

There he found the eleven at high jinks after supper, Jack Raggles shouting comic songs and performing feats of strength.—Hughes.

—**high and dry** out of the water; in a dry place; safe.

Just where the eastern curve begins stands Kingscliff, a cluster of white cottages, fronted by a white beach, whereon some half-dozen of stout fishing-smacks are hauled up high and dry.—Good Words, 1887.

—**high time** fully time. Used where a limit of time has been reached, and it is necessary to delay no more.

It was now high time (very necessary) to retire and take refreshment against the fatigues of the following day.—Goldsmith.

—**high words** an angry discussion.

Their talk that day had not been very pleasant; words, very like high words, had passed between them.—George Eliot.

—**to be on the high horse** or **the high ropes; to ride the high horse** to have a haughty demeanour; to be over-bearing.

Yes, I went there the night before last, but she was quite on the high ropes about something, and was so grand and mysterious that I couldn't make anything of her.—Dickens.

He's an amusing fellow, and I've no objection to his making one at the Oyster Club; but he's a bit too fond of riding the high horse (of being arrogant).—George Eliot.

—**high-falutin'** in a pretentious style; pompous.

His enemies have done their best to enlighten her as to the hollowness of his high-falutin' professions.—Edinburgh Review, 1882.

—**with a high hand** imperiously; arrogantly.

Mr. Tolair would have carried his mission with a very high hand if he had not been disconcerted by the very unexpected demonstrations with which it had been received.—Dickens.

—**a high tea** "tea" – the evening meal – with meats and solid food.

Miss Gray need not trouble about dress; she always looked nice. That serge she was wearing would do capitally, if she did not grudge it, for sauntering about the fields and garden, being pulled about by the children, and sharing their dinner and high tea.—Sarah Tytler.

hinges—**off the hinges** in disorder; in a disturbed state.

At other times they are quite off the hinges, yielding themselves up to the way of their lusts and passions.—Sharpe.

hip—**hip and thigh** in no half-hearted way; showing no mercy.

"Protestants, I mean," says he (the priest), "are by the ears a-drivin' away at each other the whole blessed time, tooth and nail, hip and thigh, hammer and tongs."—Haliburton.

—**to smite hip and thigh** to overthrow with great slaughter.

"We shall smite them hip and thigh" (defeat them utterly), he cried.—H. Conway.

—**to have on the hip** to gain the advantage over in a struggle. A wrestling phrase.

If I can catch him once upon the hip, I will feed fat the ancient grudge I bear him.—Shakespeare.

hit—**to hit off** to describe in a terse and clever manner.

Goldsmith concocted a series of epigrammatic sketches, under the title of Retaliation, in which the characters of his distinguished intimates were admirably hit off with a mixture of generous praise and good-humoured raillery.—W. Irving.

—*to hit it off together* to agree; to suit each other.

You should have seen Kemble and him together; it was as good as any play. They don't hit it off together so well (find each other so congenial) as you and I do.—James Payn.

—*to hit the nail on the head* to speak appositely; to touch the exact point in question.

We have already had Quintilian's witness, how right conduct brings joy . . . And Bishop Wilson, always hitting the right nail on the head in matters of this sort, remarks that, "If it were not for the practical difficulties attending it, virtue would hardly be distinguishable from a kind of sensuality."—M. Arnold.

—*to hit upon* to light upon; to discover.
I can never hit on's (recall exactly his) name.—Shakespeare.

—*to hit out* to strike with the fists straight from the shoulder; to box in a serious fashion.

hither—*hither and thither* in various directions; to and fro.

hob—*hob and nob*, or *hob-nob*. A phrase used of companions drinking together in a friendly fashion. Hence the verb *to hob-nob*, or *to hob-and-nob*.

I have seen him and his poor companion hob-and-nobbing together.—Thackeray.

hobby—*to ride a hobby* to follow a favour pursuit, or introduce a favourite subject into conversation with a childish eagerness.

Nevertheless, some ladies have hobbies which they ride with considerable persistence. Mrs. Jennynge's hobby was a sort of hearse-horse, for it consisted in a devotion to the memory of her late second husband.—James Payn.

—*to ride a hobby to death* to weary people utterly with one's peculiar notions on a subject.

Hobson—*Hobson's choice* no choice at all. Said to be derived from the name of a Cambridge livery-stable keeper, who insisted on each customer taking the horse that was nearest the door.

No university man would ride him, even upon Hobson's choice (if he could get no other to ride).—Blackmore.

hocus-pocus—*hocus-pocus* deception; underhand dealing. Said to be a play on the words Hoc est corpus, used in the Mass.

Our author is playing hocus-pocus (hoodwinking his readers) in the very similitude he takes from that juggler.—Bentley.

hog—*to go the whole hog* to have everything that can be got; to refuse to be satisfied with merely a portion. American slang.

But since we introduced the railroads, if we don't go ahead it's a pity. We never fairly knew what going the whole hog was till then.—Haliburton.

hoist—*hoist with* or *by one's own petard* destroyed by one's own machinations, framed for the destruction of others. See Shakespeare's *Hamlet*, act iii, sc. 4.

It's too disastrous a victory. I'm hoist by my own petard – caught in my own mouse-trap.—W. D. Howells.

hoity—*hoity-toity* An exclamation signifying that the person addressed has been speaking or acting petulantly and absurdly.

"Hoity-toity!" cries Honour; "madam is in her airs, I protest."—Fielding.

hold—*to hold by* to support; to approve of.

Even the paterfamilias who did not hold by stage plays made an exception in honour of the Bard of Avon.—James Payn.

—*to hold forth* to speak in public, generally in praise of something.

A pretty conjurer, telling fortunes, held forth in the market-place.—L'Estrange.

—*to hold off* to remain at a distance; to refuse to join in any undertaking.

If you love me, hold not off.—Shakespeare.

—*to hold on* to last; to continue.

The trade held on (continued) for many years after the bishops became Protestants.—Swift.

—*to hold out* to offer resistance; not to succumb or yield.

A consumptive person may hold out (not succumb to the disease) for years.—Arbuthnot.

—*to hold good* to be valid; to be applicable.

No man will be banished, and banished to the torrid zone, for nothing. The rule holds good with respect to (is valid for) the legal profession.—Macaulay.

—*to hold in play* to keep fully occupied with secondary matters while the attention is diverted from the main point at issue.

—*to hold one's own* to contend successfully; to maintain what one is struggling for.

Moreover, with all her retiring ways she was always quite capable of holding her own.—Wm. Black.

—*to hold water* to bear close inspection. A phrase generally used negatively.

Tales had gone about respecting her. Nothing very tangible; and perhaps they would not have held water.—Mrs. Henry Wood.

—*to hold in check* to restrain; to control.

We should find difficulty in supplying an army of eight thousand men at Kandahar, which would be sufficient to hold in check the advance of one hundred thousand Russians from the Caucasus.—Fortnightly Review, 1887.

—*neither to hold nor to bind* in a state of ungovernable excitement.

"I tell you in turn," said the young man, who was neither to hold nor to bind, simply because something had been said about his wife – "I tell you in turn that I mean to contest the seat all the same; and what is more, by the Lord Harry I mean to win it."—Wm. Black.

hole—*hole-and-corner* secret; underhand.

But such is the wretched trickery of hole-and-corner Buffery.—Dickens.

—*in a hole* in a difficult position.

How he is going to prove that, I want to know. I've got him in a hole, you'll see.—Justin M'Carthy.

—*in the hole* a phrase used in playing cards to signify that the player has made a minus score.

holy—*holy water* water blessed by the priests of the Roman Catholic and Greek Churches. Catholics keep it in their houses, and use it on getting up, on retiring to rest, and when about to go on a journey. It is generally placed in stone basins or fonts at the entrance of churches, and is sprinkled on the worshippers at some of the more important services of the Church.

home—*at home* familiar; on easy terms.

There was admiration, and more even than admiration, in his eyes. It was a beautiful expression that I cannot define or put into words . . . that made me feel at home (friendly) with him at once.—The Argosy, 1886.

—*an "at home"* a reception or entertainment given in the afternoon or evening.

Now it so happened that Mr. Yates the manager was going to give an entertainment he called his at homes, and this took but a small orchestra.— C. Reade.

—*to be "at home" to people* to be ready to receive visitors.

"Sir Charles Bassett!" trumpeted a servant at the door, and then waited, prudently, to know whether this young lady, whom he had caught blushing so red with one gentleman, would be at home to another. C. Reade.

—*to bring a thing home to people* to say something which interests people, and the meaning of which they fully grasp.

"You're like the wood-pigeon; it says do, do, do all day, and never sets about any work itself." That's bringing it home to people (a saying which rouses the attention of people).— George Eliot.

—*to come home to a person* to reach one's conscience; to touch one's heart.

I've heard a good deal of the clerks out of place, and now it comes home to me.—Besant.

—*to make oneself at home* to act as if one were in one's own home.

"Do untie your bonnet-strings, and make yourself at home, Miss Nipper, please," entreated Jemima.—Dickens.

—*to bring oneself home* to recover what one has previously lost.

He is little out of cash just now. However, he has taken a very good road to bring himself home again, for we pay him very handsomely.— Madame D'Arblay.

—*one's long home* the grave.

Whatever you can see in cold water to run after it so, I can't think. If I was to flood myself like you, it would soon float me to my long home (cause my death).—C. Reade.

honour—*honour bright?* do you pledge your word for it? A phrase used when a man wishes to be per-

fectly sure that he is not going to be deceived. It is also used in affirmations to mean "I do pledge my word solemnly."

"I do not mean to marry Mr. Jacomb, if that is what you mean." – "No! Honour bright?"—Wm. Black.

—*an affair of honour* a dispute involving a duel.

—*a debt of honour* a debt incurred at play, which cannot be recovered by legal process, and is therefore considered more binding in the social code of laws.

He had all along meant to pay his father's debts of honour; but the moment the law was taken of him, there was an end of honour, to be sure.—Maria Edgeworth.

—*a point of honour* a scruple arising from delicacy of feeling.

"I will not," said Lochiel, "break the ice. That is a point of honour with me."— Macaulay.

—*honours of war* the privilege granted to a defeated army to march out of a town or a camp with colours flying.

The same day, at one p.m., arrived a letter from General Stiels granting permission to the officers to retain their swords, and to the army the honours of war.—Edinburgh Review, 1886.

—*the honours rested with him* he was the most successful.

The honours of the evening would have rested with Ratcliffe, had he not lowered himself again to his ordinary level.—Edinburgh Review, 1882.

—*to do the honours* to act as host or hostess at an entertainment.

Afterwards Miss Amelia did the honours of the drawing-room.— Thackeray.

hoof—*to beat* or *pad the hoof* to walk.

Charles Bates expressed his opinion that it was time to pad the hoof.— Dickens.

hook—*by hook or by crook* by some means or other; through some device.
"I do not think," he replied coldly, after an unpleasant pause, "that William Henry cares much about Shakespeare; but he has probably asked for his holiday thus early in hopes that, by hook or by crook, he may get another one later on."—James Payn.

—*off the hooks* (a) in disorder; flurried.
*While Sheridan is off the hooks,
And friend Delany at his books.*

Swift.

—(b) dead; no longer in existence.
The attack was so sharp that Matilda, as his reverence expressed it, was very nearly off the hooks.—Thackeray.

—*on one's own hook* independently; on one's own responsibility.
The very eye-glass, which headed the cane he carried so jauntily in his hand, was out of keeping with their eye-glasses, and looked like some gay young lens who had refused to be put into spectacles, and was winking at life on its own hook.—James Payn.

—*to hook it* to run away.
Every school-boy knows that the lion has a claw at the end of his tail with which he lashes himself into fury. When the experienced hunter sees him doing that, he, so to speak, "hooks it."—H. Kingsley.

hop—*to hop the twig* to die. See **kick the bucket**.

horn—*to draw in one's horns* to be reticent or timid.
"This is not his opinion," said the doctor dryly, who having been betrayed into frankness by the other's seeming acquaintance with the subject in question, now once more seemed inclined to draw in his horns.—James Payn.

—*to show one's horns* to show signs of a devilish nature. "Hornie" is a popular name for the devil, whose characteristics, according to the popular conception, are his horns, his tail, and his cloven feet.
"A fine day, Mr. Burchell."
"A very fine day, doctor; though I fancy we shall have some rain by the shooting of my corns" (callosities on the feet).
"The shooting of your horns?" cried my wife in a loud fit of laughter.—Goldsmith.
Exp. – Mrs. Primrose suggests by her remark that Mr. Burchell had a devilish nature.

—*to be on* or *between the horns of a dilemma* to be in a position of extreme difficulty, from which there seems no way of escape.
"We never cared for the money," said Mrs. Corey. "You know that."
"No; and now we can't seem to care for the loss of it. That would be still worse. Either horn of the dilemma gores us."—W. D. Howells.

—*the horn of plenty* a horn wreathed and filled to overflowing with flowers, corn, fruit – the symbol of prosperity and peace. Known by the Latin name *cornucopia*. The goddess Ceres is frequently pictured with it.
Nature, very oddly, when the horn of plenty is quite empty, always fills it with babies.—Besant.

—*his horn is exalted* he is proud and happy. A Scriptural phrase.
As he paced the walks with Amy Shillibeer, and caused that young person's horn to be exalted for hope that his flirting chaff meant serious business, he heard nothing to which he could object.—Mrs. E. Lynn Linton.

—*to lower one's horn* to humiliate oneself; to condescend.
"If we could prevail on him to abandon this insane affair," said my Lady Jane, with the sublime self-forgetfulness of pride when it has lowered its horn as

*it skirted by ruin, and now raises it
again as it touches success.*—Mrs E.
Lynn Linton.

hornet—*to bring* or **raise a hornet's
nest about one's ears** to cause a host
of critics or enemies to rise up against
one.

*The chief offenders for the time were
flogged and kept in bounds; but the
victorious party had brought a nice
hornets' nest about their ears.*—
Hughes.

horrors—*the horrors* the symptoms of
delirium tremens.

*"It's a strange place," said the squatter
at length, speaking softly, as though
loath to break the curious stillness. "It's
enough to give one the horrors."*—*All
the Year Round*, 1887.

hors—*hors de combat* rendered useless
for fighting; disabled. A French
phrase.

*If the Board schoolmaster was placed
hors de combat by professional
scruples and professionals fatigue, the
same reservation might have applied
equally to Bennet Gray.*—Sarah Tytler.

horse—*a horse-laugh* a coarse, unmeaning laugh.

*One night, Mr. Yates being funnier than
usual, if possible, a single horse-laugh
suddenly exploded among the
fiddles.*—C. Reade.

—*to flog a dead horse* to agitate for the
revival of a creed that is extinct.

*Arguing against Tom Paine is like
flogging a dead horse.*

—*horse-play* rough amusement.

*To be sure it was a boy, not a man,
and child's-play is sometimes
preferred by the theatre-going world
even to horse-play.*—C. Reade.

—*to take horse* to journey on horseback.

*He took horse to the Lake of
Constance, which is formed by the
entry of the Rhine.*—Addison.

—*one-horse* mean; petty; in a small
way. An Americanism.

*Oh, well, Rhode Island is a one-horse
state, where everybody pays taxes
and goes to church.*—Wm. Black.

—*on one's high horse* puffed-up;
arrogant.

*Well, the colonel does seem to be on
his high horse, ma'am.*—W. D.
Howells.

host—*to reckon* or *count without
one's host* to calculate without considering fully the practicality of any
plan.

*His feelings, in fact, were precisely the
same as those on which Mr. Harris
had counted – without his host
(rashly).*—James Payn.

hot—*hot-foot* quickly.

*The stream was deep here, but some
fifty yards below was a shallow, for
which he made off hot-foot.*—Hughes.

—*in hot water* in a state of trouble or
worry.

*He was far oftener in disgrace than
Richard, and kept me, I may say, in
continual hot water, wondering what
extraordinary trick he would take it into
his head to play next.*—Annie Keary.

hour—*at the eleventh hour* just in time
and no more to obtain an advantage.

*At the eleventh hour he is compelled
to take the last chance applicant.*—
Augustus Jessopp.

—*the small hours* the morning hours
after midnight.

*He was just playing the last rubber
which possesses such elastic
attributes, and has kept many a better
man up to the small hours (out of bed
until one or two o'clock), who otherwise
makes it a principle to be in bed by
ten o'clock.*—James Payn.

—*to keep good hours* to return home
at an early hour every evening; not to
be abroad at night.

The landlady said she would have no lodger who did not keep good hours.

—in an evil hour under the influence of an unhappy inspiration; acting from an unfortunate impulse; in an unlucky moment.

house—*a house-to-house visitation* a series of visits made to neighbouring houses in regular succession.

I am struck more and more with the amount of disease and death I see around me in all classes, which no sanitary legislation whatsoever could touch, unless you had a house-to-house visitation of a Government officer.—C. Kingsley.

—to keep house (a) to maintain a separate establishment.

My mother no longer keeps house, but lives with her married daughter.

—(b) to manage domestic affairs; to act as housekeeper.

When my dear brother was alive (I kept house for him, Miss Nickleby), we had to supper once a week two or three young men.—Dickens.

—to keep open house to be hospitable to all comers.

Everybody in the country knew the colonel, and everybody knew Drinkwater Torm, and everybody who had been to the colonel's for several years past (and that was nearly everybody in the county, for the colonel kept open house), knew Polly.—Harper's Monthly, 1886.

—to cry from the house-tops to announce to the public. An eastern phrase. The roofs of the houses in Syria and the neighbouring countries are flat, and are used in the evenings as family resorts.

Gabriel, rousing himself now and again to listen, heard nothing that might not have been cried from the house-tops.—D. Christie Murray.

—house of call a house where work-

men of a particular trade meet, and where those in need of workmen can engage their services.

The inn served as a house of call for farmers returning from Exeter market.

—like a house on fire very rapidly and easily; "swimmingly."

"Yes," said Jeremiah exultantly; "I'm getting on like a house on fire."—B. L. Farjeon.

how—*how much?* a satirical expression, implying that the person who is addressed has used an absurdly learned phrase.

"The plant is of the genus Asclepiadaceæ, tribe Stapelieæ."—*"Genus how much?"*

—how is that for high? a vulgar phrase used after the telling of some wonderful story.

Mr. Berry casually remarks, "I've hanged one hundred and thirteen convicts, and only attended one inquest, when the convict's head was separated from his body, and I had to explain how the unfortunate accident occurred." How is that for high? Truly, it must be a profitable business that admits of such state and dignity in a hangman.—St. Andrews Citizen, 1889.

hub—*the hub of the solar system* or *of the universe* the central city of the world. A name often applied in jest to Boston, Massachusetts.

Calcutta swaggers as if it were the hub of the universe.—Daily News, 1886.

hue—*hue and cry* a clamour in pursuit of an offender.

A hue and cry hath followed certain men into this house.—Shakespeare.
The Dodger and his accomplished friend, Master Bates, joined in the hue and cry which was raised at Oliver's heels.—Dickens.

huff—*to take the huff* to be offended; to be sulky.

Suppose he takes the huff, and goes to some other lawyer.—C. Reade.

hug—*to hug the shore* to keep close to the shore.

—*to hug oneself* to chuckle with satisfaction.

He hugged himself at the idea of their discomfiture.

hum—*to hum and haw* to hesitate in speaking.

There came a pause, which, after humming and hawing a little, Philip was the first to break.—H. R. Haggard.

humble—*to eat humble-pie* to apologize abjectly. Humble, mumble, or umble pie was made from the umbles or entrails of the deer, and fell to the lot of the inferiors at a feast.

With the great alacrity the malcontents in France, the old Constitutional party, take up your parable. "France is eating humble-pie!" they scream out; "the tyrant is making France eat humble-pie! France is humiliated! France is suffocating!"—M. Arnold.

hundred—*not a hundred miles off* or *from* a phrase often used to avoid a direct reference to any place. The place itself or its immediate neighbourhood is always intended. It therefore is equal to "very near" or "very close to."

Scene – chemist's shop, not a hundred miles from Dumfries. Enter small girl with a bottle of cod-liver oil purchased on the previous day. Small girl: "If ye please, sir, will ye tak' this back? The man canna tak' it, for he dee'd last nicht."—St. Andrews Citizen, 1887.

Exp. – Small girl: "If you please, sir, will you take this back? The man cannot take it, for he died last night."

The phrase is also used of events not far distant in time.

From all of which wise reflections the reader will gather that our friend Arthur was not a hundred miles off an awkward situation.—H. R. Haggard.

hungry—*as hungry as a hawk* very hungry.

I made a hearty supper, for I was as hungry as a hawk.—R. L. Stevenson.

hunks—*an old hunks* a niggardly, mean fellow.

"Not one word for me in his will . . . A hunks," replied Mr. Bunker; "a miserly hunks."—Besant.

—*husband's tea* very weak tea.

hush—*to hush up* to keep concealed; to suppress.

The matter is hushed up, and the servants are forbid to talk of it.—Pope.

—*hush-money* to bribe to secure silence regarding some iniquitous transaction.

There was, besides, hush-money for the sub-sheriffs (who had been bribed to keep quiet).—Maria Edgeworth.

I

ice—*to break the ice* to commence speaking after an embarrassing silence; to begin to speak on a delicate subject.

The ice having been broken in this unexpected manner, she made no further attempt at reserve.—Thomas Hardy.

idol—*idols of the tribe* (*idola tribūs*) errors of belief into which human nature in general is apt to fall. A phrase, with the others which follow, invented by Francis Bacon.

Teachers and students of theology get a certain look, certain conventional tones of voice, a clerical gait, a professional neckcloth, and habits of mind as professional as their externals. They are scholarly men, and read Bacon, and know well enough what the idols of the tribe are.—Holmes.

Some of these (preconceived shadowy notions) are inherent in the human mind, as, for example, the general prejudice in favour of symmetry and order.... Such prejudices extend to the whole tribe of men, and may be called the idols of the tribe.—Abbott.

—**idols of the cave (idola specūs)** errors of belief into which people living apart from the world are apt to fall.

Again, individual men, circumscribed within the narrow and dark limits of their individuality, as shaped by their country, their age, their own physical and mental peculiarities, find themselves as it were fettered in a cave ... they only see the shadows of realities: such individual misconceptions or idols may be called idols of the cave.—Abbott.

—**idols of the forum** or **market-place (idola fori)** errors of belief arising from language and social intercourse.

Language is a third imposture ... tyrannizing over and moulding thoughts. It is the idol of intercourse, deriving its influence from all meetings of men, and may therefore be called the idol of the market-place.—Abbott.

—**idols of the theatre** the deceptions that have arisen from the dogmas of different schools.

In the place of the unobtrusive worship of the truth, authority substitutes the mere fictions and theatrical stage-plays (for they are no better) of the

ostentatious philosophers. It may therefore be called the idol of the theatre.—Abbott.

if—*if you please* this phrase has often a peculiar use when inserted in a sentence. It calls attention to a statement, of which the opposite might have been taken for granted, and may be translated, "Pray do not suppose the contrary."

Rank is respected, if you please, even at the East End of London; and perhaps more there than in fashionable quarters, because it is so rare.—Besant.

ignis—*ignis fatuus* deceptive light. Latin. See **will o' the wisp**.

Austria, who, beguiled by the ignis fatuus *of her great ally, had assisted in discrediting the Bund and covering it with ridicule, returned to it in her extremity.*—Quarterly Review, 1887.

ilk—*of that ilk* of the place with the same name; as, **Bethune of that ilk** = Bethune of Bethune. A Scotch phrase.

I don't mean Beatrice to marry Mr. Staunton, even if he is a Staunton of that ilk.—W. E. Norris.

ill—*it's an ill wind that blows nobody good* few events are misfortunes to every one concerned. Sickness benefits physicians; death puts money in the pockets of undertakers; fires are popular with carpenters.

Ill blows the wind that profits nobody.—Shakespeare.

imperium—*imperium in imperio* a government within a government. Latin.

improve—*to improve the occasion* to draw moral lessons from any event when it happens.

Holmes, who was one of the best boys in the school, began to improve the occasion. "Now, you youngsters," said he, as he marched along in the middle

of them, "mind this – you're very well
out of this scrape. Don't you go near
Thompson's barn again do you
hear?"—Hughes.

in—*the ins and outs of anything* its
whole working; the details of
everything.

No; if you want to know the ins and
outs of the Yankees (external and
internal characteristics of the people of
New England), I've wintered them and
summered them; I know all their points,
shape, make, and breed.—Haliburton.

—*in for it* in a critical or dangerous
situation.

There was indeed a fearful joy about
his playing at being a man of high
family. He was in for it now, and he
would not draw back.—J. M'Carthy.

—*in with a person* on friendly terms
with him.

That's the worst of being in with an
audacious chap like that old
Nickleby.—Dickens.

—*in nubibus* in the clouds; not having
an actual existence. Latin.

—*in for a penny, in for a pound* this
phrase is used when the same loss or
danger is incurred whether the previous responsibility has been great or
small. Compare the saying, "As well
be hung for a man as for a sheep."

You never know when he's done with
you, and if you're in for a penny, you're
in for a pound.—Dickens.

—*in flagrante delicto* in the very act of
guilt. Latin.

Mr. Routh, while playing hazard in Mr.
Grüntz's rooms, had been caught in
flagrante delicto, in the act of
cheating.—Edmund Yates.

—*in extremis* at the last gasp; in a hopeless condition. Latin.

The delimitation of the sphere of
influence which had been arranged,
of course, meant an agreement in
advance, whether Bulgaria or Greece

should conduct insurrections in
particular villages whenever Turkey
was in extremis, and which should
annex them whenever Turkey was
extinct.—Fortnightly Review, 1887.

—*in loco parentis* in a parent's place.
Latin.

This stately personage, probably for
Miss Burt's sake rather than his own,
was about to place himself, as
respected Miss Josceline, in loco
parentis.—James Payn.

—*in media res* right into the middle of
a subject. Latin.

At last I desperately broke the ice,
rushing in medias res (introducing the
subject abruptly).—The Mistletoe
Bough, 1885.

—*in memoriam* to the memory of.
Latin. Used like *hic jacet (q.v.).*

—*in situ* in the actual spot where anything has occurred. Latin.

It is really worth while to get a copy of
the memoirs to see how strange such
language looks in situ.—National
Review, 1888.

—*in toto* taken completely; altogether.
Latin.

If you become a nuisance, I shall either
deny your statements in toto, or I shall
take the wind out of your sails by
confessing the truth to her on my own
account.—W. E. Norris.

Indian—*Indian file* a procession in
which each person follows after the
other in a long line.

Well, sir, as the four of us were walking
in Indian file, what did the woman
suddenly do but go up to Jeremiah and
accost him.—B. L. Farjeon.

—*Indian summer* the finest part of the
autumn season in North America, a
time noted for its beauty and
mildness.

In the one case there was Mr. Josceline
wooing and winning; Mrs. Jennynge in
an Indian summer (delightful state) of

rapture; and Miss Anastasia beginning
to suspect what was going on.—James
Payn.

infra—*infra dig* a contraction for *infra
dignitatem* (Latin), "beneath one's
dignity."

Beards continued in favour until the
seventeenth century, when the
magistracy, again opposing the change
of fashion as infra dig., declined as
long and as resolutely to part with their
beards as their predecessors had
done to adopt them.—Lady Jackson.

inside—*to get the inside track of anything* to understand its workings. An
American phrase.

intention—*to heal by the first intention*
(of a wound) to close up without sup-
puration; to come together and grow
well without inflammation.

He only strapped up my cut, and
informed me that it would speedily get
well by the first intention – an odd
phrase enough.—O. W. Holmes.

inter—*inter nos* between ourselves.
Latin. Used when speaking confidentially. Compare the French *entre nous*.

I.O.U.—*I.O.U.*, "I owe you." A form
of acknowledgment of debt common
between friends. The amount borrowed and the name of the borrower
are added to these letters.

But pay? - of course he must pay; to
talk of burning I.O.U.'s was mere
child's play.—Thackeray.

ipse—*ipse dixit* a dogmatic statement
made by a writer without adducing
reasons.

Yet Sir George Trevelyan evidently
expects that, on the other hand,
Nationalist associations will be liable to
be suppressed on the ipse dixit of the
Lord Lieutenant that they are acting
illegally.—Spectator, 1887.

ipso—*ipso facto* in the fact itself. Latin.
Used where something is said to be

inherent of necessity in something
else.

Whatever the captain does is right, ipso
facto, and any opposition to it is wrong
on board ship.—R. H. Dana, Jun.

iron—*to have many irons in the fire* to
have many projects carrying on at one
time. Irons are here the bolts used in
the laundry to heat the box-iron, and
renewed from time to time.

And then he (Lamb) tells what other
literary irons are in the fire.—A. Ainger.

—*in irons* fettered.

"Overboard!" said the captain. "Well,
gentlemen, that saves the trouble of
putting him in irons."—R. L. Stevenson.

—*an inch of cold iron* a stab from a
dagger or other weapon.

—*the iron had entered into his soul* his
spirit was broken.

True, he wore no fetters, and was
treated with a grave and stately
consideration; but his bonds were not
the less galling, and the iron had not
the less entered into his soul.—G. A.
Sala.

—*to strike while the iron is hot* to act
with energy and promptitude.

"Strike the iron while it's hot, Bob,"
replied I.—Captain Marryat.

irony—*the irony of fate* the curious
providence which brings about the
most unlikely events.

By the irony of fate, the Ten Hours Bill
was carried in the very session when
Lord Ashley, having changed his views
on the Corn Laws, felt it his duty to
resign his seat in Parliament.—Leisure
Hour, 1887.

islands—*Islands of the blest* or *blessed*
imaginary islands in the West, thought
to be the abode of good men after
death.

Soon your footsteps I shall follow
To the Islands of the Blessed.
Longfellow.

issue—*at issue* (a) in controversy; disputed.

This compromise, which was proposed with abundance of tears and sighs, not exactly meeting the point at issue, nobody took any notice of it.—
Dickens.

—(b) at variance; disagreeing.

*We talked upon the question of taste, on which we were at issue.—*Southey.

—*to join Issue with* to dissent from; to find fault with; to oppose.

*I must join issue with you on behalf of your correspondent, who says that cocky is bush-slang for a small selector.—*Illustrated London News, 1887.

—*to join issues* to leave a matter to the decision of a law-court.

*Plaintiffs joined issues, and the trial was set down for the next assizes.—*C. Reade.

itching—*an itching palm* an avaricious disposition.

Let me tell you, Cassius, you yourself
Are much condemned to have an
    itching palm;
To sell and mart your offices for gold
To undeservers.

Shakespeare.

Ithuriel—*Ithuriel's spear* the weapon of the angel Ithuriel, which exposed deceit by the slightest touch.

Him (Satan) thus intent Ithuriel with his
    spear
*Miracles, the mainstay of popular religion, are touched by Ithuriel's spear. They are beginning to dissolve.—*M. Arnold.

Ixion—*the Ixionic wheel* Ixion, as a punishment for falling in love with Juno, was hurled to Tartarus, and there bound to a wheel which perpetually revolved. In the following extract the prison tread-mill is jocularly called the Ixionic wheel.

*Defendant's brothers tread the Ixionic wheel for the same offence.—*Thackeray.

J

Jack—*a Jack-at-a-pinch* a person suddenly called upon to perform some duty. Often applied to a clergyman without a fixed position, who is frequently summoned to act at a wedding or a funeral in the absence of the regular minister.

—*Jack and Jill* common names at one time among the English peasantry; *Jack* for a man, *Jill* for a woman. Occurring frequently in rhymes.

Jack shall have Jill;
Nought shall go ill;

The man shall have his mare again,
and all shall be well.

Shakespeare.

—*a Jack-in-office* a person who presumes on his official position to be pert or rude.

*I hate a Jack-in-office.—*Wolcot.

—*a Jack tar* a British seaman.

—*a Jack of all trades* a man who devotes himself to many different occupations.

He should, as I tell him, confine himself entirely to portrait-painting. As it is, he does landscapes also, "A Jack of all trades," as I ventured to remind him, "is master of none.".—James Payn.

—*a Jack with a lantern* or *Jack o' lantern* the *ignis fatuus* which flits about bogs, and often leads travellers to destruction.

He was a complete Jack o' lantern – here, and there, and everywhere.— Haliburton.

—*Jack Sprat* a diminutive boy or man. Immortalized in the rhyme,—

Jack Sprat could eat no fat,
His wife could eat no lean;
And so it was, between them both,
They licked the platter clean.

—*before you could say Jack Robinson* in an instant; immediately.

"Minerva has too bad a character for learning to be a favourite with gentlemen," said Lord Clonbrony.

*"Tut! Don't tell me! I'd get her off (secure a husband for her) before you could say Jack Robinson, and thank you too, if she had £50,000 down (in ready money), or £1,000 a year in land."—*Maria Edgeworth.

Found also under the contracted form, "Before you could say J.R."

*These men are not the warriors of commerce, but its smaller captains, who, watching the fluctuations of this or that market, can often turn a thousand pounds ere we could say J.R.—*C. Reade.

—*a cheap-Jack* a travelling vendor of goods.

*Cheap-Jacks have their carts beside the pavement.—*Besant.

—*Jack's bean-stalk* a bean-stalk which grew up in one night. The story of *Jack and the Bean-Stalk* is an old and very popular nursery tale. Compare **Jonah's gourd.**

*For the affection of young ladies is of as rapid growth as Jack's bean-stalk.—*Thackeray.

—*Jack Ketch* the hangman.

*He will come back without fear, and we will nail him with the fifty-pound note upon him; and then – Jack Ketch (he will be hanged).—*C. Reade.

—*Jack-in-a-box* something which disappears and reappears with great suddenness.

She was somewhat bewildered by this Jack-in-a-box sort of appearance.— Wm. Black.

—*Jack Horner* the self-indulgent, complacent little boy who picked out plums from the pie. Immortalized in the nursery rhyme,—

Little Jack Horner sat in a corner,
Eating a Christmas pie;
He put in his thumb, and he pulled out a plum,
And said, "What a good boy am I!"

—*Jack Frost* a playful name for frost.

"I hope you don't expect gratitude."

*"I only expect the blanket to keep out Jack Frost."—*Miss Braddon.

jail—*a jail-bird* a hardened criminal.

*The jail-birds who piped this tune were, without a single exception, the desperate cases of this moral hospital.—*C. Reade.

jar—*on the jar* ajar; partly open.

*The door was on the jar, and, gently opening it, I entered and stood behind her unperceived.—*Brooke.

jaw—*stop your jaw* be quiet.

*If you don't stop your jaw about him, you'll have to fight me.—*H. Kingsley.

Jeddart—*Jeddart* or *Jedwood justice* hanging the criminal first, and trying him afterwards.

*The case of Lord Byron was harder. True Jedwood justice was dealt out to him. First came the execution, then the investigation, and last of all, or rather not at all, the accusation.—*Macaulay.

Jericho—*to go to Jericho* to go away; to go into retirement. An expression used contemptuously. The allusion comes from the Bible: "Hanun took

David's servants, and shaved off the one half of their beards... When they told it unto David, he sent to meet them, because the men were greatly ashamed: and the king said, Tarry at Jericho until your beards be grown, and then return" (2 Sam. x. 4, 5).

Seeing her, I wished Joe's scruples had been at Jericho.—H. R. Haggard.

Jerry—*Jerry-work* unsubstantial work in building. **Jerry-builder** and **jerry-built** have this significance.

Two lumps of plaster fall from the roof of the jerry-built palace; then the curse begins to work.—Pall Mall Gazette, 1884.

—*a Jerry* or *Tom-and-Jerry shop* a public-house where only beer is sold. So called from its inferiority to a fully-licensed house.

We turned into a Tom-and-Jerry shop to have some beer, and spin a bit of a yarn about old times.—G. J. Whyte-Melville.

jeunesse—*jeunesse dorée* the "gilded youth" of a nation; its fashionable young men. French.

You could never get together a jeunesse dorée without our assistance.—H. Kingsley.

jib—*the cut of one's jib* one's personal appearance. Sailors' slang.

She disliked what sailors call "the cut of his jib."—Sir W. Scott.

jiffy—*in a jiffy* without any delay; forthwith.

In a jiffy I had slipped over the side.—R. L. Stevenson.

jingo—*by jingo* a mild oath having no definite meaning.

One of them, I thought, expressed her sentiments on this occasion in a very coarse manner, when she observed that, by the living jingo, she was all of a muck of sweat.—Goldsmith.

Job—*a Job's comforter* one who comes avowedly to comfort a friend, but who really annoys him. See the Bible (Book of Job). Job had three friends who came to him in his trouble as comforters, but spend their time in reproaching him.

"I told you so, I told you so!" is the croak of a true Job's comforter.—A. Trollope.

—*Job's comfort* consolation which irritates instead of soothing.

—*Job's news* news of calamities.

From home there can nothing come but Job's news.—Carlyle.

—*Job's post* a bringer of bad news.

This Job's post from Dumouriez reached the National Convention.—Carlyle.

—*the patience of Job* very great patience.

Mr. Pratt has certainly the patience of Job.—Maria Edgeworth.

job—*to pay a person by the job* to pay him for each separate portion of work done. A jobbing carpenter is one who is ready to do odd pieces of work when sent for.

—*to do the job for a man* to kill him.

That last debauch of his did the job for him (caused his death).

—*a bad job* said of what is hopeless or impracticable.

I will not say that he had given the whole thing up as a bad job, because it was the law of his life that the thing never should be abandoned as long as hope was possible.—A. Trollope.

jog—*to jog another's memory* or *another's elbow* to remind another of a duty or a promise apparently forgotten.

—*to jog on* to proceed lazily and heavily.

Thus they jog on, still tricking, never thriving.—Dryden.

John—*John o' Nokes and John o' Styles* ordinary peasants.

John o' Nokes and John o' Styles were now more considered than I was.—G. A. Sala.

—**John Company** a familiar name given to the East India Company (E.I.C.), which ruled in India until the mutiny of 1857.

When he had thoroughly learned this lesson he was offered a position in India, in the service of John Company.—Mrs. E. Lynn Linton.

—**John Doe and Richard Roe** dummy names used in law cases to represent the plaintiff and the defendant in an action of ejectment. This form of words was abolished in 1852.

Thus in a case lately decided before Miller, Doe presented Roe a subscription paper.—O. W. Holmes.

—**John Bull** a representative Englishman. Dr. Arbuthnot's *History of John Bull* made the expression current.

"Who is he when he is at home?"

"The Englishman's first question about every stranger," remarked Mrs. Lindsay, laughing. "What a thorough John Bull you are, Arthur!"—W. E. Norris.

—**John Orderly** the signal to shorten the performance at a show. The master, who remains on the outside platform of the booth, and takes in the money, cries to the actors, "Is John Orderly there?" This is a signal for them to cut short the performance.

Johnny—*Johnny Crapeau* a familiar term for a Frenchman, especially in use among sailors. See **Jean**.

Those vessels went armed, too, as befitted the majesty of the bunting under which old Dance had gloriously licked Johnny Crapeau.—Gentleman's Magazine, 1887.

join—*to join hands with* to take as a partner; to associate oneself with.

"When merit joins hands with

perseverance, success is certain."—James Payn.

—*to join the majority* to die. A classical phrase.

General Ward, who commanded the "Disciplined Chinese Field Force," had just joined the majority.—Pall Mall Gazette, 1887.

joint—*out of joint* in confusion and disorder.

The times are out of joint.—Shakespeare.

Jolly—*the Jolly Roger* the pirate's flag.

"Mr. Kentish, if that be your name," said I, "are you ashamed of your own colours?"

"Your ladyship refers to the 'Jolly Roger'?" he inquired with perfect gravity, and immediately went into peals of laughter.—R. L. Stevenson.

Jonah—*Jonah's gourd* a phrase applied to what grows in a night and withers with equal rapidity.

"I expect I belong to the order of Jonah's gourds," said Campion bitterly.—F. Anstey.

Jonathan—*brother Jonathan* a typical American.

An American republic in stars and stripes was also represented from Yokohama; and two brothers Jonathan, one from Tokio, another from Yokohama, supported their countrywoman.—Japan Mail, 1887.

jump—*to jump a claim* to seize upon a mining claim by force, or in the absence of one who has a prior claim.

To gain possession of this old wood and iron, and get a right to the water, Rufe proposed, if I had no objections, to jump the claim.—R. L. Stevenson.

—*to jump at* to accept with eagerness.

To his surprise, Susan did not jump at this remuneration.—C. Reade.

—*to jump or jump over the broomstick* to marry in an informal way.

Well, the other gipsy man is no other

than Joe Smith, who jumped over the broomstick with the lovely Princess Cinnaminta.—Blackmore.

justice—*to do one justice* to display one's good qualities or good looks.

In one bracelet was a photograph of dear little Charlie, taken from a picture done in oils, very like, but not doing him justice (making him appear as pretty as he actually was).—*The Mistletoe Bough*, 1885.

—*in justice to* desiring to treat fairly; doing what justice demands to.

In vain poor Lady Clonbrony followed the dowager about the rooms to correct this mistake, and to represent, in justice to Mr. Soho, though he had used her so ill, that he knew she was an Englishwoman.—Maria Edgeworth.

K

kaow—*to kaow-taow* to behave in a submissive manner. From the Chinese.

To have to kaow-taow to Arnold too, as I must do of course.—Anon.

keep—*to keep abreast of* to advance at an equal pace with; not to fall behind.

He yet found abundance of time to keep abreast of all that was passing in the world.—*Athenæum*, 1887.

—*to keep up* to continue alongside of; not to fall behind.

"Please, sir, we've been out Bigside hare and hounds and lost our way."
   'Hah! you couldn't keep up (fell behind), I suppose.''—Hughes.

—*to keep company* to have a sweetheart; to court.

This is Miss Kennedy, and I hope—I'm sure—that you two will get to be friendly with one another, not to speak of keeping company (becoming lovers).—Besant.

—*to keep an eye to* or *on* to watch.

Whilst they were eating it, leaving Mouti to keep an eye to them, he went some way off and sat down on a big ant-heap to think.—H. R. Haggard.

—*to keep in with a man* to remain on friendly terms with him.

I always told your father he thought too much of that Watson; but I would keep in with him if I were you, for they say he's coining money.—*The Mistletoe Bough*, 1885.

—*to keep one's hand in* to employ one's energies; to continue in practice.

You'll find plenty to keep your hand in at Oxford, or wherever else you go.—Hughes.

—*to keep body and soul together* to maintain bare existence.

One of the maids having fainted three times the last day of Lent, to keep body and soul together we put a morsel of roast beef into her mouth.—Maria Edgeworth.

—*to keep dark about anything* to preserve secrecy.

If you have tastes for the theatre and things, don't talk about them; keep them dark.—Besant.

—*to keep to oneself* to be retiring in one's habits; of a reserved disposition.

We do not see much of our neighbours; they live very quietly, and keep to themselves.

—*to keep in view* to have one's aim or attention fixed in a certain direction.
He had always kept in view the probability of a dissolution of the firm.

—*to keep countenance* or *in countenance* to lend moral support to.
Flora will be there to keep you countenance.—R. L. Stevenson.

—*to keep one's countenance* to preserve one's gravity; to refrain from laughing.
The two maxims of any great man at court are, always to keep his countenance, and never to keep his word.—Swift.

—*to keep house.* See **house**.

—*to keep pace with.* See **pace**.

—*to keep in* (a) to refuse to disclose; to preserve secret.
But, please, don't think old Grizzel mean for keeping in what had taken place; she was only obeying orders.—Mrs. Henry Wood.

—(b) to detail schoolboys after the regular hours as a punishment.
He was no more moved than the Roman soldiers, or than the schoolmaster is moved by the sad face of a boy kept in.—Besant.

—*to keep up appearances* to behave as if everything was right.
Captain Cuttle kept up appearances, nevertheless, tolerably well.—Dickens.

keeping—*in keeping* suitable; harmonizing.
It was in keeping (harmonized) with the scenery around.—Mrs. H. Wood.

—*out of keeping* unsuitable; inappropriate.
It was an old room on which George Dallas looked—an old room with panelled walls, surmounted by a curious carved frieze and stuccoed roof, and hung round with family portraits, which gave it a certain grim and stern air, and made the gay hothouse plants with which it was lavishly decorated seem out of keeping.—Edmund Yates.

kettle—*a kettle of fish* a confused state of affairs; a muddle. "Kettle" is here for *kiddle*, a net.
There, you have done a fine piece of work truly. . . . there is a pretty kettle of fish made on't at your house.—Fielding.

key—*the key of a position* the point whose possession gives control over a position or a district. A military phrase.

—*to have the key of the street* to be locked out.
"There," said Lowten, "you have the key of the street."—Dickens.

—*gold key* the badge of a chamberlain.
Hardly will that gold key protect you from maltreatment.—Coleridge.

keystone—*the Keystone State* a popular name for Pennsylvania.
He comes from the Keystone State.

kick—*to kick over the traces* to become violent and insubordinate. A phrase taken from horse-driving.
You must not kick over the traces, or I shall be forced to suppress you, Lady Anne. . . . You are growing a trifle too independent.—H. R. Haggard.

—*to kick the beam* to be deficient in weight; to fly into the air. Said of a scale in a balance.
But in his present survey of the age as his field, he seems to find that a sadder colour has invested all the scene. The evil has eclipsed the good, and the scale, which before rested solidly on the ground, now kicks the beam.—Gladstone.

—*to kick up dust* to carry on a valueless discussion.
Amongst the manuscript riches of the Bodleian, there was a copy of a certain old chronicler about whose very name there has been a considerable amount

of learned dust kicked up.—De Quincey.

—*to kick the bucket* to die.

"The cap'n (captain) will inherit the property after the old bird hops" (his old aunt dies).

"Hops?" repeated Josephine, not understanding him.

"Ay—kicks."

"Kicks? I don't understand."

"Hops the twig—kicks the bucket. How dull you are!"—Chambers's Journal, 1887.

—*to kick up the heels* to die.

His heels he'll kick up,
Slain by an onslaught fierce of hick-up.
Robert Browning.

—*to kick up a row* or *a shindy* to cause a disturbance; to be violent in behaviour.

Master Mash, who prided himself upon being a young gentleman of great spirit, was of opinion that they should kick up a row, and demolish all the scenery.—Thomas Day: Sandford and Merton.

—*to get more kicks than halfpence* to receive more abuse than profit; to be badly or roughly treated.

Let the sweet woman go to make sunshine and a soft pillow for the poor devil whose legs are not models, whose efforts are blunders, and who in general gets more kicks than halfpence.—George Eliot.

—*to kick against the pricks* to struggle with an overmastering force; to refuse to move in a clearly mapped-out path. The phrase is used in the Bible (Acts ix. 5).

My father had quite as little yielding in his disposition, and kicked against the pricks determinedly.—T. A. Trollope.

kidney—*of the same kidney* of the same nature.

Fellows of your kidney will never go

through more than the skirts of a scrimmage.—Hughes.

Kilkenny—*to fight like Kilkenny cats* to fight till the combatants are all torn to pieces. See **cats**.

The tactics of the Kilkenny cats by which the Sultan kept hold of the wretched island were hideously cruel.—Spectator, December 1887.

kill—*to kill two birds with one stone* to effect two results with one expenditure of trouble; to gain two objects by one exertion.

We will kill two birds with one stone—disinter a patient for our leathern gallows, and furnish a fresh incident of the Inquisition.—C. Reade.

—*to kill one's man* to fight a duel with fatal results to one's opponent.

He was a famous shot, had killed his man before he came of age, and nobody scarce dared look at him whilst at Bath.—Maria Edgeworth.

kinchin—*on the kinchin lay.* See **lay**.

kind—*(tribute) in kind* tribute paid, not in money, but in articles of produce.

The Turk, who was a man of strict honour, paid the count by embezzling the tribute in kind of the province he governed.—Beaconsfield.

King—*King's English* the standard English, such as is regarded as good by the highest authorities.

She was the most ignorant old creature that ever was known, could neither read nor write, and made sad jumble of the King's English when she spoke.—G. A. Sala.

—*King's evidence* the evidence of one of a band of criminals who, in order to obtain a pardon, informs against his fellows.

The unhappy man, to save his life, had betrayed his master and turned King's evidence.—G. A. Sala.

—*King Log* one who, having enjoyed a

short popularity, is afterwards treated with contempt. See *Æsop's Fables*, "The Frogs asking for a King." To change King Log for King Stork is to change a stupid but harmless ruler for an oppressor and tyrant.

It is a singular fact that Mr. Emerson is the most steadily attractive lecturer in America. Into that somewhat cold-waterish region adventurers of the sensational kind come down now and then with a splash, to become disregarded King Logs before the next session.—J. R. Lowell.

—*to be unwilling to call the king one's cousin* to be in a state of perfect satisfaction or elation.

He wouldn't condescend to call the king his cousin just at this present time (he is so much elated with his prosperity).—Haliburton.

—*the king of terrors* a name for death. From the Bible (Job xviii. 14).

Her rival was face to face with that king of terrors before whom all earthly love, hate, hope, and ambition must fall down and cease from troubling.—H. R. Haggard.

kingdom—*kingdom come* the next world.

If the face of the master is to be taken as a barometer, we shall all be in kingdom come before long.—Captain Marryat.

kiss—*to kiss hands* to kiss the hand of the sovereign on accepting or retiring from high office.

—*to kiss and be friends* to become reconciled.

"It is not generous of you, Mr Heigham, to throw my words into my teeth. I had forgotten all about them. But I will set your want to feeling against my want of gratitude, and we'll kiss and be friends."—H. R. Haggard.

—*to kiss the rod* to submit to punishment meekly and without complaint.

kite—*to fly a kite* to sustain one's credit by obtaining accommodation bills. A colloquial phrase among commercial men.

Here's bills plenty—long bills and short bills—but even the kites, which I can fly as well as any man, won't raise the money for me now.—Maria Edgeworth.

kith—*kith and kin* relatives, and connections by marriage.

Jason had none of his relations near him. No wonder he was no kinder to poor Sir Condy than to his own kith or kin.—Maria Edgeworth.

kittle—*kittle cattle to shoe* a difficult person to manage.

But I am not so sure that the young lady is to be counted on. She is kittle cattle to shoe.—George Eliot.

knee—*to bow the knee to Baal* to conform to the prevailing or fashionable worship of the day. See the Bible: "Yet I have left me seven thousand in Israel, all the knees which have not bowed to Baal" (2 Kings xix. 18).

Whiggism is always the scorn of thorough-going men and rigorous logicians—is ever stigmatized as a bending of the knee to Baal.—J. Cotter Morison.

—*to bow the knee before* to submit to.

In the course of the year 1859 several of those eminent Frenchmen who refused to bow the knee before the Second Empire had frequent and friendly conversations with Macaulay on the future of their unhappy country.—G. O. Trevelyan.

knife—*war to the knife* deadly strife.

War to the knife now.—C. Reade.

knock—*a knock-out* an auction where the bidders are in collusion.

There are occasional knock-outs and other malpractices in every saleroom in London.—Athenæum, 1887.

—*to knock under* to submit completely.

Our government is not going to knock under because they have suffered a few reverses.—H. R. Haggard.

—*to knock up* (a) to fatigue.

This is my only holiday, yet I don't seem to enjoy it—the fact is, I feel knocked up with my week's work.—S. Warren.

—(b) to awake by rapping at the door.

Then I knocked up old Macniven out of bed.—R. L. Stevenson.

—(c) to call upon; to visit.

He would go home some of these days and knock the old girl up.—H. Kingsley.

—*to knock on the head* to frustrate; to break up; to destroy.

Mr. Hinckley told us some very interesting facts connected with the original survey, and knocked several ignorant delusions on the head.—W. H. Russell.

—*to knock off* (a) to discontinue.

When the varlet knocked off work for the day it was observed that he was possessed of a strange manner.—Besant.

—(b) to cease work.

They gradually get the fidgets. This is a real disease while it lasts. In the workroom it has got to last until the time to knock off.—Besant.

—(c) to prepare; to get ready.

Rover, too—you might easily get up (the part of) Rover while you are about it, and Cassio and Jeremy Diddler. You can easily knock them off: one part helps the other so much. Here they are, cues and all.—Dickens.

—*to knock about* to wander; to travel without definite aim.

I am no chicken, dear, and I have knocked about the world a good deal.—H. R. Haggard.

know—*to know what one is about* to be far-sighted and prudent.

She makes the most of him, because she knows what she is about and keeps a mean.—M. Arnold.

—*to know what's what*. See **what**.

knuckle—*to knuckle down* to acknowledge oneself beaten; to submit.

We knuckled down under an ounce of indignation.—Blackmore.

I had to knuckle down to this man—to

—*to knuckle under* to yield; to behave submissively.

The captain soon knuckled under, put up his weapon, and resumed his seat, grumbling like a beaten dog.—R. L. Stevenson.

—*to rap a man's knuckles* to administer a sharp reproof.

The author has grossly mistranslated a passage in the Defensio pro Populo Anglicano; and if the bishop were not dead, I would here take the liberty of rapping his knuckles.—De Quincey.

L

labour—*a labour of love* work undertaken spontaneously, and not for pay.

That his own thoughts had sometimes wandered back to the scenes and friends of his youth during this labour of love (the composition of the Deserted Village), we know from his letters.—Black's Goldsmith.

lady—*Lady Bountiful* a charitable matron.

Every one felt that since Mrs. Armytage was playing the part of Lady Bountiful, it was better that she should go through with it.—James Payn.

laissez—*laissez-faire* let alone; allowing things to go as they will; absence of intervention or control. French.
Laissez-faire declines in favour; our legislation grows authoritative.—Contemporary Review, 1887.

lamp—*the lamp of Phœbus* a poetical name for the sun.

lance—*a free lance* one attached to no party; one who fights for his own hand.
That he (Defoe) wrote simply as a free lance, under the jealous sufferance of the government of the day.—Minto.

land—*to see how the land lies* to see in what state matters are.
Now I see how the land lies, and I'm sorry for it.—Maria Edgeworth.

—*to make the land* to come in sight of the land as the ship approaches it from the sea.
He made the land the sixth day after leaving Melbourne.

—*the land of the leal* heaven. Originally a Scottish phrase. On one celebrated occasion Mr. Gladstone used the expression erroneously, as applying to Scotland.
We'll meet and aye be fain (loving) In the land of the leal.

> Baroness Nairne.

lapsus—*lapsus linguæ* a slip of the tongue; something said by mistake. Latin.
"I will not answer for anything he might do or say. I only know—"'
"What do you know?"
"More than I choose to say. It was a lapsus linguæ" (I should not have said that I knew anything).—Florence Marryat.

large—*at large* (a) free; at liberty.

If you are still at large, it is thanks to me.—R. L. Stevenson.

—(b) in a wide sense; generally.
Their (the English people's) interests at large are protected by their votes.—W. E. Gladstone.

—*a gentleman at large* a person without any serious occupation.
He was now a gentleman at large, living as best he might, no one but himself knew how.—Miss Braddon.

lark—*to have larks* to indulge in boyish tricks.

—*when the sky falls we shall catch larks* an absurd statement, used to throw ridicule on any fanciful proposition.
The stationary state may turn out after all to be the millennium of economic expectation, but for anything we know the sky may fall and we may be catching larks before that millennium arrives.—Contemporary Review 1886.

late—*late in the day* behind time; too late. Used with reference to long periods.
"I am not going to stand your eternal visits to him."
"You have stood them for twenty years. Rather late in the day to object now, isn't it?" she remarked coolly.—H. R. Haggard.

laugh—*to laugh to scorn* to treat with ridicule.
Lochiel would undoubtedly have laughed the doctrine of non-resistance to scorn.—Macaulay.

—*to laugh in one's sleeve* to smile inwardly while preserving a serious countenance.
His simplicity was very touching. . . . "How they must have laughed at you in their sleeves, my poor Willie!" she answered pityingly.—James Payn.

—*to laugh off* to dismiss with a laugh.
Our baronet endeavoured to laugh off

with a good grace his apostasy from the popular party.—Maria Edgeworth.

—*to laugh out of the other corner or side of the mouth* to be made to feel vexation; to have the laugh turned against a leering person.

"Nonsense!" said Adam. "Let it alone, Ben Cranage. You'll laugh o' th' other side o' your mouth then."—George Eliot.

to laugh on the wrong side of one's face to be humiliated.

By-and-by thou wilt laugh on the wrong side of thy face.—Carlyle.

law—*to have or take the law of any one* to prosecute any one in a law court.

"There's a hackney-coachman downstairs, with a black eye and a tied-up head, vowing he'll have the law of you."

"What do you mean,—law?" Sedley faintly asked.

"For thrashing him last night."—Thackeray.

—*a law of the Medes and the Persians* an unalterable law.

We looked upon every trumpery little custom and habit which had obtained in the school as though it had become a law of the Medes and Persians.—T. Hughes.

—*law abiding* obedient to the laws.

Yet the road is not worthy of this reputation. It has of late years become orderly; its present condition is dull and law-abiding.—Besant.

lay—*the lay or lie of the land* the general features of a tract of country.

Fortunately, they both of them had a very fair idea of the lay of the land; and, in addition to this, John possessed a small compass fastened to his watch-chain.—H. R. Haggard.

—*to lay about* to strike on all sides.

He lustily laid about him; but in

consequence he was brought to the ground and his head cut off.—Bunyan.

—*to lay by* to save; to store away.

He had not yet, it is true, paid off all the mortgages, still less had it been in his power to lay by anything out of his income.—Good Words, 1887.

—*to lay down the law* to speak with authority.

Though it was pleasant to lay down the law to a stupid neighbour who had no notion how to make the best of his farm, it was also an agreeable variety to learn something from a clever fellow like Adam Bede.—George Eliot.

—*to lay the corner-stone* to make a regular beginning.

I verily believe she laid the cornerstone of all her future misfortunes at that very instant.—Maria Edgeworth.

—*to lay heads together* to consult.

Then they laid their heads together, and whispered their own version of the story.—Besant.

—*to lay to heart* to ponder deeply upon.

To do Alice justice, though she listens to such lessons she does not lay them to heart as she might.—Edinburgh Review, 1882.

—*to lay low* to bury.

I saw her laid low in her kindred's vault.—Shakespeare.

—*to lay violent hands on* to murder.

I do believe that violent hands were laid Upon the life of this thrice-famed duke.—Shakespeare.

—*to lay by the heels* to render powerless; to confine. Originally used of imprisonment in the stocks, a punishment inflicted on vagrants and others. The ankles were enclosed in a board, the culprit preserving a sitting posture. See **heels**.

Poor old Benjy! the rheumatiz has much to answer for all through English country sides, but it never played a scurvier trick than in laying thee by the heels.—T. Hughes.

—to lay oneself out for to direct one's energies towards.

"And now," said Mr. Colliber, "you will take chambers in Pall Mall; you will join a club—I can get you into as good a one as you have a right to expect; you will drive in your cab to the office every day; you will lay yourself out for giving dinners.—Besant.

—to be laid up to be unwell; to be confined in one's room with sickness.

He was made so rabid by the gout, with which he happened to be then laid up, that he threw a footstool at the dark servant in return for his intelligence.—Dickens.

—to lay in to store for use on an approaching occasion.

The aboriginal peasantry of the neighbourhood were laying in pikes and knives.—Macaulay.

—to lay it on to exaggerate: to do anything extravagantly.

Now you are laying it on. Surely he could not get so high a salary.

—a lay figure a human model used by an artist.

Meantime you are not to be a lay figure, or a mere negative.—C. Reade.

—to lay to (a) to cease from advancing; to stop. See **lie to**.

"Well, gentlemen," said the captain, "the best that I can say is not much. We must lay to, if you please, and keep a bright look-out."—R. L. Stevenson.

—(b) to be sure of; to be certain regarding.

"Ask your pardon, sir, you would be very wrong," quoth Silver. "You would lose your precious life and you may lay to that."—R. L. Stevenson.

—to lay anything to one's charge to accuse him of it; to hold him responsible for it. Biblical. (See Deut. xxi. 8; Rom. viii. 33).

My scoundrelly enemies did not fail to confirm and magnify the rumour, and would add that I was the cause of her insanity; I had driven her to distraction, I had killed Bullingdon, I had murdered my own son: I don't know what else they laid to my charge.—Thackeray.

—to lay out (a) to spend (of money).

Unluckily all our money had been laid out that morning in provisions.—Goldsmith.

—(b) to invest.

To crown all, Mademoiselle Beatrice is a funded proprietor, and consulted the writer of this biography as to the best method of laying out a capital of two hundred francs, which is the present amount of her fortune.—Thackeray.

—(c) to prepare a corpse for the coffin.

"What am I to do about laying her out?" asked Mrs. Evitt of the doctor.—Miss Braddon.

—(d) to be willing to undertake the charge of.

I have never laid myself out for families. Children are so mischievous.—Miss Braddon.

—the kid of kinchin lay the practice of robbing young children—a special branch of the London thieves' art. See the career of Noah Claypole in *Oliver Twist*.

"You did well yesterday, my dear," said Fagin; "beautiful! Six shillings and ninepence halfpenny on the very first day. The kinchin lay will be a fortune to you."—Dickens.

lead—to lead one a pretty dance to cause one unnecessary trouble.

"Well, my lord," cried Sir Terence, out of breath, "you have led me a pretty dance all over the town."—Maria Edgeworth.

—to lead up to to conduct to gradually and cautiously.

After a little rambling talk the lawyer led up to the subject which so disagreeably preoccupied him.—R. L. Stevenson.

—to lead off to begin.

There were, no doubt, many ardent and sincere persons who seemed to think this as simple a thing to do as to lead off a Virginia reel.—J. R. Lowell.

—to lead up a ball said of the most important couple who open the ball by commencing the dance.

Mr. Thornhill and my eldest daughter led up the ball, to the great delight of the spectators.—Goldsmith.

—to lead by the nose. See **nose.**

leaf—**to take a leaf out of another person's book** to imitate him in certain particulars.

Do you know, Arminius, I begin to think, and many people in this country begin to think, that the time has almost come for taking a leaf out of your Prussian book.—M. Arnold.

—to turn over a new leaf to begin a different mode of life.

I suppose he'll turn over a new leaf, now there's a lady at the head of the establishment.—George Eliot.

leak—**to leak out** to become gradually known (of something which has been kept a secret).

It was plain that the news of his engagement had leaked out through one of those mysterious channels which no amount of care can ever effectually close in such cases.—W. E. Norris.

—to spring a leak to let in water.

Whether she sprang a leak, I cannot find,
Or whether she was overset with wind,
But down at once with all her crew she went.

           Dryden.

leap—**by leaps and bounds** by a series of sudden and rapid advances.

The figures showing the advance by leaps and bounds of Jewish pauperism year after year are no less striking.—Spectator, 1887.

—leap year a year of three hundred and sixty-six days, occurring every fourth year. Ladies are allowed to propose marriage to gentlemen during leap years.

But I don't remember any one having given me an "engaged ring" before; and it's not leap year (the year when ladies propose) neither.—James Payn.

least—**the least said the soonest mended** it is prudent to speak little.

The old lady ventured to approach Mr. Benjamin Allen with a few comforting reflections, of which the chief were, that after all, perhaps it was well it was no worse; the least said the soonest mended.—Dickens.

leather—**leather and prunella (or prunello)** what is on the exterior; non-essential. Prunella is a cloth used by shoemakers in making the uppers of boots.

The question is, How is the book likely to sell? All the rest is leather and prunella (does not matter).—James Payn.

leave—**to leave off** (a) to cease or desist from; to abandon.

First they left off worshipping the gods of Troy.—Besant.

—(b) to discontinue wearing.

He goes in his doublet and hose, and leaves off his wit.—Shakespeare.

—to leave out in the cold to neglect; to exclude from participation in anything.

My boy was to have been her heir, but she had the disposal of her property, and she has bequeathed it all to Cornellis, so my son is left out in the cold.—Chambers Journal, 1888.

—to leave in the lurch. See **lurch.**

leek— *to eat or swallow the leek* to submit to what is humiliating.

One has heard of eating the leek, but that is nothing in comparison with that meal of the Sepoys at Dustybad.—James Payn.

left—*over the left* understand quite the reverse of what is said.

Each gentleman pointed with his right thumb over his left shoulder. This action, imperfectly described by the feeble term "over the left" when performed by any number of ladies and gentlemen who are accustomed to act in unison, has a very graceful and airy effect; its expression is one of light and airy sarcasm.—Dickens.

—*a left-handed compliment* a saying which, though apparently meant to flatter, really depreciates. An unlucky piece of flattery.

His quiet manner left his speech unpunctuated, and his fishy eyes, level voice, and immovable face put no dot to an ambiguous "i," and crossed no "t" in a left-handed compliment.—Mrs. E. Lynn-Linton.

—*on the left hand* in an irregular way.

And then this girl, this Yetta, had Clinton blood in her, if on the left hand, and sadly mixed.—Mrs. E. Lynn Linton.

—*a left-handed oath* an oath which is not binding.

"It must be a left-handed oath," he said, as he obeyed her.—Hugh Conway.

leg—*to give leg-bail* to run off; to escape.

It is by no means improbable that the marauders, with a good start and active horses under them, will have given leg-bail to (eluded) their pursuers.—Daily Telegraph, 1887.

—*on one's legs* erect; about to make a speech.

He (Major Scott) was always on his legs; he was very tedious; and he had
only one topic, the merits and wrongs of Hastings.—Macaulay.

—*on its last legs* about to perish; ready to fall.

I entirely agree with your condemnation of the London coal tax. I read with the utmost satisfaction the denunciation of it by Lord Randolph Churchill. If he holds to his position the tax must be on its last legs.—W. E. Gladstone.

—*without a leg to stand on* having no support.

And that fool Kimble says the newspaper's talking about peace. Why, the country wouldn't have a leg to stand on (would be ruined).—George Eliot.

—*to give a leg up* to help into the saddle.

His friend Tim giving him a leg up, he canters sober John past the stand.—G. J. Whyte-Melville.

—*to stand on one's own legs* to be dependent on no one.

Persons of their fortune and quality could well have stood upon their own legs.—Collier.

—*to make a leg* to bow in the old-fashioned way, drawing one leg backward.

Each made a leg in the approved rural fashion.—A. Trollope.

—*to put one's best leg foremost* to walk or run at the top of one's speed; to hurry. See **foot**.

"Now, you must put your best leg foremost, old lady," whispered Sowerberry in the old woman's ear, "we are rather late."—Dickens.

—*good sea-legs* capacity of standing the motion of a ship at sea without suffering from sea-sickness.

It was one of those doubtful days when people who are conscious of not possessing good sea-legs, and who yet enjoy a sail in moderate weather, are prone to hesitate.—James Payn.

legion—*their name is legion* they are countless; their number is infinite. A phrase taken from the Bible (Mark v. 9).

lend—*to lend a hand* to help.

You see the manufacturers. Here they are, with their wives and daughters. They all lend a hand, and between them the thing is done.—Besant.

length—*at length* (a) at last; after a long time.

And as she watched, gradually her feet and legs grew cold and numb, till at length she could feel nothing below her bosom.—H. R. Haggard.

—(b) to the full extent; omitting nothing.

"I propose to go into the subject at length after breakfast," returned Alexander.—R. L. Stevenson.

—*at full length* stretched out to the full extent.

Here stretch thy body at full length.
                      Wordsworth.

let—*to let off* to excuse; to set free.

We can't let you off, Lady Mona. It is imperative that you should wash your face in sight of us all, and dry it too.—Florence Marryat.

—*to let on* to reveal; to let people know.

"But you won't let on, Ewan, will you?" he said.—Hall Caine.

It is also used of dissimulation.

    He lets on that he is wealthy.

—*to let fly* or *let drive* (a) to discharge a missile with force.

I looked up, and there, as I thought, was the calf. So I got my rifle on and let drive, first with one barrel, then with the other.—H. R. Haggard.

—(b) to aim a blow; to strike at with violence.

He let fly with such stoutness at the giant's head and sides that he made him let his weapon fall out of his hand.—Bunyan.

—*to let out* to disclose; to make known what would otherwise be a secret.

Nave let out one day that he had remonstrated with his daughter in vain.—Mrs. H. Wood.

—*to let alone* to leave unmolested; not to approach.

It really was not poor Aleck's fault. He is gentle as a lamb when he is let alone.—H. R. Haggard.

—*to let well alone* to refuse to interfere where matters are already satisfactory.

—*let alone* a phrase signifying "much less."

I have not had, this livelong day, one drop to cheer my heart,
Nor brown (a copper) to buy a bit of bread with—let alone a tart.
                      Barham.

—*to let one in* to make one responsible without his knowledge.

He was let in for a good hundred pounds by his son's bankruptcy.

—*to let slide* to allow anything to pass unnoticed.

I call this friendly. I asked myself last night, "Will these boys come to see me, or will they let the ragged Yankee slide?" And here you are.—Besant and Rice.

—*to let go of anything* to relax one's hold of it.

He let go of Bessie in his perplexity and fear.—H. R. Haggard.

—*let be!* no matter!

    Leon. Do not draw the curtain.

    Paul. No longer shall you gaze on't, lest your fancy may think anon it moves.

    Leon. Let be, let be!—Shakespeare.

—*to let be* to leave alone.

Would it not be well to let her be, to give him his way and leave her to go hers, in peace?—R. Haggard.

letter—*the letter of the law* the exact

literal interpretation of a law or written document.

Farmer Gray had always the preference, and the hatred of Mr. Hopkins knew no bounds—that is, no bounds but the letter of the law, of which he was ever mindful, because lawsuits are expensive.—Maria Edgeworth.

—**to the letter** exactly; following instructions minutely.

He was overbearing, harsh, exacting, and insisted on his orders being carried out to the letter.—Besant.

red letter See **red**.

level—**to do one's level best** to exert oneself to the utmost of one's power.

His Level Best is the name of a work by a Mr. Hale, published in Boston in 1877.

He did his level best to get me the post.

—**to have one's head level** to be discreet; to have a well-balanced mind. American.

"The jury must be mad!"

"I guess not, Pat. They've the reputation of being a level-headed lot."—Macmillan's Magazine, 1887.

—**to level up** to bring what is lower to an equality with what is higher. First used by Lord Mayo in 1869.

The older officials with smaller salaries applied to have them levelled up to the salaries of the newcomers.

—**to level down** to bring what is higher to an equality with things that are lower.

The Government, however, did the reverse—they levelled down the salaries.

lick—**to lick into shape** to give form or method to a person or thing. The phrase owes its origin to the fable that the cubs of a bear are born shapeless, and are licked into shape by their mother.

"But," said the doctor, as he resumed

his chair, "tell me, Bonnycastle, how you could possibly manage to lick such a cub into shape, when you do not resort to flogging?"*—Captain Marryat.

—**to lick the dust** to fall in battle.

His enemies shall lick the dust. Psalm lxxii. 9.

—**to lick the spittle of** to crouch before; to be meanly servile towards.

His heart too great, though fortune little,
To lick a rascal statesman's spittle.
Swift.

lie—**as far as in one lies** as far as one is able; to the limit of one's powers.

As far as in me lies, I mean to live up to her standard for the future.—Florence Marryat.

—**to give the lie to** to contradict flatly.

When another traducer went the length of including Margaret in the indictment by the assertion that a female relative of Mr. Erin's performed the more delicate work of the autographs, he gave him the lie direct.—James Payn.

—**to lie to one's work** to work vigorously.

They lay to the work and finished it by midday.

—**to lie on hand** to remain unsold.

—**to lie on one's hands** to hang heavily.

Time lay on her hands during her son's absence.

—**to lie with any one** to belong to any one; to be the duty of any one.

The charge of souls lies upon them.—Bacon.

life—**to the life** exactly; so as to reproduce the original person or scene.

Victor Hugo, who delighted in that kind of figure, would have painted him to the life.—Spectator, 1887.

—**as large as life** of the same size as the living being represented.

He marched up and down before the street door like a peacock, as large as life and twice as natural.—Haliburton.

—*to bear a charmed life* to escape death in almost a miraculous manner.
Up and down the ladders, upon the roofs of buildings, over floors that quaked and trembled with his weight, under the lee of falling bricks and stones, in every part of that great fire was he; but he bore a charmed life, and had neither scratch nor bruise.—Dickens.

—*for my life; for the life of me* although I should lose my life as a penalty. A phrase used in strong assertions.
Lucy, for the life of her, could not help fancying there was something in it.—A. Trollope.

lift—*to lift up the eyes* or *face* to look with confidence. A Biblical phrase.
I will lift up mine eyes unto the hills.—Psalm cxxi. 2.
Thou shalt lift up thy face unto God.—Job xxii. 26.

—*to lift up the head* to rejoice; to triumph. Biblical.
And now shall my head be lifted up above mine enemies round about me.—Psalm xxvii. 6.

—*to lift up the heel against* to treat violently (and ungratefully). Biblical.
He that eateth bread with me hath lifted up his heel against me.—John xiii. 18.

—*to lift up the voice* to cry aloud in joy or in sorrow. Biblical.
And Saul lifted up his voice, and wept.—1 Samuel xxiv. 16.
They shall lift up their voice, they shall sing.—Isaiah xxiv. 14.

—*to lift up the horn* to be arrogant in behaviour. Biblical. See **horn**.
Lift not up your horn on high: speak not with a stiff neck (proudly).—Psalm bxv. 5.

light—*to see the light* to be born; to come into actual existence.
The good brother! But for him my poems would never have seen the light.—Besant.

—*to make light of* to treat as of no importance; to disregard.
But my father made light of all plebeian notions.—C. Reade.

to stand in one's own light. See **stand**.

—*to set light by* to undervalue; to despise.

—*to bring to light* to disclose; to make known.
The duke yet would have dark deeds darkly answered; he would never bring them to light.—Shakespeare.

—*to come to light* to become known.
Come, let us go; these things, come thus to light,
Smother her spirits up.
                    Shakespeare.

—*light-fingered gentry* pick-pockets.

—*to light upon* to find; to discover by accident.
M. de Bernard's characters are men and women of genteel society—rascals enough, but living in no state of convulsive crimes; and we follow him in his lively, malicious account of their manners, without risk of lighting upon any such horrors as Balzac and Dumas have provided for us.—Thackeray.

—*light of carriage* loose in conduct.
She was said to be rather light of carriage.—Captain Marryat.

like—*had like* came near. See **have**.

limb—*limb of the law* a member of the legal profession; a lawyer.
Then, when this base-minded limb of the law grew to be sole creditor over all, he takes him out a custodian on all the denominations and sub-denominations.—Maria Edgeworth.

line—*hard lines* harsh treatment; undeserved misfortune.
His wife would be the best person, only it would be hard lines on her.—A. Trollope.

—*the line of beauty* the ideal line

formed by a graceful curve of any kind.

But you know what I mean by the artistic temperament ... that way of taking the line of beauty to get at what you wish to do or say.—W. D. Howells.

—**all along the line** in every particular.

The accuracy of the supposed statements of facts is contested all along the line by persons on the spot.—W. E. Gladstone.

to read between the lines See **read.**

—**the lines are fallen to me in pleasant places** I am fortunate in my wordly surroundings (Ps. xvi. 6).

A lonely wayfarer, happy in the knowledge that his daughter's fate was no longer allied with his, that whatever evil might befall him, her lines were set in pleasant places.—Miss Braddon.

linked—**linked sweetness long drawn out** something which pleases the senses for a considerable time. A line of Milton's *L'Allegro* often quoted.

Lap me in soft Lydian airs,
Married to immortal verse;
Such as the melting soul may pierce,
In notes with many a winding bout
Of linked sweetness long drawn out.
Milton.

lion—**a lion,** or **a great lion** a very popular person.

We (Bulwer and Disraeli) are great lions here (at Bath), as you may imagine.—Disraeli.

—**the lion's share** a disproportionately large share. See Æsop's fable of the lion who went out hunting with a wild ass. "I will take the first share," he said, "because I am king; and the second share, as a partner with you in the chase."

Mr. and Mrs. Armytage had their bottle of champagne, of which the latter, it was rather ill-naturedly said, got the lion's share.—James Payn.

lip—**to make a lip** to have a sullen or mocking expression of face.

I will make a lip at the physician.—Shakespeare.

—**to keep** or **carry a stiff upper lip** to be stubborn or ill-tempered.

It's a proper pity such a clever woman should carry such a stiff upper lip (possess such a bad temper).—Haliburton.

—**to smack one's lips** to express satisfaction.

She enjoyed the supremacy of these names exceedingly, and, to use a very inappropriate (because common) expression, smacked her lips over it.—James Payn.

live—**to live down** to prove an accusation false by a consistent life.

He was beginning to live down the hostility of certain of his neighbours.—W. E. Norris, *in Good Words, 1887.*

—**to live up to anything** to prove oneself by one's life worthy of something excellent. Punch satirizes an æsthetic man and his wife who, having obtained a fine piece of old blue china, resolved "to live up to it."

And try to believe that, so far as in me lies, I mean to live up to her standard for the future.—Florence Marryat.

liver—**white-livered, lily-livered, pigeon-livered, milk-livered** cowardly; meek-tempered. The liver was considered formerly to be the seat of passion and bravery.

Curse him, the white-livered Englishman!—H. R. Haggard.

Go, prick thy face, and over-red thy fear.
Thy lily-livered boy.—Shakespeare.

loaf—**the loaves and fishes** the actual profits; the material benefits. A phrase taken from the New Testament. Christ fed a multitude with some loaves and a few small fishes. Those who followed him not for his teaching, but for the mere gratification of their appetites were said to desire the loaves and fishes.

Thenceforward he was rich and independent, and spared the temptation of playing the political game with any pressing regard to the loaves and fishes of office.—Edinburgh Review, 1887.

lock—*to lock the stable-door after the steed is stolen* to take precautions too late.

When the sailors gave me my money again, they kept back not only about a third of the whole sum, but my father's leather purse; so that from that day out (thenceforward), I carried my gold loose in a pocket with a button. I now saw there must be a hole, and clapped my hand to the place in a great hurry. But this was to lock the stable-door after the steed was stolen.—R. L. Stevenson.

locum—*locum tenens* one who holds a situation temporarily; a substitute. Latin.

And behold, he and his parishioners are given over to a locum tenens.—Nineteenth Century, 1887.

log—*log-rolling* laudatory criticisms in literary reviews bestowed on one another by private friends.

There is certainly no excuse for literary log-rolling. It is a detestable offence.—North American Review, 1887.

loggerheads—*to be at loggerheads; to come, fall,* or *go to loggerheads* to quarrel; to disagree.

A couple of travellers that took up an ass fell to loggerheads which should be his master.—L'Estrange.

loins—*to gird up the loins* to brace oneself for vigorous action.

But her father's will was law to her, and she girded up her spiritual loins and prepared for the encounter.—Mrs. E. Lynn Linton.

Lombard Street—*Lombard Street to a China orange* something very valuable staked against a thing of little value; very long odds. Lombard Street, in London, near the Bank of England, is a centre of great banking and mercantile transactions.

"It is Lombard Street to a China orange," quoth Uncle Jack.

"Are the odds in favour of fame against failure really so great?" answered my father.—Bulwer Lytton.

long—*at* or *in the long-run* eventually; before all is over.

A statesman in the long-run must yield to royal solicitation.—G. O. Trevelyan.

—*the long and the short of a matter* a matter viewed briefly in its most important aspects; the important principle, or fact, contained in any statement.

The long and short of the matter is, that on getting off the lake, after seven hours' rowing, I felt as much relieved as if I had been dining for the same length of time with Her Majesty the Queen.—Thackeray.

—*to draw* or *pull the long bow* to exaggerate.

King of Corpus (who was an incorrigible wag) was on the point of pulling some dreadful long bow, and pointing out a half-dozen of people in the room as R. and H. and L., etc., the most celebrated wits of that day.—Thackeray.

—*by a long chalk* very considerably.

Soon after Bordeaux she had words (quarrelled) with the lions. They, in their infernal conceit, thought themselves more attractive than Djek, "It is vice versa, and by a long chalk" (very much so), said Djek and Co.—C. Reade.

look—*to look after* to attend to; to pay careful attention to.

I assured you that when the trust was paid I would look after her.—Besant.

—**look you!** please observe what I am saying.

It was a place where professional singers—women, too, look you, nearly as bad as dancers, not to say actresses—came and sat on a platform and sang for money.—Justin M'Carthy.

—**to look alive, or look sharp** to hurry; to be quick; to act promptly.

"Tell young gent to look alive," says guard, opening the hind-boot.—T. Hughes.

Their life, bitter as it was, would be bitterer if they did not look sharp and learn a good many texts.—C. Reade.

—**to look sharp after** to watch carefully.

The moment I became her sole guardian, I had sworn on my knees she should never kill another man: judge whether I had to look sharp after her.—C. Reade.

—**to look blue** to show signs of disgust or disappointment.

Squire Brown looks rather blue at having to pay two pounds ten shillings for the posting expenses from Oxford.—T. Hughes.

—**to look daggers** to gaze upon with anger.

There he sits abaft the mainmast looking daggers at us.—C. Reade.

—**to look up** to improve; to grow brighter; to be in demand.

"Things are looking up, Jeremiah," he said in a tone of exultation.—B. L. Farjeon.

—**to look a person up** to visit him.

But Lucy would have me come and look you up; and I assure you I had rather face a battery of my own cannon.—The Mistletoe Bough, 1885.

—**to look in upon** to visit informally.

"I had no idea you had a visitor here, Mrs. Jennynge," he said.

"Yes; Miss Joceline was so good as to look in upon us."—James Payn.

—**to look in the face** to examine boldly; to refuse to shrink from examining.

It was many a day, however, before she could look her own misfortune in the face.—James Payn.

—**to look to** to take care of.

She hated to water her flowers now; she bade one of her servants look to the garden.—C. Reade.

—**that is your look out** you must provide against that.

If he chooses to vote for the devil, that is his look-out.—O. W. Holmes.

—**to look out** to guard against dangers; to take precautions; to be careful.

Time sometimes brings its revenges, and if it does, you may look out, Mrs. Bellamy.—H. R. Haggard.

—**to look over** (a) to read over.

Meet presently at the palace; every man look o'er his part; for, the short and the long is, our play is preferred.—Shakespeare.

—(b) to overlook; to allow to pass.

He forgave her, and looked over her conduct.—Murray's Magazine, 1887.

—**to look for a needle in a haystack** to search after anything with very little chance of finding it.

—**to look through coloured spectacles** to see things not as they really are, but distorted by one's own prejudices.

People who live much by themselves are apt to look at things through coloured spectacles.

—**to look forward to** to expect with feelings of pleasure.

The children are all looking forward to your visit.

—**to look about one** to be cautious and wary.

John began to think it high time to look about him (take precautions for the future).—Arbuthnot.

loose—*to loose one's purse-strings* to

give money towards some good object.

—*on the loose* dissipated.

Her husband is, I fear, on the loose just now.

—*a loose fish* a dissipated man.

In short, Mr. Miles was a loose fish.—C. Reade.

having a tile loose See **tile**.

lord—*a lord of creation* a man (as distinguished from a woman). The term is generally used jocularly.

No; I had rather be a woman, with all her imperfections, than one of those lords of creation, such as we generally find them.—G. J. Whyte-Melville.

lose—*to lose caste* to be no longer welcomed in the houses of respectable people.

You may break every command in the decalogue with perfect good breeding, nay, if you are adroit, without losing caste.—J. R. Lowell.

—*to lose heart* to become dispirited.

Deprived of solid support in the rear, the men in front will probably lose heart, and be easily driven away or arrested.—Fortnightly Review, 1887.

—*to lose the day* to be defeated.

You will be shot, and your houses will be burnt, and if you lose the day those who escape will be driven out of the country.—H. R. Haggard.

loss—*to be at a loss* to be unable to decide.

Jane herself was quite at a loss (quite bewildered) to think who could possibly have ordered the piano.—Jane Austen.

love—*love in a cottage* marriage without a sufficient income to live in the fashionable world.

Lady Clonbrony had not, for her own part, the slightest notion how anybody out of Bedlam could prefer, to a good house, a decent equipage, and a proper establishment, what is called love in a cottage.—Maria Edgeworth.

—*there is no love lost between them* they dislike each other.

There is no great love lost between the English Conservative Cabinet and the Bulgarian Government.—Fortnightly Review, 1887.

—*to make love to* to woo; to court.

"And you're making love to her, are you?" said Cute to the young smith.

"Yes," returned Richard quickly, for he was nettled by the question; "and we are going to be married on New Year's day."—Dickens.

luck—*down on one's luck* See **down**.

lucky—*to cut* or *make one's lucky* to run off; to decamp.

He (Fagin) might have got into trouble if we hadn't made our lucky.—Dickens.

lucus—*lucus a non lucendo* An etymological pun. *Lucus*, which means a dark grove, seems to be connected with *lucco*, to shine, but is not. This derivation rests on a principle of contradiction.

Thus Verdant's score was always on the lucus a non lucendo principle of derivation, for not even to a quarter of a score did it ever reach.—Verdant Green.

lug—*in lug* pawned.

My fiddle is in lug just now.

—*to lug in* to introduce violently; to drag in without sufficient cause.

It doesn't matter what the subject is, always provided that he can lug in the bloated aristocrat and the hated Tory.—Besant.

lump—*a lump sum* a sum which includes many small items: a sum given at one time to cover several smaller payments.

The amounts asked for should be granted in a lump sum to the imperial Government.—Daily Telegraph, 1885.

—*to make friends* to become reconciled.

He is a generous fellow, and will soon make friends with you again.

—*to make good* to make compensation for; to pay in full.

On looking into his affairs he found enough to fill him with dismay—debts, mortgages, mismanaged estates, neglected cottages, the mansion going to ruin, besides all his old arrears to be made good (paid up).—Quarterly Review, 1887.

—*to make head* or *headway against* to progress; to strive successfully against some obstacle.

I think, Mr. Goslett, that if she'd only hold her tongue and go to sleep, I might make headway with that case in the morning.—Besant.

—*to make light of* to treat as unimportant.

Up to the present time he had made rather light of the case, and as for danger, he had pooh-poohed it with good-humoured contempt.—C. Reade.

—*to make much of* to treat with great favour.

As his wife had remarked, he always made much of Gwendolen, and her importance had risen of late.—George Eliot.

—*to make of* to give a reason for; to account for.

I began to feel a pain I knew not what to make of (which I could not satisfactorily account for) in the same joint of my other foot.—Sir W. Temple.

—*to make off* to run away.

The holder of a horse at Tellson's door, who made off with it, was put to death.—Dickens.

—*to make out* (a) to discover; to find out exactly; to understand.

It is not everybody who can make her out (understand her character).—Good Words, 1887.

—(b) to establish; to prove.

There is no truth which a man may more evidently make out (prove) to himself than the existence of a God.—Locke.

—(c) to contrive.

What with foreboding looks and dreary death-bed stories, it was a wonder the child made out to live through it.—O. W. Holmes.

—*to make over* to transfer in a legal manner.

Shelley made over to her a part of his income, and she retained all that she received from her own family.—Edinburgh Review, 1882.

—*to make up for anything* to compensate for it; to supply a deficiency caused by it.

She was very hard at work—no doubt endeavouring to make up for her husband's repeated absences.—Hugh Conway.

—*to make up a quarrel* to become friendly.

He remembered, in his careless way, that there had been a quarrel, and that he wanted to make it up, as he had done many a time before—Good Works, 1887.

—*to make it up* or *make up matters* to become friendly again; to be reconciled.

Oh, how she longed to make it up with him!—Thomas Hardy.

—*to make up to* to seek the acquaintance of; to pay court to.

Young men of spirit are sadly afraid of being thought to make up to a girl for her money.—Justin M'Carthy.

—*to make up with* to become reconciled to; to regain the good will of

Many a rascally captain has made u with his crew, for hard usage, by

allowing them duff twice a week on the passage home.—R. H. Dana.

malt—*to have the malt above the wheat* or *meal* to be drunk.

When the malt begins to get above the meal (company begins to get drunk), they'll begin to speak about government in Kirk and State.—Scott.

mammon—*the mammon of unrighteousness* wealthy and worldly people. A Biblical expression.

Make to yourselves friends of the mammon of unrighteousness.—Luke xvi.9.

So Rebecca, during her stay at Queen's Crawley, made as many friends of the mammon of unrighteousness as she could possibly bring under control.—Thackeray.

man—*man alive!* an exclamation of astonishment. Used where one hears or imparts startling information.

"You are wasting my time with your silly prattle," said Meadows sternly. "Man alive! you never made fifty pounds cash since you were calved."—C. Reade.

—*to a man* every one without exception.

They had, to a man, been willing enough to give their verdict for the old man's execution.—H. R. Haggard.

—*a man of Belial* a wicked, depraved person. A Scriptural phrase in common use.

"Susan," replied Isaac, "you are good and innocent. You cannot fathom the hearts of the wicked. This Meadows is a man of Belial.'—C. Reade.

—*a man of his word* a truthful or trustworthy person. See **word**.

—*a man of straw* an unreal person; a product of the imagination.

This plotter, this deceiver of the innocent, on whom you vent your indignation, is a mere man of straw.

The reality is a very peaceable, inoffensive character.

—*a man of letters* a literary man; an author.

As a man of letters Lord Byron could not but be interested in the event of this contest.—Macaulay.

—*a man of the world* a man who is well acquainted with society and the world at large; a man whose interests lie in worldly things.

What Mr. Wordsworth had said like a recluse, Lord Byron said like a man of the world.—Macaulay.

—*the man in the moon* an imaginary person who inhabits the moon, and is supposed to be ignorant of worldly affairs.

She don't know where it will take her to, no more than the man in the moon.—Haliburton.

—*a man Friday* a faithful and subservient fellower. See Defoe's *Robinson Crusoe.*

Count Von Rechberg, according to Lord Clarendon, was Prince Bismarck's man Friday.—Athenæum, 1887.

—*every man-jack* every man, high or low; all without exception.

There happened, too, to be a man-of-war in harbour, every man-jack, or rather, every officer-jack of which, with the exception of those on watch, was there.—H. R. Haggard.

—*you'll be a man before your mother* a jocular expression of encouragement to a lad. Used on a historical occasion by Burns in addressing Sir Walter Scott, then a boy.

You mind your business half as well as I mind mine, and you'll be a man before your mother yet.—H. Kingsley.

manner—*by no manner of means; not by any manner of means* quite the contrary; in no way; on no account.

Not that he was, by any manner of

means, possessed with the greatness of his own ideas, but that Mrs. Fermitage, from a low velvet chair, looked up at him with such emphatic inquiry and implicit faith that he was quite in a difficulty how to speak or what to say.—R. D. Blackmore.

many—*too many* or *one too many* too powerful or crafty; more than a match.

"Ay! ay!" thought he; "the Irishman is cunning enough. But we shall be too many for him."—Maria Edgeworth.

mare—*to make the mare to go* to make a display of prosperity; to carry out undertakings. Generally found in the expression, "Money makes the mare to go."

I'm making the mare to go here in Whitford—without the money, too, sometimes.—C. Kingsley.

—*to find a mare's nest* to make an absurd discovery; to make a discovery which turns out to be a hoax.

He retired with a profusion of bows and excuses, while Mr. Reginald Talbot followed in silence at his heels like a whipped dog, who, professing to find a hare in her form, has only found a mare's nest.—James Payn.

—*shanks's mare* the legs.

I am riding shanks's mare (walking) to-day.

—*the gray mare* a name given to a woman who is cleverer than her husband.

There is no equalizer of sexes like poverty or misery, and then it very often proves that the gray mare is the better horse.—Burroughs.

marines—*tell that to the marines* an expression implying incredulity.

Unless you can put your information together better than that, you may tell your story to the marines on board the Pelorus.—H. Kingsley.

mark—*to make one's mark* to distinguish oneself.

The atmosphere of society is scientific and æsthetic, and its leaders, although bound to be moderately well off, have, for the most part, made their mark by their brains.—Edinburgh Review, 1882.

—*(God) bless the mark!* a superstitious utterance, originally used to avert evil. Afterwards it came to have very little meaning = "I beg your pardon."

To be ruled by my conscience, I should stay with the Jew my master, who (God bless the mark!) is a kind of devil.—Shakespeare.

—*God save the mark* an invocation to God for mercy.

I saw the wound, I saw it with my eyes—God save the mark!—here on his manly breast.—Shakespeare.

—*beside the mark* inappropriate; out of place.

There is a circle of elect spirits, to whom the whole strain of this paper will, it is most likely, seem to be beside the mark.—W. E. Gladstone.

—*to mark time* (of soldiers) to raise the feet alternately as if on the march.

With the swinging easy step of those accustomed to long and toilsome marches, the detachment moved rapidly forward, now lessening its front as it arrived at some narrow defile, now marking time to allow of its rear coming up without effort into the proper place.—G. J. Whyte-Melville.

—*up to the mark* in good condition or form.

Bob, although he had been a very short time before brutally knocked upon the top of the kitchen fire, was up to the mark, and appeared ready for action.—H. Kingsley.

marriage—*marriage lines* a marriage certificate.

All she saved from the fire was a box

containing her marriage lines and other important papers.

marrow—*to go down on one's marrow-bones* to kneel.

He shall taste it instead of me, till he goes down on his marrow-bones to me.—C. Reade.

mashed—*to be mashed upon* to be in love with; to be a devoted admirer of. A *masher* is a dandy who dresses so as to "kill".

I'm not one bit mashed to upon her, and I don't want her to be mashed upon me; and she wouldn't be in any case; but she interests me, and she's a dear little Vinnie.—Justin M'Carthy.

massacre—*the massacre of the innocents* the announcement by the leader of the House of Commons at the end of a session of the measures that are abandoned for want of time. The historical massacre of the innocents took place at Bethlehem, after the birth of Christ. Matt. ii.).

mast—*to sail* or *serve before the mast* to be a common sailor. The sailors' quarters, or forecastle, are in the bow of the vessel. Richard Henry Dana, jun., has written a well-known book, *Two Years before the Mast*—that is, two years as a common sailor. Compare "In the ranks," said of a private soldier. See **rank**.

And, indeed, bad as his clothes were, and coarsely as he spoke, he had none of the appearance of a man who sailed before the mast.—R. L. Stevenson.

matter—*a matter of course* something which naturally follows; a thing which excites no surprise or attention.

As for the certificate which Sir Henry Maine awarded us, we took it, I fear, very much as a matter of course.—Nineteenth Century, 1887.

—*matter-of-fact* unimaginative; prosaic.

Extricating her, as he seemed always to do, from her unpleasant dilemma and her matter-of-fact swain.—G. J. Whyte-Melville.

mauvaise—*mauvaise honte* awkwardness; clumsy shyness. French.

He had, he said, been always subject to mauvaise honte and an annoying degree of bashfulness, which often unfitted him for any work of a novel description.—A. Trollope.

May—*May meetings* religious meetings held yearly in Exeter Hall, London.

"Do you know, I have never been in London but once, and then to attend the May meetings."—D. Christie Murray.

mealy—*mealy-mouthed* soft-spoken; using mild language; afraid to speak out.

She was a fool to be mealy-mouthed where nature speaks so plain.—L'Estrange.

mean—*to mean well* or *kindly by* to have friendly intentions towards; to intend to aid or benefit.

He had meant well by the cause and the public.—Macaulay.

—*a mean white* a name used in the Southern States of America and elsewhere, as in South Africa, where the white race is in a minority, to signify "a white man without landed property."

—*by all means* certainly; assuredly.

Mr. Elton, just as he ought, entreated for the permission of attending and reading to them again.

"By all means. We shall be most happy to consider you one of the party."—Jane Austen.

—*by no means* certainly not.

The wine on this side of the lake is by no means so good as that on the other.—Addison.

measure—*to measure swords with*

another to fight with him, using the sword as a weapon.

So we measured swords and parted.— Shakespeare.

—to measure one's length on the ground to fall flat.

*If you will measure your lubber's length again (wish to be thrown down flat again), tarry.—*Shakespeare.

—to measure strength to engage in a struggle.

*The factions which divided the prince's camp had an opportunity of measuring their strength.—*Macaulay.

—to take the measure of a man's foot to see what is his character; to decide mentally how much a man is fit for or will venture to do.

*The natives about Mooifontein had pretty well taken the measure of John's foot by this time. His threats were awful, but his performances were not great.—*H. R. Haggard.

meet—*to meet another half-way* to come to terms with him on the basis of mutual concessions; to treat an antagonist in a conciliatory spirit.

*Margaret was indignant with her cousin that he did not respond to his father's kindness with more enthusiasm. "If he had behaved so to me, Willie, I should have met him half-way," she afterwards said reprovingly.—*James Payn.

memento—*a memento mori* something which recalls death. Strictly speaking, the phrase **memento mori** means, "remember to die."

*I make as good use of it (thy face) as many a man doth of a death's head or a memento mori. I never see thy face but I think on hell fire.—*Shakespeare.

merry—*to make merry* to indulge in laughter and joking; to enjoy oneself.

They made merry at the poor farmer's plight.

The king went to Latham to make merry with his mother and the earl.— Bacon.

miching—*miching mallecho* underhand mischief. A Shakespearian phrase (*Hamlet*, act iii, scene 2). **Miching** means hiding or skulking; **malecho** is Spanish, meaning an evil action.

His very step was thievish—miching mallecho—and his eyes shot from side to side, as though he mistrusted the darkness, as, perhaps, he did.— D. Christie Murray.

midsummer—*midsummer madness* utter lunacy.

He had shown great imprudence in paying attentions to Hester, even in her former position, but to renew them under her changed circumstances would be midsummer madness.— James Payn.

might—*with might and main* with all one's energy and resources.

*With might and main they chased the murderous fox.—*Dryden.

mild—*draw it mild* do not exaggerate.

*Draw it a little milder, Coombe, do. Make it four or five, and it will be much nearer the mark.—*Florence Marryat.

milk—*to cry over spilt milk* to indulge in useless regrets.

But it's no use crying over spilt milk.— Blackmore.

—milk-and-water tasteless; having an insipid character; feeble. Also, as a noun, what is insipid.

*A milk-and-water bourgeois (timid, feeble-minded citizen).—*C. Reade.

—the milk of human kindness natural feelings of pity, sympathy and generosity.

I fear thy nature; it is too full of the milk of human kindness to catch the nearest way.

Shakespeare.

*The milk of human kindness was not curdled in her bosom.—*A. Trollope.

miller—*to drown the miller* to put too much water in anything.

This punch is not worth drinking—you've drowned the miller.

milling—*milling in the darkness* murder at night.

Men were men then, and fought in the open field, and there was nae milling in the darkness (no midnight murder).—Scott.

mince—*to mince matters* or *the matter* to gloze over; to represent in too favourable a light; to be mealy-mouthed.

But not being a woman much given to mincing matters, she puts her meaning beyond a doubt by remarking that she had heard tell people sent to Paris for their gowns, just as though America wasn't good enough to make one's clothes.—Edinburgh Review, 1887.

mincemeat—*to make mincemeat of* to shatter; to completely destroy; to demolish.

We should have made mincemeat of them all, and perhaps hanged up one or two of them outside the inn as an extra sign-post.—G. A. Sala.

mind—*mind your eye* be careful.

"Perhaps it may be so," says I; "but mind your eye, and take care you don't put your foot in it."—Haliburton.

mint—*a mint of money* a large fortune.

She went on as if she had a mint of money at her elbow. Maria Edgeworth.

mischief—*to play the mischief with* to ruin; to over turn.

Don't you know that you will play the very mischief with our vagus nerves?—Wm. Black.

miss—*a miss is as good as a mile* a failure is a failure whether one comes very near succeeding or not.

*Had the tie parted one instant sooner, or had I stood an instant longer on the yard, I should inevitably have been thrown violently, from the height of ninety or a hundred feet, overboard; or, what is worse, upon the deck.

However, a miss is as good as a mile*—a saying which sailors very often have occasion to use.—R. H. Dana.

missing—*the missing link* a creature between a man and a monkey, the discovery of which is necessary to the establishment of the theory of the descent of men from monkeys. The name is often applied to men who resemble monkeys.

We had a tutor at college who rejoiced in the name of the "missing link."

mistletoe—*kissing under the mistletoe.* It is usual in England and other countries at the festive Christmas season to hang up a sprig of mistletoe from the ceiling. When a girl passes under the mistletoe she may be kissed. The practice is a source of much merriment.

mitten—*to get the mitten* to make an offer of marriage and be rejected.

There is a young lady I have set my heart on, though whether she is going to give me hers, or give me the mitten, I ain't quite satisfied.—Haliburton.

—*to handle without the gloves* or *without mittens* to treat unceremoniously; to deal roughly with. See **handle.**

modus—*a modus vivendi* mutual agreement under which people can live in harmony. Latin.

Surely it was possible for them to construct a sufficiently pleasant modus vivendi, even if they held somewhat different views on political matters—Wm. Black.

month—*a monthy of Sundays* an indefinitely long period.

He could easily have revenged himself by giving me a kick with his heavy shoes on the head or the loins, that would have spoiled my running for a month of sundays.—C. Reade.

moon—*a moonlight flitting* a secret removal by night of tenants who are unable to pay the rent of their house.

—*shooting of moons* the same as the above.

I bought his houses, I let his houses; I told him who were responsible tenants, I warned him when shooting of moons seemed likely.—Besant.

more—*to be no more* to be dead.

Cassius is no more.

Shakespeare.

—*more and more* with a continual increase.

As the blood passeth through narrower channels, the redness disappears more and more.—Arbuthnot.

morning—*the gray of the morning* the early morning.

But above all things, have good care to exercise this art before the master strides up to his desk in the gray of the morning.—Blackmore.

mother—*does your mother know you're out?* a quizzical expression used to a person who seems too simple and childish to take care of himself.

I went and told the constable my property to track;

He asked me if I didn't wish that I might get it back.

I answered, "To be sure I do! it's what I'm come about."

He smiled and said, "Sir, does your mother know that you are out?"

Barham.

—*mother-wit* natural sagacity; good sense.

It is extempore, from my mother-wit.—Shakespeare.

—*mother's apron strings* a phrase used to signify "watchful maternal care" of a child too young and thoughtless to take care of itself.

Little Smith, fresh from his mother's apron-strings, is savagely beaten by

the cock of the school, Jones.—H. R. Haggard.

mount—*to mount guard* to act as sentinel.

Their destination reached, they picnicked as they had arranged, and then separated, the bride and bridegroom strolling off in one direction, Mildred and Arthur in another, while Miss Terry mounted guard over the plates and dishes.—H. R. Haggard.

mountain—*to make a mountain of a mole-hill* to magnify a small matter, making it unnecessarily important.

Stuff and nonsense, Segrave! you're making mountains out of mole-hills, as you always do.—Good Words, 1887.

—*mountain-dew* Scotch whisky.

mouth—*down in the mouth* disappointed.

But upon bringing the next ashore, it proved to be only one great stone and a few little fishes; upon this disappointment they were down in the mouth.—L'Estrange.

—*by word of mouth* verbally.

The message was given by word of mouth; it was not written.

—*to have the mouth water* to have feelings of anticipated enjoyment; to look at with intense longing.

For 'tis said he lives bravely where he is; yea, many of them that are resolved never to run his hazards, yet have their mouths water at his gain.—Bunyan.

move—*to move heaven and earth* to make every possible effort.

But of course all the Plumstead and Framley set will move heaven and earth to get him out, so that he may not be there to be a disgrace to the diocese.—A. Trollope.

much—*much of a muchness* very similar; differing but slightly.

The miller's daughter could not believe that high gentry behaved badly to their wives, but her mother instructed her. "O child, men's men (men are men); gentle or simple (gentry or common people) they're much of a muchness.—George Eliot.

mud—*to throw mud at* to abuse; to speak evil of.
A woman in my position must expect to have more mud thrown at her than a less important person.—Florence Marryat.

mug—*to mug-up* to prepare for an examination. A college phrase.
I must go home and mug-up for next Saturday.

mull—*to make a mull of it* to be awkward and unsuccessful.
"I always make a mull of it," he said to himself when the girls went up to get their hats.—A. Trollope.

mummy—*to beat to a mummy* to thrash soundly; to give a severe drubbing to.
The two highwaymen caught the informer and beat him to a mummy.

mump—*mumping-day* the 21st of December, a day on which the poor were accustomed to go about the country begging. To *mump* is to "beg" or "cheat."

murder—*murder will out* a saying which refers to the great difficulty of keeping a crime secret. The phrase is now current about secret deeds which are not crimes.
Murder, the proverb tells us, will out; and although, of course, we do not know how many murders have remained undiscovered, appearances seem to lend support to the theory.—W. E. Norris.

mute—*mute as a fish* wholly silent.
Miss Kiljoy might have screamed; but, I presume, her shrieks were stopped by the sight of an enormous horse-pistol which one of her champions produced, who said, "No harm is intended you, ma'am; but if you cry out we must gag you," on which she suddenly became as mute as a fish.

mutton—*to eat one's mutton* to dine.
"Will you eat your mutton with me to-day, Palmer?" said Mr. Williams at the gate of the jail.—C. Reade.

N

Naboth—*Naboth's vineyard* a neighbour's possession coveted by a rich man. The reference is to King Ahab (1 Kings xxi, 1–10), who coveted the vineyard of Naboth the Jezreelite, and finally obtained it by foul means.
He was well aware that the little Manor House property had always been a Naboth's vineyard to his father.—Good Words, 1887.

nail—*to nail one's colours to the mast* to refuse obstinately to surrender.

"There," he said, "I've nailed my colours to the mast. That will show these gentry that an Englishman lives here."—H. R. Haggard.

—*on the nail* (a) immediately; without delay.
I'll give you twenty pounds down ... twenty pounds on the nail.—Besant.

—(b) ready money. A plate of copper on which bargains are settled in Liverpool Exchange is called "The Nail." *Remember every share you bring in* brings you five per cent, down on the nail.—Thackeray.

—*to hit the nail on the head* to say what is exactly applicable to the case; to discover the real remedy for anything.

How he hits the nail on the head! . . . What noble common sense appears in such criticism as this!—*Macmillan's Magazine*, 1887.

—*a nail in one's coffin* a facetious name for a glass of strong liquor—gin, whisky, or brandy.

name—*to name the day* to fix the day for marriage.

So, soon after, she named the day.— C. Reade.

—*to call a person names* to speak disrespectfully to a person; to use nicknames to him.

When he called his mother names because she wouldn't give up the young lady's property . . . how the ladies in the audience sobbed!—Dickens.

—*to take a name in vain* to use the name thoughtlessly or irreverently; to swear profanely by the name.

Thou shalt not take the name of the Lord they God in vain.—Exod. xx. 7. I always call Chancery "it." I would not take its name in vain for worlds.—H. R. Haggard.

nap—*to go nap* to stake all the winnings. A phrase taken from the game of nap, or napoleon.

He heard what they said. "They've squared it; it's a moral. Now's the time: I'm going nap on Morning Light" (a racehorse).—B. L. Farjeon.

napping—*to take* or *catch one napping* to find him unprepared; to surprise him when off his guard or asleep.

No, George, Tom Weasel won't be caught napping twice the same year.—C. Reade.

narrow—*the narrow house* or *home* the grave.

I feel like those would-be saints of old who bespoke their coffins years before they had occasion for them, and all day long used to contemplate their narrow home.—James Payn.

nature—*in a state of nature* naked.

The man was found in the cave in a state of nature, and raving mad.

naught—*to set at naught* to disregard.

Be you contented to have a son set your decrees at naught.— Shakespeare.

ne—*ne plus ultra* nothing further; the extreme limit. Latin.

There stood on the Spanish coast a pillar with the words ne plus ultra inscribed upon it. After the discovery of American the ne was taken out.

Of all the pleasures of the exercise of charity, the very greatest (to some minds) is the satisfaction afforded by the fact of the recipient of our bounty having once occupied a social position equal or superior to our own. This is the ne plus ultra of the delights of patronage.—James Payn.

near—*the near side of a horse* the side on the rider's or the driver's left.

—*to be near* to be stingy or parsimonious.

With all her magnificent conduct as to wasting alcoholic treasure, she was rather near.—Conway.

neat—*neat as a pin* very neat and tidy.

Everything was as neat as a pin in the house.—R. H. Dana.

neck—*neck and neck* keen and close; close together (of two competitors in a contest).

They reached the last fence neck-and-neck, Haphazard landing slightly in advance.—G. J. Whyte-Melville.

—*to break the neck of anything* to accomplish the stiffest part of it.

Blow-hard was a capital spinner of a yarn when he had broken the neck of his day's work.—Hughes.

—*on the neck of* immediately after.

> Instantly on the neck of this came news that Fernando and Isabella had concluded a peace.—Bacon.

—*neck and crop* completely.

> Finish him off, neck and crop; he deserves it for sticking up to a man like you.—Blackmore.

—*a stiff neck* obstinacy in sin. A Scriptural phrase.

> Speak with a stiff neck.—Ps. lxxv. 5.

—*neck and heels* in a hasty and summary fashion.

> There is no doubt that when the poor fellow tried to get into the pulpit, they took him and carried him neck and heels out of the church.—A. Trollope.

—*neck verse* a sentence of Scripture which, when repeated by a criminal, saved him from capital punishment. See **benefit of clergy.**

> Poor'rogue! he was soon afterwards laid by the heels and swung; form there is no neck verse in France to save a gentleman from the gallows.—G. A. Sala.

—*neck or nothing* a braving of all dangers; the risking of everything.

> "If it is neck or nothing on my side, sir, it must be neck or nothing on yours also!"
>
> "Neck or nothing by all means," said Noel Vanstone.—Wilkie Collins.

needle—*to get the needle* to get irritated.

needs—*needs must when the devil drives* one must submit, however ungracefully, to hard necessity.

> "What, you are in your tantrums again!" said she. "Come along, sir. Needs must when the devil drives."—C. Reade.

nem—*nem. con.* a contraction for *nemine contradicente* (Latin) = no one dissenting.

> This resolution was agreed to nem. con.

> The general, too, understood these details thoroughly, and therefore it was disrespectful youth voted nem con, that Newton-Hollows was "a rare shop at feeding-time."—G. J. Whyte-Melville.

Neptune—*a son Of neptune* a sailor. Neptune was the god of the sea in Roman mythology.

> This son of Neptune, dying suddenly, left all his little property to a degenerate nephew, who hated salt water.—R. Buchanan.

nest—*to feather one's nest* to provide for one's future; to lay by money.

> It may do him some harm, perhaps, but Dempster has feathered his nest pretty well (saved a considerable sum of money); he can afford to lose a little business.—George Eliot.

—*a mare's nest* See **mare**

—*a nest-egg* something laid by as a start or commencement. In a nest where hens are expected to lay, it is customary to place a real or imitation egg to tempt the hens to lay others beside it. This egg is called the *nest-egg.*

> Books or money laid for show,
> Like nest-eggs, to make clients lay.
>   S. Butler.

> At present, however, as Margaret reminded her cousin, there was not enough of them—though so far as they went they had a marine value—to become nest-eggs; they could not be considered as savings or capital to any appreciable extent.—James Payn.

never—*never say die* don't despair.

> Will you give him my compliments, sir—No. 24's compliments—and tell him I bid him never say die?—C. Reade.

—*I never did* an exclamation of astonishment.

> "I never did!" exclaimed Eliza Sampson, when her brother had read the brief letter aloud.
>
> Eliza was always protesting that she

never did. This somewhat unmeaning phrase was her favourite expression of astonishment.—Miss Braddon.

Newcastle—*Newcastle hospitality* roasting a friend to death.

Newgate—*to be in Newgate* to be a criminal. Newgate is the great prison of London.

"No doubt he ought to be in Newgate," said the other emphatically.—James Payn.

next—*next to nothing* almost nothing. *Her table the same way, kept for next to nothing.—Maria Edgeworth.*

—*next door to* very close to; almost. *She observed to that trusty servant that Colonel Arden was next door to a brute.—Theodore Hook.*

—*next one's heart* very dear to one. *They could talk unreservedly among themselves of the subject that lay next their hearts.—James Payn.*

nicety—*to a nicety* exactly; with extreme accuracy. *The room was all arranged to a nicety.*

nick—*in the nick of time* exactly at the right moment. *Things are taking a most convenient turn, and in the very nick of time.— James Payn.*

—*in the nick* at the right moment. *He gave us notice in the nick, and I got ready for their reception.—Maria Edgeworth.*

—*old Nick* the devil. *And the old man began to step out as if he was leading them on their way against old Nick.—Haliburton.*

night—*a night-cap* a warm drink taken before going to bed.

nightmare—*the nightmare and her nine-fold* frightful apparitions which appear at night. Probably *nine-fold* stands for "nine foals." See Shakespeare's *King Lear*, act iii, scene 4. *St. Withold footed thrice the old, He met the nightmare and her nine-fold.*

Stars shoot and meteors glare oftener across the valley than in any other part of the country, and the nightmare with her whole nine-fold seems to make it the favourite scene of her gambols.—Washington Irving.

nil—*nil admirari* admiring nothing. Latin. *To the last, I believe, his London nil admirari mind hardly appreciated the fact of its being real cold snow.—H. Kingsley.*

nine—*a nine days' wonder* something which causes great excitement for a short time and then is heard of no more. *King Edward. You'd think it strange if I should marry her. Gloucester. That would be ten days' wonder at the least. Clarence. That's a day longer than a wonder lasts.—Shakespeare.*

—*to the nines* to perfection; splendidly. *This gallant, good-natured soldier flattered her to the nines.—C. Reade.*

—*nine tailors make a man* a popular saying in contempt of tailors. A tailor is often called the ninth part of a man.

nip—*to nip a bung* to steal a purse. *Meanwhile the cut-purse in the throng, Hath a fair means to nip a bung. Popular Ballad, 1740.*

—*to nip in the bud* to destroy at an early state, before any mischief is done. *From the above it is quite clear that the king had ample warning of the rising, and possessed the means of nipping it in the bud.—Fortnightly Review, 1887.*

no—*no go* of no use. *"These 'lection buns are no go." said the young man John.—O. W. Holmes.*

—*no end* a very great sum; a great deal. *Times are so hard. Box at the opera no end (costs a great sum).—C. Reade.*

nob—*a nob of the first water* a very

high-class personage. *Nob* is a contraction for nobleman.

One comfort, folk are beginning to take an interest in us; I see nobs of the first water looking with a fatherly eye into our affairs.—C. Reade.

noblesse—*noblesse oblige* this phrase implies that a person in a high position is constrained to perform his duties well by a sense of his position: high rank has its obligations. A French phrase.

That fine-grained pride of place which is best expressed in those two majestic words noblesse oblige.—Mrs. E. Lynn Linton.

nod—*a nod is as good as a wink to a blind horse* there is no use repeating a sign to those who cannot or do not choose to see.

Thinks I to myself, a nod is as good as wink to a blind horse.—Haliburton.

—*the land of nod* sleep.

*But every night I go abroad
Afar into the land of nod.*

         R. L. Stevenson.

nom—*nom de guerre* a name assumed for a time. A war-name. French.

Hobart, being then a post-captain ashore with nothing to do, took a prominent part, under the nom de guerre of Captain Roberts.—Spectator, 1887.

—*nom de plume* a fictitious name assumed by an author. A pen-name. French. For example:

           nom de plume.

Marian Evans:	George Eliot.
Madame Dudevant:	George Sand.
Charles Dickens:	Boz (in his earlier writings).
William Makepeace Thackeray:	Michael Angelo Titmarsh.

Several of the pieces published in 1801

under the nom de plume of Thomas Little were written before he (Moore) was eighteen.—Encyclopædia Britannica, 9th ed.

nonce—*for the nonce* temporary; not habitual. Also used as an adverb temporarily. From "then once."

Vivian was not under the necessity of paying any immediate courtesy to his opposite neighbour, whose silence, he perceived was, for the nonce, and consequently for him.—Beaconsfield.

nose—*with one's nose at the grindstone* hard at work. Generally used of mechanical or uninteresting work.

The clerks, with their noses at the grindstone, and her father sombre in the dingyroom, working hard too in his way.—Mrs. Oliphant.

—*to snap one's nose off* to speak in a cross tone to any one; to address a person sharply.

"I observe that Mr. John's things have not been laid out for him properly, as they ought to have been," she said suddenly, snapping his nose off, as Jervis said.—Mrs Oliphant.

—*to measure noses* to meet.

We measured noses at the cross roads.

—*to make a person's nose swell* to make him jealous.

—*to turn up one's nose at* to look with contempt upon.

He has the harsh, arrogant, Prussian way of turning up his nose at things.—M. Arnold.

—*to put a man's nose out* or *out of joint* to supplant him; to mortify him. This phrase is also found in the form **his nose has lost a joint.**

He was jealous of her (the elephant)—afraid that she would get as fond of some others as of him, and so another man might be able to work her, and his own nose lose a joint, as the saying is.—C. Reade.

Perhaps Maurice may be able to drive Lanfrey out of the field—put his nose out of joint, and marry the girl himself.—Mrs. E. Lynn Linton.

—*to cut off one's nose to spite one's face* to act from anger in such a way as to injure oneself.

One of it's (jealousy's) commonest and least startling effects is that species of moral suicide which is best described by the vulgar adage of "cutting off one's nose to spite one's face," and which produces that most incomprehensible of all vagaries termed "marrying out of pique."—G. J. Whyte-Melville.

—*to lead by the nose* to influence a person so that he follows him blindly.

Though authority be a stubborn bear, yet he is often led by the nose with gold.—Shakespeare.

He showed a certain dogged kind of wisdom in refusing to be led by the nose by the idle and ignorant chatterboxes against whom he was thrown in the parlour of the public-house.—H. Kingsley.

—*to take pepper in the nose* to take offence.

—*to put* or *thrust one's nose into another's affairs* to interfere with another person's affairs unwarrantably.

I liked the man well enough, and showed it, if he hadn't been a fool and put his nose into my business—C. Reade.

—*under one's nose* in one's immediate proximity; close to one.

Poetry takes me up so entirely that I scare see what passes under my nose.—Pope.

—*to pay through the nose* to pay an extravagant price.

Sooner than have a fuss, I paid him through the nose everything that he claimed.—A. Trollope.

not—*not a bit of it* not at all; in no way.

"Well, for one thing, we ought all to be here."—"Not a bit of it," responded Dick.—Blackwood's Magazine, 1887.

note—*a note of hand* a promissory note; a paper containing a promise to pay a certain sum of money.

"Why, my dear lad," he cried, "this note of hand of Shakespeare's, priceless as it is, may be yet outdone by what remains to be discovered."—James Payn.

now—*now and then* at intervals; occasionally. Used both of place and time.

A mead here, there a heath, and now and then a wood.—Drayton.

He (Lord Byron) now and then praised Mr. Coleridge, but ungraciously and without cordiality.—Macaulay.

nowhere—*to be nowhere* to fail to secure a leading place.

In fiction, if we accept one or two historical novels, which avowedly owe their existence to a laudable admiration of Scott, Italy is literally nowhere.—Athenæum, 1887.

null—*null and void* of no effect; useless. A legal phrase.

The document began by stating that the testator's former will was null and void.—H. R. Haggard.

number—*number one* a person's self.

Some conjurers say number three is the magic number, and some say number seven. It's neither, my friend, neither; it's number one.—Dickens.

nunky—*nunky pays* the Government pays for everything. *Nunky* here stands for "Uncle", short for "Uncle Sam." The letters U.S. stamped on United States government property, were jocularly read "Uncle Sam." "Uncle Sam" thus came to mean the Government, and gave rise to the phrase **to stand Sam**, which see.

Walk through a manufactory, and you
see that the stern alternatives,
carefulness or ruin, dictate the saving
of every penny; visit one of the
national dockyards, and the comments
you make on any glaring wastefulness
are carelessly met by the slang phrase.
"Nunky pays."—Herbert Spencer.

nut—*to be nuts to* to please greatly.

To edge his way along the crowded
paths of life, warning all human
sympathy to keep its distance, was
what the knowing ones called nuts
(excessive pleasure) to Scrooge.—
Dickens.

—*to be nuts on anything* to be
extremely fond of it.

My aunt is awful nuts on Marcus
Aurelius.—Wm. Black.

—*off one's nut* crazy; mad. *Nut* is a
slang term for the head.

He was getting every day more off his
nut, as they put it gracefully.—J.
M'Carthy.

—*a hard nut to crack* a difficult problem to solve.

On the contrary, he unflinchingly faced
a third question, that, namely, of the
true wishes of the testator, whose will
had been made known some hours
before; and really this was rather a
hard nut to crack.—Good Words,
1887.

nutshell—*to lie in a nutshell* to be capable of easy comprehension or
solution.

There was no need to refer to Heimann
or any one else. The whole thing lay
in a nutshell.—Murray's Magazine,
1887.

—*in a nutshell* simply and tersely.

That one admission of yours, "he is
almost entirely dependent on his pen,"
states the whole case for me in a
nutshell.—James Payn.

O

oak—*sport one's oak*. See **sport**.

oar—*to put in one's oar* to interfere
officiously in others' affairs; to break
into a conversation uninvited.

I put my oar in no man's boat.—
Thackeray.

—*to lie or rest on one's oars* to cease
from hard work; to take an interval
of rest.

I had finished my education . . . So I
left Paris, and went home to rest on
my oars.—C. Reade.

oats—*to sow one's wild oats* to indulge
in youthful dissipation and excesses.

Dunsey's taste for swopping
(exchanging) and betting might turn
out to be something more than sowing
wild oats.—George Eliot.

observe—*the observed of all observers*
the centre of attraction. A quotation
from Shakespeare's *Hamlet*, act iii.
scene 1.

The glass of fashion and the mould of
form,
The observed of all observers!

We children admired him: partly for
his beautiful face and silver hair; partly
for the solemn light in which we beheld
him once a week, the observed of all
observers, in the pulpit.—R. L.
Stevenson, in Scribner's Magazine,
1887.

occasion—*on occasion* when necessary; at certain times.

Then they went on to give him instructions. He was to start at once—that very week, if possible; he was to follow certain lines laid down for his guidance; on occasion he was to act for himself.—Besant.

—*to take occasion* to seize an opportunity.

In rummaging over a desk to find a corkscrew, young Ludgate took occasion to open and shake a pocket-book, from which fell a shower of bank-notes.—Maria Edgeworth.

odds—*at odds* (a) opposed to; differing from.

Mr. Pilgrim had come mooning out of the house, at odds with all the festivity and tired of the crowd.—J. M. M'Carthy.

—(b) at a disadvantage.

What warrior was there, however famous and skilful, that could fight at odds with him?—Thackeray.

—*odds and ends* stray articles; casual pieces of information; things picked up in different places.

Then there was poor Jacob Dodson, the half-witted boy, who ambled about cheerfully, undertaking messages and little helpful odds and ends for every one.—T. Hughes.

—*by long odds* by a great difference; most decidedly.

He is by long odds the ablest of the candidates.

—*no odds* it's of no consequence.

"I have lost my hat." "No odds. Come without one."

odour—*in bad odour* ill spoken of; having a bad reputation.

Mat Crabtree would not be hindered from wrapping up the girls and handing them to their seats by the trifling objection that he was in bad odour with both of the women.—Sarah Tytler.

—*odour of sanctity*. It was at one time believed that the corpse of a holy person emitted a sweet perfume. The expression "odour of sanctity" is now used figuratively: "He died in the odour of sanctity" = "He died having a saintly reputation."

The whitewashed shrine where some holy marabout lies buried in the odour of sanctity.—Grant Allen, *in* Contemporary Review, *1888*.

off—*to be off* to refuse to come to an agreement.

At last when his hand was on the door they offered him twelve thousand five hundred. He begged to consider of it. No, they were peremptory. If he was off, they were off.—C. Reade.

—*well off* in comfortable circumstances.

He seemed to be very well off as he was.—Miss Austen.

—*be off with you!* go away. A peremptory order.

"Be off with you! Get away, you minx!" he shouted.—H. R. Haggard.

—*off and on* at intervals: sometimes working, sometimes doing nothing.

"Dear me! Now that's very interesting," said Mr. Josceline; "you could have got two shillings a line, if you pleased, for writing a poem that took you how long?"

"Well, perhaps two months, off and on."—James Payn.

—*off-hand* (adj.) free and easy; without stiffness.

Having a bluff, off-hand manner, which passed for heartiness, and considerable powers of pleasing when he liked, he went down with the school in general for a good fellow enough.—T. Hughes.

—(adv.) without preparation or calculation; immediately.

The strong-minded Lady Southdown quite agreed in both proposals of her son-in-law, and was for converting Miss Crawley off-hand.—Thackeray.
He can give you off-hand any information about the capital you may want.

—**off by heart** committed to memory.
A day or two afterwards, Mr. Quirk, in poring over that page in the fourth volume of Blackstone's Commentaries where are to be found the passages which are to be found the passages which have been already quoted (and which both Quirk and Gammon had got off by heart), fancied he had at last hit upon a notable crotchet.—S. Warren.

—**off one's head** crazed; distracted.
The fact was, the excellent old lady was rather off her head with excitement.—James Payn.

—**off colour** shady; disreputable.
His reputation and habits being a trifle off colour, as the phrase is, he had fallen back on a number of parasitical persons, who, doubtless, earned a liberal commission on the foolish purchases they induced him to make.—Wm. Black.

office—**to give the office** to forewarn; to tell beforehand.
Then back after me; I'll give you the office. I'll mark you out a good claim.—C. Reade.

oh—**oh yes** a corruption of *oyez* (listen), the cry of heralds making a proclamation.
Well, then, said the crier, "Oh yes! oh yes! His Majesty's—I mean her Majesty's—court is now opened.'—Haliburton.

oil—**to oil one's old wig** to make the person drunk. North of England slang.

—**to pour oil on troubled waters** to pacify matters; to act as peacemaker.
In my telegrams and letters to The Times I did all in my power to throw oil on the troubled waters, by explaining mutual misunderstandings, and combating the false accusations made on both sides.—H. Mackenzie Wallace.

—Used of the actual process
Not a barrel of water fell upon the Arno's deck. I believe this may with safety be claimed as one of the earliest recorded instances of the practical application of oil to the troubled waters.—Scribner's Magazine, 1887.

—**oil of palms** money. See **palm**.

—**to strike oil** (a) to come upon a bed of petroleum.
I knew it (the oil) was there, because I'd been in Pennsylvania and learned the signs; it was only the question whether I should strike it.—Besant and Rice.

—(b) to make a valuable discovery of any kind.

ointment—**a fly in the ointment** that which spoils the freshness or excellence of anything. See *Bible* (Eccles. x. 1).
The homely vein running through her own four daughters of whom not one was really pretty, and some were really plain, was a very blue-bottle in my lady's ointment.—Mrs. E. Lynn Linton.

o.k.—**o.k.** facetious contraction for "all correct" = "all right".

old—**old as the hills** very ancient.
My dear child, this is nothing new to me—to any one. What you have experienced is as old as the hills.—Florence Marryat.

—**an old maid** an unmarried woman who has passed the usual age for marriage, and is likely to die single.
During her papa's life, then, she resigned herself to the manner of existence here described, and was content to be an old maid.—Thackeray.

olive—*to hold out the olive branch* to make overtures of reconciliation.

The sudden appearance in these circumstances of Chamberlain with the olive branch in his mouth adds piquancy to the scene.—The Times, 1886.

—*an olive branch* a child. See Ps. cxxvii. 3. The Bible expression is olive plant. "Thy wife shall be as a fruitful vine by the sides of thy house; thy children like olive plants round thy table."

This young olive branch, notorious under the name of Timothy's Bess's Ben, had advanced beyond the group of women and children.—George Eliot.

on—*on for anything* ready to engage in it.

Are you on for a row on the river?

once—*once and for all* finally; irrevocably. Also *once for all*.

I must tell you once and for all that you will get nothing by kneeling to me.—H. R. Haggard.

—*once upon a time* a somewhat old-fashioned and pedantic phrase used to introduce an incident or story which took place at some indefinite time in the past.

Once upon a time—of all the good days in the year, on Christmas eve—old Scrooge sat busy in his counting-house.—Dickens.

—*once in a way* sometimes; at long intervals; on rare occasions. Also found in the form *once and away*.

She knew he was of no drunken kind, yet once in a way a man might take too much.—Blackmore.

—*once and again* repeatedly; often.

I have told you once and again that you must not smoke in this room.

one—*one of these days* soon; shortly.

He repeatedly reasoned and remonstrated with Mr. Titmouse on the

improiety of many parts of his conduct—Titmouse generally acknowledging, with much appearance of compunction and sincerity, that the earl had too much ground for complaint, and protesting that he meant to change altogether one of these days.—S. Warren.

—*one too many for a person* more powerful or cunning than he.

I rather fancy we shall be one too many for him.—W. E. Norris.

—*at one* agreed; in harmony; of the same mind.

We have read treatises by the dozen on style and rhetoric from Blair to Bain, and there is none that we should be inclined ourselves to adopt as a class-book. So far we are at one with Mr. Morley.—Journal of Education, 1887.

—*one-horse* third-rate; poor; insignificant.

One of them destroyed Manitoulin, my island of the blest, with a few contemptuous criticisms. It was, he declared, a very one-horse sort of place.—W. H. Russell.

open—*with open arms* gladly; with a warm welcome.

They were both received with open arms by the mayor and old Dewar.—C. Reade.

—*an open secret* a piece of information not formally declared, yet known to every one.

It was an open secret that almost every one (of Lord Palmerston's ecclesiastical appointments) was virtually made by Lord Shaftesbury.—Leisure Hour, 1887.

—*open as the day* utterly without deception or hypocrisy.

Open as the day, he made no secret of the fact that he was alone in the world.—James Payn.

—*open sesame* a phrase which causes doors to open. See, in the *Arabian*

Nights' Entertainments, the story of Ali Baba and the Forty Thieves. When Ali Baba uttered the words "Open sesame," the door of the robbers' cave opened.

*The spell loses its power; and he who should then hope to conjure with it would find himself as much mistaken as Cassim in the Arabian tale, when he stood crying, "Open wheat," "Open barley," to the door which obeyed no sound but "Open sesame."—*Macaulay.

to open the ball. See **ball**.

—*an open question* a fact or doctrine about which different opinions are permitted.

Whether the army is sufficiently organized, or sufficiently provided, or sufficiently well led, may be an open question.—Spectator, 1887.

—*to open the eyes of a person* to make him aware of the real state of affairs.

This last flagrant case of injustice opened the commissioner's eyes.

opinion— *to be of opinion* to judge; to consider.

Mrs. Sedley was of opinion that no power on earth would induce Mr. Sedley to consent to the match between his daughter and the son of a man who had so shamefully, wickedly, and monstrously treated him.—Thackeray.

orange—*orange blossoms* brides wear orange blossoms.

"How is the amiable and talented Mr. Staunton?" inquired this person jocosely; "and what has he come to this lovely retreat for? To gather orange blossoms?" (get a bride).—W. E. Norris.

—*a sucked orange* a man whose powers are exhausted.

By this time Dibdin was a sucked orange; his brain was dry.

order—*to take order* to take steps or measures; to make provision.

Is any rule more plain than this, that whoever voluntarily gives to another irresistible power over human beings is bound to take order that such power shall not be barbarously abused?—Macaulay.

—*to take orders* to become a clergyman.

Though he never could be persuaded to take orders, theology was his favourite study.—Macaulay.

—*in orders* belonging to the clerical profession.

"What!" interrupted I, "and were you indeed married by a priest, and in orders?" (a regular clergyman).—Goldsmith.

—*the order of the day* what every one is striving after.

Economy in the public service is the order of the day.—Westminster Review, December 1887.

—*the orders of the day* the list of *agenda* in a legislative body—for example, the House of Commons.

other—*the other day* lately; some time ago.

Did you see what the brigands did to a fellow they caught in Greece the other day?—H. R. Haggard.

out—*to be out* to be mistaken.

"Oh, there you are out, indeed, Cousin Wright; she's more of what you call a prude than a coquette."—Maria Edgeworth.

—*to be out with any one* to have a disagreement with the person.

If you are out with him, then I shall not visit him.

—*out-and-out* thoroughly; completely.

Now, I'm as proud of the house as any one. I believe it's the best house in the school, out-and-out.—Hughes.

—*to have it out with any one* to have

an altercation with some one on a certain subject.

One day when the two old officers return from their stroll, Mrs. Bunch informs the colonel that she has had it out with Eliza.—Thackeray.

—*out of the way* odd; quaint; unusual.

Besides, he had always something amusing to say that lessened our toil, and was at once so out of the way, and yet so sensible, that I loved, laughed at, and pitied him.—Goldsmith.

—*out of sorts* (a) indisposed; not in good bodily condition.

I am out of sorts, however, at present; cannot write. Why? I cannot tell.—Macaulay.

—(b) in bad humour; ill-pleased.

Was this the pale, sad soul who had come away from England with us, out of sorts with the world, and almost aweary of her life?—Wm. Black.

—*to out-Herod Herod* to be extravagant in one's language; to storm as an actor. Herod was a typical tyrant.

"I fancy," said he, "your praise must be ironical, because in the very two situations you mention I think I have seen that player out-Herod Herod, or, in other words, exceed all his extravagances."—Smollett.

—*out of place* unsuitable; improper.

All this delicate consideration for the feelings of an impecunious young person was deplorable and out of place.—James Payn.

—*out of pocket* (a) actually paid. As in the phrase "out of pocket expenses."

—(b) put to expense.

He was both out of pocket and out of spirits by that catastrophe.—Thackeray.

—*out of print* not now printed.

—*out of collar* without a place. Servant's slang.

The old butler has been out of collar since last autumn.

out at elbows See **elbow.**

out of the question. See **question.**

—*out of the wood* escaped from a difficulty or danger.

You are not out of the wood (safe from danger) yet.

—*an out-and-outer* a thorough-going fellow; one pre-eminent in any capacity.

Master Clive was pronounced an out-and-outer.—Thackeray.

outrun—*to outrun the constable* to become bankrupt.

A minute of the financial board, published in the Cambridge Reporter, shows that the university is in danger of outrunning the constable.—Journal of Education, 1887.

over—*over and above* in addition; besides; extra.

—*over and over* frequently, repeatedly.

She had (heard) though—over and over again. For it was Toby's constant topic.—Dickens.

—*over the left* understand the contrary of what is said.

The cook will suit you very well—over the left.

Exp.—*He will not suit you at all.*

overland—*an overland farm* a farm without any house upon it. Devonshire dialect.

owl—*to take owl* to be offended.

own—*to own up* to confess.

What do you want I should own up about a thing for, when I don't feel wrong.—W. D. Howells.

P

P—*to mind one's p's and q's* to be careful in one's behaviour.

I think that this world is a very good sort of world, and that a man can get along in it very well if he minds his p's and q's.—A. Trollope.

—*to be p and q* to be of the first quality.

*Bring in a quart of maligo, right true.
And look, you rogue, that it be p and q.*
Rowlands (1613).

pace—*to try an animal's paces; to put an animal through its paces* to find out how it goes. A horse walks, ambles, trots, canters, gallops—these are its different paces, which an intending purchaser will examine before he strikes a bargain.

I had, in the usual forms, when I came to the fair, put my horse through all its paces.—Goldsmith.

—*to try a man's paces* to see what are his qualities.

We take him (the preacher) at first on trial, for a Sabbath or two, to try his paces.—Haliburton.

—*to keep pace with* to keep alongside of; to go at the same speed as; to progress equally with.

Agriculture (in the States) has kept pace with manufacturing industry, while it has far outstripped commerce.—Edinburgh Review, 1882.

pack—*to talk pack-thread* to use improper language skilfully disguised.

—*to be packing* to go off; to leave a place.

Now, be packing; I do not wish to see you again.

—*to pack cards* to cheat; to act unfairly.

She has packed cards with Cæsar (entered into a deceitful compact with Cæsar).—Shakespeare.

—*to send a man packing* to dismiss him summarily; to send him off.

Is none of my lads so clever as to send this judge packing?—Macaulay.

pad—*a pad in the straw* something wrong.

—*to pad the hoof* to walk.

"What do you mean?" asked Lambert, staring in amazement. "You would not have Susie pad the hoof because the bank has failed?"—Sarah Tytler.

paddle—*to paddle your own canoe* to manage your own affairs without help.

*My wants are small, I care not at all
If my debts are paid when due;
I drive away strife in the ocean of life.
While I paddle my own canoe.*
H. Clifton.

paddock—*to turn paddock to haddock* to dissipate property. A provincial Norfolk phrase.

pains—*to be at pains* to take trouble; to be careful.

She delivered it for the behoof of Mr. Chick, who was a stout, bald gentleman, with a very large face, and his hands continually in his pockets, and who had a tendency in his nature to whistle and hum tunes, which, sensible of the indecorum of such sounds in a house of grief, he was at some pains to repress at present.—Dickens.

paint—*paint red*. See **red**.

pair—*a pair of stairs* a flight of stairs; a staircase.

Indeed, the hostess of that evening has since been economizing up two pair of stairs at Antwerp.—G. J. Whyte-Melville.

—*to pair* or *pair off* (a) (of a member of Parliament) to abstain from voting, having made an arrangement with a member of the opposite side that he shall also abstain. A customary Parliamentary practice.

Mr. W. B. Barbour has paired with Mr. T. Lynn Bristowe from the 14th for the remainder of the session.—The Scotsman.

—(b) to take as a partner.

He paired off with Miss Sedley, and Jos squeezed through the gate into the gardens with Rebecca on his arm.—Thackeray.

pale—*to leap the pale* to get into debt; to spend more than one's income.

palm—*to palm off anything* to pass anything under false pretences; to get another to accept ignorantly a false article.

Once upon a time a Scotchman made a great impression on the simple native mind in Natal by palming off some thousands of florins among them at the nominal value of half-a-crown.—H. R. Haggard.

—*to bear the palm* to be pre-eminent. The leaves of the palm tree were used as symbols of victory. A palm leaf or branch was carried before a conqueror.

It was certain that with Mr. Freeman for editor, the essential element of illustrative maps would not be neglected; but his own, which are admirably selected, bear the palm.—Athenæum, 1887.

—*to give the palm to* to acknowledge as superior.

Having discussed the subject of

nationality and love, Mr. Finch gives the palm without hesitation to American love.*—Literary World, August 25, 1887.

—*palm oil* money. So called because it "greases the palm."

The enterprising sight-seer who proceeds on this plan, and who understands the virtue of "palm oil" and a calm demeanour, is sure to see everything he cares to see.—C. Dickens, Jun., in Dictionary of London.

pan—*to pan out* to result; to appear in the consequences. American slang.

She didn't pan out well.—Wm. Black.

to savour of the pan. See savour.

Pandōra—*pandora's box* a collection of evils. In the legend of Prometheus, Pandora (the all-gifted goddess) is said to have brought from heaven a box containing all human ills, which, the lid having been opened, escaped and spread over the world.

Pandora's box was opened for him, and all the pains and griefs his imagination had ever figured were abroad.—Mrs. E. Lynn Linton.

paper—*a paper lord* a lord of justiciary; a judge bearing the title of lord. A Scottish phrase.

—*a paper war* a dispute carried on in writing.

par—*at par* neither above nor below the nominal value.

He (George II.) gave Englishmen no conquests, but he gave them peace and ease and freedom, the three per cents. nearly at par, and wheat at five and six and twenty shillings the quarter.—Thackeray.

pari—*pari passu* simultaneously; in a like degree. A Latin phrase.

Again, assuming that English repetition was taught in the lowest forms, and some way up the school, should it be carried on pari passu with Latin up to the sixth?—Journal of Education, 1887.

parish—*to come upon the parish*. See **come**.

parsnip—*fine words butter no parsnips* fair promises do not clothe or feed the persons to whom they are made.
Who was the blundering idiot who said that fine words butter no parsnips? Half the parsnips of society are served and rendered palatable with no other sauce.—Thackeray.

part—*part and parcel* an essential part; what is inseparably bound up with something else.
"Well, Mr. Squeers," he said, welcoming that worthy with his accustomed smile, of which a sharp look and a thoughtful frown were part and parcel, "how do you do?"—Dickens.

—*of parts* able.
The occasion was one which required a man of experience and parts to hold the office.—Edinburgh Review, 1886.

Parthian—*a Parthian shaft* a last shot; a parting missile. The Parthians, it is said, were accustomed to shoot while retiring on horseback at full speed.
Becky watched her marching off, with a smile upon her lip. She had the keenest sense of humour, and the Parthian look which the retreating Mrs. O'Dowd flung over her shoulder almost upset Mrs. Crawley's gravity.—Thackeray.

parti—*parti pris* prejudice; fondness for a cause already espoused. A French phrase.
Still, after making allowance for parti pris, and for some lack of extended inquiry, the book is valuable.—Athenæum, 1887.

pass—*to pass by* to overlook; to refrain from punishing; to excuse.
God may pass by single sinners in this world.—Tillotson.

—*to pass muster* to bear examination; to be sufficiently good not to be rejected.
An intruder in the throng, a comparative stranger and a secret spy, might pass muster and escape detection, if not absolutely, at least to a great extent.—Sarah Tytler.

—*to pass off (as)* (a) to secure acknowledgement or recognition (as).
They pass themselves off as an old married couple.—James Payn.
One of these passengers being a child still young enough to be passed off as a child in arms.—H. Conway.

—(b) to cease; to be discontinued.
For a few nights there was a sneer or a laugh when he knelt down, but this passed off soon.—T. Hughes.

—(c) to dismiss from notice; to let pass.
Work-girls are horribly afraid of gentlemen, though they pass it off with cheek and chaff.—Besant.

—*to pass over* to take no notice of; to condone.
One could see she was vain, and forgive it—she had a right to be vain; that she was a coquette, and pass it over—her coquettishness gave piquancy to her beauty.—S. Baring-Gould.

—*to come to a pretty pass* to be in a bad state.
Things are coming to a pretty pass when you take me to task for not being in earnest.

passage—*a passage of arms* a dispute; a quarrel real or playful.
As for Mrs. A. and Mrs. B., it seemed as if they were unable to encounter one another without a passage of arms.—Good Words, 1887.

passing—*passing rich* very wealthy. Passing is frequently used as an intensive by Shakespeare.
A man he was to all the country dear.

And passing rich on forty pounds a
year.
                                    Goldsmith.

—*a past-master* a thoroughly experienced person; and "old hand."
*If you are ambitious of excelling in that
line, you had better take a few lessons
from your friend Monckton, who is past-
master in the art of humbugging his
audiences.*—W. E. Norris.

patch—*not to be a patch on another
person* to be in no way comparable to
him.
*He is not a patch on you for looks
(much inferior to you in personal
appearance).*—C. Reade.

—*to patch up a reconciliation* to
return, but only in appearance, to a
formerly friendly footing; to make
a temporary truce.
*"It was perturbing, assuredly, and it
might have served, if Linda hadn't
written: that patched it up," I said,
laughing.*—H. James, Jun., *in
Harper's Monthly*, February 1888.

patrimony—*the patrimony of St. Peter*
the states of the Church; the land formerly subject to the Pope.

patter—*to patter flash* to talk thieves'
language.

pave—*to pave the way* to make ready;
to prepare the way; to facilitate the
introduction of.
*Her triumph, though, was short-lived,
and but paved the way to Lord Lytton's
final expedient.*—*Westminster Review*,
December 1887.

pay—*to pay out* to have satisfaction or
revenge from.
*"Did you see what the brigands did to
a fellow they caught in Greece the
other day for whom they wanted
ransom? First they sent his ear to his
friends, then his nose, then his foot,
and last of all his head. Well, dear
Anne, that is just how I am going to
pay you out."*—H. R. Haggard.

—*to pay court* to show flattering
attentions.
*The very circumstance of his having
paid no court to her at first operated
in his favour.*—Maria Edgeworth.

—*to pay the debt of nature* to die.
*Coleridge is just dead, having lived just
long enough to close the eyes of
Wordsworth, who paid the debt of
nature but a week or two before.*—C.
Lamb.

—*to pay one's way* to pay one's daily
expenses without going into debt; to
meet one's obligations; to live free of
debt.
*A British merchant will have to sell a
great many pounds of sugar and yards
of calico before he can have earned
enough to pay his way.*—*Spectator*,
1887.

to pay the piper. See **piper**.

—*the devil to pay* a severe penalty; very
serious consequences.
*"I must go home, else I shall be locked
out."
"There would be the devil to pay
then," says Dick, standing up too and
stretching like a big Newfoundland.*—
Rhoda Broughton.

—*to pay through the nose* to pay an
absurdly high price.
*Although that crafty and rapacious
slave-dealer would have made him
pay through the nose for his treasure,
knowing the physician to be a man of
great wealth, he forbore in very shame
from his extortion.*—G. A. Sala.

peace—*to keep the peace* a legal
phrase, signifying "to refrain from
causing a disturbance." A man who
has been guilty of an offence—for
instance, a man who has threatened
another with violence—is "bound
over to keep the peace" for a certain
period under heavy penalties.

—*bound over to the peace* obliged to

be well-behaved; under severe penalties in case of misbehaviour.

Mr. Layard, once a daring and somewhat reckless opponent of government and governments, had been bound over to the peace, quietly enmeshed in the discipline of subordinate office.—J. M'Carthy.

—*to hold one's peace* to keep quiet; to be silent.

She said, and held her peace: Æneas went Sad from the cave.—Dryden.

—*peace at any price* the name given to a party of politicians in the English Parliament who object to war under all conditions.

The well-educated, thoughtful middle-class, who knew how much of worldly happiness depends on a regular income, moderate taxation, and a comfortable home, supplied most of the advocates of peace, as it was scornfully said, at any price.—J. M'Carthy.

pearls—*to cast pearls before swine* to give what is precious to those who are unable to understand its value. A Biblical phrase.

Through him the captain offered them fifteen dollars a month, and one month's pay in advance, but it was like throwing pearls before swine.—R. H. Dana.

peep—*peep of day* the first appearance of day.

He came at peep of day.

peepers—*to close one's peepers* to shut one's eyes.

The next question was how long they should wait to let the inmates close their peepers.—C. Reade.

peg—*a peg* a drink of brandy and water. An Eastern phrase. The full expression is "a peg in one's coffin," from the deadly effects of drink on Europeans in Eastern countries.

—*to peg away* to persevere.

"Peg away, Bob," said Mr. Allen to his companion, encouragingly.—Dickens.

—*to take one down a peg* to lower a person's pretensions; to humiliate him.

The brilliant young athlete wanted taking down a peg.—Literary World, 1882.

—*to come down a peg* to be lowered or humiliated.

Well, he has come down a peg or two, that's all, and he don't like it.—H. R. Haggard.

pell—*pell mell* in confusion; heaped in disorder one upon the other.

The great force crumples up like an empty glove, then turns and gallops pell mell for safety to its own lines.—H. R. Haggard.

penny—*a pretty penny* a large sum; much money.

The owner had spent what he was wont to term playfully a pretty penny on his books.—George Eliot.

—*a penny-dreadful* the name given to newspapers devoted to the publication of accounts of murders, outrages, and such sensational news.

"You fiend in human form, what is it, I wonder, that has kept me so long from destroying you and myself too? Oh, you need not laugh! I have the means to do it if I choose. I have had them for twenty years."

George laughed again hoarsely.

"Quite penny-dreadful, I declare" (you speak, I assure you, in the style of a cheap sensational newspaper).—H. R. Haggard.

—*a penny for your thoughts* a playful remark made to one who seems immersed in thought. The full expression would be, "I'll give you a penny if you'll tell me your thoughts." *Judy looked a little bit puzzled at this. "A penny for your thoughts, Judy," says my sister.*—Maria Edgeworth.

—*penny wise and pound foolish* careful about small profits or savings, and foolishly blind to larger and more important gains.

He (the king) engaged her (the elephant) to perform gratis in the Champs Elysées during the three days' féte. Fifteen hundred francs for this.

But Huguet was penny wise and pound foolish to agree, for it took her gloss off—showed her gratis to half the city.—C. Reade.

to turn a penny. See **turn.**

—*to think one's penny silver* to have a good opinion of oneself.

—*penny gaffs* cheap places of entertainment.

Penny gaffs have a dozen audiences every night.—Contemporary Review, 1887.

pepper—*pepper-and-salt* a term applied to a kind of cloth of mingled black and white.

One was a low-spirited gentleman of middle age, of a meagre habit, and a disconsolate face, who kept his hands continually in the pockets of his scanty pepper-and-salt trousers.—Dickens.

—*to take pepper in the nose* to become irritated. Old-fashioned.

Because I entertained this gentleman for my ancient (standard-bearer), he takes pepper in the nose.—Chapman.

—*a peppercorn rent* an insignificant or nominal rent.

An admirable plan! but we will take the houses first at a peppercorn rent.—Beaconsfield.

per—*per annum* yearly.

—*per saltum* at a bound. Latin.

They imagined that, with the attainment of her political freedom, Italy ought per saltum to have regained her place among the nations.—Spectator, January 14, 1888.

—*per se* in itself; apart from other considerations. Latin.

He is always per se the duke.—Hugh Conway.

perch—*to tip over the perch* to die.

Either through negligence, or want or ordinary sustenance, they both tipped over the perch.—Urquhart.

person—*in person* not through a deputy; with bodily presence.

It is his highness' pleasure that the queen
Appear in person here in court.
                        Shakespeare.

The curt reply brought the earl in person to Becky's apartment.—Thackeray.

pet—*to take the pet* to be needlessly offended; to sulk.

You got into trouble, and when your father, honest man, was disappointed, you took the pet or got afraid, and ran away from punishment.—R. L. Stevenson.

petard—*hoist with one's petard.* See **hoist.**

Peter—*robbing Peter to pay Paul.* See **rob.**

—*Peter Funk* an auction where the bidders have a secret understanding. See **knock-out.** "Peter Funk" is the American term.

—*to peter out* to cease to produce; to fail; to come to an end by degrees.

It is said his Pennsylvania monopoly has petered out, and he is now obliged to get his supply from Canada.—The Nation, 1890.

petticoat—*petticoat government* the rule of women.

This afforded fresh subject of derision to those who scorned petticoat government.—Maria Edgeworth.

—*in petticoats* (a) still a child; still in the nursery.

An infant freethinker, a baby philosopher, a scholar in petticoats— a man, when he grew up, who knew almost everything except himself (J. Mill).—Mrs. Oliphant.

—(b) of the female sex; in the form of a woman. Opposed to "in trousers."

"But she is false, covetous, malicious, cruel, and dishonest"—what a friend in petticoats!—A. Trollope.

petto—*in petto* in secrecy; in reserve.

Whatever else they might hold undeclared in petto.—North.

Philadelphia—*a Philadelphia lawyer* the sharpest man living. "Enough to puzzle a Philadelphia lawyer" is a phrase used with reference to some very perplexing matter.

philosopher—*the philosopher's stone* an imaginary stone, sought after by alchemists, which had the property of transmuting everything it touched into gold.

That stone Philosophers in vain so long have sought.—Milton.

pick—*to pick a quarrel* to search for an occasion to quarrel.

At last Dennis could stand it no longer; he picked a quarrel with Fritz, and they had a battle-royal to prove which was master.—M. Arnold.

—*to pick holes* to find fault; to criticize.

"Hang the fellow," murmured Mr. Erin to himself, "he's beginning to pick holes already."—James Payn.

—*to pick a bone with one* to find fault with; to blame him.

Just look at my nose, and you will soon change your mind. It's broader, and flatter, and snubbier than ever. I consider that I have got a bone to pick with (reason to find fault with) Providence about that nose.—H. R. Haggard.

—*to pick up* (a) to obtain in a chance way.

He asked his friends about him, where they had picked up such a blockhead.—Addison.

—(b) to grow stronger; to recover health.

After he had eaten a little and had a swallow or two more of the brandy, he began to pick up visibly, sat straighter up, spoke louder and clearer, and looked in every way another man.—R. L. Stevenson.

—*a pick-me-up* anything taken to restore the strength; a tonic.

I find the syrup you gave me a capital pick-me-up.

—*to pick off* to kill separately; to shoot one by one.

He (the war correspondent) now marches with the van, goes out with the forlorn hope, sits down in the thick of the fight with his notebook, and takes ten men's share of the bullets. Consequently he sometimes gets picked off.—Besant.

—*to pick to pieces* to criticize harshly; to find fault with in a jealous fashion.

The ladies were drinking tea, and picking their neighbours to pieces.

—*to pick a hole in a man's coat* to find fault with him; to find a weak place in his character.

It is difficult to pick a hole in our minister's coat; he performs his duties too faithfully.

—*the pick of the basket* the very best of anything.

It cannot be pretended that we have thus far succeeded in obtaining the pick of the basket.—Daily Telegraph, 1885.

pickle—*to have a rod in pickle for any one* to have a punishment in store for any one.

I have a rod in pickle for Tom when he returns home.

Pickwickian—*in a Pickwickian sense* in a merely technical sense, not applicable elsewhere. A phrase taken from Dickens's *Pickwick Papers*: "He had used the word in its Pickwickian sense."

pie—*to go to pie* to fall in to confusion.

Your military ranked arrangements going all (as the typographers say of set types in a similar case) rapidly to pie.—Carlyle.

piece—*to give another a piece of one's mind* to speak bluntly and unceremoniously to him; to tell him unpleasant truths.

On the doorstep of the house where Hilda lodged stood her landlady, giving a piece of her mind to a butcher-boy, both as regarded his master's meat and his personal qualities.—H. R. Haggard.

—*of a piece with* similar to; like.

Scarcely any other part of his life was of a piece with that splendid commencement.—Macaulay.

—*to piece out* (a) to increase in length.

Whether the piecing out of an old man's life is worth the pains, I cannot tell.—Sir W. Temple.

—(b) to arrange from scattered materials; to put together so as to form a whole.

Piece out my history in connection with young Walter Gay, and what he has made me feel; and think of me more leniently, James, if you can.—Dickens.

—*piecework* work done and paid for by each separate article made or job finished, and not by the day or the hour.

Nothing could be a more noble spectacle than that of myself working at a lathe for nothing in the old days: would it be quite as noble at the brewery doing piecework?—Besant.

pièce—*pièce de résistance* the principal dish at a banquet; the chief article. French.

The rough fare of the ship's crew, of which the pièce de résistance was the hardest of Dutch cheese.—R. Buchanan.

pied—*a pied à terre* a place where one can alight; a convenient house of one's own. French.

Mr. Harding, however, did not allow himself to be talked over into giving up his own and only pied à terre in the High Street.—A. Trollope.

pig—*a pig in a poke* something bought without inspection; goods accepted and paid for blindly.

He would have greatly preferred to have the precious manuscript, like the others, for nothing; but, after all, what was demanded of him was better than being asked to give hard cash for a pig in a poke.—James Payn.

—*a pig's whisper* (a) a very loud whisper.

—(b) a very short space of time.

—*to drive one's pigs to market* to snore.

—*to bring one's pigs to a pretty market* to sell at a loss; to manage one's affairs badly.

"He never could have brought his pigs to a worse market," observed Sawbridge.—Captain Marryat.

—*to go to pigs and whistles* to be dissipated; to go to utter ruin.

"Do you know what has happened in your absence?"

Lambert nodded. "That the concern has gone to pigs and whistles," he said defiantly.—Sarah Tytler.

pigeon—*pigeon or pidgin English* the corrupt language, half English and half Chinese, used in commercial transactions throughout the Far East.

The grammar of pidgin English is not English but Chinese.—Sayce.

—*to pluck a pigeon* to cheat a simpleton; to fleece a greenhorn.

"Here comes a nice pigeon to pluck," said one of the thieves.—C. Reade.

—*pigeon's milk* an imaginary substance, which simple boys are sent to purchase on All Fools' Day (April 1).

pile—*to make a pile* to realize a fortune; to get wealthy.

On the other hand, if the old man should only go on for another year or two he would make that little pile, and a very comfortable little pile it would be.—Besant.

pill—*to gild the pill*. See **gild**.

to sugar the pill. See **sugar**.

—*a bitter or hard pill to swallow* a disagreeable experience to undergo; something wounding to the pride.

Sir Hamilton could not help recognizing the truth of this observation, but Metternich made him swallow another bitter pill (listen to another disagreeable truth).—Public Opinion, 1886.

pillar—*from pillar to post* from one refuge to another; hither and thither.

I'm afraid we shall be pretty well knocked about from pillar to post during the next month.—Florence Marryat.

pin—*pins and needles* the tingling sensation in a limb which has been benumbed.

A man may tremble, stammer, and show other signs of recovered sensibility no more in the range of his acquired talents than pins and needles after numbness.—George Eliot.

—*on the pin* watchful.

He was on the pin to see who should be chosen.

—*to pin one's faith* to fix one's trust.

Those who pinned their faith for better or for worse to the pack.—Field, 1885.

—*pin money* money granted to a wife for her small personal expenses. Pins formerly were costly, and formed a considerable share of such expenditure.

The day that Miss Rayne becomes Lady Coombe I will settle a thousand a year on her for her private use, and she'll be independent, and have as much pin money as she'll know how to do with.—Florence Marryat.

pinch—*at or on a pinch* in a difficulty. *They at a pinch can bribe a vote.*—Swift.

to feel where the shoe pinches. See **shoe**.

pink— *a pink coat* the dress worn by huntsmen in England.

He (the actual French dandy) has a wondrous respect for English "gentlemen sportsmen;" he imitates their clubs. . . . sports his pink out hunting.—Thackeray.

pipe—*to pipe one's eye* to weep.

He then began to eye his pipe. And then to pipe his eye.—Hood.

—*to put a person's pipe out* to disappoint his plans.

James Crawley's pipe is put out.—Thackeray.

—*put that in your pipe and smoke it* listen to that remark and think over it. This saying generally accompanies a rebuke.

"And always put this in your pipe, Nolly," said the Dodger, as the Jew was heard unlocking the door above, "if you don't take fogles and tickers."—Dickens.

piper—*to pay the piper* to defray the cost of an entertainment.

"Ay, races and balls, fine clothes and fine eating, them's the ways of the gentlefolks, and we pay the piper," growled a humble cynic.—Sarah Tytler.

—*pipers' news* stale news.

pis—*a pis aller* a desperate response; a last shift. French.

I have no idea of becoming a pis aller if this hare-brained peer should change his mind.—G. J. Whyte-Melville.

pitch—*to pitch and pay* to pay ready money. Old-fashioned.

—*to pitch a yarn* to tell a wonderful story.

> The skipper is in great glee to-night; he pitches his yarns with gusto.—*Chambers's Journal*, 1885.

—*to pitch in or into* to attack vigorously. Used either of actual blows or abusive language.

> "But if he should pitch into you, sir?"
> "Then he will pitch into a man twice as strong as himself."—C. Reade.
> "Dear Tom, I ain't going to pitch into (scold) you," said Arthur piteously.—T. Hughes.

—*to pitch it strong* to act or speak very warmly.

> I wonder he did not overdo it then, he pitched it so strong.—*Daily Telegraph*, 1885.

pitchers—*pitchers have ears* there are listeners who may hear. A proverbial expression. Also, "Little pitchers have long ears"—young persons are quick of hearing.

> Pitchers have ears, and I have many servants.—Shakespeare.
> The child might be somehow mistaken, or the old woman might have misread the address. But that was unlikely; and if it had been so, surely Miss Gray, knowing that little pitchers have ears, would have corrected the mistake.—Sarah Tytler.

place—*out of place* unsuitable.

> The words were colourless in themselves, but there was a hard, unfriendly, and superior tone in them rather out of place in a house where she was a guest.—C. Reade.

—*give place* yield; retire.

> Victorious York did first, with famed success,
> To his known valour, make the Dutch give place.
>   Dryden.

—*to give place to* to make room for.

> Dr. Swift is turned out of his stall and deanery-house at St. Patrick's to give place to Father Dominic from Salamanca.—Thackeray.

—*to take place* (a) to happen.

> It is stupidly foolish to venture our salvation upon an experiment, which we have all the reason imaginable to think God will not suffer to take place.—Atterbury.

—(b) to take precedence.

> As a British freeholder, I should not scruple taking place of a French marquis.—Addison.

—*in place* (a) present. Old-fashioned.

> Then was she fair alone, when none was fair in place.—Edmund Spenser.

—(b) suitable; appropriate.

> He did not think the remark in place.

plain—*plain as a pike-staff* very plain or evident.

> "Prune it of a few useless rights and literal interpretations of that sort, and our religion is the simplest of all religions, and makes no barrier, but a union, between us and the rest of the world."
> "Plain as a pike-staff" (that is very evident), said Pack, with an ironical laugh.—George Eliot.

—*plain work* sewing that is not ornamental.

> They understand their needle, broadstitch, and all manner of plain work.—Goldsmith.
> She does beefsteaks and plain work.—Thackeray.

plank—*to walk the plank.* See walk.

Platonic—*Platonic love* love with no mixture of sexual passion.

> There are not many men who could have observed Mrs. Lecount entirely from the Platonic point of view.—Wilkie Collins.

play—*to play the devil, deuce, or mischief with* to injure; to hurt seriously.

In short, in your own memorable words, to play the very devil with everything and everybody.—Dickens.

The master-gunner and his mates, loading with a rapidity the mixed races could not rival, hulled the schooner well between wind and water, and then fired chain shot at her masts, as ordered, and began to play the mischief with her shrouds and rigging.—C. Reade.

—*to bring into play* to give an opportunity for the exercise of.

The very incongruity of their relative relations brought into play all his genius.—A. Ainger.

—*to play one false* to deceive one.

"Now, look you here, Anne," said George in a sort of hiss, and standing over her in a threatening attitude, "I have suspected for some time that you were playing me false in this business, and now I am sure of it."—H. R. Haggard.

to play fast and loose. See **fast**.

—*to play one's cards* to carry out a scheme.

We have seen how Mrs. Bute, having the game in her hands, had really played her cards too well.—Thackeray.

—*to play into a person's hands* to act for the benefit of another person; to manage matters so that, unknowingly, another person, often an enemy, is benefited.

This is simply playing into the hands of lazy ne'er-do-wells (good-for-nothings).—Observer, 1885.

—*to play truant* to stay from school without leave; to absent oneself without leave. Properly a school phrase; elsewhere used playfully.

"What!" said George, who was, when in an amiable mood, that worst of all cads, a jocose cad, "are you going to play truant (go off without permission)

too, my pretty cousin?"—H. R. Haggard.

—*to play one person off against another* to use two people for one's own purposes; to make two people act upon each other so as to bring about a desired result.

On the occasion referred to the quick-witted old crone saw her chance in a moment, and commenced to play off one of her visitors against the other with consummate skill.—A. Jessopp.

—*to make play* to take the lead; to lead off. A phrase taken from the race-course.

Gray Parrot made play with Duke of Richmond and Florio next.—Daily Telegraph, 1885.

—*played out* of no further service; exhausted, bereft of force.

There is a popular impression, amongst the vulgar of this country and of America, that the part of sovereign has been long since played out.—Westminster Review, 1887.

—*to play the rôle or* to act the part of; to behave as. A theatrical phrase.

The fire in the cave was an unusually big one that night, and in a large circle round it were gathered about thirty-five men and two women, Ustane and the woman to avoid whom Job had played the rôle of another scriptural character.—H. R. Haggard.

—*to play one tricks* to cheat or deceive; to be untrustworthy. Used playfully.

He was now an old man, but active still and talkative. His memory played him tricks (was untrustworthy).—Besant.

—*to play a part* to be deceitful; to be double-faced; to dissimulate.

"I really am much obliged to you, my aunt," said John, utterly astonished to find that she possessed a heart at all, and had been more or less playing a part all the evening.—H. R. Haggard.

—*to play up to another* to accommodate oneself to another's peculiarities so as to gain some advantage.

There is your playing up toady, who, unconscious to its feeder, is always playing up to its feeder's weaknesses.—Beaconsfield.

—*child's play* easy work.

The work of reformation is child's play to that of making your friends believe you have reformed.—Hugh Conway.

please—*please the pigs* if all be well.

"Please the pigs," then said Mr. Avenel to himself, "I shall pop the question."—Bulwer Lytton.

if you please. See **if**.

—*pleased as Punch* highly pleased.

Old Staines is as pleased as Punch.—W. E. Norris.

plough—*to put one's hand to the plough* to commence serious work; to undertake important duties. A Biblical phrase. "And Jesus said unto him. No man, having put his hand to the plough, and looking back, is fit for the kingdom of God" (Luke ix. 62).

To have been the first publicly to proclaim this principle is no mean boast; and now that they have put their hand to the plough, the preceptors will certainly not look back.—Journal of Education, 1887.

—*to look back from the plough* to abandon work that has been seriously undertaken.

—*to be ploughed* to fail to pass an examination. College slang. *Plucked* is also used.

I am sure to be ploughed at the final examination.

pluck—*to pluck up courage* or *one's heart* or *one's spirits* to regain confidence; to throw fear aside.

Pluck up thy spirits.—Shakespeare.

Carlo sat and whimpered, and then wagged his tail, and plucked up more and more spirit.—C. Reade.

—*to pluck off* to descend in rank or title; to lower oneself.

plume—*to plume oneself upon* to be proud of; to boast regarding.

Nay, very likely Mrs. Bute Crawley thought her act was quite meritorious, and plumed herself upon her resolute manner of performing it.—Thackeray.

—*borrowed plumes* ornaments which do not belong to the wearer.

"I know some people do not care to appear in borrowed plumes," the elder woman went on.—Sarah Tytler.

pocket—*to put one's hand in one's pocket* to be charitable; to give money in charity.

I daresay Dr. Goodenough, amongst other philanthropists, put his hand in his pocket.—George Eliot.

—*to put one's pride in one's pocket* to lay aside one's pride for the time being; to be humble for the moment.

If Miss Blanche should ask you how we are getting on, Rachel, put your pride in your pocket, mind that.—G. J. Whyte-Melville.

—*to be in pocket* to be a gainer.

Yet I'm none the better for it in pocket.—Dickens.

—*to be out of pocket* to lose; to be a loser.

All idea of a peerage was out of the question, the baronet's two seats in Parliament being lost. He was both out of pocket and out of spirits by that catastrophe.—Thackeray.

—*a pocket borough* a borough where the electors are so few in number that a single powerful personage could control elections and send his own nominee to Parliament.

In the autumn of 1834 he (Disraeli) is full of his possible return for Wycombe, which was practically a pocket borough.—Edinburgh Review, 1886.

—*to pocket an insult* to submit to an

insult without retaliating or showing displeasure.

The remark was a rude one, but the man chose to pocket the insult.

Shakespeare used *pocket up* in this sense,—

Well, ruffian, I must pocket up these wrongs.

—*to pocket dibs* to receive salary or profits.

"What gives a man position," said Tommy, "is to make other beggars do the work and to pocket the dibs yourself."—Besant.

Note.—Beggars is here merely a slang term for "people," "men."

—*a pocket-pistol* a jocular name for a flask to carry liquor.

point—*to make a point of* to be very careful about; to take care not to omit.

When his sister went out to market he made a point of waiting for Sophy's coming down to the drawing-room.—James Payn.

—*to stretch a point* to make an exception; to observe a rule less strictly.

Oh, I suppose I shall have to stretch a point when I invite people to my house.—James Payn.

—*point blank* directly; plainly; explicitly.

So she refused you, Uppy—refused you point blank, did she?—G. J. Whyte-Melville.

—*to carry one's point* to obtain an object sought for; to persuade others to act as you wish.

Lady Clonbrony was particularly glad that she had carried her point about this party at Lady St. James's.—Maria Edgeworth.

—*to point a moral* to give force to a moral precept; to add to the moral force of a remark.

Here at least was a judgment ready made, to point the moral of the pious

and stimulate the fears of the timid.—Edinburgh Review, 1887.

—*to the point* apposite; applicable.

My spoken answer, like my written answer was not very much to the point.—Belgravia, 1886.

—*to come to points* to fight with swords.

They would have come to points immediately.—Smollett.

—*a case in point* a case which illustrates the subject under discussion.

He quotes instances in point from the history of Rio Grande.—Contemporary Review, 1888.

poke—*to poke fun at* to ridicule; to chaff.

One was so pleased with his tutor that he gave me a pot of beer besides my fee. I thought he was poking fun at me.—C. Reade.

—*a pig in a poke.* See **pig**

Poker—*Old Poker* the devil.

As if Old Poker was coming to take them away.—H. Walpole.

poles—*under bare poles* with no sails spread.

We were scudding before a heavy gale, under bare poles.—Marryat.

polish—*to polish off* to finish; to settle.

Well, sir, I couldn't finish him, but Bob had his coat off at once—he stood up to the Banbury man for three minutes, and polished him off in four rounds easy.—Thackeray.

pons—*pons asinorum* the name given to the fifth problem of the First Book of Euclid. See **Asses' bridge**.

What was it that so fascinated the student? Not the Pons Asinorum.—Thackeray.

pooh—*to pooh-pooh* to ridicule; to treat with contempt.

He seems to pooh-pooh the question, that it was absolutely impossible for Henry of Navarre to bring peace to the kingdom as long as he adhered to

the Church of the minority.—
Athenæum, 1887.

poor—*poor as a church mouse* very
poor; having barely enough to live
upon.
"One of your young men is just
married," Dobbin said, now coming to
the point. "It was a very old attachment,
and the young couple are as poor as
*church mice."—*Thackeray.

pop—*to pop corn* to parch or roast
maize or Indian corn until the grains
explode with a "pop." An American
phrase.

—*to pop the question* to make a proposal of marriage.
I suppose you popped the question
*more than once.—*Dickens.

position—*to be in a position to* to have
the time, opportunities, or information requisite for.
The official referred to is in a position
to know (has means of knowing).—
Daily Telegraph, 1885.

possess—*to possess oneself of* to
obtain; to secure.
We possessed ourselves of the
kingdom of Naples, the duchy of
Milan, and the avenue of France in
*Italy.—*Addison.

—*to possess one's soul in patience* to
refrain from worrying; to be patient.
"Possess your soul in patience, and in
due time you shall see what you shall
*see," answered Arthur oracularly.—*W.
E. Norris.

possession—*possession is nine-tenths*
of the law, or *possession is eleven*
points in the law, and they say there
are but twelve a dictum used to assert
the great importance which the law
attaches, in disputed cases, to actual
possession of the disputed property.
Ain't this my husband's place of
abode? Ain't possession nine points
*of the law?—*Justin M'Carthy.

—*to take possession* to occupy; to seize.

At length, having killed the defendant,
he actually took possession.—
Goldsmith.

'possum to act 'possum or *play*
'possum to dissemble. The opossum
has a habit, when pursued, of rolling itself up and pretending to be
dead.
It's almost time for Babe to quit playing
'possum.—Scribner's Magazine,
1886.

post—*to post oneself up in* to obtain
full information about; to learn
thoroughly.
Tell me all about it; what books you had
to post yourself up in for your
examinations, and how you came out
*of them.—*Sarah Tytler.

—*post-and-rails tea* tea having a
number of stalks floating in it.
The tea is more frequently bad than
good. The bad, from the stalks
occasionally found in the decoction, is
popularly known as post-and-rails
tea.—Daily Telegraph, 1886.

pot—*a pot shot* a shot taken calmly at
a sitting object.
This fanatic, having observed the
envoy seated in his tent with a light
and the door of the tent open, fetched
his long gun, squatted down at about
fifty yards, and took a pot shot at the
"nazarene infidel."—Murray's
Magazine, 1887.

—*let not the pot call the kettle black*
do no criticize your neighbours unless
you are free from blame yourself.
"Satan reproving sin."
You think it's a case of the pot calling
the kettle black, perhaps I'm black
enough, goodness knows! but you
yourself said just now that you didn't
believe I had sunk to her depth of
*infamy.—*W. E. Norris.

—*to keep the pot boiling* (a) to continue the fun.
"Keep the pot a-bilin', sir!" said Sam.

(The party were sliding on the ice.)—Dickens.

—(b) to get sufficient funds to maintain one's household in comfort. The phrase is used contemptuously by artists and literary men, of work done merely for the sake of the money to be paid for it.

Something made him unwilling to exhibit himself before her in the degrading occupation of pot-boiling (painting pictures solely for money).—James Payn.

—*to go to pot* to be ruined or wasted.

My farm, stock, and utensils, these young blood horses, and the brand-new vessels I was building, are all gone to pot.—Haliburton.

—*pot luck* ordinary fare; the meal which an unexpected guest receives.

He should be very welcome to take pot luck with him.—Graves.

pound—*to claim one's pound of flesh* to demand payment of debts due to one, even where their payment involves much suffering. The phrase comes from Shakespeare's *Merchant of Venice*, where Shylock the Jew insists upon Antonio giving him a pound of his flesh, according to an agreement previously made.

The Sultan's view of Germany is that he ought to seek for the help of German officers and of German financial guides, on the ground that all the other great powers want their pound of flesh from Turkey.—Fortnightly Review, 1887.

to pound away—to work hard.

However Goldsmith pounded away at this newly-found work—Black.

pow—*to hold a pow-wow* to have a riotous meeting.

powder—*not worth powder and shot* not worth the trouble or cost.

pray—*I pray, pray,* or *prithee* an excla-

mation which often accompanies a question.

But, pray, in this mechanical formation, when the ferment was expanded to the extremities of the arteries, why did it not break through the receptacle?—Bentley.

premium—*at a premium* much sought after; increased in value.

Servants are at a great premium, masters at a discount, in the colony.—C. Reade.

presence—*presence of mind* power of self-control and intelligent action in a crisis.

Both men changed colour but retained their presence of mind and their cunning.—C. Reade.

pretty—*a pretty time of it* a difficult or unpleasant condition of affairs.

Mr. Samuel Erin had for the present a pretty time of it. He was like a man caught in a downpour of hailstones, without an umbrella.—James Payn.

—*a pretty go* an awkward position; a critical situation.

Supposing now that some of them were to slip into the boat at night and cut the cable, and make off with her. It would be a pretty go, that would.—H. R. Haggard.

prick—*to prick up the ears* to show signs of interest; to appear attentive.

—*to prick out* to plant for the first time.

—*to prick up oneself* to make a display; to show off.

primâ—*primâ facie* at first sight; apparently. Latin.

At this stage, the learned counsel having already made his opening speech, a statement now would primâ facie be irregular, and the judge said so; whereupon Mr. Finlay turned to his learned friends, the Attorney-General and Sir Charles Russell, and showed them a letter, and conversed with them earnestly and in low tones.—St. Andrews Citizen, 1887.

primrose—*the primrose path* the pleasant and alluring road which leads to destruction.

But, good my brother,
Do not, as some ungracious pastors do,
Show me that steep and thorny way to heaven;
Whiles, like a puffed and reckless libertine,
Himself the primrose path of dalliance treads,
And recks not his own rede.
                    Shakespeare.

prizes—*to play prizes* to be in earnest. Old-fashioned.

They did not play prizes, and only pretended to quarrel.—Stillingfleet.

pro—*pro bono publico* for the public welfare; for the benefit of the whole company. Latin.

In some of the bank offices it is the custom (to save so much individual time) for one of the clerks—who is the best scholar—to commence upon the Times or Chronicle and recite its entire contents aloud pro bono publico.—Lamb.

—*pro and con* for and against; favourable and unfavourable.

Mr. Tupman and Mr. Snodgrass arrived, most opportunely, in this stage of the pleadings, and as it was necessary to explain to them all that had occurred, together with the various reasons pro and con the whole of the arguments were gone over again.—Dickens.

—*pros and cons* arguments for and against; minute discussion.

After a few pros and cons they bade her observe that her old lover, Ephraim Slade, was a rich man, and if she was wise she would look that way.—C. Reade.

—*pro tanto* so far; in itself. Latin.

That (right) does tend to attract, or rather to drive all, all ambitious or powerful men into the deliberative arena, and that pro tanto is beneficial.—Spectator, 1887.

—*pro tempore* for a short time; not permanent or permanently. Latin.

The body was then deposited, pro tempore, in St. Anne's Church, Soho.—C. Reade.

—*pro formâ* for form's sake; merely to satisfy rules. Latin.

It was merely a pro formâ meeting; the real business had already been discussed.

procrustean — *procrustean bed* an uncomfortable couch, where violent measures are necessary to insure that the person fills it. Procrustes was a famous robber who lived near Athens. He compelled his prisoners to lie down on a certain couch. If they were too long for it, their limbs were chopped off; if too short, they were stretched to the required length.

They have some particular theory to maintain, and whatever does not fit their Procrustean bed is at once condemned.—E. Whipple.

promise—*I promise you* an expression generally attached to statements about the future, and signifying "I declare to you," "You may be certain."

"Will not the ladies be afraid of the lion?"
"I fear it, I promise you."
                    Shakespeare.

proof—*to put to the proof* to test; to try in practice

My paper gives a timorous writer an opportunity of putting his abilities to the proof.—Addison.

—*the proof of the pudding* the tasting of it; the actual experience of anything.

The upshot of all discussion on this question is that, to use a vulgar phrase, the proof of the pudding will be in the eating.—*Spectator, September 17, 1887.*

proud—*proud flesh* inflamed flesh arising in wounds or ulcers.
The sores had generated proud flesh.—*Daily Telegraph, 1885.*

pull—*to pull up* to cause to stop; to come to a stop. Originally used of pulling the reins in driving, and of thus stopping a horse.
They thanked heaven they had been pulled up short (suddenly arrested) in an evil career.—*C. Reade.*

—*to pull up stakes* to remove one's residence. American slang.

—*to pull through* not to succumb; to succeed with difficulty.
You pulled through it (the punishment), and so will he.—*C. Reade.*

—*to pull a person through* to extricate him from a difficulty or danger.
His extra speed pulled him through.—*Field, 1886.*

—*to pull the strings* to set in action secretly; to be the real though hidden promoter of anything.
The men who pull the strings are down in the Cape. They want to drive every Englishman out of South Africa.—*H. R. Haggard.*

—*to pull together* to work harmoniously.
The new director and the professors are said not to pull together.

—*to pull oneself together* to rally; to prepare for a fresh struggle.
Joe retired to the bar, where he had a glass of brandy neat, and tried to pull himself together, but with small success.—*Besant.*

—*to pull faces* to make grimaces.

—*to pull a long face* to look melancholy.
Sarah returning at this moment, shaking her head, and pulling a long face at the ill-success of her search, devoted herself to administering sal volatile.—*Murray's Magazine, 1887.*

pulse—*to feel one's pulse* (a) to discover the beat of the heart by pressing an artery.

—(b) to sound a person; to try to discover a person's secret opinions.
So much matter has been ferreted out that this Government wishes to tell its own story, and my pulse was felt (I was sounded in the matter).—*Southey.*

purchase—*his life is not worth a year's purchase* he is not likely to survive more than a year.

purple—*born in the purple* born a prince. Purple is the imperial colour.
To think of that dear young man (Prince Louis Napoleon), the apple of his mother's eye, born and nurtured in the purple, dying thus, is too fearful, too awful.—*Queen Victoria.*

—*to marry into the purple* to marry a prince or a nobleman.
Now I had not the slightest wish for my dear Helena to marry into the purple.—*Mistletoe Bough, 1885.*

purpose—*on purpose* designedly; with full intention.
Where men err against this method, it is usually on purpose, and to show their learning.—*Swift.*

—*with the purpose of* with the intention of (followed by the participle of gerund).
He left with the purpose of following her.

—*to the purpose* appositely; pointedly; sensibly; (also as an adjective) sensible; practical.
He was wont to speak plain and to the purpose.—*Shakespeare.*

—*to small purpose* for very little good; without much practical benefit.
To small purpose had the council of Jerusalem been assembled, if once

their determination being set down, men might afterwards have defended their former opinions.—Hooker.

purse—*purse-proud* arrogant because of wealth; puffed up through being wealthy.

What is so hateful to a poor man as the purse-proud arrogance of a rich one?—Observer.

I wish we had never seen those odious, purse-proud Osbornes.—Thackeray.

—*to make up a purse* to collect subscriptions on behalf of some individual; to get together a sum of money.

Some friends who took an interest in me made up a purse for me, by which I was enabled to pay my passage-money in advance.—G. A. Sala.

push—*to be put to the push* to be tested by difficult circumstances.

Once he is put to the push, his native energy will appear.

—*to come to the push* to be seriously tested.

'Tis common to talk of dying for a friend; but when it comes to the push (people are actually tested) 'tis no more than talk.—L'Estrange.

put—*put about* anxious; annoyed; in a flurry.

Tom was rather put about by this speech.—T. Hughes.

—*to put oneself about* take trouble.

Mr. Treverton was a person for whom people must be expected to put themselves about.—Miss Bradon.

—*to put about a ship* to turn it round.

The Stella was put about, and the other broadside given without a return from her opponent.—Captain Marryat.

—*to put by* (a) to thrust aside; to neglect.

A presence which is not to be put by.—Wordsworth.

—(b) to save; to lay aside.

Eight thousand servants, fed, and half-

clothed at their masters' expense, have put by for forty years, and yet not even by aid of interest and compound interest have reached the Rubicon of four figures (goal of £1,000).—C. Reade.

—*hard put to (it)* in great trouble; sore beset.

For if he, though a man, was so hard put to it, what canst thou, being but a poor woman, do?—Bunyan.

—*put to it* tested; tried; placed in a difficulty.

But Gingham worked for the whole family as a woman will when put to it.—G. J. Whyte-Melville.

—*put on* feigned; hypocritical.

Sir Charles obeyed this missive, and the lady received him with a gracious and smiling manner, all put on and cat-like.—C. Reade.

—*to put out* or *put out of countenance* to discompose; to make uncomfortable; to confuse; to disconcert.

She interested him, intensely, to say the least of it, and, man-like, he felt exceedingly put out (annoyed), and even sulky, at the idea of her departure.—H. R. Haggard.

—*to put out* to dislocate.

She put her shoulder out.—Field, 1887.

—*to put two and two together.* See **two**

—*to put that and that together* to reason; to draw an inference.

Young as I was, I also could put that and that together.—Captain Marryat.

—*to put in a word* to recommend; to use one's influence.

Well, sir, if he thinks so well of Mr. Poyser for a tenant, I wish you would put in a word for him to allow us some new gates (recommend that he should allow us some new gates).—George Eliot.

—*to put in an appearance* to be present; to attend a meeting.

Half an hour afterward they sat down

as usual to supper. *Bessie did not put in an appearance till it was a quarter over, and then was very silent through it.*—H. R. Haggard.

—*to put heads together* to consult; to plot; to arrange a plan.
Those two ladies now put their heads together.—C. Reade.

—*to put off* (a) to postpone.
Let not the work of to-day be put off till to-morrow, for the future is uncertain.—L'Estrange.

—(b) to baffle; to get rid of by temporizing.
Mrs. Wallace was not to be put off by jest.—James Payn.

—(c) to set out from the shore.
Three of them put off in a boat to visit the brig.

—*to put down* to suppress; to quell; to crush.
He does me the favour to inquire whether it will be agreeable to me to have Will Fern put down.—Dickens.

—*to put on* to dress oneself with.
The little ones are taught to be proud of their clothes before they can put them on.—Locke.

—*to put up a person* (a) to give him accommodation; to lodge him.
His old college friend Jones lived there, and offered to put him up for a week.

—(b) to proclaim his marriage banns.
We are to be put up in Church next Sunday, and it takes three Sundays.—Captain Marryat.

—*to put up a horse* to tie it up or put it in a stable. The American word is hitch—"he hitched his horse."
He rode into Newborough, and putting up his horse, strolled about the streets.—C. Reade.

—*to put up* to stop; to rest.
I wondered at what house the Bath coach put up.—Dickens.

—*to put up to* to incite; to instigate; to teach a dodge or trick.
"We will practise it in the morning, my boy," said he, "and I'll put you up to a thing or two worth knowing."—Thackeray.

—*a put-up affair* a concocted plot; an affair which is not what it pretends to be.
A suspicion of the whole affair being what the police call a put-up one, was passing through his mind.—James Payn.

—*to put up with* to suffer; to pass over without resentment.
Whatever may be the case with Hungary, it must be admitted that Austria will put up with a good deal from Russia rather than fight.—Fortnightly Review, 1887.

—*to put upon* to deceive; to treat unfairly or deceitfully; to make one do more than a fair share of work.
Take care never to know anything about leather, and you won't be put upon (gulled or bullied).—Besant.

—*to put to the blush* to shame; to vanquish.
Flattering himself that by this stroke of magnanimity he had put the old quiz to the blush, he stalked out of the office with the paper in his pocket.—Thackeray.

—*to put to death* to execute.
Teuta put to death one of the Roman ambassadors.—Arbuthnot.

—*to put out of court* to make one's evidence of no value; to disqualify one from speaking with authority.
The fact that they were believed to be opposed on principle to all wars put them out of court in public estimation, as Mr. Kinglake justly observes, when they went about to argue against this particular war.—Justin M'Carthy.

Q

quality—*the quality* the upper class; the gentry. Old-fashioned, and now vulgar.

By degrees the quality gave up going, and the fair, of course, became disreputable.—Athenæum, 1887.

quarter—*to give* or *show quarter* to act with clemency; to be merciful; to be lenient.

To the young, if you give any tolerable quarter, you indulge them in their idleness and ruin them.—Collier.

Queen—*Queen's English* the standard English. The same as *King's English*. See **King**. *A Plea for the Queen's English* is the title of a book by Dean Alford.

—*Queen Anne is dead* that is stale news. A phrase used sarcastically. The Americans says "Rats," or "That's an awful chestnut," when a stale story is told.

Lord Brougham, it appears, isn't dead, though Queen Anne is.—Barham.

—*Queen of the May* the village girl who was chosen, as the fairest in the village or district, to be queen of the revels on the first of May, known as May-day.

"I thought that you were the spirit of the place, or," he added gracefully, pointing to a branch of half-opened hawthorn bloom she held in her hand, "the original Queen of the May."—H. R. Haggard.

—*to turn the Queen's evidence* to turn informer for the sake of a pardon. See **King**

I hate a convict who turns Queen's evidence.—H. Kingsley.

—*Queen's heads* postage stamps.

"I must buy some stamps; I am run out of Queen's heads."

"That is precisely what I want money for," said Trip testily. *"I have neither paper nor envelopes nor stamps."*—S. Baring-Gould.

Queer—*to be in Queer Street* to be in unfortunate circumstances.

No, sir, I make it a rule of mine—the more it looks like Queer Street, the less I ask.—R. L. Stevenson.

question—*in question* referred to; under discussion.

But at this moment Hawes came into the cell with the bed in question in his arms.—C. Reade.

—*to call in question* to express doubts regarding; to find fault with.

When religion is called in question because of the extravagances of theology being passed off as religion, one disengages and helps religion by showing their utter delusiveness.—M. Arnold.

—*out of the question* impracticable; unworthy of discussion.

Intimacy between Miss Fairfax and me is out of the question.—Jane Austen.

—*a burning question* a subject causing widespread interest; a question demanding solution.

The people like to be roused by red-hot, scorching speeches; they want burning questions, intolerable grievances.—Besant.

—*to beg the question*. See **beg**.

qui—*on the qui vive* eager, watchful; alert. *Qui vive* is the summons addressed by French sentinels to those who approach them.

Every one was on the qui vive, as Mrs. Jennynge expressed it, to see the new-comers.—James Payn.

quid—*a quid pro quo* something given in return; a recompense. Latin.

Unfortunately, in this prosaic world, one cannot receive cheques for one thousand pounds without, in some shape or form, giving a quid pro quo.—H. R. Haggard.

quits—*to be quits with a person* to have paid another all you owe him; to have a clear account with him. Used both of money dealings and of injuries to be revenged.

My spade shall never go into the earth again till I'm quits with him (I have had my revenge).—C. Reade.

—*to cry quits* to acknowledge that one's account with another is clear; to cease struggling.

But will he get her to marry him, I wonder. If he does, I shall cry quits with him indeed.—H. R. Haggard.

quod—*to put in quod* to imprison.

Do you really mean to maintain that a man can't put old Diggs in quod for snaring a hare without all this elaborate apparatus of Roman law?—M. Arnold.

R

R—*the three R's* reading, (w)riting, and (a)rithmetic. These subjects were formerly considered the necessary parts of an ordinary education.

Fortunate indeed were the youngsters who for a brief season tasted even of the rich delights of the three R's, as an alderman of that epoch (1850) is said to have designated the mysteries of reading, writing, and arithmetic.—Edinburgh Review, 1887.

rack—*on the rack* (a) in a state of torture, of pain, or of bodily or mental discomfort.

A cool behaviour sets him on the rack (makes him miserable) and is interpreted as an instance of aversion or indifference.—Addison.

—*to go to rack and ruin* to fall into utter disrepair; to go to destruction.

So we must go to rack and ruin, Kate, my dear.—Dickens.

—*to be* or *live at rack* (or *heck*) *and manger* to live extravagantly; to spend money heedlessly.

John Lackland . . . tearing out the bowels of St. Edmundsbury Convent (its larders, namely, and cellars) in the most ruinous way by living at rack and manger there.—Carlyle.

racket *to be on the racket* to spend one's time in frolic or dissipation.

He had been off on the racket, perhaps for a week at a time.—Daily Telegraph, 1885.

—*to stand the racket* to take the consequences; to be responsible.

He is as ready as myself to stand the racket of subsequent proceedings.—Daily Telegraph, 1882.

rag—*gentlemen of the order of the rag* military officers. The rag refers to their red uniform.

It is the opinion which, I believe, most

of you young gentlemen of the order of the rag deserve.—Fielding.

—**rag-tag and bob-tail** the dregs of the people; those loungers about a city who are always ready to flock together and make a mob. Found also in the more correct form, *tag-rag and bob-tail*. See **tag**.

Mr. Gladstone, in fact, is tired of being out in the cold. The pleasure of leading the rag-tag and bob-tail proves but so-so, compared with the pleasure of commanding the House of Commons.—St. Andrews Citizen, 1887.

rage—*all the rage* extremely popular.

Uncle Tom, to the surprise of many that twaddle traditional phrases in reviews and magazines about the art of fiction, and to the surprise of no man who knows anything about the art of fiction, was all the rage.—C. Reade. Note.—Uncle Tom's Cabin, by Mrs. H. Beecher Stowe.

rain—*it never rains but it pours* a phrase often used when a rapid succession of events occur. It signifies somewhat the same as "misfortunes never come singly," but has a wider application by its reference to all kinds of events.

Nevertheless—for, in spite of the proverb, "It never rains but it pours," good fortune seldom befalls us mortals without alloy—there were drops of bitterness in his full cup.—James Payn.

—*a rainy day* a time of trouble and difficulty.

Mr. Punch, in a cartoon, is represented as advising the British workman to avoid the gin-palace, and put by for a rainy day.—Fortnightly Review, 1887.

raise—*to raise one's back* to grow obstinate; to rebel.

He had raised his back more than once against orders emanating from the palace in a manner that had made the hairs on the head of the bishop's

wife to stand almost an end.—A. Trollope.

—*to raise the wind.* See **wind**.

raison—*raison d'être* claim to exist; right to have an existence. A French phrase.

In the conviction that no real amalgamation could ever exist between the two will be found the raison d'être of the high character with which some of the men of the tiers état were credited.—National Review, 1886.

ramp—*on the ramp* wild; in a state of excitement. See **ran-tan**.

It is apropos of a re-issue of Messrs. Cassell's serial, British Battles by Land and Sea, that Lord Wolseley goes anew on the ramp.—Scottish Leader, August 5, 1890.

rampage—*on the rampage* drunk.

ran—*on the ran-tan* excited; roaming about furiously.

John had been (as he was pleased to call it) visibly "on the ran-tan" the night before.—R. L. Stevenson.

rank—*the rank and file* the undistinguished mass; the private soldiers of an army.

While the rank and file of his parliamentary opponents sought to shout or laugh him down, he tells his sister that he was receiving the most flattering testimonies of approval from discriminating judges.—Edinburgh Review, 1886.

—*in the ranks* serving as a private soldier.

Specimens (of gentlemen) are to be found at the plough, the loom, and the forge, in the ranks, and before the mast, as well as in the officers' mess-room, the learned professions, and the Upper House itself.—G. J. Whyte-Melville.

—*to rise from the ranks* to be promoted to the position of a commissioned

officer after having served as a private
soldier.

rap—*to rap out* to speak violently; to
utter loudly. Generally used with the
word "oath" as object.

*Frank rapped the words out sharply.
Mordle looked the picture of
surprise.*—Hugh Conway.

—*to rap over the knuckles* to administer a sharp reproof; to censure
sharply.

*The author has grossly mistranslated a
passage in the* Defensio pro populo
Anglicano; *and if the bishop were not
dead, I would here take the liberty of
rapping his knuckles.*—De Quincey.

rara—*rara avis* something seldom
seen. Latin. Literally, a "rare bird."

*He had brought from India a favourite
native servant, his khitmutgar,
Supashad; a man who was indeed a
rara avis among English-speaking
khitmutgars, being very intelligent, and
only a moderate thief.*—Mistletoe
Bough, 1886.

rate—*at any rate* in any case; whatever
be the circumstance.

*If he could once reach the cave he
would at any rate get shelter and a dry
place to lie on.*—H. R. Haggard.

raw—*a raw recruit* an awkward or
simple fellow; one who has not yet
learned his trade or profession; one
who is "green."

*For example, if Sir Barnet had the good
fortune to get hold of a raw recruit, or
a country gentleman, and ensnared
him to his hospitable villa, Sir Barnet
would say to him on the morning after
his arrival, "Now, my dear sir, is there
anybody you would like to know?"*—
Dickens.

reach—*reach-me-downs* second-
hand clothes. So called in London
because an intending purchaser of
such clothes asks the shopman to

"reach-him-down" them in order to
try them on.

read—*to read a lesson* to scold or reprimand.

*Oh, you can speak to my Aunt
Molineux and she will read you a fine
lesson.*—C. Reade.

—*to read between the lines* to see a
writer's concealed meaning.

*He has not enough experience of the
way in which men have thought and
spoken to feel what the Bible writers
are about—to read between the lines,
to discern where he ought to rest his
whole weight, and where he ought to
pass lightly.*—Matthew Arnold.

ready—*ready money* money which can
be immediately made use of; money
in one's hands.

*No ready money was required by the
new heir.*—Maria Edgeworth.

rear—*to bring up the rear* to come last.

*At half-past ten, Tom Moody, Sir
Huddlestone Fuddlestone's
huntsman, was seen trotting up the
avenue, followed by the noble pack of
hounds in a compact body—the rear
being brought up by the two whips
clad in stained scarlet.*—Thackeray.

reckon—*to reckon without one's host*
to calculate blindly; to enter rashly
upon any undertaking.

*We thought that now our troubles were
over and our enemy's beginning; but
we reckoned without our host (were
mistaken).*—Macmillan's Magazine,
1887.

—*to reckon on* or *upon* to expect.

*You reckon upon losing (expect to lose)
your friends' kindness.*—Sir W.
Temple.

—*to reckon with* to call to punishment;
to settle accounts with.

*Antony and Lepidus, too, had to be
reckoned with. J. A. Froude.*

record—*to beat, break,* or *cut the*

record to do a distance in less time than it has ever been done before.

Speechly proceeded to cut the three miles' record nearly by twelve seconds.—Referee, 1886.

red—*red-handed* in the very act of committing a crime. No doubt referring to stains of blood.

"By taking the place of your servant, and so selling you into the power of my friend Count Perètekoff,"—and here he laughed a low, cruel laugh,— "I was enabled to take these wretches red-handed, and so insure the fate they have so long richly deserved."— Murray's Magazine, 1887.

—*red tape* officialdom; useless official formalities.

Unlike a minister in England who steps into an office with the red tape cut and dried for him, Lord Wellesley had no one to advise him.—Asiatic Quarterly Review, 1887.

—*the Red Book* the peerage list.

And let us, my brethren, who have not our names in the Red Book, console ourselves by thinking how miserable our betters may be, and that Damocles, who sits on satin cushions, and is served on gold plate, has an awful sword hanging over his head.— Thackeray.

—*a red-letter day* an auspicious or happy day.

All my holidays, I feel as if I had none, as they do in heaven, where 'tis all red-letter days."—Charles Lamb.

—*painted red* (of a village or town) given over to merriment and high jinks. An American phrase.

Singapore has been in trouble. During the greater part of three days—22nd, 23rd, and 24th of February—the town was "painted red" by Chinese rowdies, and the air was full of bludgeons and buckshot.—Japan Mail, 1887.

—*a red cent* used, like "a brass farthing," to signify the least piece of money. American.

Now the colonel, in short and sharp sentences, interrupted by a good deal of writhing and hard swearing, said he would not leave a brass farthing—a red-cent was what he actually mentioned—to any of his relatives who had known him in England.—Wm. Black.

—*a red rag to a bull* what especially provokes and irritates.

He (George II.) hated books, and the sight of one in a drawing-room was as a red rag to a bull.—Temple Bar, 1887.

reductio—*a reductio ad absurdum* a particular case which proves the absurdity of a general statement. Latin.

Certainly that appears to us the reductio ad absurdum of the theory of fortuitous variation.—Spectator, February 2, 1888.

reed—*a broken reed* a support which will fail you.

Though Mr. Crawley was now but a broken reed, and was beneath his feet, yet Mr. Thumble acknowledged to himself that he could not hold his own with this broken reed.—A. Trollope.

reel—*off the reel* in uninterrupted succession.

refusal—*to have the refusal of anything* to be allowed to buy it before any one else; to have the first offer of it.

Mrs. Flint will never let Mrs. Steel have the refusal.—Haliburton.

reins—*to give the reins* to allow unrestrained freedom; to release from control.

But how could he thus give reins to his temper.—James Payn.

removed—*once or twice removed* separated by one or two steps of family relationship. A person is cousin once removed to the full cousin of one of his parents, or to the child of one of his full cousins.

Our cousins, too, even to the fortieth remove, all remembered their affinity.—Goldsmith.

respects—*to pay one's respects to any one* to make one a polite visit; to meet one with courtesy.

Every day Miss Swartz comes you will be here to pay your respects to her.—Thackeray.

resurrection — *resurrection pie* a pie composed of the odd bits of meat that have been cooked already.

return—*to return to our muttons* to return to the main subject of our narrative. The translation of a proverb taken from the old French farce of *Pierre Patelin.*

To return to our muttons—this mode of progression
At length upon Spanking Bill made some impression.

Barham

rhyme—*neither rhyme nor reason* wanting in sense and every other valuable quality. Sir Thomas More advised an author, who had sent him his manuscript to read, "to put it into rhyme," which, when he had done, Sir Thomas said, "Yes, marry, now it is somewhat, for now it is rhyme; before it was neither rhyme nor reason."

—*without rhyme or reason* inexplicably; from no cause to be easily understood.

When a person on whom one is accustomed to depend for most of that social intercourse and those pleasant little amenities that members of one sex value from another, suddenly cuts off the supply without any apparent rhyme or reason, it is enough to induce a feeling of wonder, not to say of vexation, in the breast.—H. R. Haggard.

ribbon—*a red ribbon* or *riband* the order of the Bath. The knights of the Bath wear a crimson ribbon with a medallion bearing the motto, *Tria juncta in uno* (three joined in one).

He (Hastings) *had then looked forward to a coronet, a red riband, a seat at the Council Board, an office at Whitehall.*—Macaulay.

—*a blue ribbon* the order of the Garter, the most distinguished of the English orders. The phrase is used to signify a "distinction of the highest kind."

In 1840 he was elected to a fellowship at Oriel, then the blue ribbon of the university.—Athenæum, 1887.

rich—*rich as a Jew* very rich.

Poverty prevails among the London Jews to a much greater extent that was imagined—sufficient, certainly, to shake considerably popular faith in the truth of the old saying, "Rich as a Jew."—Spectator, 1887.

Richmond—*another Richmond in the field* another unexpected adversary. The phrase is taken from Shakespeare's *Richard III.*, act v., scene 4. At the battle of Bosworth, King Richard replies to his attendant Catesby, who urges him to fly, "I think there be six Richmonds in the field. Five I have slain to-day instead of him."

This time it was a rival suitor who made his appearance, and Brian's hot Irish temper rose when he saw another Richmond in the field.—Fergus W. Hume.

rift—*the rift in the lute* the small defect or breach which will gradually spoil the whole.

Some little rift had taken place in the lute of her diplomacy.—James Payn.

rig—*to rig the market* to buy shares of a stock in which one is interested, in order to force up the price; a common practice. A stock-broking phrase.

So you make your mine by begging—
(modern miners never dig),—
And you float a gorgeous company.
The shares go spinning up;
But you never rig the market,
(What an awkward word is rig.)
And you drain success in bumpers
from an overflowing cup.

Punch.

right—*to put* or *set to rights* to arrange;
to rectify; to set in order; to cure.
*She put her curls to rights, and looked
as pleased as fun.*—Haliburton.
*When I had put myself somewhat to
rights at the hotel, I hired a fly and
drove to Herr Kûcher.*—Leisure Hour,
1887.
*Was it not well, then, that he should
see a letter which put that mystery to
rights?*—R. L. Stevenson.
*Old Cooper has set him to rights
(caused him to recover from sickness)
by this time, you may depend on it.*—
James Payn.

—*by rights* properly; according to strict
justice.
*Had it not been for the pre-occupied
and uncomfortable state of his mind,
Arthur should by rights have enjoyed
himself very much at Madeira.*—H. R.
Haggard.

—*a right arm* one's staunchest friend;
the principal supporter of any one.
*Sir Launcelot, my right arm, the
mightiest of my knights.*—Tennyson.

—*a right-hand man* a very serviceable
person; a friend on whom one chiefly
depends.
*He's his royal highness's right-hand
man.*—Thackeray.

—*his heart is in the right place* he is
faithful and true-hearted.
*My daughters are plain, disinterested
girls, but their hearts are in the right
place.*—Thackeray.

—*right as a trivet* safe and sound; in a
thoroughly satisfactory condition.

*Don't you hear me tell you that we have
found out all about the cheque, and
that you're as right as a trivet?*—A.
Trollope.

ring—*to form a ring* to make a union
of manufacturers of a certain article,
so as to keep up the price.
*Experience has shown that the
operation of these trusts, or rings, or
syndicates, is completely baneful.*—
The Scotsman, 1890.

riot—*to run riot* to roam wildly and
without restraint; to be lawless in
conduct.
*And as he was whirled along on the
London and North-Western, how the
young soldier's thoughts ran riot in
the future.*—G. J. Whyte-Melville.

rise—*to take* or *get a rise out of a
person* to amuse oneself by making
another angry or excited; to play a
trick on another. Originally, no doubt,
taken from angling, where one casts
a fly to get a fish to "rise."
*On one occasion I took what we used
to call a "rise" out of Calverley.*—
Temple Bar, 1887.

road—*a royal road* a road without difficulties.
*There is no royal road to learning; no
short cut to the acquirement of any
valuable art.*—Trollope.

—*in the road* forming an obstruction.
The same as "In the way."
*Although as strong as a horse, he
looked neither heavy nor yet adroit,
only leggy, coltish, and in the road.*—
R. L. Stevenson.

roast—*to rule the roast* or *roost* to be
supreme. See **rule.**

rob—*to rob Peter to pay Paul* to take
what rightfully belongs to one person
to pay another. The origin of this
expression is as follows: In 1540 the
abbey church of St. Peter's, Westminster, was advanced to the dignity
of a cathedral by letters patent; but

ten years later it was joined to the diocese of London again, and many of its estates appropriated to the repairs of St. Paul's Cathedral.

How was he to pay for it? The horse was not his. To leave it would be to rob Peter to pay Paul.—Leisure Hour, 1887.

robe—*gentlemen of the long robe* judges and barristers.

The genteel world had been thrown into a considerable state of excitement by two events, which, as the papers say, might give employment to the gentlemen of the long robe.—Thackeray.

rock—*rocks ahead* a phrase signifying that some danger menaces. The title of one of Mr. Greg's books is *Cassandra, or Rocks Ahead*—that is, "the Prophetess of Evil, or Danger looming near."

"Take him away again, sir. Don't let him stay. Rocks ahead, sir!" Mr. Bunker put up his hands in warning.—Besant.

—*on the rocks* hard up; having no money left.

—*rock-bottom prices* the lowest possible price.

The largest stock of United States stamps of any dealer, at rock-bottom prices.

Roger—*the Jolly Roger* the black pirate's flag.

The Hispaniola still lay where she had anchored; but, sure enough, there was the Jolly Roger—the black flag of piracy—flying from her peak.—R. L. Stevenson.

roi—*roi fainéant* a do-nothing king; a sovereign only in name. The later Merovingian kings of France allowed all power to pass into the hands of the mayors of the palace, and themselves became *rois fainéants*, or sluggard kings.

It was the old story—the young Sultan

who leaves everything to his grand vizier, and finds himself a roi fainéant dethroned and imprisoned.—Mistletoe Bough, 1887.

rolling—*a rolling stone gathers no moss* a person who is always shifting about makes no money; a restless wanderer remains poor. A proverb of Thomas Tusser's (1523–80). Mr. Laurence Oliphant described his experiences, as a traveller, in a series of articles in *Blackwood's Magazine*, entitled "Moss from a Rolling Stone."

He had been a rolling stone, which, if it had gathered no moss, had rolled on it (made no money, had used plenty of it).—James Payn.

Rome—*Rome was not built in a day* great results cannot be obtained in a short period; patience is required in the production of anything valuable.

"Yes," said Ella, amused by this very moderate compliment to her artistic skill; "it is the one with the coastguard station on it; but I have not had time to put that on it yet.

"I see; Rome was not built in a day, was it?"—James Payn.

—*when at Rome do as the Romans do or as the pope does* an ancient proverb recommending prudence in behaviour. We must adapt ourselves to the prejudices and customs of others. St. Augustine found on arrival at Rome that they fasted on Saturday; he complied with this custom, though it was strange to him.

room—*room and to spare* plenty of accommodation; ample room.

—*to prefer another's room to his company* to wish another to leave you; to dislike his society.

When one is not en rapport with one's friends about any particular subject in which for the time they are interested, it is better to leave them, for it is certain they would rather have our

room than our company.—James
Payn.

root—*the root of all evil* the love of
money. So called in the New Testament (1 Tim. vi. 10).

—*the root of the matter* sound religious
principle; deep-seated religious faith.
A phrase much used by the Puritans
and borrowed from the Old Testament: "Seeing the root of the matter
is found in me" (Job xix. 28).

*Thou dost not believe but what the
Dissenters and the Methodists have
got the root of the matter as well as the
Church folks.*—George Eliot.

rope—*give a rogue rope enough and he
will hang himself* a wicked man is
sure to bring about his own
destruction.

*He is a bad man, and a dangerous
man, but let him be. He is taking plenty
of rope, and he will hang himself one
of these days.*—H. R. Haggard.

—*with a rope round one's neck* in imminent danger of a violent death.

*This (hanging) was the usual fate
which followed failure in this country
(Central America); and those who
fought in it knew they were doing so
with a rope round their necks—which
doubtless improved their fighting
qualities.*—Blackwood's Magazine,
1886.

—*a rope of sand* something which has
an appearance of strength, but is in
reality useless.

*Where he (Love) sets his foot, the
rocks bloom with flowers, or the
garden becomes a wilderness
according to his good-will and
pleasure, and at his whisper all other
allegiances melt away like ropes of
sand.*—H. R. Haggard.

rose—*under the rose* privately; secretly;
in confidence.

*The Alsatians and we have some
common enemies, and we have,*

under the rose, some common
friends.—Scott.

—*a bed of roses* a luxurious place; a
very comfortable situation.

*Life could not have been a bed of roses
for any of them.*—Mrs. Henry Wood.

rot—*rot or all rot* humbug; nonsense.
A favourite schoolboy phrase in
England.

*Let's stick to him, and no more rot
(nonsense), and drink his health as
the head of the house.*—T. Hughes.

rouge—*rouge et noir* a well-known
game of cards. French. Literally, "red
and black."

*Those who are interested in the
mysteries of rouge et noir.*—
Beaconsfield.

rough—*to rough it* to endure hard-
ships; to do without comforts or
luxuries.

*Take care of Fanny, mother, she is
tender; and not used to rough it like
the rest of us.*—Jane Austen.

—*rough on* hard lines for; a hardship
to; unfortunate for.

*There was a universal feeling, he
assured his ward, of sympathy for him.
Everybody felt that it was rough on
such a man as himself to find that he
was not of illustrious descent.*—
Besant.

—*a rough customer* an unpleasant individual; one whose manners are
coarse.

—*a rough diamond* a person with an
unattractive exterior, who possesses
good qualities of mind and heart.

*As for Warrington, that rough diamond
had not had the polish of a dancing-
master, and he did not know how to
waltz.*—Thackeray.

—*the rough side of the tongue* rebuke;
abuse.

*Johnson, after the manner of critical
bears, often licked with the rough side
of his tongue.*

round—*a round o* nothing.

Alfred told her the round O, which had yielded to "the duck's egg," and was becoming obsolete, meant the cipher set by the scorer against a player's name who is out without making a run (at cricket).—C. Reade.

—*to go the round* to circulate; to be carried to the different members of a society.

In spite of the stories which have lately gone the round of the European press as to Russian mobilization on the frontier of Roumania, it is probable that Russia will no longer pursue the policy of tearing off bits of Turkey.—Fortnightly Review, 1887.

—*in round numbers* mentioning an approximate sum which has no small figures or fractions.

The cost, in round numbers, will be £3,200.

—*a round robin* a document, signed by a number of individuals, which has the names radiating from the centre so that no name heads the list.

Their names were reduced to writing to be respectfully submitted to Johnson. But such was the awe entertained of his frown, that every one shrank from putting his name first to the instrument; whereupon their names were written about in a circle, making what mutinous sailors called "a round robin."—Washington Irving.

—*to round on a person* to prove unfaithful to him; to behave treacherously to him.

"Jeremiah, if that venomous wretch Phœbe Farebrother had married you, would you be in danger now?"

"No; there would be nothing to trouble me, if she hadn't rounded on me.—B. L. Farjeon.

row—*a row of pins* used to signify what is of small value or importance.

"True," would be my mournful reply;

"but he doesn't amount to a row of pins" (is a very insignificant person).—Robert Grant, quoted in Edinburgh Review, 1882.

rub—*to rub down* to groom a horse.

When his fellow beasts are weary grown,
He'll play the groom, give oats, and rub 'em down.

Dryden

—*to rub up* to renew; to refresh; to brighten.

I shall be glad of the opportunity of rubbing up my classics a bit; I have been neglecting them lately.—H. R. Haggard.

—*there's the rub* that is the point which causes me trouble. A quotation from Shakespeare—Hamlet's soliloquy.

"How does your account with him stand?"

"My account! ah, there's the rub."—Edmund Yates.

Rubicon—*to cross* or *pass the Rubicon* to take a decisive step; to venture on a great and dangerous understanding. The Rubicon is a small river which separated republican Italy from Cisalpine Gaul. Cæsar, whose military command was limited to the latter province, arrived at this river, and after some hesitation crossed it. By doing so he broke the law, and became an invader of his country.

The die was thus cast, the Rubicon crossed.—Quarterly Review, 1887.

rule—*to rule the roost* or *roast* to manage; to govern; to have the chief say in everything. Probably *the roost* (meaning an assembly of fowls) is the original phrase.

The new-made duke that rules the roast.—Shakespeare.

Mrs. Nash was ruling the roast at Caromel's farm, being unquestionably both mistress and master.—Mrs. Henry Wood.

He cruised around in the rivers and inlets and sounds of North Carolina for a while, ruling the roost.—Harper's Monthly, 1887.

rum—*a rum start* a strange condition of affairs.

"Come," said Silver, struggling with his ashen lips to get the word out, "this won't do. Stand by to go about. This is a rum start."—R. L. Stevenson.

—*a rum customer* a person difficult to deal with.

run—*to run to seed.* See **seed.**

—*to run riot* to roam wildly. See **riot.**

—*to be run out of anything* to have no more in stock or in one's possession.

I must buy some stamps; I am run out of Queen's heads.—S. Baring-Gould.

—*to run short* to be insufficient.

However, the house was finished at length and furnished—furnished quietly and scantily, because the money ran short.—Chambers's Journal, 1887.

—*several days running* several days in succession.

Fine ladies would never consent to be asked for three Sundays running in the parish church.—Trevelyan.

in the long run. See **long.**

—*to run amuck* or *amok* to rush ahead violently; to go at a headlong pace. A Malay phrase. Generally associated with violent and angry collisions.

Ready to run amuck with any one who crossed him.—Disraeli.

—*to run to earth* to secure the capture of; to hunt down.

It looks extremely ugly, to say the least of it, that all the men who helped to run to earth the various members of the Ruthven family were richly rewarded.—Spectator, January 7, 1888.

—*the run of one's teeth* as much as one can eat.

It was an understood thing that he was

to have the run of his teeth at Hazelhurst, and that his use was to supply all other wants.*—Miss Braddon.

—*the run of people; the common run* ordinary folks; the average of people.

Perhaps I am scarcely an example of what is popularly called the common run of visitors at the "Ultramarine."—James Payn.

—*to be run after* to be popular and admired.

"She gives herself wonderful airs, it seems," said Bassett, rather bitterly.

Marsh flared up. "So would any woman that was as beautiful, and as witty, and as much run after as she is."—C. Reade.

—*to run down* (a) (of a vessel or any body in motion) to sink or overturn it by collision.

As he trotted on, he would call out to fast postmen ahead of him to get out of the way, devoutly believing that in the natural course of things he must inevitably overtake and run them down.—Dickens.

—(b) to speak against; to criticise unfavourably.

"How could you, could you deceive me so?" cried Ella pitifully. "Suppose I hadn't liked the poems?"

"Well, then, I should never have told you about them. But didn't you guess the truth when Felspar used to run them down, and protest that they were not half good enough for the illustrations?"—James Payn.

—(c) to discover; to hunt after and find.

"Now, look here," said the captain; "you've run me down; here I am. Well, then, speak up: what is it?"—R. L. Stevenson.

—(d) to stop through want of winding (of a watch).

The mechanism of the miller's life stopped, but that of the watch went

on, for Joe wound it up that same
evening, and it had not since been
allowed to run down.—S. Baring-
Gould.

—**run down** in a low state of health.
*This evening, especially, he was much
run down, and the unexpected chop
brought a sense of physical comfort
which he had not known for a great
while.—Besant.*

—**run on** a phrase used in printing, to
signify that a paragraph is to be continued without a break.

—**a run upon a bank** a sudden rush of
depositors and holders of notes anxious to obtain their money.
*Jessop's bank has such a number of
small depositors, and issues so
many small notes. He cannot cash
above half of them without notice. If
there comes a run, he must have to
stop payment this very day.—Miss
Mulock.*

—**to run for it** to make off; to hurry
away. *For it* does not refer to any
object, but is a mere extra phrase.
*But just then — crack! crack! crack!—
three musket-shots flashed out of the
thicket. Merry tumbled head-foremost
into the excavation; the man with the
bandage spun round like a teetotum,
and fell all his length upon his side,
where he lay dead, but still twitching;
and the other three turned and ran for
it with all their might.—R. L. Stevenson.*

—**to run up a score** to buy articles on
credit.

*Run up a score with that Jellico! No;
she'd not be such an idiot as that.—
Mrs. H. Wood.*

—**to run on anything** (of the mind) to
be occupied with thoughts of it.
*In England everybody's head runs on
dukes.—James Payn.*

—**to run a rig; to run one's rigs** to play
a trick; to be riotous.
*While I live you shall be kept straight
and like a lady; and when I'm gone I
shan't be none (any) the wiser if you
go wrong and run your rigs as you
have done.—Mrs. E. Lynn Linton.*

—**to run over** (a) to overflow.
*He fills his famished maw, his mouth
  runs o'er
With unchewed morsels, while he
  churns the gore.*
                                    Dryden.

—(b) to read or consider in a hasty
manner.
*If we run over the other nations of
Europe, we shall only pass through so
many different scenes of poverty.—
Addison.*

—**to run out** (a) to come to an end.
*When a lease had run out, he
stipulated with his tenant to resign up
twenty acres without lessening his
rent.—Swift.*

—**to run up** (of a building) to erect
speedily; to build in a short time.
*This whole street was run up in three
months' time.*

rush— **not worth a rush** of no value.
*John Bull's friendship is not worth a
rush.—Arbuthnot.*

S

sack—*to get the sack* to be dismissed from employment. A phrase common in French, were *sac* (sack) means knapsack. It has, therefore, reference to the "marching off" of a soldier.
*I say, I wonder what old Fogg 'ud (would) say, if he knew it. I should get the sack, I s'pose (suppose), eh?—*Hugh Conway.

sackcloth—*in sackcloth and ashes* in grief and repentance. This is a Scriptural expression, and comes from the habit of Eastern nations on occasions of sorrow and remorse.
*A deplorable error and misfortune, for which humanity should mourn in sackcloth and ashes.—*J. Mill.

sad—*a sad dog* a merry fellow; a gay man; a man given to joking.
I am afraid, ma'am, your son is a sad dog.

safe—*safe bind, safe find* what is packed up securely will be easily got again.
*Safe bind, safe find—you know the proverb.—*Wilkie Collins.

sail—*to sail close to the wind* to go very near to impropriety or danger. Said of a ship when nearly running into the wind.
*He had always been so especially hard on a certain kind of young English gentleman, who has sailed too close to the wind at home, and who comes to the colony to be whitewashed.—*H. Kingsley.
—*to make sail* (a) to start (of a sailing vessel).
The captain gave orders for unmooring ship, and we made sail, dropping
down slowly with the wind and tide.—R. H. Dana, Jun.
—(b) to start; to go off.
*The signal to make sail for the drawing-room was given, and they all arose and departed.—*Thackeray.
—*to strike sail* (a) to lower the sails.
—(b) to be more humble; to lessen one's pretensions.
*Margaret
Must strike her sail, and learn awhile
    to serve
While kings command.*
                    Shakespeare.
—*sail of the line* warships.
*Before he left Egypt he (Nelson) burnt three of the prizes. They could not have been fitted for a passage to Gibraltar in less than a month, and that at a great expense, and with the loss of the service of at least two sail of the line.—*Southey.

to set sail. See set.

sake—*for sake's sake* for old times; because of previous acquaintance. Equal to the Scotch "for auld lang-syne."
*I've a-been (I have been) long minded to do't for sake's sake.—*T. Hughes.
*Yet for old sake's sake she is still, dears,
The prettiest doll in the world.*
                    C. Kingsley.

salt—*above the salt* in a position of honour. The salt-cellar in the dining-hall of former times was placed half-way down the table, and marked the division between the equals of the master in rank and his inferiors.

—*below the salt* in an inferior position. His lordship's business, however, lies chiefly with those, so to speak, below the salt.—G. J. White-Melville.

—*to eat a man's salt* to partake of his hospitality; to be his guest. It is, among the Arabs especially, constituted a sacred bond between host and guest. It is considered unseemly for a person to eat a man's salt and then to speak ill of him.
One does not eat a man's salt, as it were, at these dinners. There is nothing sacred in this kind of London hospitality.—Thackeray.

—*to salt a mine* to sprinkle some precious ore about it, so that it may appear rich and productive. A common trick.
If it hadn't been for the Dutchman's story, they would never have known the mine was salted at all.—St. Louis Democrat, April 17, 1888.

—*to throw salt on the tail* a ludicrous phrase, applied to the attempted capture of something difficult to catch. Children are told they may catch birds if they succeed in throwing salt upon their tails, as in the nursery rhyme,—
Simple Simon went a-hunting
  For to catch a quail;
He got a pennyworth of salt
  To throw upon its tail.
His intelligence is so good, that were you coming near him with soldiers or constables or the like, I shall answer for it you will never lay salt on his tail.—Scott.

—*the salt of the earth* the wholesome portion of a community; that portion of a community which has a good influence upon the rest. The expression is taken from Matthew v. 13: "Ye are the salt of the earth."
We require to call up before us the dissenting community of the period, with its strong underlying sense, not only that it was the salt of the earth, but that its bounden duty was to prove itself so.—Mrs. Oliphant.

—*to spill salt* This is considered unlucky. It is also considered unlucky to help another to salt at table: "Help to salt, help to sorrow."
Some of these eggs were for breakfast, and I ate them with a good appetite; but in helping myself to salt I spilled it, on which she started up with a scream.—Thackeray.

—*worth one's salt* of value; serviceable.
Every man who is worth his salt has his enemies.—T. Hughes.

—*true to one's salt* faithful to one's employer.
Faithful as they were to their salt, they had never so much as dreamed that the master whom they had served so loyally could betray them.—J. A. Froude.

with a grain of salt. See **grain.**

sam—*to stand Sam* to entertain friends; to pay for refreshments Sam is a contraction for "Uncle Sam," a jocular name for the U.S. Government. The phrase, therefore, originally means to pay all expenses, as the government does.

Samaritan—*a good Samaritan* one who behaves in a kind and compassionate manner to those who have no claim upon him. See the parable of the Good Samaritan (Luke x. 29).
It is seldom that debtors or good Samaritans waylay people under gas-lamps in order to force money upon them, so far as I have seen or heard.—J. R. Lowell.

same—*all the same* (a) no difference.
"It must be late in the afternoon, then," said the lawyer rather crossly.
    "All the same to me," acquiesced the Pater.—Mrs. H. Wood.

—(b) nevertheless.

He may be a reformed character. All the same, I cannot employ him.

sanctum—*sanctum sanctorum* a private retreat; the room in a house set apart for one's private use. Latin.

"If I might be allowed to propose," said Lazarus, "I would suggest your following me into my sanctum sanctorum."—S. Baring-Gould.

sand—*the sand has run out* the appointed term has come to an end. *Sand* is here the sand in the hourglass, by which time was formerly measured.

"Hush, my child—never talk of dying. Please God, you may have many years of life before you."

She shook her golden head a little sadly, "No, doctor, my sand has run out; and perhaps it is as well.'—H. R. Haggard.

sang—*sang froid* cold blood; calmness in the presence of excitement or of danger. French.

Then Robinson, who had never lost his presence of mind, and had now recovered his sang froid, made all four captives sit round together on the ground in one little lot.—C. Reade.

sans—*sans façon* without observing strict etiquette. French.

"Will you both come and dine with me to-night, sans façon; there will be nobody except Agatha and Mr. Heigham?" asked Mrs. Carr.—H. R. Haggard.

satin—*a yard of satin* a glass of gin. London slang.

sauce—*what is sauce for the goose is sauce for the gander* like things demand like treatment.

Now, what's sauce for the goose is sauce for the gander: if you put a pressure on one class to make it train itself properly, you must put a pressure on others to the same end.—M. Arnold.

sauve—*sauve qui peut* This phrase is used when, in a time of danger, every one looks out for his own safety. French.

If Swift had not been committed to the statesmen of the losing side, what a fine satirical picture we might have had of that general sauve qui peut (scramble out of danger) amongst the Tory party.—Thackeray.

savoir—*savoir vivre* knowledge of polite life. French.

Miss Nugent had always seen him in large companies, where he was admired for his savoir vivre and entertaining anecdotes.—Maria Edgeworth.

say—*to say one's say* to say all one has to say; to tell one's own story in one's own way.

Ladies and gentlemen, the workman has said his say, and I hope the company have been amused.—C. Reade.

scarce—*to make oneself scarce* to retire; to withdraw; to go off.

When a lady tells you decidedly she can't stop to talk to you, and when she appears up to her eyes in cleaning house or something of that sort, the next thing to do is to make yourself scarce.—George Eliot.

scarlet—*the scarlet woman* the Church of Rome. A term borrowed from the Bible (Rev. xvii. 4).

The latter old lady (Rome) may be the Scarlet Woman, or the beast with ten horns, if you will.—J. R. Lowell.

schoolmaster—*the schoolmaster is abroad* good education is spreading everywhere. Often, but wrongly, used in the opposite sense—to imply that the schoolmaster is absent, and is much needed.

Let the soldier be abroad if he will, he can do nothing in this age. There is another personage—a personage less imposing in the eyes of some, perhaps insignificant. *The schoolmaster is abroad, and I trust to him, armed with his primer, against the soldier in full military array.*—Lord Brougham.

scissors—*scissors and paste* the implements of a newspaper sub-editor, who cuts out extracts from other journals for his own.

They saw in the applicant for the editorship merely an inferior, whose duty had probably lain in the scissors and paste department.—Besant.

scot—*scot free* quite uninjured.

I could not name a single woman of my acquaintance of whom I have not heard some story or other. Even dear, good, old Hester doesn't come off scot free.—Florence Marryat.

scotch—*scotch fiddle* the itch.

—*a scotch marriage* an irregular marriage. The Scotch marriage law required very few formalities. The village of Gretna Green, on the Border, was famous for such marriages.

A good many years ago, when I was very young, and a most consummate fool, I got myself entrapped into a Scotch marriage.—Miss Braddon.

—*a scotch mist* a drizzling rain.

"Drop, drip, drip!" cried Celia, pettishly; "one of those odious Scotch mists, that is as likely to last for a week as for an hour.—Miss Braddon.

Scotland—*Scotland Yard* the London police headquarters.

He'll bleed you to your last sixpence, and, as likely as not, when you're cleaned out he'll write to Scotland Yard.—D. Christie Murray.

scrape—*to scrape acquaintance with any one* to insinuate oneself into terms of familiarity; to make friends in a chance way.

screw—*a screw loose* something wrong; a disturbing element. Said when two friends have a difference, or when

something wrong or unpleasant happens in one's affairs.

Our landlady turned pale;—no doubt she thought there was a screw loose in my intellect.—O. W. Holmes.

—*an old screw* a miserly fellow.

This gentleman and the guard knew Sir Pitt very well, and laughed at him a great deal. They both agreed in calling him an old screw, which means a very stingy, avaricious person.—Thackeray.

—*to draw one's screw* to draw one's salary.

He's a reporter on the News, and draws a handsome screw.—Besant.

—*to screw one's courage to the sticking-place* to resolve to act decisively; to summon up boldness to strike. A quotation from Shakespeare (*Macbeth* act i. scene vii. line 60): "But screw your courage to the sticking-place, and we'll not fail."

He either did not fear him, or had screwed his courage to the sticking-place.—James Payn.

—*to put on the screw* to limit one's credit; to be less bold and venturesome in business undertakings.

—*to put under the screw* to coerce or compel.

—*to put the screw on* to bring pressure to bear on; to apply force to.

He knew where he could put the screw on George.—Thackeray.

—*regularly screwed.* drunk.

sea—*at sea* in a state of perplexity; unable to give any explanation or solution.

I could not have been more at sea had I seen a Chinese lady from Pekin.—Mrs. H. Wood.

—*half seas over* the worse for liquor.

—*to get one's sea-legs on* to be able to walk steadily on shipboard.

Give him a little time to get the use of his wits in emergencies, and to know the little arts that do so much for a patient's comfort—just as you give a young sailor time to get his sea-legs on and teach his stomach to behave itself—and he will do well enough.—O. W. Holmes.

—**beyond seas** on the other side of the ocean.

The husband or lover may have been out of the way—beyond seas, perhaps—a sailor, very likely.—Miss Braddon.

—**sea-horses** the white breakers on the sea-coast.

Alice's eyes are fixed on the white sea-horses.—Austen Pember.

—**the son of a sea-cook** a contemptuous term in use among seamen.

If he got any more cheek from him, or any other post and rail son of a sea-cook.—H. Kingsley.

sear—**the sear and yellow leaf** old age.

My way of life
Is fallen into the sear, the yellow leaf.
Shakespeare.

The baby in whose honour they had all met is a matron in the sear and yellow leaf.—Thomas Hardy.

season—**in season and out of season** at suitable times and at unsuitable times.

He made many enemies by these things, uttered in season and out of season.—Macmillan's Magazine, 1887.

second—**to come off second best** to be defeated.

The Koh-i-noor, as we named the gentleman with the diamond, left us, however, soon after that "little mill," as the young fellow John called it, where he came off second best.—O. W. Holmes.

see—**to see double** to be drunk.

—**to have seen better days** to have been in a higher social position; to have been in a better condition. Used both of persons and things.

He's an Englishman, and, I guess, has seen better days.—Haliburton.

—**to see to anything** to attend to it; to take care of it.

She (Lady Palmerston) saw to everything.—Public Opinion, 1886.

—**to see off** to accompany to the place of departure; to witness the departure of.

Before he could say any more, in came Bessie herself, saying that the driver was waiting, and they went out to see her sister off.—H. R. Haggard.

—**to see well and good** to think fit; to be willing; to consent.

An' if your reverence sees well and good, I'll send my boy to tell 'em as soon as I get home.—George Eliot.

seed—**to run to seed** (a) to grow rank; to become weak by excess of growth.

Mr. Monks is aware that I am not a young man, my dear, and also that I am a little run to seed.—Dickens.

—(b) to become seedy, or worn out.

seek—**to seek** lacking; deficient.

The Germans in Greek
Are sadly to seek.
Porson.

sell—**to sell another man** to deceive him.

Did I ever tell you how the young vagabond sold me last half?—T. Hughes.

—**to sell a man up** to force him to become bankrupt; to compel him to have his property brought to auction.

Then he would send in his bills, sue her, sell her up, and drive her out of the place stripped to the last farthing.—Besant.

—**to sell out** (a) to leave the army. This phrase was used when commissions in the army were bought and sold, a system abolished by Mr. Gladstone's government in 1869.

It was in this period that he quitted the

Guards, and sold out of the army.—
Thackeray.

—(b) to get rid of investments; to take ready money in place of investments.
Still a great loss would be incurred by selling out of them at a period of depression.—C. Reade.

—**to sell off** to part with the whole of anything.
George heard of a farmer who was selling off his sheep about fifty miles off near the coast.—C. Reade.

send—**to send to Coventry** to exclude from companionship. "Sent to Coventry" signifies in disgrace or disfavour with one's associates. Most used by schoolboys, who inflict the punishment frequently on their fellows. See **boycott**.
In fact that solemn assembly, a levy of the school, had been held, at which the captain of the school had got up, and given out that any boy, in whatever form, who should thenceforth appeal to a master, without having first gone to some prepositor and laid the case before him, should be thrashed publicly and sent to Coventry.—T. Hughes.

—**to send one about one's business** to dismiss peremptorily.
Upon this I was, naturally, mollified, and sent him about his business, hoping to have seen the last of him at Highmore.—C. Reade.

seniores—**seniores priores** elders first; let the older people take precedence. Latin.
We say at school, Seniores priores (let favour go by seniority).—C. Reade.

sere. See **sear**.

serve—**to serve a person out** to retaliate upon him for real or fancied wrongs; to wreak revenge on him.
"Little brute," cried Hawes viciously; "I'll work him; I'll serve him out."—C. Reade.

—**to serve a man right** to be a right treatment for him; to punish him deservedly.
He knocked him clean off his legs on to the deck, where he lay stunned and bleeding. "Serve him right," cried Charlie from the hatchway.—G. J. Whyte-Melville.

—**to serve one's turn** to be useful on occasion; to assist or prove serviceable when needed.
His connection with the press serves our turn, Harry, doesn't it?—Edmund Yates.

—**to serve one a bad turn** to do him an injury.
You mean well, I have no doubt; but you never in your life served me a worse turn than when you prevented me from hitting that man.—W. E. Norris.

set—**to set about** to commence; to made preparations for.
They gave him hints that he might set about doing something to provide himself with a living.—William Black.

—**to set one's cap at** (of a woman) to try to captivate; to try to obtain as a husband.
"You won't like everything from India now, Miss Sharp," said the old gentleman; but when the ladies had retired after dinner, the wily old fellow said to his son, "Have a care, Joe; that girl is setting her cap at you."—Thackeray.

—**to set one's face against** to oppose resolutely.
Nor was it in the least on æsthetic grounds that he had set his face against the whole scheme.—Good Words, 1887.

—**to set the teeth on edge** to irritate; to grate upon the feelings.
His nails also were flat and shapeless, and he used to be continually gnawing them till he had succeeded in getting

them down to the quick, and they were
a sight to set a Christian's teeth on
edge.—S. Warren.

—*to set one's face like a flint* to be
resolute and determined.
They were a couple of lion-like men;
they had set their faces like a flint.—
Bunyan.

—*to set against* or *over against* to place
on the opposite side from, so as to
counterbalance or make even.
In fact, one vice is to be set over
against another, and thus something
like a balance is obtained.—R. H.
Dana.

—*to set on foot* to start; to begin.
He did not stop to set on foot an inquiry
into his train of thought or state of
feeling.—Dickens.

—*to set the Thames* (or *a river*) *on fire*
to be conspicuously able; to be a man
of light and leading.
I hardly expect him to set the Thames
on fire; but I hope his mother will never
have reason to be ashamed of him.—
W. E. Norris.

—*well set up* well built; having a powerful frame.
He was well set up; a big, handsome
fellow, with brown hair straight and
short, a smooth cheek, and a full
moustache.—Besant.

—*to set off* (a) to start.
He set off for Bedford early that
morning.—C. Reade.

—(b) to embellish; to show to advantage.
That is a becoming glass, Gwendolen;
or is it the black and gold colour that
sets you off?—George Eliot.

—*a set-off* what counter-balances.
Others talked of the shop as infra dig;
the set-off against which was the
education and beauty of the bride.—
Captain Marryat.

—*to set in* to become settled in a particular state.

The afternoon set in dull, and toward
evening the sea freshened sufficiently
to send most of the passengers
below.—H. R. Haggard.

—*to set sail* to start on a voyage.
Henry had taken the child she brought
him in his arms, and set sail in a vessel
bound for Africa.—Mrs. Inchbald.

—*to set up for* to pretend to be.
Henry White swore he would take
rooms at the Tremont House and set up
for a gentleman.—R. H. Dana, Jun.

to set store by see **Store.**

—*to set little by* to value slightly; to
despise.
His prince, the lord of that country, will
shortly come into these parts and will
know the reason, if they have any, why
his neighbours set so little by him.—
Bunyan.

—*a set-to* a fight.

—*at a dead set* in a state of stagnation;
at a standstill.

settle—*to settle a man's hash* to kill
him.
He received some terrible kicks on the
back and legs. "Give it him on the
head!"—"Kick his life out!—"Settle his
hash!"—C. Reade.

—*to settle down* to adopt a regular
mode of life; to engage in one's life-
work; to cease to wander about.
"Surely," thought Angela, "he is settling
down; he will soon find work."—Besant.

seven—*the seven deadly sins* pride,
envy, wrath, sloth, covetousness, glut-
tony, and lust.
Sure, it is no sin;
Or of the deadly sins it is the least.
                                  Shakespeare.
Vulgarity is an eighth deadly sin, added
to the list in these later days.—J. R.
Lowell.

—*seven-league boots* boots which carried their wearer at an extraordinarily
rapid rate. An expression borrowed
from a well-known fairy tale.

Mr. Carlyle would be much better if he didn't take health by the throat (as it were), bathing as if he were a little boy in the Serpentine, walking as if he had seven-league boots.—Jane Carlyle.

—*the seven sleepers* seven Christian youths who fled from persecution in the third century, and fell asleep in a cave. They did not awake until their discovery more than two hundred years later. The story occurs in various forms.

A roasted ox and a lethargy like that of the seven sleepers would scarce restore you to the use of your refreshed and waking senses.—Scott.

—*a seven days' wonder* something which absorbs public interest for a short time and then is forgotten. See **nine**.

The seven days' wonder about the boy had almost died away.—Hugh Conway.

sewn—*sewn up* intoxicated.

He took care to tell you that some of the party were pretty considerably "sewn up" too.—Thackeray.

shade—*to fall into the shade* to cease to attract attention.

But, finally, the original Semite fell more and more into the shade. The Aryan came to the front.—H. R. Haggard.

shake—*to shake a leg* to dance.

I explain that the stage is ready for them, if they like to act; or the concert-room, if they will sing; or the dancing-room, should they wish to shake a leg.—Besant.

—*to shake one's head* to indicate disapproval, doubt, or dissent.

When he read the note from the two ladies, he shook his head, and observed that an affair of this sort demanded the utmost circumspection.—Goldsmith.

—*no great shakes* of little value or account.

Oatmeal is no great shakes at best. It ain't even so good for a horse as real yellow Indian corn.—Haliburton.

—*to shake by the hand* or *shake hands* to salute by grasping the hand.

He said, "I wish you to abstain from writing to Sir Charles, and him to visit you only once more before his marriage, just to shake hands and part, with mutual friendship and good wishes.—C. Reade.

—*to shake the elbow* to gamble with dice.

—*to shake the dust off one's feet* (a) an act showing one's displeasure with any place and a determination never to return thither.

He (Beaust) had been regarded by the Austrians as the author of their misfortunes, and wrote from their capital to a friend in Saxony: "Tomorrow I leave Vienna. I will shake the dust off my feet. I will not return there in a hurry."—Quarterly Review, 1887.

—(b) to cease travelling.

At length the pilgrim shook the dust off his feet at Heidelberg.—Beaconsfield.

—*to shake in one's shoes* to be in a state of apprehension or fright.

The children's copybooks, etc., were laid out for inspection, while the embryo scholars manifestly shook in their shoes before the verdict to be pronounced on their halting performance.—Sarah Tytler.

sharp—*sharp practice* grasping behaviour; conduct which is defensive on legal grounds, but is yet considered ungenerous.

"I call this," said Tommy, in a great rage, "confounded sharp practice."—Besant.

sheep—*to cast* or *make sheep's eyes* to look at with amorous eyes.

The horrid old colonel, with a head as bald as a cannon ball, was making sheep's eyes at a half-caste girl there.—Thackeray.

—*black sheep* bad characters.

"We are as liable to have black sheep here as elsewhere," the archdeacon replied.—A. Trollope.

sheet—*three sheets in the wind* half-intoxicated.

Captain Cuttle, looking, candle in hand, at Bunsby more attentively, believed that he was three sheets in the wind, or, in plain words, drunk.—Dickens.

shelf—*laid* or *put on the shelf* no longer engaged in active work; set aside to make room for more active workers.

What is a man to do when he's put on the shelf and has no home?—Good Words, 1887.

shell—*to shell out* to pay out money.

We can always make the old villain shell out, as he ought.—Mrs. E. Lynn Linton.

shield—*the other side of the shield* the other side of any question. The story is told of two knights who, meeting at a post from which a shield was suspended, fell to quarrelling about the material of which the shield was composed. The one held it to be gold, the other silver. From words they came to blows. After a bitter struggle they discovered that both were right, since the one side was gold, and the other side silver.

shift—*to make shift* to contrive with difficulty.

By my other labours I make shift to eat and drink and have good clothes.—Goldsmith.

shilling—*to take the Queen's shilling* or *get the shilling* to become a soldier. Soldiers on enlisting received a shilling from the recruiting sergeant as a sign of the bargain having been concluded.

It was then that, not caring what became of me, I took the Queen's shilling, and became a soldier.—B. L. Farjeon.

shine—*to take the shine out of* to surpass; to outshine; to outvie. Also, but less correctly, off of.

You will become a rival potentate to my governor. You will take the shine out of him directly.—C. Reade.

He is the first man of the age; and it's generally allowed our doctors take the shine off all the world.—Haliburton.

ship—*when one's ship comes in* or *home* when one's fortune is made.

The wealthy relative, of whom he borrowed for Douglas's sake, proposed to supply him with an income of a hundred pounds per annum until the major's next expected ship should come in.—D. Christie Murray.

—*ship-shape* neatly arranged.

—*the ship of the desert* the camel.

shoe—*to shoe a goose or a gosling* to engage in a foolish or fruitless undertaking.

"The smith that will meddle with all things may go shoe the goslings," is an old proverb.—Maria Edgeworth.

—*to die in one's shoes* to die on the scaffold.

And there is Mr. Fuse, and Lieutenant Treegooze,

And there is Sir Carnaby Jenks of the Blues,

All come to see a man die in his shoes. Barham.

—*to stand in another's shoes* to occupy the position held by another.

Don't think, if you value your peace of mind, to stand in my shoes when they are vacant.—Thackeray.

—*to thread the shoes straight* to be upright in one's conduct.

—*to throw an old shoe after one* This is done at weddings to wish good luck to the person. An old shoe means "long life."

—*to shake in one's shoes* to be in a state of nervous terror.

When Mrs. Proudie began to talk of the souls of the people he always shook in his shoes.—A. Trollope.

—*to be in another person's shoes* to be in the same position as another.

"Oh, would I be in Arthur's shoes after fourth lesson?" said the little boys to one another.—T. Hughes.

—*to step into another person's shoes* to take the position previously occupied by another.

"That will do, sir," he thundered; "that will do. It is very evident now what would happen if you stepped into my shoes after my death."—Good Words, 1887.

—*to wait for another's shoes* to look forward with expectation to his death.

Cornelis, the eldest, who had made calculations of his own, and stuck to the hearth, waiting for dead men's shoes.—C. Reade.

—*quite a different pair of shoes* an altogether different cause. Probably a corruption of the French *tout autre chose*, "an altogether different thing."

Promise and performance are a very different pair of shoes.—Blackmore.

—*where the shoe pinches* where the difficulty or cause of discomfort lies.

"I do not believe it; and, anyhow, I will not have you flirting with her in my presence."

"Ah, that is where the shoe pinches."—Florence Marryat.

shoot—*to shoot the pit* to cheat a landlord by leaving without paying the rent. Compare "moonlight flitting" and "shooting of moons," which see.

shooting of moons see **moon**.

shop—*to talk shop* to speak exclusively of one's own business or professional affairs.

"When he had a few clergymen round

him, how he loved to make them happy!"

"Never talked shop to them, did he?" said the archdeacon.—A. Trollope.

short—*a short cut* a quick path; a path which saves distance; a method which saves time.

"See yonder, how our young people are enjoying themselves!" and he pointed with his whip to where Ella and Anastasia, accompanied by Vernon and Felspar, could be seen approaching them by a short cut.—James Payn.

—*short shrift* little time to repent; but a small interval before the infliction of punishment. *Shrift* was the priest's absolution.

The neighbours would form a posse in a twinkling, and chase the thief night and day till they secured him; and then short shrift for the poor wretch.—Macmillan's Magazine, 1887.

—*the short and the long of it* the whole matter stated briefly; the sum and substance of the matter.

And the short and the long of the matter was, that while we could get several who were willing enough to ride to Dr. Livesey's, which lay in another direction, not one would help us to defend the inn.—R. L. Stevenson.

shot—*shot in the locker* funds in hand.

"As long as there's shot in the locker, she shall want for nothing," said the generous fellow.—Thackeray.

shoulder—*to turn, show, or give the cold shoulder* to treat coolly; to repulse.

Since I discarded him for Nave, he has turned the cold shoulder upon me.—Mrs. Henry Wood.

I'm afraid people are rather inclined to show them the cold shoulder.—Good Words, 1887.

Some time ago you had a friend whose companionship I thought was doing you no good, and I gave him the cold shoulder.—James Payn.

—*to have an old head on young shoulders* to be wise beyond one's years.

You appear to have an old head upon very young shoulders.—Captain Marryat.

—*to rub shoulders* to come into close contact.

Here was a dreary outlook for persons who knew democracy, not by rubbing shoulders with it lifelong, but merely from books.—J. R. Lowell.

—*with one's shoulder to the collar* hard at work.

Have I not always had my shoulder to the collar?—A. Trollope.

—*to put one's shoulder to the wheel* to commence working in earnest.

"Still, you have only to put your shoulder to the wheel," insisted the secretary. "Time and patience conquer everything."—James Payn.

show—*to show the door* to dismiss without ceremony.

The upshot of the matter for that while was, that she showed both of them the door.—R. L. Stevenson.

—*to show off* to make a vain display; to display for the purpose of exciting admiration.

For this year the Wellesburn return match and the Marylebone match are played at Rugby, to the great delight of the town and neighbourhood, and the sorrow of those aspiring young cricketers who have been reckoning for the last three months on showing off at Lord's ground.—T. Hughes.

—*to show in* to conduct into a house.

Without suffering me to wait long, my old friend embraced me with the most cordial welcome, showed me in, and assured me that he considered himself peculiarly fortunate in having

under his roof the man he most loved on earth.—Goldsmith.

—*to show to a room* to conduct thither.

She was so fatigued with the journey, she wished to be shown to her room at once.—Florence Marryat.

—*to show one's teeth* to display signs of anger.

—*to show one's hand* to reveal one's plan of action.

From time to time a man must show his hand, but save for one supreme exigency a woman need never show hers.—W. D. Howells.

—*to show a person up* to reveal to the world a person's real character; to disclose a person's villainy or hypocrisy.

"You are a liar, Uncle Coetzee," was the cool answer. "English with the English, Boer with the Boer. You blow neither hot nor cold. Be careful lest we show you up."—H. R. Haggard.

—*a show of hands* a display of right hands in voting. A chairman, wishing for the decision of a question by a meeting, often calls for a show of hands.

shut—*to shut up* to be silent.

"True for you, old man," said Trevor, good-naturedly laughing. "Pitch that fellow Dick over the arm of the chair and make him shut up."—Blackwood's Magazine, 1886.

—*to shut a person up* to silence him.

Though we agree with Mr. Skelton in wishing that we had also Maillard's account of it, we cannot doubt that the reformer (to use the colloquial expression) shut him up.—Athenæum, 1887.

—*to shut the stable door when the steed is stolen* to take precautions when too late.

And then it all came out—the old story of shutting the stable-door on the stolen steed, and separation, when the mischief of constant

companionship had been done.—
Mistletoe Bough, 1887.

—*to shut up shop* to close business; to
cease working.

*About this time, in the beginning of
1824, the Jamaica Ginger Beer
Company shut up shop—exploded, as
Gus said, with a bang!*—Thackeray.

sight—*out of sight* incomparably;
beyond comparison.

*She was walking back through the
quiet streets of the old-fashioned
market-town to the Bank House, with
its peculiar importance and dignity, out
of sight the best house in Newton.*—
Sarah Tytler.

—*a bill at sight* a bill which will be
cashed when presented, and not after
three or six months.

*I'll pay you off that kiss with interest; I'll
answer a bill at sight for it (pay at
once), I will, you may depend.*—
Haliburton.

—*a sight of things* a great number of
things.

*Bought a sight of furniture—couldn't
hardly get some of it upstairs.*—O. W.
Holmes.

—*a sight for sore eyes* a pleasant object;
something pleasant to see.

*"I hope," said she, "my lady will come
and see me when my lamb is with me;
a sight of her would be good for sore
eyes."*—C. Reade.

silent—*silent as the grave* wholly silent;
saying nothing; making no noise.

*"Livesey," said the squire, "I'll be as
silent as the grave."*—R. L. Stevenson.

silk—*to make a silk purse out of a
sow's ear* to make a handsome article
out of coarse and inferior materials.

*He flung the Phänomenologie to the
other end of the room, exclaiming,
"That smart young fellow is quite right!
it is impossible to make a silk purse
out of a sow's ear."*—M. Arnold.

—*the silken tie* the soft and invisible
bonds of love and affection.

*True love's the gift which God has
given.
To man alone beneath the heaven . . .
It is the secret sympathy,
The silver link, the silken tie,
Which heart to heart, and mind to mind,
In body and in soul can bind.*
                                        Scott.

—*to take silk* to be made a King's
Counsel (K.C.) at the English bar,
and be entitled to wear a silk robe.

*Weston became a distinguished
barrister and in due course took silk.*

silver—*every cloud has a silver lining*
there is always some ray of hope in
the darkest condition of affairs.

*"I have a bad headache to-day," said
Helen, by way of excuse for her tears.
"It has been gloomy weather lately."*

*"Gloomy within and without," he
assented, giving a meaning to her
words that she had not meant to imply.
"But in every cloud, you know,
however dark it may be, there is a silver
lining."*—Mrs. H. Wood.

—*a silver wedding* the celebration of
the twenty-fifth anniversary of a
wedding.

*The jubilee of her Majesty will be
immediately followed by the year
marking the heir apparent's silver
wedding.*—Fortnightly Review, 1887.

**born with a silver spoon in one's
mouth.** See **spoon.**

—*the silver-fork school* a name used by
Thackeray for the school of novelists
who describe only elegant life and
fashionable society.

*Up to the heights of fashion with the
charming enchanters of the silver-fork
school.*—Thackeray.

sine—*sine die* without fixing any future
date; indefinitely. Latin.

*Our old friend was even now balancing
on the brink of that eventful plunge (a*

proposal of marriage), which, if not made before the grand climacteric, it is generally thought advisable to postpone sine die.—G. J. Whyte-Melville.

—*a sine quâ non* an essential; what is absolutely requisite. Latin.

"Besides, sir," he added, turning to the warder with an assumed air of deference, "I believe it is a sine quâ non—*I mean it is indispensable—that for some time I must report myself to the police once a month."*—Hugh Conway.

sinews—*the sinews of war* money; funds.

Widow Maxey had only become reconciled to her abdication, because, as was well known, she had remained in possession of the sinews of war—that is, the actual proprietorship of the horse and cart, in addition to her savings.—Sarah Tytler.

sink—*leave him to sink or swim* do not aid him, but let him fail or succeed by his own efforts.

Her husband told her that she must sink or swim with him.—Edmund Yates.

sit—*to sit up for any one* to await a person's return after the usual bedtime.

Her own maid should sit up for her.—George Eliot.

—*to sit out anything* to refrain from taking part in it.

Frank danced beautifully, but somehow we had given up dancing together lately, and used to sit out our dances together.—The Mistletoe Bough, 1885.

—*to sit out* to stay longer in one's seat than another can. Often used in accounts of drinking parties.

On coming into the estate he gave the finest entertainment ever was heard of in the country; not a man could stand

after supper but Sir Patrick himself, who could sit out the best man in Ireland.—Maria Edgeworth.

—*to sit on the rail or fence* to refuse to support any party; to reserve one's decision as a voter. An American phrase.

In the American political slang, he (Henry IV.) was always sitting on the rail between Catholics and Huguenots.—The Times.

—*to sit under a clergyman* to attend his church.

She, after a time, sat under him, as the phrase is, regularly thrice a week.—Thackeray.

six—*six of* or *to one, and half a dozen of* or *to the other* essentially the same; differing in nothing.

There's been a good deal of fun made of rabbinical fables; but, in point of fables, my opinion is, that all over the world it's six of one and half a dozen of the other.—George Eliot.

Also in the shorter form—**six and a half dozen.**

"What do they say about his chance?"
"Six and a half dozen, sir."—H. Kingsley.

—*at sixes and sevens* in disorder; ill-arranged.

Its vicinity (the presence of soldiers in a town), in our own experience, has invariably over-roasted our mutton, multiplied our cobwebs, and placed our female establishment generally at sixes and sevens.—G. J. Whyte-Melville.

sixty—*like sixty.* See **statice.**

skeleton—*the skeleton in the house or cupboard* the secret cause of grief or shame in a household.

After that first and last visit, his father's name was never mentioned in Pitt's polite and genteel establishment. It was the skeleton in the house, and all the family walked by it in terror and silence.—Thackeray.

skin—*to skin a flea for its hide* to be excessively mean and avaricious.
"*Generous!*" *I exclaimed; "why, he's the meanest little hunks that ever skinned a flea for the hide and fat.*"—G. A. Sala.

—*to skin a flint* to be excessively grasping. Hence the term skinflint for a miser.
Just as the toper squeezes the empty bottle and the miser skins the flint.—Besant.

—*to escape by the skin of one's teeth* to escape very narrowly; to come within an ace of falling a victim.
It is true that ten years before this he had, after an almost heroic resistance, yielded to accept office in the Palmerston Ministry, and escaped only by the skin of his teeth.—Leisure Hour, 1887.

—*to save one's skin* to get off without bodily hurt.
We meet with many of these dangerous civilities, wherein it is hard for a man to save both his skin and his credit.—L'Estrange.

skip—*to skip over* to pass unnoticed.
A gentleman made it a rule in reading to skip over all sentences where he spied a note of admiration at the end.—Swift.

sky—*to sky a picture* to place it in an exhibition high up on the wall.
This flight of Eastern imagery was due to his picture having been skied in the academy.—James Payn.

—*to laud* or *praise to the skies* to be loud in praise of.
Indeed he was lauded by many persons to the skies.—James Payn.

slap—*a slap-bang shop* a low eating-house. A London term.
They lived in the same street, walked into town every morning at the same

hour, dined at the same slap-bang every day.—Dickens.

—*slap-up* very fine; elegant.
More slap-up still, have the two shields painted on the panels with the coronet over.—Thackeray.

sleeping—*a sleeping partner* a member of a firm who takes no share in its management, but receives part of the profits.
In most businesses there are sleeping partners.—Captain Marryat.

—*let sleeping dogs lie* do not refer to unpleasant events of the past.
Peter Scott was a jealous man to begin with, and it was best to let sleeping dogs lie.—St. Andrews Citizen, 1887.

—*to sleep upon anything* to defer action until next morning. Cautious people often prefer to wait at least twelve hours before they commit themselves to a course of action.
Still he went in to breakfast with some slight hope that, now Mrs. Glegg has "slept upon it," her anger might be subdued enough to give way to her usually strong sense of family decorum.—George Eliot.

sleeve—*to laugh in one's sleeve.* See **laugh**.

—*to carry a thing on one's sleeve* to reveal it to the public gaze. See **heart** and **wear**.
He (the poet) should talk well, but not with an obvious striving after epigram; he should be sensitive, but not carry his vanity openly on his sleeve for the daws to peck at.—Besant.

—*in one's sleeve* secretly.
Mostly used of secret laughter. "No, not that woman," said Mr. Harding, enjoying his joke in his sleeve.—A. Trollope.

sleight—*sleight-of-hand* manual dexterity; clever use of the fingers.
Vivian, you are a juggler; and the deceptions of your sleight-of-hand

tricks depend upon instantaneous motions.—Beaconsfield.

slide—*to let things slide* to refuse or neglect to interfere; to leave matters to develop themselves.

She was not one of those diplomatists who advocate a masterly inaction, and let things slide.—James Payn.

sling—*to sling one's hook* to move on.

slip—*to give the slip* to escape secretly.

"I wonder the writs haven't followed me down here," Rawdon continued, still desponding. "When they do, we'll find means to give them the slip," said dauntless little Becky.—Thackeray.

—*to slip through one's fingers* (a) to die unexpectedly and without a struggle. Said of a sick person.

He would not let the thing slip through his fingers . . . a debtor never yet escaped him, and never should.—Maria Edgeworth.

—(b)to escape from a person's grasp.

—*there's many a slip 'twixt the cup and the lip* men cannot count on anything until it is actually in their grasp.

"The original," says Charles Reade, "is Greek, and comes down to us with an example. To the best of my recollection, the ancient legend runs, that a Greek philosopher was discoursing to his pupil on the inability of man to foresee the future—ay, even the event of the next minute. The pupil may have, perhaps, granted the uncertainty of the distant future, but he scouted the notion that men could not make sure of immediate and consecutive events. By way of illustration he proceeded to fill a goblet. 'I predict,' said he sneeringly, 'that after filling this goblet, the next event will be that I shall drink the wine.' Accordingly he filled the goblet. At that moment his servant ran in in—Master! master! a wild boar is in our vineyard!' The master caught up his javelin

directly, and ran out to find the boar and kill him. He had the luck to find the boar, and attacked him with such spirit that Sir Boar killed him, and the goblet remained filled. From that incident arose in Greece the saying, "Polla metaxu pelei kulikos kai cheileos akra.' "

slough—*a slough of despond* a state of utter despondency. See Bunyan's *Pilgrim's Progress*, "The First Stage."

She seemed to be stuck in a slough of despond, and could not move in any direction to get out of it.—C. Reade.

slow—*a slow coach* a lazy or inactive person.

He's not very quick in temper, or in anything else; he's what we call a slow coach.—Captain Marryat.

sly—*on the sly* secretly.

He was beginning to doubt this clerk who attended that meeting on the sly.—C. Reade.

small—*a small-beer chronicle* a record of insignificant domestic events. The phrase comes from Shakespeare, *Othello*, act ii., scene 1 line 161: "To suckle fools, and chronicle small-beer."

—*Small hours* the hours after twelve; midnight.

Although a fog rolled over the city in the small hours, the early part of the night was cloudless. —R. L. Stevenson.

—*small talk* conversation about unimportant things, like the weather or the every-day events of life.

His voice was soft and low, and he had a way of placing his white, plump glistening hand on the region of his heart as he spoke, that gave a sort of dramatic earnestness to what would otherwise have been small talk.—James Payn.

smell—*to smell a rat* to detect something wrong.

Of his attachment to the doctrine of the Trinity the Bishop of Exeter may make what protestations he will. Archdeacon Denison will smell a rat in them.—M. Arnold.

smoke—*to end in smoke* to come to no practical result.

—*to smoke the calumet, or the pipe of peace* to be formally reconciled. The phrase comes from a Red Indian custom.

This dinner was essentially a well-dressed pow-wow to witness the burying of the hatchet and the smoking of the calumet.—Mrs. E. Lynn Linton.

snail—*at a snail's gallop* very slowly.

And if he happened not to feel
An angry hint from thong or steel,
He by degrees would seldom fail
T' adopt the gallop of a snail.
                              Combe.

snap—*to snap one's fingers at* to defy; to show one's contempt for.

You live with me, and snap your fingers at Hawes and all his crew.—C. Reade.

—*to snap a man's nose off* to speak sharply to him.

Well, well, you needn't snap a man's nose off! Come, what has the young man been doing?—Good Words, 1887.

sneeze—*to sneeze at a thing* to despise it; to think little of it.

A buxom, tall, and comely dame
Who wished, 'twas said, to change her name,
And if I could her thoughts divine,
Would not perhaps have sneezed at mine.
                              Combe.

snuff—*to take it in snuff* to take offence.

You'll mar the light by taking it in snuff;
Therefore I'll darkly end my argument.—Shakespeare.

—*in snuff or in the snuff* offended.

He dares not come there for the candle, for, you see, it is already in snuff.—Shakespeare.

"Hoot, hoot," said Uncle Ebenezer, "dinna [don't] fly up in the snuff at me."—R. L. Stevenson.

—*to snuff pepper* to take offence.

I brought them in, because here are some of other cities in the room that might snuff pepper else.—Old Play.

—*up to snuff*—crafty; knowing.

A rough and tough, and possibly an up-to-snuff old vagabond.—Dickens.

—*to snuff out* to die.

so—*only so-so* very indifferently; not well.

"How do you find yourself, my dear fellow?"

"Only so-so," said Mr. John Spanker.—Dickens.

—*and so on* and the like; and other similar words, acts, or events.

He heard of a house here or a house there, and went to see it, but it was too large; and of another, but it was too small; and of a third, but it was not convenient for her purpose; and so on.—Besant.

—*so-and-so* a phrase used when exact particulars are referred to but not actually given.

It would also have been considerate, at least, had Mr. Browning given the dates of dispatches referred to by Lord Hawkesbury as No. So-and-so, when answering them or acknowledging their receipt.—Spectator, December 17, 1887.

—*so to speak*—(a) An apologetic phrase generally used with statements which are not literrally true.

Sometimes the home is visited by the committee, who go round and taste the soup, so to speak, confer as to the accounts, and consider the case of those ill-advised young people who have requested permission to stay out for an hour later than is allowed by the rules.—Besant.

—(b)if the phrase may be used. Attached to statements that must not be taken literally.

If an old man has to go hungry, he grows melancholy, because the situation is permanent, so to speak.

soap—*how are you off for soap?* A meaningless, bantering phrase, at one time common in England.

Or put their heads into his shop, and asked how he was off for soap.—S. Baring-Gould.

soft—*soft sawder* flattery

It is done by a knowledge of soft sawder and human nature.—Haliburton.

—*soft soap* complimentary speeches. A person of insinuating manners is said to be *soapy.*.

soi—*soi-disant* self-named; self-appointed. French.

Charges of seduction trumped up by young women like Annette Harchoux and their soi-disant patrons must be subjected to a very searching investigation.—Saturday Review, 1887.

some—*some of these days* soon; before very long.

son—*son of a sea-cook* a term of contempt used by sailors to their companions.

Of course, in the use of sea-terms you'll not wonder
If I now and then should fall into some blunder,
For which Captain Chamier or Mr. T. Cook
Would call me a lubber and son of a sea-cook.

Barham.

song—*to sell for a song* or *an old song* to sell very cheap.

A skeleton clock and a couple of bronze figures, picked up in one of the

slums of Covent Gardens for a song.—Miss Braddon.

sop—*to throw a sop to Cerberus* to try to pacify a greedy enemy by granting him favours. Cerberus, in Roman mythology, was the three-headed dog that watched Pluto's palace in the infernal regions.

To Cerberus they give a sop
His triple barking mouth to stop.

Swift

sore—*a sight for sore eyes* a welcome sight.

Well, the very sight of the Yankee girls is good for sore eyes, the dear little critters (creatures).—Haliburton.

sotto—*sotto voce* in a subdued voice; in a whisper. Italian.

"She's worn out and upset, poor little thing!" he said sotto voce.—Murray's Magazine, 1887.

sour—*sour grapes* a thing despised because it is unattainable.

A famished fox once saw some clusters of ripe black grapes hanging from a trellised vine. She resorted to all her arts in vain, for she could not reach them. At last she turned away, beguiling herself of her disappointment, and saying, "The grapes are sour, and not ripe as I thought."—Æsop's Fables.

sow—*to sow wild oats* to be wild and extravagant when young.

"Upon my honour," exclaimed Sir Brian, "your excuse seems to me to be your condemnation. If you were a spendthrift, as young fellows often are, there would be a chance of your sowing your wild oats."—Good Words, 1887.

—*to sow the wind and reap the whirlwind* to behave recklessly and wickedly, and suffer a dreadful punishment. From the Bible (Hosea viii. 7).

In Stevenson's The Misadventures of

John Nicholson, *the heading to chapter i. is* "In which John sows the wind" *and to chapter ii.,* "In which John reaps the whirlwind." *His portrait of the poor crazy-brained creature, Lord George Gordon, who sowed the wind which the country was to reap in whirlwind, is excellent.*—F. Marzials, in *Life of Dickens,* "Great Writers" Series.

sow—*to have the wrong sow by the ear* to have captured the wrong individual. Also "the right sow."
However, this time he'd got the wrong sow by the ear.—T. Hughes.
"It's all right old fellow," he said, clapping his hand on Crawley's shoulder; "we've got the right sow by the ear at last."—A. Trollope.

spade—*to call a spade a spade* to use plain language; to be straightforward in the terms one uses.
Viola, when will you leave off using such terrible words? Our poor father always said he never knew such a girl for calling a spade a spade.—Florence Marryat.

Spanish—*a Spanish castle* something visionary and unreal. See chateaux en espagne.
Nellie le Strange, with her light heart, her tumble-down Spanish castles (dreams never to be realized) and her silly little tender jokes, has gone away.—Rhoda Broughton.

speak—*to speak volumes* to furnish ample testimony.
Does it not, then, speak volumes as to what the instinctive revolt of the attitude is, to find her taking it quite as a matter of course that a high-bred, well-behaved young lady of eighteen should be roused to an outbreak like the following?—Spectator, 1887.

—*to speak of* worth mentioning.
They have no institutions of their own to speak of, no public buildings of any importance.—Besant.

spear—*Achilles' spear* It was said that this spear could both wound and cure.
Whose smile and frown, like to Achilles' spear.

Is able with the change to kill or cure.—Shakespeare.

Sphinx—*the Sphinx's riddle* the Sphinx was a she-monster who is said to have proposed a riddle to the Thebans, and to have murdered all who failed to guess it. Œdipus was finally successful in guessing it, whereupon she killed herself.
What solution, if any, have you found for the labour question? It was the Sphinx's riddle of the nineteenth century.—E. Bellamy.

spick—*spick and span* very neat and trim.
A spick and span new gig at the door.—Haliburton.

spin—*to spin a yarn* to tell a story. A sailor's phrase.
Blow-hard (as the boys called him) was a dry old file, with much kindness and humour, and a capital spinner of a yarn.—T. Hughes.

spirits—*out of spirits* melancholy; gloomy; sad.
He was out of spirits; he had grown very silent; he did not read; it seemed as if he had something on his mind.—R. L. Stevenson.

spliced—*to get spliced* to be married. A sailor's phrase.

split—*to split on a friend* to inform against him; to reveal a scheme in which he was concerned; to betray him.
Robinson sighed. "What is the matter?" said his master, trying to twist his head round.
"Nothing, only I am afraid they—they won't split. Fellows of that sort don't

*split on a comrade where they can get
no good by it".*—C. Reade.

—to split with to quarrel with; to separate from.

—to split hairs to indulge in over-
refined arguments.

No splitter of hairs was he.—C. Reade.

spoil—*to spoil the Egyptians* to get
supplies from one's enemies. A Scriptural phrase (Exod. xii. 36).

*More, he might even be able to spoil
that Egyptian George, giving him less
than his due.*—H. R. Haggard.

—to spoil for a fight to be very anxious
for a fight.

*"You seem to be spoiling for a fight?"
remarked Bracknell. "I don't know that I
have any grievance against you, but I'll
try my best to indulge you by
discovering one."*—W. E. Norris.

spoke—*to put a spoke in another's
wheel* to arrest his progress; to hinder
his schemes.

*You have put a most formidable spoke
in my wheel by preventing the
extension of the borough.*—W. E.
Norris, in Good Words, 1887.

sponge—*to sponge upon another* to get
money or food in a mean way; to take
advantage of another's good nature
to obtain money from him, or a place
at his table.

*He could not allow people to say of him
that it was an easy matter to abandon
his own income, as he was able to
sponge on that of another person.*—
A. Trollope.

—to throw up the sponge to confess
oneself vanquished; to yield. In pugil-
istic encounters the two principals are
accompanied by seconds. After each
round these seconds wipe the faces of
the principals and prepare them for
the next round. When a principal refuses to enter for another round, his
second throws up the sponge.

Had it not been for her, French would

*have collapsed, and perhaps would
have thrown up the sponge.*—Mrs. E.
Lynn Linton.

spoon—*it takes a long spoon to sup
with him* he is a devil or an evil spirit.
The proverb runs, "It takes a long
spoon to sup with the devil"—that is,
the devil is so crafty that if one forms
a league with him, most of the profits
are sure to go with him.

   "Bespeak a long spoon."

   "Why, Dromio?"

   *"Marry, he must have a long spoon
that must eat with the devil."*—
Shakespeare.

*He had voluntarily supped with the
devil, and his spoon had been too
short.*—Mrs. E. Lynn Linton.

**—born with a silver spoon in one's
mouth** born in wealth and luxury.

*"What! the settlement I have made is
more than enough—five thousand
pounds more than enough. One can
see, young fellow, that you were born
with a silver spoon in your mouth."*—
Longmans' Magazine, 1886.

spooney—*spooney on a girl* foolishly
fond of her.

*George is getting spooney on that girl,
or she is getting spooney on him.*—
Florence Marryat.

spot—*on the spot* just there; instantly;
without change of place.

*Though they had caused the death of
many men during the last two years,
they had not yet, as it happened,
murdered a single one on the spot.*—
C. Reade.

*It was determined upon the spot,
according as the oratory on either side
prevailed.*—Swift.

spout—*up the spout* at the pawnbroker's.

*I haven't a suit of clothes fit to go in,
even my (barrister's) wig and gown
are up the spout together.*—D. Christie
Murray.

sprat—*to throw a sprat to catch a whale* to venture something small in order to obtain a large return.

"What are you at? Are you mad, Tom? Why, there goes five pounds. What a sin!"

"Did you never hear of the man that flung away a sprat to catch a whale?"—C. Reade.

spread—*spread-eagleism* boastful American patriotism. Compare it with English Jingoism and French Chauvinism.

When we talk of spread-eagleism we are generally thinking of the United States; but the real spread-eagleism is that, not of the American Republic, but of the Russian Empire.—Fortnightly Review, 1887.

spring—*to spring a mine upon one* to surprise one: to lay a plot and announce suddenly its completion.

"But, my dear Samuel, this is so altogether unexpected."

"So is the discovery of the manuscript," put in the young fellow with pitiless logic.

"It is like springing a mine on me, my lad.—James Payn.

—*to spring to one's feet* to rise suddenly up.

He sprang to his feet, and pushed the woman, a buxom party of about thirty, from him.—H. R. Haggard.

spur—*on the spur of the moment* acting under the first impulse, without reflection.

The criticism offered on the spur of the moment had been, in reality, advanced by way of protest against the whole document.—James Payn.

—*to win one's spurs* to gain a reputation. Originally used of feudal warriors who, by doing some deed of valour, won the spurs of knighthood.

The encounter in which Charles Townshend won his spurs was only a preliminary skirmish.—Trevellyan.

square—*all square* all right; quite satisfactory.

"Sit still; it will be all square."

But in his heart he knew that it was not all square, and that they were in imminent danger of death from drowning.—H. R. Haggard.

—*on or upon the square* honourable; fair; even; honourably; fairly.

If you think it fair
Amongst known cheats to play upon the square,
You'll be undone.

　　　　　　　　　　　　Rochester.

—*to square* to settle; to adjust.

Lady Parker will square accounts by sending you a card for a garden party next July.—Miss Braddon.

—*to square up* to take the attitude of a boxer; to clench the fists and prepare to fight.

The speaker proceeded to square up to George in a most determined way.—H. R. Haggard.

—*to square anything to or with* to make it agree with.

Eye me, blest Providence, and square my trial
To my proportioned strength.—Milton.

—*a square meal* a full meal which satisfies.

Talleyrand, even at the age of eighty, ate but one square meal a day.—Saturday Review, 1888.

—*square-toes* a contemptuous name for a person of strict morals. The Puritans wore shoes of this shape.

I never shall forget the solemn remonstrance of our old square-toes of a rector at Hackham.—Thackeray.

—*to call it square* to consider matters settled; to make no further claim.

I don't think I ever did Rogers any wrong, and I never did think so; but if I did do it—if I did—I'm willing to call it square, if I never see a cent of money back again.—W. D. Howells.

stable—*to lock or shut the stable-door when the steed is stolen* to take precautions when too late.

The emperor of Austria, who has given a great deal of time and patient labour to the reorganization of the Austria-Hungary army, is, it is understood, pleased with the recent development of the powers of mobilization of the Austrian cavalry. But this is rather a case of shutting the stable-door when the steed is stolen. The Russians had a very long start, and it is probably they still maintain it.—Fortnightly Review, 1887.

stage—*a stage whisper* a whisper that can be heard by many.

stake—*at stake* in peril; about to be contended for.

He wrote to tell the king that the honour of himself and his brother sovereigns, whose consciences they directed was at stake.—National Review, 1887.

"Do not speak of him, Johnny."

"I must speak of him. A man isn't to hold his tongue when everything he has in the world is at stake."—A. Trollope.

stand—*to stand by*—(a) to be faithful; to assist in a difficulty.

The man that stands by me in trouble I won't bid him go when the sun shines again.—C. Reade.

—(b) to be ready; to hold oneself in readiness. A nautical use.

"What did you say, Captain Cuttle?" inquired Walter.

"Stand by!" returned the captain thoughtfully.—Dickens.

—*to stand at ease* to take the restful position allowed to soldiers in the intervals of drill.

By their rattles and slaps they're not standing at ease.—Barham.

—*to stand on end* to stand erect. Generally said of the hair of a person who has got a fright.

When I think of the souls of the people in that poor village, my hair literally stands on end.—A. Trollope.

—*to stand to reason* to be logically certain; to be an undoubted fact.

It stands to reason that I just either be driven along with the crowd or else be left behind.—A. Trollope.

—*to stand on ceremony* to act with reserve; to be stiff and ceremonious in behaviour; to be backward.

Mordecai absolutely refused (this bond), declaring that now he had the power he would use it to obtain the utmost penny of his debt; . . . that a man lying on his death-bed was not going to stand on ceremony about disturbing a gentleman in his last moments.—Maria Edgeworth.

—*to stand in one's light* to hinder his advancement.

Don't stand in the poor girl's light; for pity's sake, George, leave us in peace.—C. Reade.

—*to stand in need of* or require; to be in want of.

I stood in need of a comfortable dinner.—Goldsmith.

—*to stand to*—(a) to uphold; to be faithful to.

"My lady, whatever I say you'll stand to?"

"Whatever you say I'll stand to."—C. Reade.

—(b) to oppose in a duel; to be a match for.

"A regular Turk," answered Fagan; adding, "I never yet knew the man who stood to Captain Quin."—Thackeray.

—*to stand treat* to pay the expenses of any feasting or merriment.

He ordered in a glass of negus from the adjoining public-house, after some discussion, which ended in an agreement that he should stand treat that night, and Titmouse on the ensuing one.—S. Warren.

—**to stand in good stead** to be useful; to prove of good service.

"I pique myself on my wisdom there, Arthur, and as an old fellow to whom wisdom has become cheap, I can bestow it upon you."

"Thank you. It may stand me in good stead some day."—George Eliot.

—**to stand up for** to champion; to speak in defence of.

You are always standing up for the black people, whom the Boers hate.—H. R. Haggard.

—**a standing dish** a dish or article of diet which regularly appears at table.

—**standing orders** general rules or instructions constantly in force.

star—**his star is in the ascendant** he is lucky; fortune favours him.

His feelings of resentment became more lively, and not the less so because the expression of them had been stifled, while he had considered the star of Titmouse to be in the ascendant.—S. Warren.

—**a man's good star** a lucky influence affecting his life.

"Yes," said Ella patiently; "she was, of course, the Pre"—(her good star just saved her from saying the Pretender)— *"Prince Charlie in disguise."*—James Payn.

—**the Stars and Stripes,** or **the Star-spangled banner** the flag of the United States.

I don't want to see my husband walking into his proper place in Westminster with Stars and Stripes flying over his head.—Besant.

Being a sharp fellow, he has acquainted himself thoroughly with the geography of that country, and the amount of capital requisite to enable a man to set up for himself under the

Star-spangled banner.—G. J. Whyte-Melville.

stare—**to stare in the face** to be very evident; to threaten; to be ready to overwhelm.

Is it possible for people without scruple to offend against the law, which they carry about them in indelible characters, and that stares them in the face whilst they are breaking it?—Locke.

statice—**like statice or stacia or sixty** A phrase used in comparing or estimating things. Statice is a plant that grows among rocks by the sea-shore.

It is the most costly government in the world, considering our means. We are actually eaten up by it; it is a most plaguy sore, and has spread like statice till it has got its root into the very core.—Haliburton.

status—**the status quo** the position in which affairs actually are; the present situation of affairs. Latin.

It was hardly further thought, a little more consideration of future probabilities, would have led to the maintenance of the status quo.—Good Words, 1887.

stave—**to stave off** to prevent; to keep back for a time with difficulty.

I have more influence in the land than you know of. Perhaps, even, I could stave off the war.—H. R. Haggard.

steal—**to steal a march upon** to gain an advantage over an enemy or a competitor without his knowing it; to act before another is aware.

At last, one morning, happening to awake earlier than usual, he stole a march on his nurses, and taking his stick, walked out and tottered into the jail.—C. Reade.

stick—**a stick-in-the-mud** a slow person who is wholly without the spirit of enterprise or adventure.

This rusty-coloured one is that

respectable old stick-in-the-mud, Nicias.—T. Hughes.

—*to stick by* to be faithful to; not to desert.

He thought what a savage, determined man Osborne was, and how he stuck by his word.—Thackeray.

—*to stick to one's colours* to be faithful to a cause; to refuse to yield.

The lady had made a great mistake in putting her supremacy to a test so crucial, but, having made it, she stuck to her colours.—James Payn.

—*to stick up for* to champion; to speak in defence of.

I'll stick up for the pretty woman preaching.—George Eliot.

—*a poor stick* a person without character or energy.

He was a poor stick to make a preacher on (of).—Haliburton.

—*to stick in* to persevere.

—*a stiff'un* a corpse.

stile—*to help (a lame dog) over a stile* to assist a poor fellow in a difficulty.

I can help a lame dog over a stile (which was Mark's phrase for doing a generous thing).—C. Kingsley.

still—*still waters run deep* silent and undemonstrative people have generally great powers of thought and action.

"What, kissing her hand, and he a clergyman!" said Miss Dunstable. "I did not think they ever did such things, Mr. Robarts."

"Still waters run deepest," said Mrs. Harold Smith.—A. Trollope.

stir—*stir-up Sunday* the Sunday just before Advent. The Collect or Church prayer for this day begins with the words, "Stir up, O Lord, we beseech thee." Schoolboys who are looking forward at this time to the Christmas vacation irreverently "stir up" or poke each other's side on this day.

—*a stock phrase* an expression in constant use by a person, so that it has become a mannerism.

And the poor boy seemed to see under the humble stock phrases in which they talked of their labours of love, and the future reward of their present humiliation, a deep and hardly hidden pride.—C. Kingsley.

—*stock-in-trade* marketable articles; the goods which merchant wishes to dispose of. Also used of the accomplishments or possesions which a man can turn into money.

All his show was on his back, as he said. His carriage, with the fine gelding, was a part of his stock-in-trade.—Thackeray.

—*to take stock of* to observe and estimate; to watch minutely.

"You seem to have observed him very closely considering your opportunities."

"I have. It is my trade to take stock of my fellow-creatures."—James Payn.

stolen—*stolen fruit* said of something which is very sweet.

It was so sweet to hear Edward praised by one who did not know us; it was like stolen fruit.—C. Reade.

stone—*stone-throwing* finding fault with one's neighbours. No doubt taken from Christ's saying, "He that is without sin among you, let him first cast a stone at her" (John viii. 7).

The stone-throwing spirit, the self-depreciation of the capital, and the occasional outbursts of Nihilism, are only the natural results of the autocratic system.—Fortnightly Review, 1887.

—*stone-blind* completely blind.

He is considered a rich man, and, being stone-blind, he sent for this girl.—Captain Marryat.

—*a stone's-throw* a short distance; a hundred yards or more.

Rebecca and her husband were but a few stone's-throws from the lodgings which the invalid Miss Crawley occupied.—Thackeray.

—*to leave no stone unturned* to adopt every possible method of search or inquiry; to take every possible means towards gaining an object. A phrase borrowed from the Greek dramatist Euripedes, Polycrates asked the Delphic oracle how best to find the treasure buried by Mardonius, the general of Xerxes, on the field of Platea. The oracle replied, "Turn every stone" (*Panta kinesai petron*).

But Mr. Irwine 'll leave no stone unturned with the judge—you may rely upon that, Adam.—George Eliot.

stool—*to fall between two stools* to adopt two plans of action, and to fail; to lose oneself by trusting to two supports instead of boldly choosing a single one.

What on earth should she do? Fall to the ground between two stools? No; that was a man's trick, and she was a woman, every inch.—C. Reade.

store—*to set store by* or *on* to value; to think highly of.

An artist sketched a likeness of the young declaimer, on which, in after days, those who were fondest of him set not a little store.—George Eliot.

—*in store* ready; waiting; soon to disclose itself.

If he portrays persons generally as well as he does places (as I do not doubt), there must be another treat in store for us.—James Payn.

story—*weak in the upper story* crazy; feeble-minded.

stove—*the stove-pipe hat* the tall silk hat.

About the only monstrosity I saw in the British man's dress was the stove-pipe hat.—Burroughs.

straight—*a straight tip* private and correct information.

We got the straight tip; that's all you need know.—Miss Braddon.

strain—*to strain at a gnat* to make difficulties about something insignificant. A Scriptural phrase (Matt. xxiii. 24).

You are just the chap to strain at a gnat and swallow a camel.—Haliburton.

strait—*a strait jacket or waistcoat* an article of dress put on a madman when he is unruly.

George Gaunt is accredited to a keeper, who has invested him with the order of the Strait Waistcoat.—Thackeray.

Exp.—*George Gaunt, instead of going as a secretary of legation to a foreign court, has been intrusted to a keeper, and is watched as a madman.*

straw—*the last straw* that which finally causes a catastrophe; an event simple in itself, but able, in conjunction with other things, to cause a calamity. The proverb runs: "It is the last straw which breaks the camel's back."

Identification would mean loss of credit, the last straw in many cases.—Spectator, 1887.

—*not to care a straw or two straws* to be perfectly indifferent. A straw is the symbol of what is worthless.

I don't think she could have cared two straws about the woman.—Murray's Magazine, 1887.

—*a man of straw* a creature evolved from the fancy, and wholly unlike the real person; an unreal person; a dummy.

You bring me a party that will give me enough for those mills to clear me of you, and I'll talk to you. But don't come you here with any man of straw.—W. D. Howells.

Strephon—*Strephon and Phyllis* a pair of rustic lovers, generally taken as typical of a sentimental young man and his sweetheart.

He brought his lovely wife to a romantic-looking cottage, covered with roses and myrtle, and there their Strephon and Phyllis-like existence had commenced.—Florence Marryat.

strike—*to strike work* to refuse to work until better terms are promised.

A number of functions, in fact, struck work.—H. Drummond.

—*to strike one's colours or flag* to surrender.

Anastasie was aware of defeat; she struck her colours instantly.—R. L. Stevenson.

—*strike me luck or lucky.* An old phrase, used when a bargain was made, and money exchanged in token thereof.

"Come, strike me luck with earnest, and draw the writings."

"There's a God's penny for thee."—Beaumont and Fletcher.

—*to strike a bargain* to conclude a bargain. The striking of hands was a sign of a bargain being concluded.

Mr. Miles answered by offering to bet he should make the best servant in the street; and, strange to say, the bargain was struck, and he did turn out a model servant.—C. Reade.

—*strike while the iron is hot* do not miss a favourable opportunity; act when the conditions are favourable.

"Let George cut in and win her," was his advice. "Strike while the iron's hot, you know—while she's fresh to the town.—Thackeray.

—*to strike up* to begin; to set on foot. Generally said of music.

I fancy it requires more than ordinary spirit now for a good old gentleman, at the head of his family table, to strike up a good old family song.—Thackeray.

—*to strike in* to make an abrupt entry into a conversation. See *cut in.*

But at this moment the lieutenant struck in. "Oh, that is quite foolish!" he cried.—Wm. Black.

struck—*struck upon* attracted by. An Americanism.

"But that young man had perfect ways."

"Seem struck upon Irene?" asked the colonel.—W. D. Howells.

stuck—*stuck up* proud; conceited.

"They didn't seem stuck up," urged his wife.—W. D. Howells.

stump—*to stump up* to pay out money.

Why don't you ask your old governor to stump up?—Dickens.

suaviter—*suaviter in modo* possessing tact; having a pleasant mode of dealing. Latin. The full phrase is *suaviter in modo, fortiter in re*, "Pleasant in the manner of carrying out an enterprise, firm in the business itself."

Let Mr. Slope be the fortiter in re, he himself would pour in the suaviter in modo.—A. Trollope.

sub—*sub rosa* in confidence; secretly. The Latin form of "Under the rose." See *rose.*

By-the-bye, I wonder some of you lawyers (sub rosa, of course) have not quoted the pithy line of Mandeville.—S. T. Coleridge.

such—*such and such* certain. An adjective phrase, which saves the need of using a definite numeral or other adjective.

She had written to him to say that she would be at her father's on such and such a morning, and he had gone to her there.—A. Trollope.

sugar—*a sugar-plum* something very nice.

For this pretty toy Mr. Conway Dalrymple had picked up a gilt sugar-

plum to the tune of six hundred pounds.—A. Trollope.

sui—*sui generis* peculiar; belonging to a class apart; not like anything else. Latin.

Not a Clinton, nor yet a Carew, she was sui generis, and supreme.—Mrs. E. Lynn Linton.

sunshine—*to have been in the sunshine* to be drunk.

He was in that condition which his groom indicated with poetic ambiguity by saying, that "master had been in the sunshine."—George Eliot.

sup—*to sup with Pluto* to die. Pluto was the Latin god of the infernal regions, where the spirits of the dead existed.

sure—*as sure as a gun* certainly; without fail.

"As sure as a gun," said she, "that must be the knock of the post."—Macaulay.

—*to be sure* certainly; no doubt. An exclamation having no decided force or meaning.

Lord! what a life mine is, to be sure.—S. Warren.

swallow—*one swallow does not make a summer* we must not frame a general law from one single phenomenon.

"One swallow does not make a summer, for all that."—C. Reade.

swear—*to swear by another* to be an imitator or admiring follower; to admire all his actions; to have full confidence in.

"I suppose I oughtn't to say it before you," observes Miss Smiles presently, "because of course, you swear by everything British.—Florence Marryat.

—*to swear in* (of a magistrate) to engage formally the services of men for the government.

Governor Lanyon is sending Raaf down with power to swear in special

constables, and enforce the law at Potchefstroom.—H. R. Haggard.

—*to swear like a trooper* to use profane language freely.

She was perfectly tipsy, screaming and fighting like a Billingsgate fish-woman, and swearing like a trooper.—Florence Marryat.

—*to swear out* to renounce; to give up. Old-fashioned.

Your grace hath sworn out housekeeping.—Shakespeare.

sweat—*the sweat of one's brow* or *face* hard labour.

In the sweat of thy face shalt thou eat bread, till thou return unto the ground.—Gen. iii. 19.

In this practice, indeed, he imitated some of the most renowned geniuses of the age, who have laboured in secret with the sweat of their brows for many a repartee.—Smollett.

sweet—*sweet on* or *upon* attached to; having a fancy for.

"Mark my words, Rawdon," she said. "You will have Miss Sharp one day for your relation."

"What relation—my cousin, hey, Mrs. Bute? James sweet on her, hey?" inquired the waggish officer.—Thackeray.

—*a sweet tooth* a liking for sweetmeats and dainties.

I know she has a sweet tooth still in her head.—Maria Edgeworth.

—*one's sweet will* uncontrolled wishes; the unrestrained desires of one's heart. A phrase generally used somewhat sarcastically.

If only the idealists can have their way, and work out the yearnings of their own sweet will, we shall soon be a teetotal, vegetarian, and none-tobacco-smoking people.—Family Herald (quoted in Edinburgh Review, 1887).

swell—*the swell mob* people of bad

character; men who prey on the vices or follies of others.

The fact was that he had been one of the swell mob.—Captain Marryat.

swim—*in the swim* in the current of events; acquainted with all that is going on.

swing—*in full swing* very busy; working busily.

The street market was in full swing.— Besant.

—*to give full swing to* to indulge freely; to let loose; to free from control.

But let us return to Nature: do you mean that we are to give full swing to our inclination, to throw the reins on the neck of our senses?—M. Arnold.

—*to have full swing* to be allowed free and uncontrolled exercise.

Every one has his full swing, or goes to the devil his own way.—Hazlitt.

swoop—*at one fell swoop* with one unlucky blow; by a single catastrophe.

At one fell swoop it had cleared the sideboard of glasses, decanters, silver waiters.—Wilson.

sword—*at swords' points* bitterly hostile.

This the captain took in dudgeon, and they were at swords' points at once.— R. H. Dana

—*the sword of Damocles* Damocles was a courtier in the palace of Dionysius the Elder, ruler of Syracuse. Having extolled the felicity of princes, he was answered in the following fashion by his master. He was invited to a sumptuous banquet, and arrayed in a royal robes, was given the principal seat; but over his head hung a sword supsended by a single-horse-hair. By this Dionysius meant to intimate the precarious nature of the power and felicity of princes.

When it is said to be the Czar's wish that the aged Emperor of Germany's end should be peaceful, and that it is only because he would not that his last moments should be disturbed by the clash of arms that he desists from action, it will be seen how thin is the thread by which the sword of Damocles is suspended.—St. Andrews Citizen, 1887.

—*to put to the sword* to kill.

—*at swords drawn* bitterly hostile. See **dagger.**

Giovanni belonged to a family who, from the earliest times, had been at swords drawn with the government.— Marion Crawford.

T

T—*to a t* exactly. Perhaps from a *T-Square.*

"Well," said I, "there is a pretty show of girls, that's certain; but they wouldn't condescend to the like of me. I was thinking there were some of them that would just suit you to a T."— Haliburton.

table—*to turn the tables* to reverse the position of two rival parties.

It was no light act of courage in those days, my dear boys, for a little fellow to say his prayers publicly, even at Rugby. A few years later, when Arnold's manly piety had begun to leaven the school, the tables turned.

Before he died, in the school-house at least, and I believe in the other houses, the rule was the other way.—T. Hughes.

—*table d'hôte* the public dining table at a hotel. A French phrase. Literally, the "host's table," from the custom of the landlord presiding at the public dinner.

I was very fond of dining at table d'hôte anywhere.—The Mistletoe Bough, 1885.

—*upon the table* known to every one—a matter of public discussion.

I will not, however, take up the time of this—I mean your time—by recapitulating all that I told you on that occasion; the facts are, so to speak, all upon the table, and I will merely touch upon the main heads of the case.—H. R. Haggard.

tableaux—*tableaux vivants* "living pictures;" dumb representations, generally of historical scenes, in which the figures are real people. French. A favourite amusements in social gatherings.

On the 26th of January 1500, having accomplished the first half of his task, he (Cæsar Borgia) entered Rome, as a conqueror, on which occasions a representation was given of the triumph of Cæsar, with the various episodes of the life of the Roman Cæsar, shown in tableaux vivantes suggested by the painter Mantegna.—Blackwood's Magazine, 1888.

tag—*tag-rag and bob-tail* the ill-dressed rabble. See *rag-tag.*

He invited tag-rag and bob-tail to the wedding.—L'Estrange.

tail—*to keep the tail in the water* to thrive; to prosper.

—*to turn tail* to retreat in an undignified way.

"Never thought I should live to turn tail in this way," growled one soldier to

another as they passed out.—English Illustrated Magazine, 1887.

tailor—*nine tailors make a man* an old saying. See *nine.*

I believe Pinchin's father to have been a tailor. There is no harm in the craft, honestly exercised; but since the world began nine tailors have made a man, and you cannot well see a knight of the shears without asking in your own mind where he has left his eight brethren.—G. A. Sala.

take—*to take aback* to bewilder; to astonish; to surprise.

"A what?" asked Hardy rather taken aback.—Dickens.

—*to take back* to recall words that have been spoken; to retract.

"I've disgusted you, I see that; but I didn't mean to. I—I take it back."

"Oh, there's nothing to take back," said Corey.—W. D. Howells.

—*to take home to oneself* to understand completely.

Jael did not at all take home to herself the peculiar meaning of her friend's words.—A. Trollope.

—*to take after* to resemble; to imitate.

Thank God, you take after your mother's family, Arthur.—George Eliot.

—*to take the cue* to understand a hint.

The ladies took the cue and retired.—C. Reade.

—*to take down* (a) to humiliate to lower the pretensions of.

"The fact is," went on the other, "that I thought you wanted taking down a peg."—Good Words, 1887.

—(b) to take the place of a scholar higher up in the form. A school phrase.

—(c) to commit to writing spoken words as they are uttered.

He wrote letters and took down instructions in shorthand.—Besant.

—*to take flight* to go off.

My good Matilda, I am sick of this. I

have been bored to-night, and what is
much worse, I have been snubbed.
Suppose we take flight for Cannes?—
Good Words, 1887.

—*to take in good part* to hear or
receive willingly.

I will just add one little word, Utterson,
that I'm sure you'll take in good part.
This is a private matter, and I beg of
you to let it sleep.—R. L. Stevenson.

—*to take anything to heart* to bear it
seriously; to be much affected by it.

The next day he called at Grasmere,
Susan met him all smiles, and was
more cheerful than usual. The watchful
man was delighted. "Come; she does
not take it to heart." He did not guess
that Susan had cried for hours and
hours over the letter.—C. Reade.

—*to take in hand* to undertake; to commence working with.

But that acquaintances—mere
acquaintances—should have taken it in
hand to give her pecuniary assistance,
was a humiliation indeed.—James
Payn.

—*to take hold of* to seize; to occupy.

But there was something in the delicate
handwriting and perfume of the letter
that took hold of my imagination.—
Mistletoe Bough, 1885.

—*to take in* (a) to deceive; to delude.

Here were two battered London rakes,
taking themselves in for a moment,
and fancying they were in love with
each other like Phyllis and Corydon.—
Thackeray.

—(b) to escort to a room.

As for Miss Huntly, she rather prided
herself upon her immunity from "airs,"
and would have been quite content to
accept Mr. Buswell's arm, had that
person been requested to take her in
to dinner.—*Good Words*, 1887.

—(c) to comprehend; to absorb
mentally.

It is not to be supposed that he took in
everything at one glance.—Dickens.

—*to take off* (a) to mock at; to make
sport of; to mimic.

I know the man I would have; a quick-
witted, outspoken, incisive fellow . . .
delights in taking off bigwigs and
professional gowns, and in the
disembalming and unbandaging of all
literary mummies.—O. W. Holmes.

—*to take oneself off* (a) to go away.

The stranger suddenly took himself off,
and was no more seen by the young
lady.—A. Trollope.

—(b) to commit suicide.

"You argue," said Mrs. Wallace, "that
in the case of wicked people, they very
best thing they can do is to take
themselves off, as you call it, since in
so doing they do the world a
service."—James Payn.

—*to take on* to be affected; to be overcome by one's feelings.

"Dear heart! Dear heart!" cried the
squire, who was deeply attached to
his sister; "don't take on so, my dear
good Joan."—Blackmore.

—*to take it out of a person* to exhaust
his energies.

So they tried back slowly and
sorrowfully, and found the lane, and
went limping down it, plashing in the
cold puddly ruts, and beginning to feel
how the run had taken it out of them.—
T. Hughes.

—*to take part* to share; to act along
with others.

Take part in rejoicing for the victory
over the Turks.—Pope.

—*to take place* to happen.

Whether anything of the nature of a
family collision had taken place on the
occasion of her doing so, John
Lawrence did not know.—*Murray's
Magazine*, 1887.

—*to take stock in*. See *stock*.

—*to take by storm* to secure by one

great effort; to overcome by one single blow.

In face and manner and speech she was of those sweetly innocent girls who take men's hearts by storm.—Mrs. H. Wood.

—*to take to* apply oneself to; to conceive a liking for.

Miss Betsy won't take to her book.—Swift.

Men of learning who take to business discharge it generally with greater honesty than men of the world.—Addison.

The squire took to her very kindly (was very well pleased with her).—A. Trollope.

—*to take to one's bed* to be prostrated by illness.

It is quite true that at times he took to his bed.—Letter quoted in *Nineteenth Century,* 1887.

—*to take to one's heels* to commence running; to start off at a rapid pace.

I gave a view halloa, took to my heels, collared my gentleman, and brought him back.—R. L. Stevenson.

—*to take to task* to reprove; to lecture; to find fault with.

"Still," urged Mrs. Armytage, irritated at being taken to task—and, as was evident, with the approval of the company—by a lady so inferior to her in the social scale—"the truth must be told, we are taught, even of the dead."—James Payn.

—*to take too much* to get drunk.

She knew he was of no drunken kind, yet once in a way a man might take too much.—Blackmore.

—*to take in tow* to conduct; to take charge of. Originally a sea phrase.

Sir Brian stood in the middle of Pall Mall shaking his stick at the cabman, whose number he took, and causing some interruption to the traffic, until he was courteously but firmly taken in tow

by a policeman, who remarked that the roadway was intended for wheeled vehicles and the pavement for foot passengers.*—Good Words,* 1887.

—*to take turns* to engage in anything alternately, each one in succession being allowed to take part.

I think a good way will be for each of them, even the youngest, to take turns in ordering the dinner and seeing it prepared.—Besant.

—*to take up* (a) to put in jail.

For many a time, when they take a man up, they spread it about that he's turned informer like the rest.—Charles Lever.

—(b) to help; to aid; to patronize.

He told his story from the beginning; how he had experienced nothing but failure and disappointment; how he had been taken up by the queer old fellow at the chop-house, etc.—Besant.

—(c) to engross; to comprise.

I prefer in our countryman the noble poem of Palamon and Arcite, which is perhaps not much inferior to the Ilias, only it take up seven years.—Dryden.

—(d) to reply to; to interrupt with a criticism.

One of his relations took him up roundly for stooping so much below the dignity of his profession.—L'Estrange.

—*taken up* wholly occupied; engrossed.

Mr. Fraser did not answer him immediately, so taken up was he in noticing the wonderful changes a week had wrought in his appearance.—H. R. Haggard.

—*to take up arms for* to defend; to champion.

Miss Smiles takes up arms at once for Mrs. Beverley.—Florence Marryat.

—*to take upon oneself* to venture (in a moral sense); to undertake a responsibility.

"Well, well, well!" he murmured. "But it

doesn't do it to say so, you know, Mr. Segrave. At times, I confess, he appears to me to take too much upon him."—Good Words, 1887.

—*to take a man at his word* to believe what he says.

"It seems a pity," Harry chimed in, "that so much protesting was in vain. Perhaps Mr. Messenger took him at his word."—Besant.

—*to take a telling* to receive advice or a rebuke patiently.

—*to take it into one's head* to conceive a sudden intention; to resolve upon without any apparent reason. Generally used of a capricious whim.

Mrs. Crumpe took it into her head that she could eat no butter but of Patty's churning.—Maria Edgeworth.

—*to take up with* to be friendly with; to seek the society of; to keep company with.

Do you suppose that Penelope Lapham is a girl to take up with a fellow that her sister is in love with, and that she always thought was in love with her sister, and go off and be happy with him?—W. D. Howells.

talk—*to talk a person's head off* to be excessively talkative; to weary another with talking.

I only hope, Heigham, that old Pigott won't talk your head off; she has got a dreadful tongue.—H. R. Haggard.

—*to talk over* (a) to persuade a person by talking; to induce a person to change his opinion by talking with him.

Miss Kennedy looked embarrassed. She had betrayed herself, she thought. "I know—I know. But he talked me over."—Besant.

—(b) to discuss a subject.

tangent—*off at a tangent* this phrase is used of quick and sudden movements, where a person breaks away unexpectedly. Especially used of conver-

sations; but also, as in the second example, of one's thoughts.

She could scarcely say ten words, except about herself; so when Bassett questioned her about Sir Charles and Lady Bassett, she said, "Yes," or "No," or "I don't know," and was off at a tangent to her own saying and doings.—C. Reade.

Tantalus—*a Tantalus cup* a cup in which the water vanishes as soon as the thirsty person attempts to drink. Tantalus was a tyrant who, for his many crimes, was tortured in the infernal regions by having water ever at his lips. As soon as he tried to drink, however, the water slowly receded, and left him more thirsty than ever.

Nothing occurred to interfere with the plan of action decided on by Hilda and Philip; no misadventure came to mock them, dashing the Tantalus cup of joy to earth before their eyes.—H. R. Haggard.

tantrums—*in one's tantrums* in a bad humour.

When he saw Dobbs Broughton he told that gentleman that Mrs. Van Siever had been in her tantrums.—A. Trollope.

tape—*tape* or *red tape* official routine; official delay and obstruction.

The frost and reserve of office melted like snow in summer before the sun of religion and humanity. How unreal and idle appeared now the twenty years gone in tape and circumlocution.—C. Reade.

tapis—*on the tapis* under discussion. *Tapis* is French for "carpet."

The Schleswig-Holstein question comes on the tapis and no one seems to know much of anything about this place geographically.—Fortnightly Review, 1887.

—*tarring and feathering* a punishment inflicted upon an unpopular person.

Joseph Smith, the founder of Mormonism, was so treated. King Richard Cœur de Lion, before sailing for the Holy Land, had a law enacted in the fleet that "a robber, who shall be convicted of theft, shall have his head cropped after the manner of a champion, and boiling pitch shall be poured thereon, and then the feathers of a cushion shall be shaken out upon him, so that he may be known, and at the first land at which the ships shall touch he shall be set on shore."

—*tarred with the same brush* or *stick* possessing the same peculiarities; marked by the same qualities.

As a sample of the self-trained and self-educated amateur, he was, however, tarred with the same brush as John Lawrence.—Murray's Magazine, 1887.

Tartar—*to catch a Tartar* to capture what proves to be a troublesome prisoner; to seize hold of what one would afterwards willingly let go.

Reckless Reginald soon found he had caught a Tartar in his new master.—C. Reade.

task—*to take to task* to reprove; to find fault with.

Mrs. Baynes took poor madame severely to task for admitting such a man to her assemblies.—Thackeray.

tattoo—*the devil's tattoo* beating, usually with the fingers, on a table or other flat surface. Generally a sign of impatience or of ill-humour.

"Ah, what shall I do, Lord Steyne, for I am very, very unhappy?'

Lord Steyne made no reply except by beating the devil's tattoo and biting his nails.—Thackeray.

tea—*a storm in a teacup* a petty squabble; a disturbance marked by much noise, but of no importance.

For all that, his sympathies had been entirely with her in the recent

squabble. *"What a ridiculous little storm in a tea-cup it was!" he thought with a laugh.—Murray's Magazine,* 1887.

teens—*in one's teens* between the ages of twelve and twenty.

He (the great Condé) was a ripe scholar even in his teens, as the Latinity of his letters proves.— Edinburgh Review, 1887.

teeth—*to cast* or *throw anything in one's teeth* to reproach one with anything.

You've got the girl, and we must keep her; and keep her well too, that she may not be able to throw it in your teeth that she has made such sacrifice for you.—Blackmore.

—*to have cut one's teeth* or *eye-teeth* to be crafty.

He and I were born the same year, but he cut his teeth long before me.—C. Reade.

tell—*to tell on* or *upon* to affect; to influence.

"His previous exertions had told on his constitution.—Quarterly Review, 1807.

to tell tales out of school to repeat in public what has passed in the company of intimates; to reveal private matters.

"Look here, Duffham," he went on: "we want you to go with us and see— somebody: and to undertake not to tell tales out of school."—Mrs Henry Wood.

ten—*ten to one* ten chances to one; almost certainly.

Whenever the reader lights upon the title which Fox had waded through so much to earn, it is ten to one that within the next half-dozen lines there will be found an allusion to the gallows.— Trevelyan.

—*one of ten thousand* an exceptionally excellent person.

She did not know that she herself was a woman of ten thousand. She spoke believing herself to be a common type of humanity.—James Payn.

—**the upper ten** or **ten thousand** those moving in the highest London society.
Lord Swansdown has had some dealings with him in an agricultural way, and wishing to show him civility on his accession to the upper ten, desired his wife to send him an invitation for the shooting season.—Florence Marryat.

tenterhooks—**on tenterhooks** in a state of discomfort or agony. Tenterhooks are the hooks on which a web of cloth is stretched by the selvages on a frame.
I must say I should like to have it settled as soon as possible, because it keeps a man on tenterhooks, you know, and feeling like a fool.—Florence Marryat.

terms—**on good** or **excellent terms** friendly; intimate.
I am not on good terms with Sir Charles.—C. Reade.

—**to come to terms** to make bargain.
When George returned to the farmer, the latter, who had begun to fear the loss of a customer, came at once to terms with him.—C. Reade.

terra—**terra firma** dry land. Latin.
Another foaming breaker, supplemented by a vigorous shove from their stalwart arms, sends their unwieldy craft up high and dry, and the spray-splashed passengers can step out on terra firma.—Scribner's Magazine, 1887.

tête—*a tête-à-tête* a confidential conversation. French.
*"You will forgive me, Philip, for interrupting your tête-à-tête, but may I ask what is the meaning of this?"
Philip returned no answer.*—H. R. Haggard.

tether—*to the end of one's tether* as far as one is able to proceed.
I tell you plainly I have gone pretty well to the end of my tether with you.—C. Reade.

Thames—*to set the Thames on fire.* See *set.*

thanks—*thanks to this* or *that* this is the cause; the result is due to this.
If we are to believe the book, thanks to the American social system, she had a series of wonderful escapes from ill-considered matches.—Edinburgh Review, 1882.

that—*at that* a phrase in common use in America, signifying that certain conditions are conceded.
John, looking at him, guessed that he could not weigh less than seventeen stone, and he was well within the mark at that (if he allowed him such a weight).—H. R. Haggard.

thick—*through thick and thin* through every obstacle; daunted by nothing.
The first dawn of comfort came to him in swearing to himself that he would stand by that boy through thick and thin, and cheer him and help him and bear his burdens.—T. Hughes.

—*thick-skinned* not sensitive; not easily rebuked.
There was something in his companion's astounding thickness of skin that tickled his humour.—James Payn.

thin—*the thin end* or *edge of the wedge.* See *wedge.*

thing—*the thing* exactly right; just what ought to be.
Where energy was the thing, he was energetic enough.—All the Year Round, 1887.

—*to know a thing or two* to be wise or cunning.
"Mr. Levi," said he, "I see you know a thing or two; will you be so good as to answer me a question?"—C. Reade.

thingumbob—*thingumbob, thingumebob, thingummy,* or *thingamy* a word used to replace a name that is forgotten. "What d'ye call him?" is sometimes used in this way.

The merchant who discharged his clerk last week because he never could remember the word mucilage, and persisted in saying thingummy, has got another who is unsound on the word chronometer, and calls it a watch-you-call-it.—St. Andrew Citizen, 1887.

There was Mr. So-and-So and Mrs. Thingamy.—Wilson.

think—*to think better of it* to change one's mind; to abandon a resolve.

"I said plainly that I will not marry him.'
"I know you did, my dear; but Mrs. Garnier and I fancied you might have thought better of it."—Florence Marryat.

—*to think no end of a person* to have a very high opinion of his character.

thirty—*thirty-nine articles* the statement of the doctrines of the Church of England which every clergyman must sign. Theodore Hook, when asked if he was ready to sign the Thirty-nine Articles, replied flippantly, "Yes; and forty if you wish."

Mr Punch like Theodore Hook, had not any great reverence for the Thirty-nine Articles.—Fortnightly Review, 1887.

Thomas—*a very Thomas* an unbelieving, incredulous person. The disciple of our Lord who bore that name refused for a time to believe in Christ's resurrection. See John xx, 24, 25.

Moreover, when he sees the lock of hair and the love-letter—and perhaps there may be other discoveries by the time he returns—he must be a very Thomas not to believe such proof.—James Payn.

thorn—*to sit on thorns* to be in a position of excessive discomfort; to be troubled in mind.

She did not say anything at the breakfast-table, though Anna sat upon thorns lest she should; Helen was so apt to speak upon impulse.—Mrs Henry Wood.

—*A thorn in the side* or *the flesh* a perpetual source of annoyance.

There was given to me a thorn in the flesh.—2 Cor. xii. 7.

Sir Charles demurred. "Oh, I don't want to quarrel with the fellow; but he is a regular thorn in my side with his little trumpery estate, all in broken patches. He shoots my pheasants in the unfairest way."—C. Reade.

thousand—*a thousand and one* a very large number; an innumerable collection.

The servant girl entered, bringing a slip of paper upon a salver, the name, no doubt, of one of those thousand and one persons who were now always coming to ask permission to see the manuscript.—James Payn.

thread—*to take up the thread of* to commence again where a stoppage has taken place; to resume the treatment or discussion of.

Harry possessed a ready sympathy; he fell easily and at once into the direction suggested by another's words. Thus, when Angela talked about the palace, he also took up the thread of invention, and made believe with her as if it were a thing possible—a thing of brick and mortar.—Besant.

—*to hang by a thread* to be an imminent danger; to be ready to fall.

A fate which has already overtaken one living, and hangs by a thread over others.—Spectator, 1887.

throw—*to throw the great cast* to venture everything; to take a step of vital importance.

In a word, George had thrown the great cast.—*Thackeray.*

—*to throw dust in the eyes of* to confuse; to mislead.

It is not an honourable occupation to throw dust in the eyes of the English reader.—Contemporary Review, 1887.

—*to throw the handkerchief* to propose marriage; to choose a wife. The Sultan is said to select women for his harem in this fashion.

Her highly-flattered mother falls straightway in love with him, and he might have been encouraged to throw the handkerchief at once, had the frivolous Alice been equally impressionable.—Edinburgh Review, 1882.

—*to throw dirt* or *mud at* to abuse; to speak evil of.

A woman in my position must expect to have more mud thrown at her than a less important person.—Florence Marryat.

—*to throw oneself at* or *at the head of* (of a woman) to show a man that she is eager to receive a proposal of marriage.

They say that unless a girl fairly throws herself at the young men's heads she isn't noticed.—W. D. Howells.

—*to throw over* to abandon; to cease to aid or acknowledge.

"Look here, Musselboro; if you're going to throw me over, just tell me so, and let us begin fair."

"I'm not going to throw you over; I've always been on the square with you."—A. Trollope.

They say that he is engaged to a girl in England, and has thrown her over for the widow.—H. R. Haggard.

—*to throw stones* to find fault with other people.

There is an old proverb about the inexpediency of those who live in glass houses throwing stones, which I
always think that we (who are in society) would do well not to forget.—*Florence Marryat.*

—*to throw up the sponge.* See *sponge.*

—*to throw upon one's hands* to give one the responsibility of.

In spite of his warning the mother had been left behind, and he was in the unenviable position of having a child thrown upon his hands until the next stoppage.—Hugh Conway.

thumb—*rule-of-thumb* measurement of calculation without the aid of precise instruments; rough and ready calculation.

The real truth is, Winterborne, that medical practice in places like this is a very rule-of-thumb matter.—Thomas Hardy.

—*under the thumb of* completely subservient to; quite under the control and direction of.

From the death of Louis XI. female influence was constantly on the increase, and we may designate the century from 1483 to 1580—with the exception of Louis the Twelfth's reign—as the era of the ascendency of women and favourites. The kings were either nobodies, or were under the thumb of their wives or mistresses.—National Review, 1887.

—*to turn the thumbs up* to decide against. A classical phrase. The Romans in the amphitheatre turned their thumbs up when a combatant was not to be spared.

They had unanimously turned their thumbs up, "Sartor," the publisher acquainted him, "excites universal disapprobation."—R. Garnett.

—*to bite one's thumbs at* to show contempt for.

tick—*on tick* on credit; not paid for. Abbreviated from "On ticket", on credit.

There are few, I guess, who go upon tick as much as we do.—Haliburton.

ticket—*to go any ticket* to vote for any cause. An American political phrase.
Yes; I love the Quakers. I hope they'll go the Webster ticket.—Haliburton.

—*ticket-of-leave* a warrant given to convicts who are allowed their liberty on condition of good behaviour.
I suppose he's out now on a ticket-of-leave.—Huigh Conway.

—*that's the ticket* you have done the right thing; that's well done. From the winning ticket in a lottery.

tickle—*to tickle to death* to amuse exceedingly.

tide—*to tide over* to overcome a difficulty temporarily.
Such questions as these are sometimes very anxious ones in a remote country village, where every pound spent among the inhabitants serves to build up that margin outside the ordinary income of the wage-earners which helps the small occupants to tide over many a temporary embarrassment when money is scare.—Nineteenth Century, 1887.

tile—*a tile* or *a slate loose* something wrong with the brain; a disordered brain.
Do you think I am as mad as he is? Attack a man who has just breakfasted with me, merely because he has a tile loose!—C. Reade.

time—*at times* occasionally.
She knew that at times she must be missed.—Miss Austen.

—*in no time* very quickly; with great speed.
They listened a moment; there was no fresh sound. Then Brutus slipped down the front stairs in no time; he found the front door not bolted.—C. Reade.

—*from time to time* at intervals.

She lived with them entirely, only visiting her grandmother from time to time.—Miss Austen.

—*in time* (a) after a season; when some years have passed.
Emma was now in a humour to resolve that they should both come in time.—Miss Austen.

—(b) punctual or punctually; not behindhand.
Impey posted back to Calcutta, to be in time for the opening of term.—Macaulay.

—*to have a good time* or *a real good time* to enjoy oneself. An American phrase.
An American, when he has spent a pleasant day, will tell you that he has a good time.—A. Trollope.
How you will enjoy it! I guess you'll have a real good time, as our cousins say.—Florence Marryat.

—*for the time being* temporarily; for the particular season or occasion only.
It is the leading boys for the time being who give the tone to all the rest, and make the school either a noble institution for the training of Christian Englishmen, or a place where a young boy will get more evil than if he were turned out to make his way in London streets, or anything between these two extremes.—T. Hughes.

—*time out of mind* from a remote date; longer than any one can remember.
Having, out of friendship for the family, upon whose estate, praised be Heaven! I and mine have lived rent free, time out of mind, voluntarily undertaken to publish the memoirs of the Rack-rent Family, I think it my duty to say a few words, in the first place, concerning myself.—Maria Edgeworth.

—*to take time by the forelock* to act promptly; to make no unnecessary delay.

Now, sir, it's got to come to blows sooner or later; and what I propose is, to take time by the forelock, as the saying is, and come to blows some fine day when they least expect it.—R. L. Stevenson.

—*at this time of day* at so late a date; in our present stage of civilization. The phrase refers to a *period*, not to a day of twenty-four hours.
More than anything else, at this time of day (now that she was an elderly woman), I was sorry for her.—Henry James, Jun.

—*time and again* very frequently.
Time and again I've had my doubts whether he cared for Irene any.—W. D. Howells.

timeo—*timeo danaos et dona ferentes* I fear the Greeks even when they bring gifts. A line from the Latin poet Virgil, signifying that an enemy is to be feared even when he professes friendship.
"Come in here—there's a good fellow—I want to speak to you."
"Why is he so infernally genial?" reflected Philip. "Timeo Danaos et dona ferentes."—Thackeray.

tip—*to tip the wink* to give the signal.
For without putting on his fighting face, he calmly replied that he had seen Mr. Metaphor tip the wink, and whisper to one of his confederates, and thence judged that there was something mysterious on the carpet.—Smollett.

—*on the tip of one's tongue* ready to be uttered; on the point of utterance.
It had been on the tip of my tongue to say where I had just seen Jellico; and the trade he was doing.—Mrs Henry Wood.

—*to tip up* to pay money; to open one's purse.
"I should have liked to make her a little present," Osborne said to his friend in

confidence, "only I am quite out of cash until my father tips up."—Thackeray.

tiptoe—*on tiptoe* in eager expectation; in a state of excited suspense.
The news that Smike had been caught and brought back in triumph ran like wildfire through the hungry community, and expectation was on tiptoe all the morning.—Dickens.

tip-top—*tip-top* first-class.
One of those tip-top firms in the city would have gone straight off to take counsel's opinion.—Miss Braddon.

tit—*tit for tat* something given in return; just retaliation.
"Tit for tat! tit for tat!" they cried.
"Squire, you began it, and you have your due."—Blackmore.

to—*to and fro* backwards and forwards.
Speckled spiders, indolent and fat with long security, swing idly to and fro in the vibration of the bells.—Dickens.

—*a to-do* a commotion; a noise and confusion.
His mother, inside the vehicle with her maid and her furs, her wrappers, and her scent-bottles, made such a to-do that you would have thought she never had been in a stage-coach before.—Thackeray.

toe—*the light fantastic toe* a phrase used with reference to dancing.
Come, and trip it as you go
On the light fantastic toe.
                                    Milton.

—*to toe the mark* to be careful in one's conduct.
Now you know what I am! I'll make you toe the mark, every soul of you, or I'll flog you all, fore and aft, from the boy up.—R. H. Dana, Jun.

token—*by the same token* moreover; likewise; nay more.
Why, I caught two of their infamatory treatises in this very house. By the same token, I sent them to the executioner at Marseilles, with a

request that he would burn them publicly.—C. Reade.

—*more by token* moreover; in truth.
Whether it were St. George, I cannot say, but surely a dragon was killed there; for you may see the marks yet where his blood ran down, and more by token the place where it ran down is the easiest way up the hillside.—T. Hughes.

Tom—*Tom, Dick and Harry* ordinary, insignificant people; the multitude.
If that girl isn't in love with you, she is something very like it. A girl does not pop over like that for Dick, Tom, or harry.—H. R. Haggard.

—*Tom Tiddler's ground* said to be a contraction for *Tom the Idler's ground.* An imaginary garden of ease and wealth, where children pick up gold and silver.
Now the spacious drawing-room, with the company seated round the glittering table, busy with their glittering spoons and knives, and forks and plates, might have been taken for a grown-up exposition of Tom Tiddler's ground, where children pick up gold and silver.—Dickens.

tongue—*with the tongue in the cheek* mockingly; insincerely.
And if statesmen, either with their tongue in their cheek or with a fine impulsiveness, tell people that their natural taste for the bathos is a relish for the sublime, there is more need to tell them the contrary.—Matthew Arnold.

—*to hold the tongue* to be silent.
'Tis seldom seen that senators so young
Know when to speak and when to hold their tongue.
                                    Dryden.

—*to give tongue* to speak out.
Only when Mary fired a broadside into her character, calling her a bold bad,

brazen-faced slut—only then did Mrs. Richard give tongue on her behalf.—Mrs. E. Lynn Linton.

tooth—*tooth and nail* with great energy; violently; fiercely. As if attacking both with the teeth and with the nails.
There are men that roll through life, like a fire-new red ball going across Mr. Lord's cricket-ground on a sunshiny day; there is another sort that have to rough it in general, and, above all, to fight tooth and nail for the quartern loaf, and not always win the battle.—C. Reade.

—*a sweet tooth* a liking for sweet things. See **sweet.**

—*in the teeth of* (a) in direct opposition to; in spite of.
But when we fly antagonistically in the teeth of circumstances, bent on following our own resolute path, we take ourselves out of God's hands, and must reap the consequences.—Mrs. Henry Wood.
much disheartened about the whole business.—H. R. Haggard.
—(b) in presence of; with something right before one.
He was not, in most people's opinion, a very estimable man, but he had the talent—by no means a despicable one—of maintaining his personal dignity in the teeth of the most adverse circumstances.—Murray's Magazine, 1887.

top—*the top of the morning to you!* a morning salutation. Now old-fashioned.
"You, doctor? Top of the morning to you, sir!" cried Silver, broad awake and beaming with good nature in a moment.—R. L. Stevenson.

—*to the top of one's bent* fully; wholly; to the farthest limit.
They fool me to the top of my bent.—Shakespeare.

Accordingly Goldsmith was fooled to the top of his bent.—W. Irving.

—*a top-sawyer* a first-rate fellow. Of the two men who work a frame-saw in a saw-pit, the one who stands above is called the top-sawyer.
Well, he may be a top-sawyer, but I don't like him.—C. Reade.

—*at the top of the tree* in the foremost place; at the head of one's profession.
He's had wit enough to get to the top of the tree, and to keep himself there.—A. Trollope.

—*the top notch* the highest point.
It is two weeks since they (the locusts) first appeared in that county, and the effect of their blighting touch has not yet reached the top notch.—New York Herald, 1888.

—*to top up with* to finish with.
What'll you drink, Mr. Gargery, at my expense, to top up with?—Dickens.

torch—*to hand on the torch* to continue the work of enlightenment. A classical phrase.
Though Italy now (in the sixteenth century) ceases to be the guiding light of Europe, her work has been done among the nations, and in their turn France, England, and Germany hand on the torch, and the warmth and radiance survive still, and are reflected in the Italy of our own day.—Quarterly Review, 1887.

toss—*to toss up* to decide in a chance way, as by throwing up a coin.
It is a queer picture—that of the old prince dying in his little woodbuilt capital, and his seven sons tossing up who should inherit and transmit the crown of Brentford (petty crown).—Thackeray.

touch—*touch and go* said of a critical situation, where a very small influence will turn the scale.
"It was touch and go (my escape was a narrow one), doctor, was it?"

inquired the other with a seriousness as strangely foreign to the phrase as the phrase itself was to the speaker's usual manner of expressing himself.—James Payn.

—*in touch with* having a delicate appreciation and intimate knowledge of; in sympathy with.
Certainly this is inherent in the office and function of the country parson, that he is not quite in touch with any one in his parish if he be a really earnest and conscientious parson.—Nineteenth Century, 1887.

tour—*a tour de force* a feat of strength or of skill. French.
"That is not worthy of a mathematician," said Mr. Fraser with some irritation: "it is nothing but a trick, a tour de force."—H. R. Haggard.

tout—*the tout ensemble* the whole taken together. French.
"What a lovely woman this is!" said Mrs. Bellamy, with enthusiasm to Miss Lee, so soon as Philip was out of earshot. "Her tout ensemble positively kills one."—H. R. Haggard.

tow—*to take in tow* to take charge of.
Dr. Blimber accompanied them; and Paul had the honour of being taken in tow by the doctor himself—a distinguished state of things, in which he looked very little and feeble.—Dickens.

town—*a man about town* a fashionable gentleman; a man who spends his life in city clubs and in pleasure.
"Why should I give her pure heart to a man about town?"
"Because you will break it else," said Miss Somerset.—C. Reade.

tracks—*to make tracks* to go off; to depart quickly.
"I am glad that the old gentleman has made tracks," said John.—H. R. Haggard.

trade—*two of a trade* two people in the same business or profession.
It is proverbial that two of a trade seldom agree.—*Edinburgh Review*, 1886.

trail—*to trail off* to move heavily; to lose impetus. The example given refers to a novel that had been begun with some spirit.
How was it that, after this, A Heart of Gold began to trail off?—B. L. Farjeon.

tread—*to tread the boards* to be an actor; to follow the stage as a profession.
The theatres occupied a much higher position in society. Kemble and his majestic sister, Mrs. Siddons, trod the boards.—James Payn.

—*to tread on a man's corns* to annoy or hurt him.
"Only," he added, "I'm glad I trod on Master Pew's corns," for by this time he had heard my story.—R. L. Stevenson.

—*to tread on another's toes* to annoy or exasperate him.
The old West Indian families are very proud and sensitive, but there is much possibility of their having their toes trodden upon in anything like the way that made Mr. Froude's last book the subject of such an outcry by some of our antipodean friends and relations.—*Spectator*, 1887.

—*to tread on eggs* to walk with the utmost care; to be very circumspect.
"It's a real mean of him, isn't it?" says Miss Smiles. "Why, it might come to her husband's ears any day, and poor Emily will feel as if she was treading on eggs all her life."—Florence Marryat.

treasure—*treasure-trove* treasure hid away and accidentally discovered.
And so Farmer Caresfoot became the lawful owner of Cratham Abbey with its two advowsons, its royal franchises of treasure-trove and deodand, and

more than a thousand acres of the best land in Marlshire.—H. R.Haggard.

treat—*to stand treat* to entertain at a public place; to pay the holiday expenses of a party.
They went out to Versailles with their families; loyally stood treat to the ladies at the restaurateurs.—Thackeray.

tree—*up a tree* in a fix; cornered; unable to do anything.
I'm completely up a tree this time.—Haliburton.

trice—*in a trice* without delay; very quickly.
If she gives him proper encouragement, he'll pay the money in a trice.—Maria Edgeworth.

trip—*to trip up* to cause to fall.
Paddy was tripped up.—Beaconsfield.

—*to catch a man tripping* to discover a man making some error or committing some offence.
Though the police know him, and would give their eyes to catch him tripping, he never tumbles into their trap.—Miss Braddon.

Triton—*a Triton of* or *among the minnows* a man who appears big because his companions are so small. Triton was a sea-god, the trumpeter of Neptune.
Hear you this Triton of the minnows?—Shakespeare.

Trojan—*like a Trojan* gallantly; bravely.
He had lain like a Trojan behind his mattress in the gallery; he had followed every order silently, doggedly, and well.—R. L. Stevenson.

trot—*to trot out* to show for inspection; to exhibit to a company.
"Come, come," said James, putting his hand to his nose and winking at his cousin with a pair of vinous eyes, "no jokes, old boy; no trying it on me. You

want to trot me out, but it's no go."—Thackeray.

truant—*to play truant* to be absent without leave.

"He'll be back on the 15th," said the knight, "unless he means to play truant."—A. Trollope.

true—*true blue* thoroughly faithful and trustworthy; staunch.

Squire Brown, be it said, was a true blue Tory to the backbone.—T. Hughes.

—*true as steel* faithful; steadfast; wholly to be trusted.

Thank Farmer Meadows, for he 'twas that sent Tom to the prison, where he was converted, and became as honest a fellow as any in the world, and a friend to your George, as true as steel.—C. Reade.

trump—*to hold trumps* to be lucky; to be sure of victory. Trumps are the winning cards at whist. The word is a form of "triumph".

You never hold trumps, you know: I always do.—George Eliot.

—*to play one's trump card* to use one's best chance of success.

He was a man with power in reserve; he had still his trump card to play.—Besant.

—*to turn up trumps* (a) to prove successful; to be fortunate.

There are plenty of instances, in the experience of every one, of short courtships and speedy marriages which have turned up trumps—I beg your pardon—which have turned out well after all.—Wilkie Collins.

—(b) to prove of signal service; to prove very useful.

When he turned up trumps I let things be.—H. Kingsley.

—*to trump up* to fabricate; to make up with an evil motive.

"The girl has gone mad."

"Good heavens! you don't say so!"

"Yes, I do, though; and I'll tell you what it is. Bellamy, they say that you and your wife went to Madeira and trumped up a story about her lover's death in order to take the girl in."—H. R. Haggard.

trumpet—*to blow one's own trumpet* to speak boastfully.

After such a victory our old friend the archdeacon would have blown his own trumpet loudly among his friends.—A. Trollope.

try—*to try it on* to see how far one may venture with impunity; to test one's power.

Well, then, he is trying it on with Miss Rayne. There is no doubt of that. I watched them through the tableaux.—Florence Marryat.

—*to try on* to see if clothes fit.

In the conduct of the show-room and the trying-on room she has all her own way.—Besant.

—*to try one's hand at* to venture upon for the first time; to make a beginning with.

He had on several occasions been induced to try his hand at écarté.—S. Warren.

tuck—*to tuck into* to eat heartily of.

"I won't myself," returned Squeers; "but if you'll just let little Wackford tuck into something fat, I'll be obliged to you."—Dickens.

—*to tuck up* to draw tight round one; to roll up so as not to drag or hang.

"Why," said Lord Jocelyn, with a shudder. "you will rise at six; you will go out in working-clothes, carrying your tools, and with your apron tied round and tucked up."—Besant.

—*a tuck-out* a feast; an eating of dainties. A "tuck-shop" is a confectioner's.

Old Dobbin, his father, who now respected him for the first time, gave him two guineas publicly, most of which he spent in a general tuck-out for the school.—Thackeray.

tug—*the tug of war* the hardest part of any undertaking; the real struggle. The name is also given to a favourite athletic pastime, where two sides pull at the opposite ends of a rope.

When Greeks joined Greeks then was the tug of war.—N. Lee.

It was when the ladies were alone that Becky knew the tug of war would come.—Thackeray.

tune—*to the tune of* to the amount of. A surprisingly large sum of money is generally mentioned after the phrase.

Then Mr. Titmouse ventured to apply to Mr. O'Gibbet, that gentleman being Mr. Titmouse's debtor to the tune of some five hundred pounds.—S. Warren.

turf—*on the turf* engaged in horse-racing.

"My dear Digby, you talk like a racing-man," said Mrs. Brabazon. "You should remember that we are not all of us on the turf."—James Payn.

turn—*to turn in* to retire for the night.

"Well, I'll turn in; I'm pretty tired," said Larry, rising and laying his hand on the old man's shoulder.—All the Year Round, 1887.

—*to turn out* (a) to prove in the sequel; to result.

£37,000 was private capital sunk in the land without any prospect of seeing the capital again, and, as things have turned out, without even getting the interest.—Spectator, 1887.

The tidings turned out to be correct.—Dickens.

—(b) to eject; to evict.

—*to turn out in the cold* to repulse; to reject; to remove from a pleasant situation.

It was a warm evening, as his father had observed; but in one sense he

had been turned out in the cold, and he felt it bitterly.—James Payn.

—*to turn up* to show oneself; to appear; to happen unexpectedly.

He had come over to England to be an apothecary, or anything else that might turn up.—Dickens.

He's turned up, by Jove, a trump (nice fellow) all of a sudden.—S. Warren.

But something might turn up; and it was devoutly to be hoped that Dr. Tempest would take a long time over the inquiry.—A. Trollope.

—*to turn up one's nose at* to show contempt for.

When first Chaldicotes, a very old country-seat, had by the chances of war fallen into their hands and been newly furnished, and newly decorated, and newly gardened, and newly green-houses, and hot-watered by them, many of the country people had turned up their noses at them.—A. Trollope.

—*to take turns.* See **take**.

—*by turns* alternately; one after another.

*They feel by turns the bitter change
Of fierce extremes; extremes by
   change more fierce.*

                      Milton.

—*to turn one's coat* to be a renegade; to join the party one has opposed.

I never turned my coat, as some fine gentlemen who have never been to Constantinople have done. I never changed my principles.—G. A. Sala.

The celebrated Sir John Urie, a soldier of fortune like Dalgetty, who had already changed sides twice already during the Civil War, and was destined to turn his coat a third time before it was ended.—Scott.

—*to turn one's back on* to refuse to acknowledge; to repulse.

He could not consent to turn his back upon helpless travellers.—W. Irving.

—*to turn a deaf ear* to refuse to listen.

The Russian government, in the last few years, made repeated applications to the governments of France and England for protection against Nihilist conspirators who made Paris or London their residence; but the English government has turned a deaf ear to the requests made for legislation.—Fortnightly Review, 1997.

—*to turn one's hand* to be ready to work at.

I can turn my hand to anything.—W. Irving.

—*to turn the head of* to intoxicate; to destroy the moral balance of.

He was but a stripling of sixteen, and being thus suddenly mounted on horseback, with money in his pocket, it is no wonder that his head was turned.—W. Irving.

—*to turn in one's grave* a phrase used with reference to dead people, when something happens which would have annoyed them exceedingly when alive.

O William Slagg, you must have turned in your grave.—Hugh Conway.

to turn the corner to pass a critical point; to change for the better.

For the present this young man (although he certainly had turned the corner) lay still in a very precarious state.—Blackmore.

—*to turn over* to transfer.

'Tis well the debt no payment does demand.
You turn me over to another hand.
            Dryden.

—*to turn on one's heel* to go off with a gesture of contempt.

A very dry recognition on Miss Anna Maria's part replied to the effort I made to salute her, and, as she turned on her heel, she said to her brother. "Breakfast's ready," and left the room.—C. Lever.

—*to turn over a new leaf* to commence a new course of life; to improve in conduct.

Then, in a private postscript, he condescended to tell us that all would be speedily settled to his satisfaction and we should turn over a new leaf.—Maria Edgeworth.

—*to turn one round one's little finger* to manage with ease.

"But he turns you and me round his little finger, old boy—there's no mistake about that." And East nodded at Tom sagaciously.—T. Hughes.

—*to turn a penny* to earn money.

I attend sales, and never lose a chance of turning a penny.—C. Reade.

—*to turn the tables.* See **table**.

—*to turn tail* go to off; to turn back.

That night two supers turned tail. An actress also, whose name I have forgotten, refused to go on with her.—C. Reade.

—*to turn to account* to make good use of; to profit from.

It is possible that he would turn them to good account.—Thackeray.

—*to do a good turn* to be of service.

Indeed, I tried, at Angela's suggestion, to do you a good turn with Philip Caresfoot.—H. R. Haggard.

—*to do a bad* or *an ill turn* to injure.

Go to Crawley. Use my name. He won't refuse my friend, for I could do him an ill turn if I chose.—C. Reade.

—*to turn the stomach* to cause sickness or loathing.

The stomach turns against them.—Hazlitt.

—*to turn upon* to prove unfaithful to; to desert.

But he (George IV.) turned upon twenty friends. He was fond and familiar with them one day, and he passed them on the next without recognition.—Thackeray.

turned—*turned out of* educated at.

Indeed, he knew that the arguments of

those who hold the doctrine of predestination and its correlative reprobation, are logically unanswerable by the best theologian ever turned out of Oxford.—Hugh Conway.

turtle—*to turn the turtle* to capsize.

Yes, Mr. Keene; but turning the turtle is not making a quick passage—except to the other world.—Captain Marryat.

tweedle—*Tweedledum and Tweedledee* two things which differ very slightly, and are very insignificant at best.

Some say, compared to Bonocini,
That Mynheer Handel's but a ninny;
Others aver that he to Handel
Is scarcely fit to hold a candle.
Strange all this difference should be
'Twixt Tweedledum and Tweedledee.
                              John Byrom.

twig—*to twig a person* to comprehend him; to understand his meaning; to know what his intention is.

"Stay," cried he; "if he is an old hand he will twig the officer."—C. Reade.

two—*in two twos* immediately; without any delay.

"Do they, indeed?" says I; "Send them to me, then, and I'll fit the handle on to them in two twos."—Haliburton.

—*to put or lay two and two together* to reason logically; to draw a logical conclusion.

The young fellows in Dublin, too, by laying two and two together, began to perceive that there was a certain dragon in watch for the wealthy heiress.—Thackeray.

Gwendolen was a woman who could put two and two together.—George Eliot.

—*to have two strings to one's bow* to have two things to rely upon; to have a second resource to fall back upon.

You have now, as you see, what it is always well to have—two strings to your bow.—James Payn.

The American heiress is both powerful and wealthy, and Hester Beverley knows well the advantage in this world of having two strings to your bow.—Florence Marryat.

—*to make two bites of a cherry* to divide something so small as not to be worth a division.

If I was in your place, I wouldn't make two bites of a cherry.—C. Reade.

—*two can play at that game* another person can retaliate in the same way.

"Woman, what do you mean?" cries the visitor, rising to her feet.

"Now, don't you call me any names, or you will find that two can play at that game."—Florence Marryat.

Mr. Bassett had invoked brute force in the shape of Burdock. "Well, sir," said he, "it seems they have shown you two can play at that game."—C. Reade.

—*two upon ten* two eyes on ten fingers—that is, "keep a watch on his movements or he may steal." This watchword is often passed round a shop when a suspicious character has entered it.

twopence—*to want twopence in the shilling* to be weak in the brain; to be crazy. The head is called sarcastically a man's "two-penny;" as in the game of leap-frog, where the boy stooping down is told to "tuck in his twopenny."

twopenny—*twopenny-halfpenny* of small value; insignificant.

The next day we took a prize called the Golden Sun, belonging to a creek on the main, a twopenny-halfpenny little thing, thirty-five tons.—G. A. Sala.

Those twopenny-halfpenny lights which make so good an effect in the garden.—Mrs. E. Lynn-Linton.

U

ugly—*an ugly duckling* something which is despised for its want of beauty, but which afterwards wins admiration. In the fable from which the phrase is taken the ugly duckling proved to be a swan.

"Well," said Campion, "you see I was one of the ducklings myself."

"Oh, ah, so you were," said Babcock, perfectly unabashed, "but we'll hope you'll turn out more in the ugly duckling line."—F. Anstey.

And then we all get into our carriages, with the "ugly duckling," transformed within the last quarter of an hour into a swan, leading the way.—Rhoda Broughton.

—*an ugly customer* an unpleasant individual to deal with: a person to be afraid of.

Some of these good-looking young gentlemen are ugly customers enough when their blood is up, and Cousin Charlie, like the rest, had quite as much "devil" in his composition as was good for him.—G. J. Whyte-Melville.

—*as ugly as sin* repulsive in appearance.

Why, she is as ugly as sin! Though she is my friend, I must acknowledge that.—Maria Edgeworth.

uncle—*my uncle's* the pawnbroker's.

"If you won't lend me, I must starve."

"Go to my uncle's," Titmouse groaned aloud.—S. Warren.

—*Uncle Sam* the people or government of the United States.

'We call," said the clockmaker, "the American public Uncle Sam, as you call the British John Bull."—Haliburton.

She was called the Catalina, and, like the vessels in that trade, except that Ayacucho, her papers and colours were from Uncle Sam.—R. H. Dana, Jun.

unction—*to lay a flattering unction to the soul* to soothe oneself with a pleasant fancy. A Shakespearean phrase (*Hamlet*, act iii, scene 4).

And he had answered her, that she sent him straight to the devil; that when she heard in after times that vaurien, George Ruthven, had shot himself, or gone to the dogs, she might lay the flattering unction to her soul that she had sent him there.—Florence Marryat.

union—*the Union Jack* the flag of the United Kingdom of Great Britain and Ireland.

The weighted corpse, wrapped around with a Union Jack, was borne along by the sailors to the stern of the ship.—Wm. Black.

up—*all up* certain destruction; a hopeless condition of affairs.

John realized that it was all up, and that to stop in the cart would only mean certain death.—H. R. Haggard.

Pippin was as white as death, and I thought it was all up myself.—C. Reade.

'Tis all up with the villains.—S. Warren.

—*up and about* no longer in bed; dressed and moving about.

It was then a little after five, and there was already a stir, an occasional

footfall along the principal streets. By
the time he got to the Whitechapel
Road there were a good many up and
about.—Besant.

—*up in arms* enraged; ready to quarrel.
The squire would have been up in
arms, no doubt, if he had known it.—
Mrs. Henry Wood.

—*up a tree* in a dilemma; thoroughly
perplexed.
"Worse than that," replied Jacques,
looking very grave; "I'm in a regular
fix—up a tree, by Jove."—G. J. Whyte-
Melville.

—*ups and downs* prosperity and
adversity; successive rises and falls.
The ups and downs of the rival parties
furnished subjects for two excellent
cartoons.—Fortnightly Review, 1887.

—*up to a thing or two* knowing; skilful.
As King Solomon says,—and that man
was up to a thing or two, you may
depend, though our professor did say
he wasn't so knowing as Uncle
Sam,—it's all vanity and vexation of
spirit.—Haliburton.

—*up to something* about to carry out a
scheme.
Old Jacobson was as curious as
anything over it, and asked the squire,
aside, what he was up to, that he must
employ Crow instead of his own
man.—Mrs. Henry Wood.

—*up to the eyes* completely; to its full
extent.

Splatchett's farm is mortgaged up to
the eyes.—C. Reade.

—*up to the mark* in excellent condition
or health; not below the average.
Generally used negatively.
"Come, Balfour," said Mr. Bolitho
brightly, "have a glass of sherry and a
cigar. You don't look quite up to the
mark this morning."—Wm. Black.

upper—*the upper hand* the control;
power of governing.
Finally, the reports were that the
governess had come round
everybody, wrote Sir Pitt's letters, did
his business, managed his
accounts—had the upper hand of the
whole house.—Thackeray.

—*the upper ten* or *upper ten thousand*
the highest circle of society.
Next comes "The History of a Crime"
(pace, Victor Hugo), of the high-falutin'
order, intended, we suppose, to give
one a glimpse of the iniquities of the
upper ten.—Edinburgh Review, 1887.

—*the upper story* the head or brain.
You see, the point we should gain
would be this,—if we tried to get him
through as being a little touched in the
upper story,—whatever we could do
for him, we could do against his own
will.—A. Trollope.

upset—*an upset price* the price at
which an article at an auction is
started by the auctioneer.
The upset price was one pound an
acre, payable at once.—H. Kingsley.

V

vadë—*a vade mecum* a useful book of reference that can be carried about; a constant companion. Latin: "Go with me."

> The fact is, I can't say I am versed in the school
> So ably conducted by Marryat and Poole;
> (See the last-mentioned gentleman's "Admiral's Daughter."
> The grand vade mecum for all who to sea come).—Barham.
> All these things will be specified in time,
> With strict regard to Aristotle's rules,
> The vade mecum of the true sublime,
> Which makes so many poets and some fools.—Byron.

Væ—*væ victis!* woe to the vanquished! Latin.

> Væ victis being of old the only regret expressed towards those against whom the fortune of war had turned.—Chamber's Journal, 1887.

valet—*valet de chambre* bedroom servant; personal attendant. French.

> We are not the historic Muse, but her ladyship's attendant, tale-bearer—valet de chambre—for whom no man is a hero.—Thackeray.

veil—*to take the veil* to become a nun.

> He had, as he said, taken orders as a nun takes the veil, to get rid of the wicked world.—R. Garnett, in *Life of Carlyle*.

—*beyond the veil* in the other world; in the regions of the dead.

> The tale was finished in London on the 3rd of November 1844, and early in December read by him from the proofs ready for publication at Forster's rooms to a little party of friends, including Maclise and Stanfield, Dyce, Laman Blanchard, Douglas Jerrold, and Thomas Carlyle. Reader and hearers are beyond the veil; there is not one left to us now.—Henry Morley.

—*to draw a veil over* to conceal.

> There may be whole pages, close-written and full of stirring matter, which I have chosen to conceal; there may be occurrences which it is best, at this time, to draw a veil over.—G. A. Sala.

vengeance—*with a vengeance* extremely; forcibly; unmistakably.

> He could be logical with a vengeance—so logical as to cause infinite trouble to his wife, who, with all her good sense, was not logical.—A. Trollope.
> The Hispaniola reached Bristol just as Mr. Blandly was beginning to think of fitting out her consort. Five men only of those who had sailed returned with her. Drink and the devil had done for the rest, with a vengeance.—R. L. Stevenson.

ventre—*ventre à terre* at the greatest speed. French. Literally "with the belly on the earth."

> We ride at speed, we drive at speed . . . are married, divorced, robbed, ruined, and enriched, all ventre à terre!—G. J. Whyte-Melville.

verbum—*verbum sap* a word is enough. A contraction of the Latin phrase *verbum sap sapienti*, "a word is enough for a wise man."

> I say no more. Verbum sap.—Wilkie Collins.

via—*via media* a middle path; a course between two opposite extremes. Latin.

It must be unconditional surrender, or the last attempt at conciliation. There was no via media.—Mrs. E. Lynn Linton.

vial—*to pour out the vials of one's wrath* to give vent to one's anger; to express one's indignation.

She pours out the vials of her mental wrath on the head of Mrs. West for encouraging Staunton to come to Norman House.—Florence Marryat.

vice—*vice versâ* making an interchange of positions; placing two things each in the place of the other. Latin. Literally "the terms being exchanged."

They never laugh when they ought to weep, or vice versa (weep when they ought to laugh).—James Payn.

victory—*a cadmean victory* a victory in which the victors suffer as much as their enemies.

vin—*vin ordinaire* ordinary red wine, such as is supplied free of charge at meals in a French hotel. French.

I suppose those toadies of his have supplied him with a vin ordinaire at a hundred and twenty shillings a dozen.—Wm. Black.

virgin—*virgin soil* what is fresh and unused.

I am convinced that comic opera, or rather operatic comedy, has an immense future before it in this country. One may almost call it virgin soil.—Good Words, 1997.

virtue—*to make a virtue of necessity* to do willingly what cannot be avoided to submit with a good grace to what is inevitable.

Making a virtue of necessity, there are many in England who begin no longer to regard Constantinople as a British interest of the first magnitude.—Fortnightly Review, 1887.

viva—*vivâ voce* using the voice and not the pen as the medium of communication. Latin. The literal signification is "with the living voice."

Dr. Johnson seems to have been really more powerful in discoursing vivâ voce in conversation than with his pen in his hand.—S. T. Coleridge.

The sole examination is vivâ voce and public, but, I was assured, of not the least importance.—Journal of Education, 1887.

voice—*at the top of one's voice* loudly; in a high voice.

volte—*volte face* a complete change of position; a reversal of conduct or policy. French.

Nothing in the last two years had happened to justify the conference in executing a volte face.—Journal of Education, 1887.

volumes—*to speak volumes* to be important testimony; to be very significant.

Bella, you know it is the same woman. You recognized her in a moment. That speaks volumes.—C. Reade.

The epithet so often heard, and in such kindly tones, of "Poor Goldsmith," speaks volumes.—W. Irvine.

W

wait—*to wait upon* (a) to pay a formal visit to.

> *The countess had actually come to wait upon Mrs. Crawley on the failure of her second envoy.*—Thackeray.

—(b) to attend to the wants of a person.

> *She had been so long used to be humoured and waited upon, by relations and servants, that she considered herself a sort of golden idol.*—Maria Edgeworth.

—*to wait for another's shoes.* See **shoe.**

walk—*to walk the plank* a punishment frequently imposed by pirates on their captives. The unfortunate victims were made to walk along a plank partly overhanging the water. After a few steps the plank tilted, and they were shot into the sea.

> *It is also to be deplored that pirates should be able to exact ransom by threatening to make their captives walk the plank.*—Macaulay.

> *I had to take it, or walk the plank.*—C. Reade.

—*to walk one's chalks* to go off.

> *The prisoner has cut his stick, and walked his chalks, and is off to London.*—C. Kingsley.

—*a walk over the course*, or *a walk over* an easy victory; a victory gained without any real competition.

—*to walk the chalk line* to be particular in one's conduct.

> *Make him walk the chalk line.*

—*to walk the hospital* to prosecute medical studies with the view of becoming a physician. Before medical colleges were introduced into England, students attached themselves to one or other of the London hospitals.

> *Lor', no; it's quite a stranger; a young man that's just been walking the 'orspital; but they say he's very clever.*—Miss Braddon.

wall—*to go to the wall* to fail; to be unsuccessful.

> *Quacks prosper as often as they go to the wall.*—Thackeray.

> *Charles's hopes had had to go to the wall.*—Mrs. Henry Wood.

—*the finger* or *handwriting on the wall* the announcement of a coming disaster. See **handwriting.**

> *This inexplicable incident, this reversal of my previous experience, seemed, like the Babylonian finger on the wall, to be spelling out the letters of my judgment.*—R. L. Stevenson.

wallaby—*to go on the wallaby track* to go up country in search of work. An Australian term.

war—*war to the knife* a bitter and deadly struggle.

> *Which war old Lady Lufton, good and pious and charitable as she was, considered that she was bound to keep up, even to the knife, till Dr. Proudie and all his satellites should have been banished into outer darkness.*—A. Trollope.

—*to put on the war-paint* to dress oneself up in a conspicuous fashion; to wear one's finest clothes.

> *"Have you seen the hero of the evening?"*

"Who?" Do you mean the Portuguese governor in his war-paint?"—H. R. Haggard.

warming—*a warming-pan* a person who holds a post until a minor is ready to occupy it.
We used to call him in my parliamentary days W. Adams, in consequence of his being warming-pan for a young fellow who was in his minority.—Dickens.

warrant—*a warrant officer* a petty officer in the navy as distinguished from a "commissioned officer."
What is surprising is to find my self a warrant officer.—Captain Marryat.

wash—*to wash one's hands of* to refuse to have anything more to do with.
To look at me, you would hardly think "Poor Thady" was the father of Attorney Quirk. He is a high gentleman, and never minds what poor Thady says, and having better than fifteen hundred a year, landed estate, looks down upon honest Thady; but I wash my hands of his doings, and as I have lived so will I die, true and loyal to this family.—Maria Edgeworth.
"And I think he said it was a cruel business—nay, I'm sure he did; and that as for him, he washed his hands on't" (of it). Mr. Aubrey seemed confounded.—S. Warren.

—*to wash one's dirty linen in public* to speak in public of unpleasant private affairs; to discuss unpleasant private matters before strangers.
"I have been so pressed since my marriage" he said, "that it has been impossible for me to keep things straight."
"But Lady Alexandrina—"
"Yes, of course, I know. I do not like to trouble you with my affairs—there is nothing, I think, so bad as washing one's dirty linen in public; but the truth is, that I am only now free from the

rapacity of the De Courcys."—A. Trollope.

—*washed out* pale and bloodless in appearance.
She noticed that the young man who sat beside him looked rather pale and washed out.—Hugh Conway.

wasp—*a wasps' nest* a place where there are plenty of enemies; a place where one is unwelcome.
It was into a wasps' nest that the imprudent Louise thrust herself.—Illustrated London News, 1887.

watch—*watch and watch* taking alternative watches.
We will fight the schooner watch and watch till daylight.—Captain Marryat.

water—*to throw cold water on an enterprise* to discourage its promotion: to speak slightingly of it.
It was to be hoped Mr. Godfrey would not to go Tarley and throw cold water on what Mr. Snell said there.—George Eliot.
Colman threw cold water on the undertaking from the very beginning.—Wm. Black.
Among them was Aurelia Tucker, the scoffer and thrower of cold water.—Besant.

—*in deep water* in difficulties; puzzled how to act.
Once he had been very nearly in deep water because Mrs. Proudie had taken it in dudgeon that a certain young rector, who had been left a widower, had a very pretty governess for his children.—A. Trollope.

—*of the first water* of the highest type; very excellent. A term originally applied to precious stones.
One comfort, folk are beginning to take an interest in us. I see nobs of the first water looking with a fatherly eye into our affairs.—C. Reade.

—*to hold water* to be tenable; to be supported by facts.

Tales had gone about respecting her. Nothing very tangible, and perhaps they would have held water.—Mrs Henry Wood.

He was secretly conscious that the theory of the evergreen tree would not hold water.—James Payn.

—**to make the mouth water** to be excessively alluring; to cause desire and longing.

I could tell you things that would make your mouth water about the profits that are earned in the musical branch of our own trade.—Good Words, 1887.

—**to be in hot water** to be in trouble or difficulties; to have people angry with one.

Tom was in everlasting hot water as the most incorrigible scapegrace for ten miles round.—T. Hughes.

—**to water stock** to give away a proportion of the shares in a company at a large discount or gratis.

But there's no use crying over spilt milk, or watered stock either.

—**to back water** to reverse the forward motion of a boat in rowing; to row backwards.

The captain gave orders to back water, and none too soon, for we just avoided a collision.—R. H. Dana.

—**the water-works** or **the water pumps** the shedding of tears.

"Oh, Miss B—, I never thought to have seen this day;" and the waterworks began to play.—Thackeray.

"Thank you, Dobin," he said, rubbing his eyes with his knuckles, "I was just— just telling her I would. And, O sir, she's so kind to me." The water-pumps were at work again (he again commenced to shed tears).—Thackeray.

wax—**to wax fat and kick** to become unruly and hard to manage through too great prosperity. A Biblical phrase (Deut. xxxii. 15).

During the prosperous period when our revenue was advancing by leaps and bounds, it is to be apprehended that waiters as well as sailors waxed fat and kicked.—Blackwood's Magazine, 1886.

—**in a wax** angry.

when she's in a wax there's nowhere a finer stringer of big ones (lies).—Besant.

"You needn't get into a wax over it, old chap," said my father.—H. Kingsley.

way—**in a way** (a) somewhat; in a certain sense.

The people of the boarding-house continued to amuse him, partly because they were in a way afraid of him.—Besant.

—(b) agitated; much concerned.

The poor father is in a way about his son's misbehaviour.

—**once in a way** rarely; occasionally.

Once in a way a man might take too much.—Blackmore.

—**in a fair way of** likely to; with every likelihood of.

Rothsay had come back to England in a fair way, for the first time in his life, of making money.—Wilkie Collins.

—**in a good way** prosperous; prosperously.

He quitted the militia and engaged in trade, having brothers already established in a good way in London.—Maria Edgeworth.

—**to make one's way** to be prosperous; to rise.

He (Disraeli) is determined to make his way.—Edinburgh Review, 1886.

—**to make way** to step aside so as to leave a passage; to give place.

Make way there for the princess.—Shakespeare.

Every one shifting, and shuffling, and staring, and assisting in that curious and confusing ceremony called making way.—Beaconsfield.

—**to go the way of all flesh** to die.

His former retainer, Phil Judd, had gone the way of all flesh.—Murray's Magazine, 1887.

They nodded to each other by way of breaking the ice of unacquaintance, and the first stranger handed his neighbour the family mug—a huge vessel of brown ware, having its upper edge worn away like a threshold by the rut of whole generations of thirty lips that had gone the way of all flesh.—Thomas Hardy.

—**in the way** proving an obstacle; causing an obstruction; not wanted; not welcome. Compare "in the road."

You may be (you are) a charming person, but just now you are a little in the way. They resent your presence.— James Payn.

It may seem strange that I felt in the way in their company.—Mistletoe Bough, 1885.

—**out of the way** strange; eccentric.

In her drama, which was so effective on the stage, Djek did nothing out of the way.—C. Reade.

—**under way** in motion.

Arthur was perfectly charmed with everything he saw, and so was Agatha Terry, until they got under way when she discovered that a mail steamer was a joke compared with the yacht in the matter of motion.—H. R. Haggard.

—**to be way of being** to be able to be classed as; to come into the category of.

Phipps was by way of being something of a musician.—Good Words, 1997.

—**by the way** a phrase used with remarks made incidentally, and not belonging to the main subject.

With this, and showing the tricks of that dog, whom I stole from the sergeant of a marching regiment (and, by the way, he can steal too upon occasion). I make shift to pick up up a livelihood.— H. Mackenzie.

—**to give away** (a) to yield; to submit.

I have never seen the bridegroom's male friends give way to tears.— Thackeray.

—(b) to break down; to lose control of oneself.

"I see how it is," said poor Noggs, drawing from his pocket what seemed to be an old duster and wiping Kate's eyes with it as gently as if she were an infant; "you're giving way now."— Dickens.

—**to go a very little way with** to have small influence upon.

Her well-meant apology for her father went, indeed, but a very little way with her companion.—James Payn.

—**ways and means** necessary funds and the manner of procuring them.

This passionless character is illustrated by Lewis's position in the Cabinet as Chancellor of the Exchequer during the height of the Crimean War and to its close, and he was therefore responsible for finding the ways and means for carrying it on.—Westminster Review, 1887.

When money has to be raised, the House of Commons resolves itself into Committee of Ways and Means.

weak—**weak as a cat** very feeble. Always of physical weakness.

John looked round, and for the first time a sense of hope began to creep into his heart. Perhaps they would survive after all.

"Let's go up and see. It is no good stopping here; we must get food somewhere. I feel as weak as a cat.'— H. R. Haggard.

—**as week as water** very feeble. Used both of moral and of physical weakness.

Sir, I am only just getting well of a fever, and I am as weak as water.—C. Reade.

Away from you I am as weak as water,

excepting where she is concerned.—
Florence Marryat.

wear—*wear and tear* damage resulting from constant use and from occasional accidents.

The increasing wear and tear of life, reducing leisure and making brevity in letter-writing a primary consideration, supplies a third reason.—Macmillan's Magazine, 1887.

The castle walls have stood the wear and tear of centuries.—Edinburgh Review, 1887.

—*to wear on* to pass slowly (of time).

After the Bellamy's departure, the time wore on at Madeira without bringing about any appreciable change in the situation.—H. R. Haggard.

—*to wear one's heart upon one's sleeve for daws to peck at* to expose one's private feelings to unfeeling criticism. A Shakespearian phrase. See **heart** and **sleeve**.

She is, in fact, a fair specimen of an English maiden—upright, fearless, and wholesome-looking. What more may be in her, her intimate friends alone know, for she is not a woman to wear her heart upon her sleeve for daws to peck at.—Florence Marryat.

weather—*the weather eye* the eye of a keen observer. A sea phrase.

Job returned in a great state of nervousness, and kept his weather eye fixed upon every woman who came near him.—H. R. Haggard.

But you keep your weather eye open, Jim.—R. L. Stevenson.

wedge—*the thin end* or *edge of the wedge* the first small beginning, which may lead to what is serious and important.

How or when he (Thackeray) made his very first attempt in London, I have not learned; but he had not probably spent his money without forming "press" acquaintances, and had thus formed

an aperture for the thin edge of the wedge.—A. Trollope.

It was the thin edge of the wedge, in good truth, and the driving home had to come.—Mrs. E. Lynn Linton.

In this way the thin edge of the wedge had been inserted for French influence at the back of Marocco.—Grant Allen, in Contemporary Review, 1888.

weeping—*to return by weeping cross* to regret deeply some undertaking; to be in a state of lamentation.

The lawyers' harvest-term is o'er
Which to their purses brought good
  store;
But many clients, to their loss,
Do return home by Weeping Cross.
         Poor Robin, 1755.

weigh—*under weigh* in motion.

We were soon under weigh again.—C. Lever.

well—*well, I never!* an exclamation of surprise.

This almost caused Jemima to faint with terror. "Well, I never!" said she. "What an audacious—" Emotion prevented her from completing either sentence.—Thackeray.

"Well, I never!" said the old man. "My stay-at-home Jess wanting to go away, and without Bessie, too! What is the matter with you?"—H. R. Haggard.

—*well-to-do* in comfortable circumstances.

Moreover, she had a distillery of rum and arrack in Kingston itself, and everybody agreed that she must be very well-to-do in the world.—G. A. Sala.

—*well and good* a common consequent in a conditional sentence, signifying that the result is satisfactory.

If it come up a prize, well and good; and if it come up a blank, why, well and good too.—Maria Edgeworth.

—*truth lies at the bottom of a well* a

saying which refers to the difficulty of finding out the truth.

In his simple opinion the depth of the well, at the bottom of which truth is hid, was nothing to the unfathomableness of his designs.—J. Maclaren Cobban.

wet—*to wet one's whistle* to take a drink of liquor.

"Musselboro, reach me down the decanter and some glasses. Perhaps Mr. Crosbie will wet his whistle."

"He don't want any wine—nor you either, said Musselboro.—A. Trollope. "But if you'll believe me, sir, they don't so much as wet their whistles.—A. Trollope.

whack—*to take one's whack* to drink liquor.

Dinner parties, where the guests drank grossly, and even the schoolboy took his whack, like licorice-water.—R. L. Stevenson.

what—*I tell you what.* this phrase calls the attention of the listener to some important statement.

I know something about that place (the House of Commons), I think; and I tell you what besides, that if there had not been this interruption, Mr. Disraeli might have made a failure.—Sheil.

—*what not* various things difficult to mention severally.

In these rooms in Wine Office Court, and at the suggestion or entreaty of Newbery, Goldsmith produced a good deal of miscellaneous writing— pamphlets, tracts, compilations, and what not, of a more or less marketable kind.—Wm. Black.

—*to know what's what* to be intelligent and well-informed.

If, perhaps, such men as Louis Philippe and Monsieur A. Thiers, minister and deputy, and Monsieur François Guizot, deputy and excellency, had, from interest or conviction, opinions at

all differing from the majority, why, they knew what was what, and kept their opinions to themselves.— Thackeray.

—*what-do-you-call-'em* a phrase used like *Thingamy*, because one forgets the exact name, or does not wish to utter it.

"I might feel it was a great blow," said Miss Snevellicci, "to break up old associations and what-do-you-call-'ems of that kind, but I would submit, my dear, I would indeed.— Dickens.

"Well," I said, "three guineas, which I shall have over, will buy me a pair of what-d'ye-call 'ems.—Thackeray.

—*what's-his-name* used like the previous phrase.

My dearest Edith, there is such an obvious destiny in it, that really one might almost be induced to cross one's arms upon one's frock and say, like those wicked Turks, there is no What's-his-name but Thingummy, and What-you-may-call-it is his prophet.— Dickens.

wheel—*to go on wheels* to advance smoothly and rapidly; to make rapid progress.

The thing went on wheels. Richard Bassett was engaged to Jane Wright almost before he was aware.—C. Reade.

—*to put a spoke in a man's wheel* to interrupt his career of success; to embarrass him.

You have put a most formidable spoke in my wheel by preventing the extension of the borough.—Good Words, 1887.

while—*to while away* to pass in amusement; to spend for purposes of amusement.

And so he went on riding with her, and copying music and verses in her album, and playing chess with her very submissively; for it is with these simple amusements that some officers in India are accustomed to while away their leisure moments.—Thackeray.

whip—*the whip-hand* the control; the power of ruling.

Why, Anne, do be reasonable. If I gave you those letters, I should never be able to sleep in peace. For the sake of my own safety, I dare not abandon the whip-hand I have of you.—H. R. Haggard.

The secret of all success is to know how to deny yourself. If you once learn to get the whip-hand of yourself, that is the best educator. Prove to me that you can control yourself, and I'll say you're an educated man; and without this all other education is good for next to nothing.—Mrs. Oliphant.

whistle—*to pay dear for one's whistle* to pay too much for some coveted possession or pleasure.

We went off in very great state, but still having to pay with needless heaviness for our whistle.—G. A. Sala.

—*to wet one's whistle.* see **wet**.

—*to whistle for anything.* this phrase is used when there seems to be no reasonable chance of obtaining the thing desired.

If we only got what we deserved—Heaven save us!—many of us might whistle for a dinner (go dinnerless).—Thackeray.

white—*at a white heat* in an intense passion; very angry or excited.

They let their thinking be done for them, in all critical moments, by Parisian journalists at a white heat.—Contemporary Review, 1887.

—*a white lie* or *fib* a statement which is verbally true, but really and essentially false.

Between them both, Helen was in a corner. She might have been capable of telling a white fib and saying she had

not the letter, rather than let her father see it.—Mrs. Henry Wood.

—*white as a sheet* intensely pale.

Next second a terrible crash resounded from the other end of the room. George turned white as a sheet, and sank into a chair.—H. R. Haggard.

When they took him out of the black hole after six hours' confinement, he was observed to be white as a sheet and to tremble violently all over.—C. Reade.

—*white soup* the substance which is obtained by putting silver plate, etc., into the melting pot. A term used by London thieves.

Gold watches, silks and shawls and trinkets, yards of brocade, ells of lace, and last, not least, a caldron always on the boil for the manufacture of that all-absorbing fluid which is called "white soup," and is sold by the ounce, surrounded the once virtuous Gingham in her respectable home.—G. J. White-Melville.

—*white caps* waves having their tops white through the wind breaking them into foam. Also known as "white horses".

It was no gale, but only a fair wind; the water foamed along the ship's sides, and as her bows descended, shot forward in hissing jets of spray; away on every side flocked the white caps.—W. D. Howells.

—*a whited sepulchre* something outwardly fair but inwardly corrupt. A Scriptural phrase (Matt. xxiii, 27).

So that (bad as I may be, Lady Swansdown) I consider myself a better woman than you (and such as you) are. Oh yes! I know you don't stand alone. I know there are plenty like you in the best society—whited sepulchres, fair without, and rottenness and dead men's bones within.—Florence Marryat.

—*the white feather*. See **feather**.

whole—*upon the whole* taking everything into consideration.

Upon the whole, Emma left her with softened and charitable feelings.—Jane Austen.

wide—*there is a wide gulf fixed* there is a great and permanent cause of separation. The phrase is taken from the New Testament. See the parable of Dives and Lazarus (Luke xvi.).

Lady "Pat", as she is called by her familiar friends, would seem to be a fitter companion, both in station and age, for Lady Swansdown than Mrs. Beverley; but between the countess and Lady Pat there is a great gulf fixed.—Florence Marryat.

—*wide awake* smart; clever.

Sir Bate Coombe likes to be admired, even by an old maid; but he is too wide awake to let her see it.—Florence Marryat.

—*to give a wide berth* to avoid.

Always give the redcoats a wide berth, my dear.—G. A. Sala.

wigging—*to get a wigging* to be scolded.

However, it did not take him long to pardon John Monckton, while, as for the tremendous wigging which he would doubtless receive from his father, he had no difficulty at all about pardoning that in advance.—Good Words, 1887.

wild—*a wild-goose chase* a foolish and fruitless search.

"Wouldn't to-morrow do for this wild-goose chase?" inquired Wheeler.—C. Reade.

will—*will he, nill he* whether he wishes or not.

An imprudent marriage is a different thing, for then the consequences are inevitable when once the step has been taken, and have to be borne, will he, nill he.—Mrs. Oliphant.

—*will-o'-the-wisp* the *ignis fatuus*, or phosphorescent light which hovers over marshes; anything which deludes or deceives.

"I am very, very miserable; give me hope, the light of hope."

"It would be a will-of-the-wisp, Willie."—James Payn.

willow—*to wear the willow* (a) to occupy the lowest place or seat.

—(b) to be in mourning; to be in grief.

This went on until the summer of the year 1657, when her father gently put it to her that she had worn the willow (grieved for her lover) long enough, and would have to ally herself with some gentleman of worth and parts in that part of the country.—G. A. Sala.

But as high an estimate of Hazlitt is quite compatible with the strongest political dissent from his opinions, and with a total freedom from the charge of wearing the willow for (deploring the death of) painting.—Macmillan's Magazine, 1887.

—(c) to be forsaken.

Miss Grantley's approaching marriage, Ludovic?" she asked.

"Oh yes; it's at all the clubs. I have been overwhelmed with presents of willow branches."—A. Trollope.

win—*to win the day* to be successful.

Yet if, on the one side, there stood cold science, and on the other a suffering girl, it is ridiculous to acknowledge that the girl always won the day.—Besant.

—*to win at a canter* to gain an easy victory.

Petty finery without, a pinched and stinted stomach within; a case of Back versus Belly (as the lawyers would say) the plaintiff winning in a canter.—S. Warren.

wind—*in the wind* about to happen; talked of as probable.

All of a sudden the coach stopped.

"Hallo," said my uncle, "what's in the wind now?"—Dickens.

He never has a kind word to say of me even when we're alone; I believe there's some one else in the wind.—Florence Marryat.

"Such things never happen to such a poor devil as me," exclaimed Huckaback with a sigh.

"What is in the wind, I wonder?" muttered Titmouse.—S. Warren.

—**to get wind** to be talked about; to circulate as news.

His return had got wind, and every farmer under fifty had resolved to ride with him into Huntercombe.—C. Reade.

"And now, since we are to go," said Lady Clonbrony, "pray let us go immediately, before the thing gets wind, else I shall have Mrs. Dareville, and Lady Langdale, and Lady St. James, and all the world coming to condole with me, just to satisfy their own curiosity."—Maria Edgeworth.

—**to get wind of** to obtain news regarding; to learn about.

I could get wind of the amount given, now, if I wanted.—Macmillan's Magazine, 1887.

Luckily Mr. Hodge speedily got wind of our misfortune.—G. A. Sala.

—**to go to the winds** to be dissipated; to be utterly lost.

Few men can bear to see a sweet and pretty woman in tears, and this little incident was too much for John, whose caution and doubts all went to the winds together, and have not since been heard of.—H. R. Haggard.

At this all young Fielding's self-restraint went to the winds.—C. Reade.

—**in the wind's eye** right in the face of the wind; pointing directly to the quarter from which the wind comes.

At last, however, she fell right into the wind's eye, was taken dead aback,

and stood there awhile helpless, with her sails shivering.—R. L. Stevenson.

—**to raise the wind** to obtain necessary funds.

To raise the wind some lawyer tries.—J. and H. Smith.

—**betwixt wind and water** the part of a ship betwixt wind and water is that portion which is below the waterline, except when the shop heels over under the pressure of the wind. There is of course great danger when a shot strikes here. The phrase is used figuratively.

That shot was a settler; it struck poor Sall right atwixt wind and water (in the most susceptible place).—Haliburton.

—**to take the wind out of another's sails** to anticipate another; to gain a clever advantage over a competitor.

Ex-Baillie Laverock announced the important fact that one gentleman had offered him two-thirds of the £12,500 loan at 3½ per cent, and another gentleman had offered him £500 at the same rate. This quite took the wind out of the sails of the party in power. They looked aghast at each other, and it was evident from their countenances that the ex-baillie's statement had a terribly depressing effect on the majority.—St. Andrews Citizen, 1886.

By the way, I flatter myself that I have rather taken the wind out of Mr. Buswell's sails.—Good Words, 1887.

—**it's an ill wind that blows nobody good** few calamities are harmful to all concerned.

But it is an ill wind that blows nobody good. This storm raised George Fielding's better part of man.—C. Reade.

This very sensible view of the matter reassured Brian, who thought to himself, "It's an ill wind that blows nobody good, perhaps when she is Mrs. Dubbin she won't want to sing in

the choir any more."—*Good Words,*
1887.

—*to take wind* to become known.

*I could easily have brought her
ladyship to her senses, however; but my
scheme had taken wind, and it was
now in vain to attempt it.*—Thackeray.

—*to the four winds (of heaven)* completely irrecoverable.

*"Heaven knows," answered John,
carelessly; "given to Tom, Dick, and
Harry—scattered to the four winds. I
have not kept one of them."*—Miss
Braddon.

wind—*to wind up* to settle; to bring to
a conclusion. Generally used of the
formal settlement of the affairs of a
business firm that is broken up.

*If you like to retire and leave me to
wind up the concern, a cheque for
£10,000 is at your service.*—*Mistletoe
Bough,* 1885.

*With this beautiful metaphor I shall
wind up* (bring my remarks to a close).

wing—*to clip another's wings* to
hamper his movements; to lessen his
power of action.

—*to take under one's wing* to protect;
to patronize.

*We heard you were under Lady
Patrick's wing, and felt that you were
safe.*—Florence Marryat.

*As for you, Miss Ella, with your papa's
permission, I shall henceforth take you
under my wing.*—James Payn.

—*to lend wings to* to increase the speed
of; to hasten.

*I could hear hails coming and going
between the old buccaneer and his
comrades, and this sound of danger
lent me wings.*—R. L. Stevenson.

—*the wings of azrael.* See **azrael.**

—*to take wing* to fly off suddenly; to
depart without warning.

*So Beauchamp took wing; and whether
Lady Bracknell was annoyed or*

relieved by his flight I cannot venture
to say.—W. E. Norris.

wink—*to wink at* (a) to signal to with
the eye in token of a mutual understanding.

*"But now your mother's not by you
know," said Mrs. Dolly, winking at the
landlady; "now your mother's not by—"*

*"Yes; nobody will tell of you," added
the landlady.*—Maria Edgeworth.

—(b) to pretend not to see; to take no
notice of.

*Later on the emperors were fain to wink
at what they would not sanction and
could not extirpate.*—*Fortnightly
Review,* 1887.

—*to wink on* the same as *to wink at* (a).

*"Very well, sir," cried the squire, who
immediately smoked him (quizzed
him), and winked on the rest of the
company to prepare us for the sport;
"if you are for a cool argument upon
the subject, I am ready to accept the
challenge."*—Goldsmith.

winking—*like winking* quickly;
eagerly.

*Nod away at him, if you please, like
winking.*—Dickens.

wish—*to wish to goodness* to be very
desirous.

*"And to be lying all the time horribly
sick in your berth, and wishing to
goodness you were back again in the
schoolroom learning about the feudal
system," Lady Mordaunt suggested.*—
Murray's Magazine, 1887.

—*to wish one joy of anything* a phrase
generally used sarcastically to intimate that the person who has the
object will find it a troublesome possession.

*The apothecary's apprentice wished
Mrs. Corney joy of her job, and took
himself off on tiptoe.*—Dickens.

wit—*at one's wit's end* in a state of
utter perplexity; wholly puzzled how
to act.

Mr. Felspar was almost at his wit's end how to act.—James Payn.

—*to have one's wits about one* to be observant; to be quick at seeing and acting.

Cripps, if his wits had been about him, must have yielded space and bowed.—Blackmore.

Whatever might be urged about William Henry, it could not be said that he had not his wits about him.—James Payn.

witch—*to be no witch* to be quite sharp.

The editor is clearly no witch at a riddle.—Carlyle.

—*the witch is in it* there is some mysterious, supernatural influence at work.

She had never heard of the fate that was once supposed to appoint the sorrows of men irrespective of their blamelessness or blame, before the time when it came to be believed that sorrows were penalties; but in her simple way she recognized something like that mythic power when she rose from her struggle with the problem, and said aloud to herself. "Well, the witch is in it."—W. D. Howells.

withers—*our withers are unwrung* we are not hurt or irritated. The metaphor is taken from a galled horse, the withers being the ridge between the shoulderbones.

Let the galled jade wince; our withers are unwrung.—Shakespeare.

"I know you are," said Robarts, who knew the man well, and cared nothing for his friend's peculiarities when he felt his own withers were unwrung.—A. Trollope.

wolf—*to cry "wolf"* to call out for help when none is needed, until one's friends get disgusted, and do not come at a real crisis.

"O Beavis!" exclaimed the duke; "this is Beavis's cry of wolf, is it?"

"Papa," said Lady Grace, in urgent tones," when the wolf did not come the cry was disregarded."—S. Baring-Gould.

—*to keep the wolf from the door* to obtain sufficient to sustain life; to avoid dying of hunger.

Giving the people that employment to which they had always been accustomed, and without which, they would, in many cases, have found no little difficulty in keeping the wolf from their humble doors.—Murray's Magazine, 1887.

—*a wolf in sheep's clothing* a dangerous person who pretends to be quite harmless.

"There are three thousand men in the British army," announced the old vrouw oracularly, and casting a severe glance at the wolf in sheep's clothing, the man of blood who pretended to farm.—H. R. Haggard.

wonder—*for a wonder* strangely enough; contrary to expectations.

For a wonder he was not sea-sick.—C. Reade.

wood—*out of the wood* free from danger; escaped from a difficulty.

Mr. Josceline had merely observed indifferently, "I think we may be quite comfortable as to our young friend's getting out of the wood" (recovering from his dangerous illness).—James Payn.

Not being a man of invention, he could not see his way out of the wood at all.—C. Reade.

wooden—*the wooden spoon* the prize supposed to be conferred on the lowest graduate in a college list.

Here is something about a wooden spoon that he says he quite expected to have won for a prize, but the examiners have gone and given it to

Mr. Richard Lutbridge instead.—Annie Keary.

—**wooden nutmegs** citizens of Connecticut State in America. The name arose from a swindling transaction successfully carried out by a merchant of Hartford, the capital of Connecticut. The people of this state are noted for their sharpness in commercial transactions.

He called me a Yankee peddler, a cheating vagabond, a wooden nutmeg.—Haliburton.

wool—*to draw* or *pull the wool over one's eyes* to cheat or hoodwink him.

"Ahab," said I, "I have but a few minutes to stay with you, and if you think, to draw the wool over my eyes, it might perhaps take a longer time than you are thinking on, or than I can spare."—Haliburton.

I don't propose he shall pull the wool over my eyes, or anybody else.—W. D. Howells.

—*to go a-wool-gathering* to go astray; to be bewildered.

"What misconception?" asked the Pater, whose wits, once gone a-wool-gathering, rarely came back in a hurry.—Mrs. Henry Wood.

—*to be wool-gathering* to be in an absent-minded state.

Mr. Robarts had come round, to the generally accepted idea that Mr. Crawley had obtained possession of the cheque illegally, acquitting his friend in his own mind of theft, simply be supposing that he was wool-gathering when the cheque came in his way.—A. Trollope.

word—*to have words* or *a word* to have an angry discussion; to quarrel.

He is a poor, sneaking creature, and my brother George he caught Crawley selling up some poor fellow or other, and they had words.—C. Reade.

"We were a very happy little company,

Johnson," said poor Crummles. "You and I never had a word."—Dickens.

—*a man of his word* a man to be depended on; a trustworthy man.

As for himself, Mr. Osborne, he was a man of his word.—Thackeray.

—*to take the word* to commence speaking. A French phrase.

The colonel, left alone with his wife for the first time, since he had come to town, made haste to take the word.—W. D. Howells.

—*upon my word* certainly; surely; I assure you.

Upon my word, you answer as discreetly as she could do herself.—Jane Austen.

—*by word of mouth* orally; with the tongue.

That noble instrument (the organ) was saying to her something which the player did not venture to say by word of mouth.—Good Words, 1887.

The chance of entrapping Magdalen by word of mouth.—Wilkie Collins.

work—*to work the ropes* to control; to manage a scheme without being observed.

How our mutual friend worked the ropes is more than I can tell you.—H. R. Haggard.

—*to work up* to investigate thoroughly and with a special purpose.

Having some private means of his own, he had gone out to India for the purpose of working up certain still obscure problems.—Murray's Magazine, 1887.

—*to make short work of* to finish quickly; to gain an easy victory over.

We all thought he would make short work of the soldier-officer.—G. A. Sala.

world—*all the world and his wife* every one without exception.

Miss. Pray, madam, who were the company?

Lady S. *Why, there was all the world
and his wife.*—Swift.

—*a man of the world* a man well
acquainted with public and social life.
*"I am not at all a man of the world," he
said; "and of the law I know
nothing."*—Blackmore.

—*the world, the flesh, and the devil*
love of pleasure, sensual indulgence,
and vicious propensities.
*He renounces the world, the flesh, and
the devil, preaches and prays day
and night.*—Haliburton.

worm—*to worm out information* to
obtain information by subtle devices.
*By the aid of liquor he wormed out their
story.*—C. Reade.
*By these means he wormed out of Mr.
G. the whole story of his
adventure.*—G. R. James.

worse—*the worse half* a playful name
for a husband. "Better half" is a
common name for a wife.
*It would be a nice amusement for some
of these long evenings, and the
preparations would serve to occupy our
time, whilst our worse halves are out
shooting.*—Florence Marryat.

worst—*if the worst comes to the worst*
in the event of things turning out very
badly.
*"If the worst comes to the worst,"
Becky thought, "My retreat is
secure."*—Thackeray.

worth—*worth one's while* advan-
tageous; profitable.
*Upon the face of the thing, it looks as
if it might be worth your while.*—*Good
Words,* 1887.

—*worth one's salt* efficient; a good
workman.
*It was plain from every line of his body
that our new hand was worth his
salt.*—R. L. Stevenson.

would—*would-be* in intention; anxious
to be considered this or that.
The would-be wags among the boys

*racked their brains to find the means
of tormenting her through her name.*—
S. Baring-Gould.

wrapped—*wrapped up in* wholly
devoted to.
*Lork, Mrs. Richards, no; her pa's a deal
too wrapped up in somebody else.*—
Dickens.

wreck—*wreck and ruin* complete ruin.
See **rack** and **ruin**.
*The whole estate is going to wreck and
ruin because my uncle won't have the
rabbits killed down.*—Wm. Black.

wrinkle—*a wrinkle on one's horn* a
valuable hint.
*"Now," says the major, "I'll give you,
Slick, a new wrinkle on your horn."*—
Haliburton.

write—*to write anything up* to praise
in a systematic manner through the
press.
*"Pray, Mr. Grey, is it true that all the
houses in Russell Square are
tenantless?*
*"Quite true. A perfect shame, is it
not! Let us write it up."*—Beaconsfield.

wrong—*the wrong side of sixty or seventy* more than sixty or seventy years
of age.
*The old woman answered, "That
though her master was a deal on the
wrong side of seventy, yet he was as
alert, and thought no more of going
about than if he was as young as the
gentleman who was now speaking to
her."*—Marie Edgeworth.

—*to have got up on the wrong side of
the bed* to have got out of bed the
wrong way. This is said of a person
who is in a cross humour during the
day.
*There is a pleasing nursery fiction that
accounts for many disagreeable
things by a theory on the right and the
wrong way of getting out of bed.
Valentine remembered this, and felt
quite certain that Sam, Melanda, and*

Lizzie had all three got out of bed the
wrong way that morning. There was

going to be a row, and one of uncertain
dimensions.—Besant.

X

X—*double X* a superior quality of
beer.

And I said, "A pint of double X, and
please to draw it mild!"—Barham.

Y

yarn—*to spin a yarn*. See **spin**.

year—*years of discretion* an age when
one is able to judge between what is
right and what is wrong.
*A mere boy; a very lad. Not come to
years of discretion yet; and never will,
if he goes on raging in this manner.—*
G. A. Sala.
*I'm afraid the cat got out of the bag
when Mrs. Pasmer came to the years
of discretion.—W. D. Howells.*

—*year of grace* year dating from the
birth of Jesus Christ. Equivalent to
Anno Domini, or year of our Lord.
*My story begins in the year of grace
seventeen hundred and sixty-four.*

yellow—*Yellow Jack* the yellow fever.
*I have been in places hot as pitch, and
mates dropping round with Yellow
Jack.—R. L. Stevenson.*

yeoman—*yeoman's duty* or *service*
excellent work.
*The shattering of the false image had
done him yeoman's service.—A.
Trollope.*
*In the gratitude of his heart, George
would willingly have given a thousand
pounds towards the erection of a statue*

to Hilda Caresfoot, whose outraged
pride and womanly jealousy had done
him such yeoman service.—H. R.
Haggard.
Indeed, it is quite certain that he
(Benvenuto Cellini) performed more
than yeoman's duty as a gunner all
through the period of the sack of
Rome.—J. A. Symonds.

Yorkshire—*to come Yorkshire over a
man* to cheat or swindle him. Yorkshire jockeys were known for their
tricky dealings in the sale of horses.
See Macaulay's *Warren Hastings*:
"And the crime for which Nuncomar
was about to die was regarded by
them in much the same light in which
the selling of an unsound horse for a
sound price is regarded by a Yorkshire jockey."
*Surely," said John, "what I say I stick
by."*
*"And that's a fine thing to do, and
manly, too," said Nicholas, "though it's
not exactly what we understand by
coming Yorkshire over us in
London."—Dickens.*